Language
Intervention
with
Young Children

Language
Intervention
with
Young Children

Marc E. Fey, Ph.D.

Department of Communicative Disorders
The University of Western Ontario

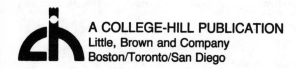
A COLLEGE-HILL PUBLICATION
Little, Brown and Company
Boston/Toronto/San Diego

College-Hill Press, Inc.
A Division of Little, Brown and Company (Inc.)
34 Beacon Street
Boston, Massachusetts 02108

Library of Congress Cataloging in Publication Data
Main entry under title:

Fey, Marc E., 1952-
  Language intervention with young children.

  Bibliography: p.
  Includes index
  1. Language disorders in children. 2. Language disorders in children—Treatment, I.
  Title.
  RJ496.L35F49 1985   618.92'855   85-14887
ISBN 0-316-28134-4
Printed in the United States of America

To Mrs. Jane A. Wells—a truly grand parent—and her great-grandson, Marshall

The circle remains unbroken.

CONTENTS

Preface

The proliferation of books on early language impairment and intervention over the last few years has been impressive. The formula for most of these books has been to present information on language acquisition, language assessment, and then, language intervention. Although this formula has given rise to the production of some very useful books, it has always seemed to me that something else was needed by students, working clinicians, and academicians interested in language intervention processes. I undertook the writing of this book because I believe that language intervention itself involves significant clinical and theoretical issues that deserve a careful and comprehensive treatment. I have assumed, then, that readers of the book will have knowledge of language development and of procedures commonly used to evaluate children suspected of having language impairments. Holding this assumption has left me free to cover practical and theoretical problems that are often excluded from books that really provide only an introductory survey to the study and practice of language intervention.

It often has been stated that clinicians do not need and should not want a cookbook to tell them what to do in their intervention sessions and how to do it. Preplanned therapy "recipes" can never meet the needs of all language impaired children. I am in complete agreement with this claim—but clinicians need to make decisions regarding what might be the best course of treatment for each client, and they need a knowledge base from which such decisions can be made. It is this knowledge base that I have attempted to provide in this book.

My primary aims in the book can be summarized as follows:

1. To make clear the relationship between theory and clinical decision-making and to demonstrate that the theoretical perspectives that the clinician adopts will have a significant impact on the decision-making process;
2. To present a scheme for analyzing intervention processes that will assist the clinician in the development of effective intervention plans (e.g., the selection of goals, procedures, and goal attack strategies and the development of intervention activities);
3. To describe a broad array of intervention procedures in detail that is sufficient to enable clinicians to put those procedures into practice;

4. To present a balanced, critical analysis of the available literature on intervention (i.e., to determine with whom specific procedures have and have not been successful and why) that will assist the clinician in evaluating the merits of particular intervention approaches with children exhibiting specific types of language impairments.

To extend the cookbook analogy one step further than it is usually taken, it is my hope that individuals who read this book will not become simply "short-order cooks" who lay on their clinical tables the standard fare of an ordinary therapy recipe. Rather, I hope the information provided herein prepares them to become "gourmet cooks" who are capable of modifying existing procedures and activities and experimenting with new ones to yield a product that is especially created to suit a particular child and occasion.

I have many people to thank for their assistance in the preparation of this book. I have profited a great deal from discussions with Donna Corcoran, Sandy Fey, Carla Johnson, and Cynthia Shewan on what makes a good speech-language pathologist. Sandy Fey, Laurie Lemieux, Larry Leonard, Daniel Ling, Patti Sorenson, and an anonymous reviewer read all or parts of drafts of the manuscript and made helpful comments that make the book much more readable than it otherwise would have been. Sheila MacDonald provided expert technical assistance in the preparation of the reference list. John Fracasso and Jim Stouffer made computer equipment available which enabled me to meet deadlines that had already been extended well beyond their original dates. The staff of College-Hill Press has been extremely helpful and has given me the freedom to develop the book to my own specifications rather than to some preconceived notion of their own. The careful editing of Catherine Fix of College-Hill Press is especially appreciated. Special thanks go to my mentor, collaborator, and pal, Larry Leonard, for his continued support and encouragement, which led to my undertaking this task. Finally, *very* special thanks go to my wife, Sandy, whose acceptance and tolerance of me, my chronic forgetfulness, and my selfishness over the period of time during which this book was written made the preparation of the book the most important and satisfying experience of my professional career.

Chapter 1

The Role of Theory in Intervention

To the student or practicing clinician interested in getting to the heart of language intervention, beginning this book with a chapter on theories of language acquisition may seem to be a familiar and altogether unnecessary digression. This is certainly understandable. Most students have sat patiently in classes through weeks of presentations of theories and discussions of the basic literature only to discover that the promised lectures on intervention have been reduced to a list of readings and a brief survey of the approaches that reflect the instructors' own biases. But the relationship between theory and practice is not always clear and, as a result, many clinicians do not use their backgrounds in theory to their best clinical advantage. In fact, some talented language clinicians have claimed that theories were for ivory-tower academics, not clinicians. These individuals operate under the maxim "find something that works and use it."

Such an empirically based approach is admirable, and I don't think a theorist of any persuasion would disagree with it as long as success could be demonstrated unambiguously. The problem, of course, lies in knowing how to find a procedure that works. How does the clinician go about such a task? Trial and error is possible, but it is inefficient and unreliable. As an alternative, the hundreds of available programs can be perused and one or more possibilities can be selected for personal use. Most of these programs, however, have not been tested in any scientifically acceptable manner (Connell, Spradlin, and McReynolds, 1977). Therefore, simply picking the one that appears to be the most effective and efficient on the basis of test data is a luxury usually not afforded to the clinician. Even when this can be done, not everyone agrees on what effective and efficient intervention actually is (cf. Muma, 1978a). What, then, can be viewed as a rational means of program selection?

Another alternative is to rely on one's own experiences in the past; what has worked in the past may work now as well. But as any

1

clinician knows, every child is different, and in actuality methods applied in the past are *not* always successful for every child.

Every clinician needs to modify her procedures at one time or another to fit the needs of an individual child and to exploit learning opportunities that arise spontaneously. Whether it is acknowledged or not, each clinician makes such modifications on the basis of the principles and assumptions that she believes are critical to learning—that is, on the basis of her own theory of language learning. If we acknowledge those theoretical underpinnings, we can study and analyze the implications that our beliefs have for our approaches to intervention. Then, by carefully evaluating other theories and their implications, we may find that the options open to us within our existing theoretical framework are highly restricted and that modification of our present theory or adoption of another is warranted.

Most importantly, careful analyses of our views on language and language learning make it possible for us to generate and test hypotheses concerning ways in which we can modify our existing procedures. This process of clinical hypothesis testing makes our intervention approaches more effective and efficient. Also, with this knowledge comes greater flexibility and adaptability to the specific needs of our individual clients. When we are faced with new clinical problems, we can create new solutions by analyzing the problems from our chosen theoretical perspective. Johnston (1983) regards this creative potential as being similar to the creative nature of language.

> Clinical proficiency likewise requires an infinite range of intervention acts. If our knowledge of language intervention is abstract, or theoretic, in nature, we can be productive and creative therapists. No longer stuck with formulas, no longer hopeful imitators, we can use our intervention "rules" to generate activities that are thoroughly responsive to the client and the moment. (p. 56)

Perhaps these claims are no more convincing than the last-minute proclamations of a professor who has tried to crowd too much information into too little time. Therefore, in the rest of this chapter, I will demonstrate how different theoretical perspectives can guide us in fundamentally different directions in the ways in which we approach intervention. To accomplish this goal, the general principles underlying four different theoretical accounts of language acquisition are presented: operant learning theory, social learning theory, the interactionist view of language learning, and the developmental perspective of the theory of transformational generative grammar. *This list is not exhaustive,* and even within these four theoretical perspectives, there is room for much disagreement on critical issues. Space does not permit a thorough discussion of any of these viewpoints. Instead, I have tried to capture the essence of each proposal as it can be related to language intervention. Following a presentation of each theory, I will point out the ways in which those particular theoretical assumptions can influence differentially both our perception of our role as interventionists and the goals that we view as appropriate for our clients.

OPERANT LEARNING THEORY

Since the early 1960s, operant theory, or behaviorism, probably has had a greater impact on intervention practices than any other theory. The following discussion, based largely on Winokur's excellent description (1976) of the radical behaviorist view, should provide some insight into why clinicians have found the theoretical principles of operant conditioning so useful. To obtain a much more detailed account from an avowed behaviorist, Winokur's book is strongly recommended. For a clear and concise critique of the theory, the book by Moulton and Robinson (1981) should serve as an excellent starting point.

Rudiments of the Theory

A critical principle that underlies the operant analysis is that verbal behavior is nothing more than a particular example of behavior in general, and as such, it is subject to the same "laws" that govern the nonverbal behavior of humans and other animals. In other words, language is accorded no special status under this theory. Since the behavior of animals is observable through the senses or through sensitive instruments such as electromyographic equipment that aid in measuring otherwise undetectable behavior, it follows that language behavior must also be observable through these same media. In the operant account, there is no need to infer the existence of central processing mechanisms, abstract instruments of thought, or hierarchically organized linguistic categories. Winokur (1976) summarizes succinctly this theme, which underlies all aspects of the theory: "Minds and brains, grammars and intentions, ideas and cognitions have been shown unnecessary for a complete, causal, naturalistic account. Man himself has been eliminated as a causal variable; he is just a place where causal variables interact to produce talking" (p. 152). The learner is passive within this theory, acquiring knowledge and skills automatically through the influences of the environment.

The most basic element in operant theory is the *operant*. The *verbal operant* comprises a *stimulus* and a *verbal response*. The stimulus-response relationship is a causal one. In other words, a verbal response is produced as a direct result of the presentation of a particular stimulus or stimulus complex. For example, a child presented with a glass of juice may say "juice." In this case, the response "juice" probably resulted from a number of stimuli present in the context, such as the glass, the smell and sight of the juice, the refrigerator, the child's caregiver, and perhaps a number of other factors.

It is important to recognize, however, that the causal relationship between a verbal response and a stimulus complex is not predetermined in any way; it is learned. Operant learning occurs through a very well outlined sequence of events. For example, in the presence of a nonverbal stimulus, such as a glass of juice, the child hears someone say "juice." The child then imitates this word. This imitative response to a verbal stimulus is a type of operant called an *echoic*. The relationship between the nonverbal stimulus and the word would never develop without the assistance of some knowledgeable person, usually an adult, who then reinforces the child's output. According to the theory, a *reinforcer* is any stimulus that functions to increase the likelihood that the response will occur again under a similar set of circumstances. In other words, reinforcement serves to strengthen the relationship between the stimulus, in this case the verbal stimulus "juice," and the child's response. The relationship between a discriminative stimulus, a response, and a reinforcing stimulus can be represented in the following manner (Bandura, 1977):

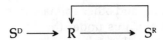

$$S^D \longrightarrow R \longrightarrow S^R$$

The strengthening effect of the reinforcer is automatic—that is, not mediated by central cognitive processes. By this definition of reinforcement, almost anything could be viewed as a reinforcer in a particular case. In the "juice" example, reinforcement might come in the form of a drink of juice, continued adult attention, a hug, a confirmation such as "yeah, juice," or any number of other potential reinforcers.

The effect of this and repeated examples under similar circumstances would be that the response "juice" would come under the control of the nonverbal *discriminative stimuli* that are typically present, particularly the juice itself, since it would virtually always be present in the earliest episodes. On subsequent occasions when these stimuli are present, the probability that the child will say "juice" even without an imitative stimulus is increased. The child's continued use of this response depends on two highly interactive processes, stimulus generalization and response generalization. *Stimulus generalization* occurs when stimuli that differ slightly from those previously associated with the verbal response take on controlling properties for that response. It is through this process that the child will use the word under different stimulus conditions, such as when she sees a picture of juice or when she is a given a different kind of juice than the one that was originally associated with the response. *Response generalization* occurs when the conditioning of one response leads to the increased probability of responses similar to the original. For example, the child may originally learn the word "juice" to make a comment or to label the object. With no further experience or reinforcement, she may begin to use the response to get a drink of juice from an adult when she is thirsty or perhaps even to inquire whether the glass that is being prepared for her contains juice (e.g., "juice?"). These generalized responses that result from the conditioning of an isolated response form what is referred to as a *response class*. Generalization is a process that does not need to be learned. It is a basic process that is characteristic of all animals, but especially humans and other primates (Winokur, 1976, p. 139).

There are several different types of operants that can develop under similar stimulus-response-reinforcement situations. *Mands* are typically requests, demands, or hints that help the speaker obtain some desired object or service. They have as their controlling stimuli deprivation, such as thirst, or the presence of some aversive stimulus. The utterance of the mand under these circumstances results in the listener's providing the desired object or service or removing the aversive stimulus. Thus, mands seem to specify the very acts that will reinforce them; for example, the child says "juice" when thirsty and is reinforced by the very stimulus that was specified in the mand.

A *tact* has as its controlling variable a discriminative stimulus, as described above. The reinforcement for a tact is administered by a listener because of a conventional correspondence between the verbal response and the discriminative stimulus. For example, a child learning English is likely to be reinforced for saying "juice" in the presence of a pitcher of juice, but is not likely to receive reinforcement if she is looking at the cookie jar. Thus, children's tacts are selectively reinforced until the only tacts used are those that conform to the conventions of the speech community in which they live.

One obvious problem with these types of operants is that the stimuli evoking a response must be present in the speaking context. What about situations in which a stimulus is tacted, but the referent for the tact is not physically present? For example, a child might say something like "daddy coming home" when her daddy is not present. A behaviorist might explain this with the concepts of stimulus generalization and stimulus clustering. Suppose the primary controlling variable for the response of the child just mentioned is the appearance of her father emerging from his car in the driveway. Through stimulus generalization, she might also produce the response after seeing a picture of her father or perhaps upon observing some man who is not her father in a car either while watching television or while looking out the window. *Stimulus clustering* is a powerful construct that results because many stimuli are present on those occasions when responses such as "daddy coming home" are produced and reinforced. For example, along with the father's return home, the child hears the car door slam, the clock tolls the time of day, she is beginning to feel hungry, and so forth. When these stimuli occur consistently in correspondence with the return of the father, they too become capable of "causing" the response "daddy coming home." Reinforcement of these responses throughout the day strengthens the relationship between the stimuli, which were not discriminative from the outset, and the response.

Two other types of verbal operants should be mentioned. *Intraverbals* are operants that have as their controlling variables the speaker's own previous verbal responses. Responses on free association tasks are intraverbals. The response "daddy" may evoke the related responses "mommy," "Norm," "Suzanne," and so forth. Similarly, the production of a given word in a sentence serves as a stimulus for subsequent words. These intraverbal responses are not believed to be thought out, but are related through their common reinforcement histories, stimulus generalization, stimulus clustering, and related processes.

The final operant to be discussed is the autoclitic. *Autoclitics* are operants that have as their discriminative stimuli other operants. For example, given two responses "mommy" and "sick" to relevant discriminative stimuli, the autoclitic then operates on these responses before they are uttered to somehow modify the shape of the utterance. Autoclitics take on a number of different shapes and forms including function words, such as the copula, prepositions, and conjunctions. In such cases, their function is frequently to relate two or more verbal responses (e.g., *"Mommy* is *sick"*).

Perhaps the most important function of autoclitics, however, is their ordering of verbal responses so that long strings can occur in a highly consistent order. Essentially, what is proposed to happen is this: A child is affected by a stimulus complex such that she is predisposed through prior learning to produce the verbal response of one or more operants. For example, the observation that her brother is stealing cookies from the cookie jar might evoke the verbal responses "Richie," "stealing," and "cookies," simultaneously. The autoclitic is a relationship between these stimuli and an ordering response. Thus, the primary verbal responses, as yet not uttered, are ordered in a sequence that has been reinforced in the past. In English, the sentence "Richie is stealing cookies" is highly probable, given a prior history of these types of stimulus conditions and reinforcement.

A major problem with the notion of autoclitic ordering is that it appears that only those specific strings that have been reinforced could be produced. Such a proposal could not explain the fact that language users, including young children, typically create novel strings that they have never before heard or produced. Again, the behaviorists attempt an explanation. The child first produces a number of isolated utterances that are similar in their structure (e.g., "Susie running," "Don laughing," "Jimmy crying"). These responses and the order in which their components appear are reinforced. The individual constituents of these combinations eventually generalize into larger classes of responses. Using the examples given previously, these classes could be characterized as actors and actions. When the combination of these more general classes into an actor–action sequence is also generalized through the influences of stimulus and response generalization, the order is autoclitic. From this point onward, the child can respond to stimuli in ways that are consistent with this pattern. Each specific string need not be conditioned separately, primarily because of this process. What is commonly viewed as the child's grammatical system is said to develop in just this fashion.

Implications for Intervention

The behaviorist's position on language and learning has enormous implications for all aspects of intervention. Its greatest impact has been on how clinicians perceive their roles in the intervention process. This should come as no surprise, since the theory is quite specific in its description of the mechanisms of development. Since all learning depends on the relationships between a stimulus complex, a response, and the stimuli that follow the response, a language clinician should be able to teach language by manipulating these very elements of the learning process. For example, sentences like "Jack has eaten his dinner" should be trainable by (1) presenting relevant antecedent nonverbal stimuli such as a real boy named Jack who has just cleaned up his plate, or by showing a picture of this type of event; (2) simultaneously presenting the verbal stimulus "Jack has eaten his dinner"; (3) encouraging the child to imitate the verbal stimulus; and

(4) reinforcing the correct imitative production and punishing (e.g., "no!") or ignoring incorrect responses.

Once the child has mastered this imitative task, the imitative stimulus could gradually be removed or *faded,* leaving only the nonverbal stimuli and thereby increasing the complexity of the task. As we will see in Chapter 8, there are innumerable variations on this theme. Nevertheless, all training is the result of the clinician's selection of highly specific and carefully defined target responses to be learned, creating relevant antecedent events, and following correct responses with reinforcement. For the most part, the learning process is controlled by the clinician. After presenting several nonverbal and verbal stimuli that are similar to the original (e.g., "The boy has won the race," "The man has washed the dishes") in this fashion, generalization might be expected to occur readily. When it does not, more stimuli that differ in significant ways from those originally used, different reinforcement contingencies, or, generally, more practice, perhaps involving other intervention agents, would be the anticipated remedies to the problem.

It is interesting that, although operant theory emphasizes the functions that language serves (mands, tacts, etc.), most of the efforts to modify language behaviors using operant technology have involved teaching new language forms. Operant theory provides very little assistance to the clinician in determining what forms should be taught and the order in which selected goals should be presented. This is because the theory is highly noncommittal with respect to the nature of language structure.

An example should help here. Examine the four sentences below.

1. I really like hard candy.
2. Give me some hard candy.
3. Do you like hard candy?
4. Candy that's hard, I like.

Each of these sentences contains five words and either six or seven syllables. They all contain labels for the same objects, attributes, and people. Assuming then, that the child knows all of these labels, there is no reason, a priori, to suspect any one sentence to appear developmentally before another. In reality, sentences like examples 1 and 2 are likely to appear in the speech of children before sentences like example 3, and sentences like example 4 are very unlikely to occur at all; these facts must be explained by factors like varying frequencies of exposure, varying numbers of opportunities to imitate, and different numbers of opportunities for reinforcement to be administered. In other words, some sentences are more likely to be found earlier than others in children's speech because the sentences have different reinforcement histories. There is no claim that these sentences differ markedly in their internal structure and that this structure could pose different levels of difficulty for the child.

Now suppose that we are faced with a language impaired child who produces none of these sentence types. Under this theory, each sentence type should be equally easy or difficult to train, provided that measures are taken to see that equivalent numbers of stimuli are presented and that identical reinforcement contingencies apply. Of course, no behaviorist would select a sentence like example 4 for training because the child would have fewer models for this structure outside the clinic. Furthermore, sentences 1, 2, and 3 can serve similar functions (e.g., tacts or mands) for the child in her everyday environment. But we do not need to look far into the experimental literature to see that this aspect of the theory is taken seriously. Severely and profoundly mentally retarded and autistic individuals who were previously nonverbal or functioning at very low linguistic levels have been trained to produce plural inflections (Guess, 1969; Guess and Baer, 1973), comparative and superlative inflections (Baer and Guess, 1973), past tense inflections (Schumaker and Sherman, 1970), subject–verb–object sentences (Lutzker and Sherman, 1974), and complex sentences (Stevens-Long and Rasmussen, 1974). Very imaginative programming steps are often required to reach these impressive goals. We will discuss many of these attempts in Chapter 8. What is important for this discussion is that advocates of the other three theories to be presented would not have considered these attempts very promising. In fact, they probably would have predicted failure.

Devotees of behaviorism thus have a great deal of flexibility in terms of what they teach and in the sequence with which new forms are presented. Generally, they select language forms that they believe are most functional for the children with whom they deal. The most effective and efficient sequence of training is considered to be an empirical matter. More will be said about this in Chapter 6.

SOCIAL LEARNING THEORY

Although clinical procedures derived from principles of social learning theory have been used much less extensively than those based on operant theory, significant contributions have been made from within this theoretical paradigm as well. These contributions appear not to be too well known, however, since major textbooks relating to intervention can still be found with no references to the major clinical works in this area (e.g., Cole, 1982; McCormick and Schiefelbusch, 1984). The discussion that follows borrows heavily from Bandura's (1977) lucid presentation of the theory.

Rudiments of the Theory

As a point of departure from operant theory, Bandura (1977) notes that

> Detailed analysis of how external influences affect conduct provides confirmatory evidence that behavior is indeed subject to external control. However, limiting the scope of scientific inquiry to certain psychological processes to the neglect of other important ones can reinforce a truncated image of the human potential. (p. vi)

The other important processes to which Bandura refers are several internal factors that interact in a very complex reciprocal fashion with the social and physical environments. These internal, cognitive factors enable individuals to do more than simply respond to stimuli; they provide the capacity for selection, organization, and transformation of stimuli to the behavioral advantage of the individual. Thus, the individual is seen as a more active force in the learning process.

A basic tenet of social learning theory is that learning does not depend on performance; in fact, the theory holds that most human behavior is acquired through observation of modeled events. How much the child gains from observing a modeled event depends at least partly on her level of development of four interdependent processes: attention, retention, motor reproduction, and motivation. Learning and performing complex behaviors depends on each of these processes. A deficit in one of these components reduces the probability of the child's production of the appropriate behavior, and improvements in any of the areas positively influence the other processes so that observational learning is enhanced. The relationship between these four processes and their influence on learning is illustrated in Figure 1-1.

Attention to modeled stimuli is essential for learning. It is a function partly of characteristics of the stimuli themselves and partly of the characteristics of the observer. For example, words containing syllables that are greater in duration and that are produced with greater frequency and intensity than neighboring words and syllables (i.e., words that contain syllables with nuclear stress) are likely to be more distinctive to the child. The fact that these words often refer to objects, people, actions, and other things that are important in the child's everyday circumstances also increases their functional value and, consequently, the likelihood that they will be attended to. On the other

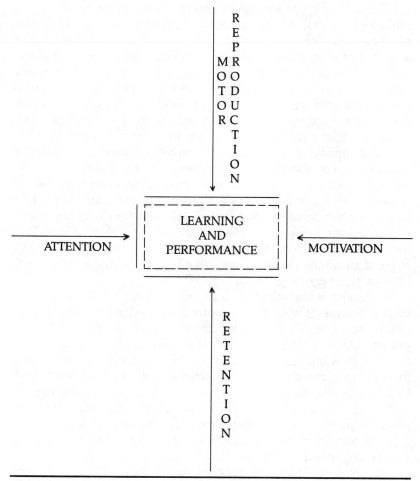

Figure 1–1. Component processes for observational learning and performance of a new behavior, according to social learning theory.

hand, what is attended to also depends on the child's sensory capabilities, the extent to which the modeled behavior has been associated with reinforcement in the past, and the child's arousal level, as well as other internal factors.

Through *retention processes,* the child can rehearse and retain experiences mentally. Later, stored images and verbally coded information can be accessed to guide behavior. In complex tasks, these processes enable the child to organize and rehearse a behavior mentally before enacting it overtly.

Social learning theory, like operant theory, must be able to account for the fact that much behavior, especially language behavior, is novel and creative, even though it is highly patterned and not random. The storing of images relating to specific events and their associated verbal codings does not necessarily lead to innovative behavior. However, according to the theory, events and the words used to represent those events are not stored individually. Bandura (1977) describes the process of *abstract modeling* to account for generative language behavior. Following the observation of many events and the verbalizations accompanying them, the child derives common principles that underlie the specific verbal performances. "In abstract modeling, observers extract the common attributes exemplified in diverse modeled responses and formulate rules for generating behavior with similar structural characteristics" (Bandura, p. 41). Although imitation of individual responses may play a role in learning, "It is abstract modeling, with its perceptual, cognitive and reproductive component processes, rather than simple verbal mimicry, that is most germane to the development of generative grammar" (p. 174).

Motivation is also viewed as a criterion of learning. Unlike operant theory, however, the sources of motivation need not be external reinforcement alone. *Vicarious reinforcement,* the observation of another person being reinforced for an act, is viewed as a powerful influencer of behavior. Consistent with the view of the individual as an active force in the learning process, the learner herself can also provide feedback concerning the adequacy of her performance. Thus, through external, vicarious, and self-reinforcement, in combination with the other processes described above, the child learns to anticipate which types of acts, linguistic and otherwise, are likely to have the desirable effect in a given circumstance.

Bandura (1977) represents stimulus, response, reinforcing, and cognitive events with the following formula:

$$S^R \text{ (anticipated)} \longrightarrow \text{attention} \longrightarrow S^D \longrightarrow \begin{array}{l} \text{Symbolic} \\ coding \\ \text{Cognitive} \\ organization \\ \text{Mental} \\ rehearsal \end{array} \longrightarrow R$$

Here, the prospect of reinforcement (external or self) motivates the individual to attend to stimuli selectively and to operate on them actively through symbolic representation and organization and rehearsal of those symbols. Learning can take place *before* any response or external reinforcement. The automatic strengthening of a response, characteristic of the behavioral view of reinforcement, is viewed as nonsignificant within social learning theory.

Finally, through *motor reproduction* symbolic representations are transformed into actions. Just observing and storing modeled events is not enough. The child must also produce linguistic acts in ways that are consistent with the pattern that has been modeled repeatedly (e.g., agent–action–object, "Sue kiss doggie"). This ability depends to a large extent on the availability of component responses (e.g., agent–action, action–object). When these more basic components are not represented mentally in a stable form, reproduction of more complex behaviors is likely to be faulty.

Implications for Intervention

Like operant learning theory, social learning theory provides an explicit technology for teaching; however, it places much greater importance on the ways in which social and self-generated factors can influence a child's attention and motivation processes and, consequently, the ability to learn and retain information of all kinds. Generally, anything that the clinician can do to motivate the child to attend closely to the target linguistic behavior and to improve retention of a modeled event should facilitate learning even of abstract linguistic rules. The steps typically taken to achieve this objective include (1) selecting a model with whom the child closely identifies, such as a parent or a peer; (2) having the model produce numerous examples of the target language behavior (e.g., subject–verb–object constructions to describe pictures with varying content); (3) reinforcing the model for correct productions; (4) after the presentation of several uninterrupted models, encouraging the child to "talk just like the model"; and (5) reinforcing the child for correct productions of the target.

Steps 1 and 3 should motivate the child to attend carefully to determine what types of behaviors receive reinforcement. By having the child attend to several uninterrupted models of the target form in step 2, she is provided with the opportunity to rehearse mentally the models and to extract and organize their common underlying attributes. Finally, reinforcement of the child's correct productions serves to help the child to regulate her behavior, providing feedback concerning the accuracy of her hypotheses and further motivating her to use the abstracted structure to generate upcoming responses.

It should be noted that immediate imitation, the hallmark of the behavioral approach, is not used in this paradigm. In fact, Courtright and Courtright (1976) argued that allowing the child to imitate each modeled stimulus interferes with the child's internal processing of the sentences' shared grammatical properties, thereby reducing the effectiveness of the models. This is a fundamental difference between the two learning theory approaches. Whereas the behaviorist must have immediate confirmation of the effects of teaching efforts in the form of an overt response, a social learning theorist can operate under the assumption that internal symbolic processing and consequent learning can go on independently of an overt response.

A clinical example might be helpful here. In a naturalistic intervention context, when an appropriate situation for language usage by the child arises, a behaviorist must feel compelled to prompt the child to produce a *complete* target response. In contrast, a social learning theorist may feel content to (1) provide models of the target, some of which are overtly reinforced; (2) see that other children produce models of the target response under similar circumstances; and (3) model the correct response, following the child's incorrect attempts. It is not essential for the child to produce a response to assume that learning is taking place. All that is necessary is that the environmental (social and physical) conditions be modified such that the child is highly motivated to pay attention to these models and the objects, states, events, and relations to which they refer. The clinician's role is changed from one of elicitor and reinforcer of specific responses to one of modeler and motivator of language usage.

If this notion rubs you the wrong way, your behavioristic assumptions about learning may be showing. This is not bad, but it should be edifying. Your stance on the behavioral approach to learning may have precluded use of methods that follow naturally from another theoretical account. Whether or not these methods are indeed effective requires subjecting them to clinical test.

Social learning theory is like operant learning theory in that it was not designed specifically to account for language development. Consequently, although its proponents speak frequently of the generative nature of grammar and of abstract rules, the theory is not associated with any theory of language in particular. What language is and how it is structured is not well described. Therefore, clinicians adopting a social learning approach have no theoretical basis for selecting goals that have a syntactic basis (e.g., subject–verb–object), a semantic basis (e.g., agent–action), a pragmatic basis (e.g., topic–comment), or other basis. The theory is quite explicit, however, in its claim that ease of learning depends on the status of the child's component processes, attention, retention, motivation, and motor reproduction. Therefore, verbal goals that are well within the individual child's own internal processing capacities should be selected. It is likely, then, that whatever the nature of the goals selected, intervention will proceed in a manner that is highly consistent with patterns of normal development.

THE INTERACTIONIST VIEWPOINT

The interactionist perspective outlined in this section is essentially that presented by Bloom and Lahey (1978). Although it includes aspects of theories of cognitive development and of language, it differs from the other theories presented in this chapter in that it represents an attempt to account for language development on its own terms, rather than as one aspect of a broader and more inclusive theory.

Rudiments of the Theory

From an interactionist perspective, language must be understood as a complex system involving three separate but highly interdependent knowledge bases. These include language content, form, and use. *Language content* consists of two kinds of knowledge: *referential* and *relational*. Referential knowledge involves the child's understanding of the particular objects, events, and relations that underlie the meanings of the words we use (e.g., the critical defining features of concepts such as *cat, rat, chase, eat, red, silly*). Relational knowledge involves the child's understanding of the roles that objects can play in the context of actions or states of affairs as well as the ways in which events can relate to one another. For example, examine the three sentences below.

5. The cat chased the rat.
6. The rat was chased by the cat.
7. Did the cat chase the rat?

These sentences are different, but they are not different by virtue of their language content. In each case, the event that is being described involves an agent, or initiator of an action (e.g., the cat), an action (e.g., chasing), and a patient, or an animate object affected by the action of the verb (e.g., the rat). The fact that the action takes place in the past is also part of the semantic content of these sentences.

In the following three sentences, reference is made to the same objects and actions, but the meaning of the sentences is no longer the same.

8. The rat chased the cat.
9. The cat was chased by the rat.
10. Did the rat chase the cat?

Clearly, the meanings of the words "cat" and "rat" have not changed in this second group of sentences. They still have the same referential meaning as before. It is the relational meanings that distinguish the two groups of sentences. In the second group, the rat is the agent of the action and the cat is the patient. The change in meaning results from a change in the semantic relationships among the constituents in the sentence.

Many different objects can fill the same semantic role in sentences. That is, many different objects, actions, attributes, and so forth, can be viewed as functionally equivalent for the purposes of linguistic encoding. For example, people, cats, cows, and birds can all initiate actions and, therefore, can play the role of *agent* in an event (e.g., *"John/the cat/the cow* jumped the fence"). Furthermore, the same objects can enter into other types of semantic relationships. For example, people, cats, cows, and birds can be affected by actions and serve the role of *patients* (e.g., "The truck hit *John/the cat/the bird)*, they can be associated habitually with other objects, thus serving as *possessors* (e.g., *"John's/the cat's/the cow's* house), they can all be the recipients of objects or actions and serve as *datives* (e.g., "I gave the carrot to *John/ the cow/the bird)*, and so forth. Finally, semantic relations between different states or events can be encoded using a variety of forms including compound and complex sentences. For example, the sentence "I will go when I'm ready" encodes a temporal relationship between the action of "going" and the state of "readiness." Similarly, the sentence "I like it, but I don't have the money to buy it" explicitly represents an adversative relationship in which one state ("liking") is contrasted with another ("lack of money"). In short, language content refers to the knowledge of the concepts (objects, states, and events) and of the relationships between concepts that underlie the words and sentences that we use.

The second area of linguistic knowledge that must be considered is *language form*. To communicate content, an individual must also have knowledge of the code that is used to represent that content linguistically. Language form includes the sounds, words, syntactic forms, and morphological inflections that the language users of a given speech community have accepted as standard means of representing language content. Form represents the system of rules designed to relate sounds and sequences of sounds to meaning. For example, the child learning English must learn that, usually, the word representing the agent of an event is placed before the word denoting the action. The patient or object then follows the verb. Note that examples 6 and 9 given earlier are exceptions to this canonical pattern. These passive utterances are not used or understood until long after children have been using sentences in the active voice, as in examples 5 and 8. The observed gap in the time of acquisition for these forms cannot be due to the types of language content that are expressed by each sentence type. Rather, it results from differences in the complexities of the language forms themselves and from differences in the speaking conditions under which each sentence type can be used appropriately.

In sum, to create meaningful sentences, the child must learn how content and form interact. The outcome of this learning gives the child the potential to use language in a highly flexible and creative manner. Once rules for relating content and form have been acquired, the child has the potential to understand and produce meaningful strings of words and morphological inflections that have never been heard or expressed before.

This brings us to the third dimension of language discussed by Bloom and Lahey (1978), *language use*, often referred to as *pragmatics*. This component reflects the social nature of language. Although language can be used for many purposes, its primary function is communication. Within interactionist theory, language can be neither conceived nor understood without consideration of (1) the social functions that language serves and (2) the influences of the social context on the topics that are discussed and on the forms that are selected by the speaker in a particular speaking situation.

Assuming that an individual has available language content and knowledge of the forms that can be used to encode that content, the only other ingredient necessary for the production of a speech act would be the presence of some perceived need to communicate. In some cases, the speaker intends to share information or to modify the attitudes, beliefs, and information system of another person (e.g., "Chuck is sick," "I hate exams"). In other cases, the speaker may request action or information, make promises, tease or insult a partner, claim authority, and so forth (e.g., "Have you heard Dewie and the Big Dogs?" "Please get over here").

A child must learn that language can be used to serve a number of different social functions. To acquire this kind of knowledge, the child must discover the ways in which content, form, and use interact. Examples 1 and 3 encode the same content. They have different forms, however—one is a declarative and one is an interrogative. The child must learn that, typically, if a person wants to make an assertion about an event, a declarative form is used. If information is being requested, the interrogative is the canonical form.

This type of rule represents only one aspect of language use. The child must also learn that features of the speaking context have a pervasive influence on what can be talked about as well as on the forms that are used to encode expressible language content. For example, the speaker must consider her social role with respect to the listener. If the child is talking to a peer, a command like "Give me that candy!" might be maximally efficient in achieving the intended function of the speech act. When addressing an adult, however, a less direct and more polite form is probably more desirable (e.g., "May I have candy, please" or "Boy, I love that kind of candy!"). As these examples illustrate, the relationship between form and use is not direct—the same language form can be used to serve a number of different functions. Conversely, the same function can be served by a number of different forms.

The speaker must also determine the amount of relevant background information that is shared by the listener. If the listener has a great deal of information, the speaker's language form can take on an abbreviated form. Consider the following examples:

11. Speaker 1 approaches Speaker 2, who is admiring a painting on the wall of an art gallery.

    Speaker 1:   It's terrific!

    Speaker 2:   Isn't it, though.

12. Some time after the museum visit, at school. Speaker 2 enters the room and Speaker 1 approaches her.

    Speaker 1:   Do you remember when we went to the museum last month?

    Speaker 2:   Yeah.

    Speaker 1:   Do you remember that Van Gogh self-portrait?

    Speaker 2:   Sure.

    Speaker 1:   That was terrific!

    Speaker 2:   It really was.

In example 12, Speaker 1's intentions were essentially the same as in example 11—to assert an opinion of a painting. In example 12, though, Speaker 1 cannot assume that Speaker 2 will know what she is talking about. She uses two turns to orient Speaker 2 to the event, and then makes an evaluative assertion. Imagine the problem that would have arisen if, in her first speaking turn in example 12, Speaker 1 would have said "It's terrific." This is an example of how the speaker must adapt to the needs of the listener if her goals for speaking are to be attained.

According to the interactionist viewpoint, competent use and understanding of language depends on a very complex interaction between knowledge in each of the three dimensions of language: content, form, and use. Along the road to communicative competence, the child's knowledge in each of these areas is undergoing a continual process of developmental change. Changes are believed to occur as a result of the child's interactions with the physical, social, and linguistic world. Through interactions with the environment, the child becomes aware that the objects and events that are experienced do not behave randomly. Rather, certain events are predictable and relationships between the individual objects of experience can be identified. The one principle that is common to all forms of an interactionist model of language learning is that the child actively explores the world in an effort to interpret and understand it. With continued exploration and experience, the child's attention becomes more focused on the regularities and consistencies to be found in both the nonlinguistic and linguistic environments. The child's major task in learning language is to induce the relationships between language content, form, and use.

Viewed in this way, it can be seen that knowledge of language content, form, and use are not only the *objectives* of the child's exploration of the environment; at any given point, the child's incomplete knowledge in each of these areas and her knowledge of the nonlinguistic world serve as the forces *guiding* the child's exploration of the environment and interpretation of experience. To be sure, the environment has a tremendous impact on the child's learning; but which aspects of the environment are attended to and which contexts present opportunities for learning depend to at least an equal extent on the child and what she *knows* about the world.

A complete account of the specific learning mechanisms and processes that lead to developmental changes in the child's language knowledge would be very complex and has not been fully developed. To illustrate some possible ways in which learning could occur, however, two general types of situations that should lead to language learning, according to this theory, are presented. A more complete delineation of possible learning situations is beyond the scope of this discussion.

In the first scenario, the child is in a situation in which the need to express available linguistic content is present, but the knowledge of the syntactic form needed to express that content is not. In such a situation, the child might be motivated to begin an active search in the environment for ways in which this type of content can be encoded.

> The child observes a dog licking the child's plate. The child has knowledge of agents, actions, and objects, and can coordinate all three mentally. The child does not have knowledge of the semantic-syntactic pattern, agent–action–object, however.

Child: Dog lick. Dog plate.
Adult: Yeah, the dog is licking the plate.
Child: Dog lick plate.

In her first utterance the child used available knowledge to produce an utterance that encodes only part of her intended message. A second utterance is required to encode the aspect of language content that was omitted from the original sentence. The adult's sentence *expands* the child's two utterances and provides the child with a model for how the agent, action, and object can be combined in one sentence. Under the conditions present in this example, this type of expansion would appear to make the relationship between content and form maximally salient. The child's spontaneous imitation that follows may also have a positive influence on learning (Bloom, Hood, and Lightbown, 1974; Scherer and Olswang, 1984), but it is not believed to be necessary for learning to occur.

Within the same situation just presented, the child might also perform in an alternative fashion. For example, given the motivation to communicate and the support from the context, the child may be able to expand on her own existing knowledge base and formulate a type of sentence never before produced (e.g., "doggie lick plate"). In this case, the adult's expansion or other related response would serve to inform the child that such strings of utterances are acceptable means of expressing this type of content. This information might motivate the child to look for examples of expressions of action relations involving agents and objects in the environment. It might also encourage the child to attempt the agent–action–object form on future occasions to satisfy the need to encode these relations.

In all likelihood, it is not always the case that a child who is motivated to speak intends to mean more than her existing formal abilities will enable her to encode. On some occasions, each aspect of the language content that the child intends to express will be represented in the child's sentence. Under these circumstances, the adult's expansion or even a contingent question might force the child to attend to aspects of the situation that were not originally part of the child's mental plan for speaking. This type of situation is illustrated in the example below.

The child looks out the window and watches her brother, Jay, playing.
Child: Jay play.
Adult: He's playing in the sandbox.
Child: Play sandbox.
Or, alternatively,
Adult: Where's Jay playing?
Child: Sandbox.

Through these types of interactions, the child may not only be led to new ways to combine words, but she may be led to the very cognitive relations on which more complex utterances depend.

Implications for Intervention

Acceptance of an interactionist position will have a significant influence on how clinicians view their role as interventionists and, indeed, on what they are willing to call intervention. Bloom and Lahey (1978) suggest that the term "facilitator" of language is more appropriate than "teacher" or "trainer" for an individual engaged in intervention. The necessary inductions relating language content, form, and use cannot be taught directly. But it may be possible to manipulate the social, physical, and linguistic environments in ways that facilitate the child's perception of consistencies across these three environmental domains. Below are some implications for intervention procedures and activities that seem to follow naturally from the interactionist assumptions about language and language learning.

1. Language form should *never* be divorced from the underlying meanings that it represents or from the social contexts in which the forms may be used appropriately. In other words, models should be presented in meaningful contexts, and the child should be expected to produce the target behavior only under conditions in which there is a need to communicate using the target content-form interactions. Requiring a response from the child would be a last resort procedure. Even then, a response should not be required outside of a meaningful context.

2. The child's goal behaviors should be modeled very *frequently* for the child in meaningful contexts. The same linguistic pattern should be modeled to encode a variety of nonlinguistic stimulus situations. This should facilitate the child's induction of abstract patterns (e.g., agent–action–location, "The boy is playing outside," "The lady is working in the garden").

3. To increase the likelihood that the child will induce relations between contextual events and language form and content, language should be used to describe the objects and events to which the child is attending.

4. Appropriate nonverbal consequences (e.g., providing objects and actions solicited by the child) and contingent verbal responses, such as expansions, should follow the child's utterances in a highly consistent manner.

5. Generally, the complexity of the adult's speech should be adjusted to reflect the child's existing capacities in order to increase the saliency of new content categories or new forms. For example, the regular past tense might be modeled more effectively in sentences like

"You moved it" rather than "You moved it behind the couch, didn't you."

6. Activities should be selected based on the *child's* interests since these are the conditions in which the need for communication is most likely to arise frequently and naturally.

Differences between these suggestions and those derived from operant learning theory are not difficult to see. There is no effort to secure a response from the child, although attempts are made to see that opportunities to make functional use of the target responses occur frequently. Furthermore, there is never any effort to reinforce the child with anything other than the natural consequences available within a typical speaking situation.

Most of these procedures are consistent with, if not directly derivable from, the assumptions of social learning theory. The greatest differences between the clinical implications of social learning theory and the interactionist position presented in this chapter arise from the fact that the interactionist theory is much more complete in its description of what language is (i.e., what it is that must be learned). This makes possible a much more careful delineation of the goals of intervention and the sequence in which they should be targeted.

Whereas the operant or social learning theorist might attempt to train the use of a particular word or sentence pattern (e.g., "cow" or "milk" or noun–verb–noun), the interactionist will always be equally concerned with the social context in which the form is used, the function that the form serves within that context, and the semantic content that it transmits. Five sample goal statements written from this perspective are given to illustrate possible ways in which the content of intervention would be affected by these concerns:

1. To facilitate the use of the word "cow" to *label* a referent in *response to questions* such as "what's that?"

and as a spontaneous *request* (e.g., the child reaches for the toy cow, looks at the adult, and says "cow").

2. To facilitate the use of the form "-ed" to *comment* about *actions* that took place in the distant *past*.

3. To encourage the child's appropriate elliptical use of "will" to indicate *willingness to perform some act* (i.e., in *response to questions*, such as "Who will pour the juice?" "I will").

4. To facilitate the child's *spontaneous comments* that encode the semantic relations of *agent, locative action*, and *location* (e.g., "John went [to the] store").

5. To encourage the child's more *frequent use of requests for clarification* of all types (e.g., "What?" "Huh?").

TRANSFORMATIONAL GENERATIVE GRAMMAR

Both operant and social learning theory are broadly based in that they attempt to account for learning of all kinds. Neither of these theories is specific in what it considers to be the structure of language. Interactionism is much more detailed in terms of its claims about what must be acquired during language acquisition. The child must acquire knowledge of language content, form, and use to be a competent language user. In contrast, work in developmental psycholinguistics from within the framework of transformational generative grammar (Chomsky, 1957, 1965, 1975) has focused primarily on the acquisition of syntax. Erreich, Valian, and Winzemer (1980) recognize the importance of nonsyntactic aspects of language use; "however, these related areas supplement but do not supplant syntax" (p. 157). Therefore, acquisitions in nonlinguistic cognition, the lexicon, relational semantics and pragmatics do not figure significantly in most developmental formulations of the theory. The theoretical account described in the following paragraphs is taken largely from Erreich and colleagues (1980). Moulton and Robinson (1981) present a very readable summary and critique of the transformational theory, including its developmental aspects. A more thorough presentation of the standard theory can be found in Akmajian and Heny (1975).

Rudiments of the Theory

In their theoretical account of language acquisition, Erreich and colleagues (1980) claim that what the child must eventually acquire is a transformational grammar, including a phrase structure component that serves to generate deep structures and a set of transformational rules that performs basic operations on deep structures to yield surface structures. Phrase structure rules provide descriptions of the ways in which grammatically well-formed sentences are structured. Some sample phrase structure rules are given below.

Sentence $\longrightarrow$ Noun phrase–Verb phrase
Noun phrase $\longrightarrow$ Article–Noun
Verb phrase $\longrightarrow$ Verb–Noun phrase
Article $\longrightarrow$ "the," "a"
Noun $\longrightarrow$ "rat," "cat," "ball," "John"
Verb $\longrightarrow$ "chase," "fall," "see," "love"

The syntactic units used in these rules do not simply reflect the combinatorial properties of the language. For example, in the sentence "The cat chased the rat," "the" and "rat" seem intuitively to be more closely related than "chased" and the second "the." This is represented in the phrase structure rules by the statement that articles and nouns group together (i.e., as noun phrases) and verbs group with the noun phrase unit to make up an even larger unit (i.e., a verb phrase). Phrase structure rules reflect a competent speaker-hearer's intuitions about how closely the individual constituents in the sentences are related. The output of these rules is called the *deep structure* of a sentence.

Whereas phrase structure rules operate on a single sentence unit at a time (e.g., sentence, noun phrase, verb phrase), transformational rules operate on entire strings of sentence elements. They are very useful in demonstrating many intuitions of speakers, such as the relatedness of sentences that appear to be different on the surface. For example, most adults view the following sentences as being highly related.

13. "The Blue Jays will win the game."
14. "Will the Blue Jays win the game?"
15. "The game will be won by the Blue Jays."

According to the theory of transformational grammar, the deep structures are highly similar; that is, they are generated by the same phrase structure rules. (Actually, there are some differences in the deep structures of the three sentences, but these need not concern us here.) The particular shape that sentences take on the surface (i.e., their *surface structure*) is due to the additions, deletions, and permutations imposed on the deep structure to turn a sentence like example 13 into a question, as in example 14, or into a passive sentence, as in example 15.

Erreich and colleagues (1980) argue that humans are innately endowed with the capacity to formulate and test hypotheses concerning the structure of language. This genetic endowment is the fundamental mechanism through which a transformational grammar could be acquired. Thus, the child must observe linguistic input and generate hypotheses concerning the structure underlying that input. These hypotheses must then be tested by evaluating new input and by comparing the structures generated by the child's own grammar with those of adults. Those hypotheses that continue to yield sentences conforming to the surface structure of sentences in the linguistic environment will be maintained; those that generate output inconsistent with input will be modified or otherwise abandoned.

The fundamental problem, from the transformationalist's viewpoint, concerns how a child can learn the basic properties of a complex transformational grammar in such a short time with apparently little or no explicit teaching. It must be remembered that a transformational generative grammar has both underlying and surface structures; yet the child is exposed only to surface structures. For such a grammar to be learnable, even for a child who is an active hypothesis tester, the learning task must be simplified. Erreich and co-workers (1980), following Chomsky (1965, 1975), claim that this can only be done by proposing that the child begins the task with some built in "knowledge" that guides her hypothesis-formulating activity. This genetic endowment is claimed to comprise those properties of grammar that are found universally, across all languages of the world.

Although exactly what is universal is still a very moot issue, it is generally acknowledged that purely syntactic categories, such as "subject," "object," "noun phrase," and "sentence," are abstract categories that are universal. These categories are presumed, therefore, to be innately endowed. In a way, syntactic categories are viewed as basic motivational forces for the child's task of acquiring language. Searching for evidence of and testing hypotheses about these categories, then, could be viewed as a means of assuaging these predetermined needs, much as finding and indulging in a source of food will satisfy the child's hunger.

Reinforcement is not necessary within this theory. Invoking reinforcement as a necessary component of the theory would make no more sense than to say that a child must be reinforced in order to learn to walk! Furthermore, it is not clear how reinforcement of the child's actual surface level productions could assist her in learning what is necessary: an abstract system of linguistic categories and rules. According to Erreich and colleagues (1980), the child is never required to learn or be reinforced for using the universal properties of language, she must only discover how the properties are represented in the particular language that is being learned.

The specific transformations found from language to language differ greatly, but the basic operations that they perform, e.g., moving, inserting, and deleting elements of deep structure, seem to be universal. Furthermore, there is a universal constraint on which elements of language may be copied, inserted, deleted, etc. This constraint is called *structure dependency*. It asserts that only syntactic categories such as noun phrases, adverbial phrases, verb phrases, or auxiliary verbs may be manipulated by the basic operations. Thus, we may observe a transformation that involves the interchanging of subject and object noun phrases (e.g., the passive), but not operations such as "interchange any word beginning with /b/ and any word beginning with /l/ in the deep structure" or "take the third word in the deep structure and move it in front of the first word." In this theory, it is proposed that universal properties of transformations make up part of the child's genetic inheritance and that this "knowledge" assists the child's development by precluding the formulation of transformations that violate these universal constraints. In a sense, the child is genetically programmed to avoid wasting time by testing hypotheses concerning transformational rules that are never found in any language of the world. The task of determining which specific transformations from the universal repertoire are found in the language to be learned is believed to be induced through hypothesis generation and testing.

Implications for Intervention

Transformational accounts of language and language learning have influenced intervention most significantly by encouraging clinicians to focus on syntax in selecting goals for intervention. To learn language, the child must acquire information on syntactic categories, such as grammatical subject and object, noun phrase and verb phrase, as well as phrase structure and transformational rules. Furthermore, the child's syntactic learning is viewed as being relatively independent of other types of learning. Therefore, in intervention, efforts should be directed toward acquisition of these types of syntactic goals. Under the influence of this theory, the trend for speech pathologists, prior to 1960, to concern themselves primarily with articulation and vocabulary gave way to a strong emphasis on language structure (McLean, 1983).

Yet even with the embellishments of Erreich and co-workers (1980), transformational theory lacks critical details concerning the mechanisms responsible for a child's movement from point A to point B in development. This is accented in cases of language impairment. In these cases, it can be assumed that the child has suffered some insult to the neurological centers that are central to her hypothesis generating and testing capacity. It is unclear just how a clinician could intervene to the child's best advantage under these circumstances, given the abstract, autonomous nature of syntax. Consequently, the transformational theory has had little impact on the procedures used by language clinicians to facilitate language growth (Craig, 1983), especially in the early stages of development.

Perhaps the most significant procedural development emanating from this theoretical perspective can be found in types of sentence play tasks advocated by Muma (1971, 1978b). In many of these tasks, words and sentences are given to the child, who is required to somehow transform them into some alternate sentence. For example, a child faced with the problem of learning relative clauses might be given two sentences, one of which can be embedded in the other.

Clinician: The boy had a sore toe. The boy lost the race.
Child: The boy who had a sore toe lost the race.

Although these tasks may be useful in facilitating a child's metalin-guistic knowledge as well as her creative and flexible usage of newly acquired principles and rules, performance of such tasks indicates that the necessary linguistic rules are already part of the child's lin-guistic repertoire. Therefore, these rules must be acquired through some other means.

Although the transformational position has not been particularly productive in helping clinicians know what to do to facilitate language growth in language impaired children, it has strong implications for what will *not* be effective. Because language is viewed as an abstract set of specifically linguistic categories and rules, manipulations of the child's overt language performances through imitation and reinforce-ment have little likelihood for success. In other words, if reinforce-ment of surface level behaviors has any lasting effect at all on lan-guage learning, the child's subsequent language use would be highly restricted and inflexible—that is, not characteristic of the creative, rule-governed language use of normally developing individuals. Whatever the role taken by the transformational grammarian in intervention, it would *not* be that of the highly programmed behavioral technician.

CONCLUSION

In this chapter, four different theories of language learning were presented, along with some of the implications that each has for lan-guage intervention. For the most part, I have been uncritical of these theories. It has not been my intent to convince anyone of the superior-ity of one over the other. It is not necessary to read too far beyond this chapter, however, to recognize that my own biases reflect an interac-tionist perspective. I believe that all language goals and procedures must take into account the content that is being communicated, the language form needed to express that content, and the social circum-stances that make the performance of a particular speech act truly functional and socially appropriate.

It should be pointed out, however, that none of the four theories presented is an entirely adequate description of the variables critical to language learning, and none satisfactorily explains how relevant vari-ables interact to enable most children to acquire language with rela-tively little effort. Furthermore, although other theoretical positions also exist (see, for example, Bates and MacWhinney, 1982; Maratsos and Chalkley, 1980; Moulton and Robinson, 1981; Rice and Kemper, 1985), they all have limitations in some respects. Neither the basic strength of these theories nor the success of the clinical procedures emanating from these views warrants a blind commitment from clinicians.

How, then, can interventionists make maximal use of their knowledge of theory in clinical contexts? In my view, they can do this by considering themselves to be clinical researchers rather than clinical technicians. Let me explain briefly.

When a speech-language pathologist assesses a young child and determines that intervention is required, she is operating under three assumptions: (1) the child is abnormally slow in one or more aspects of language development or has certain biological or behavioral characteristics that place her at risk for such a delay in development; (2) language intervention of the type selected can facilitate the child's growth of linguistic abilities and may even help her catch up to peers; and (3) without this intervention, the child is not likely to catch up on her own and, indeed, may continue to grow further behind, increasing the probability of problems in social, cognitive, and educational development as well. Each of these assumptions must be accepted before intervention begins; yet the degree of confidence that can be held in any of these assumptions is regrettably low. We simply do not have enough information about language impaired children to know precisely who should receive treatment, how it should be administered, and when it should begin to be optimally effective. So, every time these assumptions are made, the clinician is, in effect, beginning an experiment.

The success of our clinical experiments depends on our ability to generate sound clinical hypotheses and to design our clinical experiments in ways that can put these hypotheses adequately to the test. These hypotheses will grow out of three interrelated variables: our past clinical experience, our knowledge of the intervention literature, *and* our own theoretical orientations regarding what language is and how it is acquired. We can test these hypotheses through our intervention efforts. Just how this can be done is the subject of much of the rest of this book (see especially Chapter 7).

As a profession, we must begin to test more carefully and thoroughly the real and durable effects that intervention has on our clients' ability to communicate. As individual clinicians, we must begin to test our own individual clinical hypotheses in experimental fashion and, on the basis of our results, modify our procedures and the theoretical notions from which they emerge. The clinician who acts as an experimenter, constantly challenging her theoretical positions through clinical hypothesis testing, is, in my view, in the best position to help children. Furthermore, because greater attention is paid to the details of the experiment, she is in the best position to demonstrate the effects of her efforts.

Chapter 2

Identifying Language Impaired Children

Because this book is about intervention with children who are language impaired, it is imperative that this group of children be carefully defined. This task would not seem to present much difficulty. After all, every clinician who works with children spends a good bit of time identifying language impairments and admitting clients to therapy on the basis of such identification, then dismissing clients when intervention objectives have been reached. Unfortunately, deciding on what constitutes language impairment is not simple at all. Although there are probably no issues that are more fundamental to the needs of the practicing speech-language pathologist, deciding when to apply the diagnostic label "language impaired" to a child is one of the most controversial issues in this field.

As a working definition, language impairment will be considered to be a significant deficit in the child's level of development of the form, content, or use of language. This definition reflects my admitted bias to an interactionist view of language learning. In most language impaired children, deficits manifest themselves as delays in the onset of use of various linguistic forms and expressions of semantic content. For example, language impaired children are often late in their production of their first words, their first semantic-syntactic constructions, and their first morphological inflections. In addition, these same aspects of language are typically mastered over a protracted developmental period (Johnston, 1982a; Johnston and Schery, 1976; Leonard, 1979; Leonard and Fey, 1979; Liebergott, Bashir, and Schultz, 1983; Morehead and Ingram, 1973; Snyder, 1984). Recent studies of these children have indicated that significant delays in the use of language in social contexts are also common (Fey and Leonard, 1983; Gallagher and Prutting, 1983; Johnston, 1982a; Snyder, 1984; Wollner, 1983).

On the surface, this general definition may seem innocuous and, perhaps, even beyond dispute. The term "significant" is subject to a variety of interpretations, however, and this is where the controversy begins. Each interpretation leads to differences in the size and constitution of the group of children described as language impaired. Our task is really doubly complex. We must try to identify all of those children who have or are likely to have difficulties in speech and language skills that present real obstacles to communication and, perhaps, to later educational and social development. On the the other hand, we must be aware of the tremendous amount of variability found among normal children in language acquisition. A large group of children who are considered "below average" in their development are still well within the range of what may be called "low normal" (Snyder, 1982).

All of the different interpretations of "significant delay" in our proposed definition seem to be based on two different underlying philosophies about what constitutes an "impairment," "sickness," or "disorder" in any health related profession: normativism and neutralism (Tomblin, 1983). These positions will be described, and their implications for the language clinician will be discussed, in the remainder of this section. The chapter will close with some conclusions regarding how language impairment can be defined and which children should receive priority for admittance into a language intervention program.

THE NORMATIVIST POSITION

It is possible to define language impairment in broad terms that consider not only the child's performance on linguistic and cognitive tasks but also society's views on this behavior and on the linguistic, social, psychological, educational, and economic consequences with which certain levels of linguistic performance are likely to be related. The value or lack of value that society places on the presenting condition (for example, a mild problem with inflectional morphemes or adequate use of syntax in the face of extreme avoidance of conversational situations) and future conditions that are possibly related (such as certain difficulties with reading or the development of positive peer relations) are actually parts of the definition of impairment within this philosophical position called normativism (Tomblin, 1983). Advocates of this position would maintain that the concept of language impairment cannot be understood without a consideration of what society views as a handicapping condition.

Tomblin (1983) suggests that what may be important is *not* the child's level of language skill per se but whether the child's level of language skill places her at risk for social disvalue.

> Specifically, a language disorder exists for an individual when that person is at some level of risk for disvalue in one or more domains of life function because of the person's current or projected language abilities . . . . A mild language disorder is one that presents the person with only limited risk for disvalue while a severe problem represents a high probability for disvalued life functions . . . . The clinician who states that a child has a severe language disorder in this definition is making a claim about the likelihood and degree of unpleasant events for this child because of the characteristics of the child's language development. (pp. 105–106)

Using this normativist type of definition, it would be possible to consider a child to be language impaired even when she falls within what is typically viewed as the normal range on standardized tests. In this case, the child's overall communicative skills would be judged to be sufficiently poor with respect to other abilities as to hinder development in areas on which society places great value (e.g., saying what one wants to communicate without undue frustration, reading fluently, getting a particular kind of job, developing friendships through communicative interaction with peers).

This procedure for evaluating children's communicative ability and potential within a broader social, physical, psychological, and educational framework is intuitively very appealing. The accuracy of judgments made on this basis could be enhanced by an interdisciplinary assessment effort. Through consultation with parents, educators, physicians, psychologists, and, in some cases, physical and occupational therapists, the speech-language pathologist may be better able to determine what the child's present condition is and the extent to which this condition is likely to result in disvalue in any identifiable life functions. At present, however, reliable prognosticators within education, psychology, and speech-language pathology are not easy to find. In their discussion of children judged to be at risk for language impairments, Liebergott and colleagues (1983) concluded "Unfortunately, the important question 'will the noted language difference affect the child's achievement of educational and social success?'—was left unanswered and remains so to this day" (p. 41).

It is not difficult to predict that a child of $2^{1/2}$ or 3 years of age who is using no words will continue to show some language learning problems. Furthermore, if attempts to remediate these problems are not successful, the child is at risk for future problems in social and educational development (Aram, Ekelman, and Nation, 1984; Aram and

Nation, 1980; DeAjuriaguerra et al., 1976; Hall and Tomblin, 1978; King, Jones, and Lasky, 1982; Nippold and Fey, 1983; Weiner, 1974). When the child's problems are less marked, however, such predictions become increasingly difficult to make. Leonard's (1972) comments of over a decade ago are still relevant today.

> It is the future linguistic behavior of children who use restricted utterances made up of early-developing structures that proves difficult to predict. If such a child is three or older, it is not worth the risk of waiting to see whether his language develops further, for the social and educational developments in his near future will demand a more sophisticated linguistic system. And if the child is not yet three years of age? Many of us may not treat such a child because he may be a "late developer." A few of us may recommend some sort of language intervention, but all of us are only guessing. (p. 441)

Based on the normativist account, it becomes important to distinguish between those who are viewed as language impaired and those who are actually admitted to intervention. For example, the child in the borderline case referred to previously by Leonard (1972) could be viewed as mildly impaired, because his pattern of development suggests only a limited probability that his problems will persist and become a source of social disvalue. The determination of whether intervention is appropriate for such a child is made no less difficult by this account, but it can be viewed as a distinct problem. This issue will be brought up again in the conclusion to this chapter.

THE NEUTRALIST POSITION

More commonly, speech-language clinicians, researchers, and educators have argued that language impairment may be defined operationally through reference only to the child's level of language functioning. First, the child's level of language functioning is measured using standardized and nonstandardized tests, developmental scales, and behavioral observation (Miller, 1978). The child's performance is then compared to the performance of other children of the same chronological or mental age (CA or MA) and sociocultural, linguistic, and economic background. Children who fall below a certain preestablished criterion are then viewed as language impaired.

This method of determining who is language impaired is based on an underlying philosophy called *neutralism*. "The term neutralism in fact refers to neutrality with regard to social values" (Tomblin, 1983, p. 87). Regardless of the health-related field in which it is applied, neutralism has as its foundation the notion of "significant deviation from the norm." Therefore, any definition of language impairment that is grounded in neutralism must confront three difficult problems: (1) How shall the child's language be measured to determine the normal standard? (2) How shall the reference population to which the child's performance is compared be selected? and (3) What shall be considered a significant discrepancy from the norm? Each of these questions poses a significant challenge to speech-language pathologists.

How Shall the Child's Language Be Measured

It is often suggested that standardized testing offers the best method for determining the existence of a language impairment. Nonstandardized observations and descriptions are used to help the clinician to determine what standardized tests should be administered, to supplement knowledge gained through standardized testing, and to provide more in-depth information into the nature of the child's linguistic difficulties so that appropriate intervention goals and procedures can be developed (Bloom and Lahey, 1978; Lund and Duchan, 1983). Although this approach is prudent and guards against many problems inherent in language assessment, it is not without problems of its own, and these should be acknowledged.

Comparisons between a child's level of linguistic performance and the performance of a normative group depend on the use of valid and reliable means for measuring such performance. However, our working definition of language impairment includes deficits in language use. Because very few standardized tests take relevant pragmatic factors into consideration, and because the child's linguistic skills are tested outside typical communicative contexts, these tests often distort the child's true linguistic abilities.

An even more serious problem is that the vast majority of tests of speech and language performance do not meet even minimal requirements for the standardization of psychometric instruments (McCauley and Swisher, 1984). Comparisons of a child's performance with that of other children are not likely to be valid and reliable when the validity and reliability of the instruments used to measure that performance are not well established. Standardardized testing is often necessary and illuminating, but its shortcomings must be recognized.

Acceptance of a neutralist position does not restrict the clinician to the exclusive use of standardized tests and procedures to aid in the identification of language impairment. It is possible to make use of descriptive, criterion-referenced measures for purposes of identification as well as for characterization of the child's problem and to aid in goal selection. Practitioners using such procedures, however, should have a healthy respect for the amount of individual variation that can be found among normal children in the speed, order, and pattern of linguistic development within various dimensions of language (syntax, morphology, semantics, phonology, pragmatics) and across those dimensions. The clinician's determination of what is normal often must be based on descriptions of extremely small samples of children reported in the literature on normal development (e.g., Brown, 1973). Furthermore, even if the behaviors of these few children could be viewed as the norm, there is a great deal of room for error because the children reported in the literature often have come from exemplary backgrounds, and they have been observed over very long periods of time in a number of contexts (e.g., Brown, 1973). In many clinical contexts, longitudinal observation and analysis for purposes of diagnosis is not possible, no matter how desirable it may be.

What Should Serve as the Normative Standard

After the methods for observing and reporting the child's communicative behaviors have been selected, the clinician still has some formidable decisions to make. To determine if a deficit in development exists, a comparison must be made between the child's performance and some reference group. The clinician must decide who this reference group will be. There are two such comparisons commonly used in practice: chronological age referencing and mental age referencing. Two other possibilities to be discussed include intralinguistic referencing and the regression discrepancy method.

Chronological Age (CA) Referencing. With CA referencing, language impairment is defined as a clinically significant departure from what is expected for children of the child's own CA. This definition has broad implications for practicing clinicians. For example, Bangs (1982), who recommends this procedure, notes quite correctly that "With this interpretation, mentally retarded children are language delayed as are deaf children who have had insufficient language training" (p. 3). To take the CA referencing definition to its logical extreme, children with chronic and severe seizure disorders, all severely multiply handicapped children, all autistic children, as well as many others, must be included. This may be acceptable, and even desirable, for some clinicians. It is important to observe, however, that this definition implies not only that these children should be considered candidates for language intervention but also that the objectives of intervention would be to bring the child's communicative abilities to an age-equivalent level (Miller, 1981a,b). Unfortunately, this is frequently an unrealistic expectation for many of the children. A final problem with this procedure involves unusually bright children who are performing at an average language level for their age, but who are markedly deficient in certain language areas with respect to other cognitive and academic areas. Under the foregoing definition, these children could not be viewed as language impaired and likely would not be eligible for intervention.

Mental Age Referencing. Some of the problems with CA referencing just discussed can be avoided by comparing the child's performance with children of the same mental age (MA). This position is based on the presumed relationship between nonlinguistic cognitive development and language development. The nature of this relationship seems to be correlational rather than causal (Bates, Benigni, Bretherton, Camaioni, and Volterra, 1977; Miller, 1981b; Miller, Chapman, Branston, and Reichle, 1980). In other words, specific cognitive developments (for example, the attainment of object permanence or the development of symbolic play) are neither necessary nor sufficient for the development of specific levels of linguistic performance; however, a given child's development on linguistic parameters is not likely to diverge greatly from development on related cognitive parameters.

Miller (1981a,b) and Westby (1980) are two of the strongest advocates of MA referencing. Miller (1981b) states the empirical and practical rationale for this position especially clearly.

> The practical significance of the correlational view of the cognition hypothesis is the value of mental age over chronological age in determining whether the child has a problem in acquiring language at an appropriate rate. The data to date clearly support MA as the general pacesetter for language acquisition. As a result, we cannot judge performance status as deficit unless we have measures of nonverbal mental age. The alternative, chronological age, leads us to conclude that all retarded children have language deficits that can be remediated to CA level. (p. 336)

This procedure has the practical advantage of not overidentifying children as language impaired when their problems in all areas of cognitive and social behavior parallel their delays in language development. In addition, it makes it possible to identify children as language impaired when a significant verbal-cognitive performance gap is observed, regardless of whether the child is high or low on the IQ continuum. Under this proposal, the basis for terminating intervention would presumably be attainment of a level of language skills approximately equivalent to those expected for the child's mental age.

Because the relationship between language and cognition has been studied in normal and developmentally disabled children most intensely between birth and 24 months, Kemp (1983) adopts MA referencing only for children in this age range. As children grow older, components of cognition become increasingly complex and difficult to measure. Therefore, Kemp argues that the procedure is not appropriate for older children.

Leonard (1983) raises objections to MA referencing on slightly different grounds. Leonard notes that some normally and abnormally developing children with linguistic abilities more highly developed than their nonlinguistic cognitive skills have been observed (Folger and Leonard, 1978; Greenwald and Leonard, 1979; Ingram, 1981; Miller, 1981a,b). Therefore, it is conceivable that language intervention of some type could help a given child's language to develop beyond expected levels based on MA. In fact, the correlational version of the cognitive hypothesis makes it possible for language to lead the way and even facilitate indirectly the development of cognitive structures. Therefore, if MA referencing is used to determine when an impairment exists, other factors should be used to determine which children will be admitted to intervention programs and on what basis intervention will be terminated.

Intralinguistic Referencing. Kemp (1983) adopts a third neutralist position that involves comparison of a given child's performance in each area of language (e.g., phonology, semantics, syntax, pragmatics) with performance in all other areas. Children who show significant deficits in one or more areas with respect to the remaining areas would be considered language impaired. For example, a 3½ year old child with normal intelligence would be considered by Kemp to be "language disordered" if her measured vocabulary and phonological skills reached age-equivalent levels and syntactic and morphological skills were commensurate with the abilities of younger children. Kemp regards this pattern as truly abnormal, not just delayed, and therefore finds such a pattern to be highly significant clinically. Under this model, children with synchronous patterns of delay (for example, all language skills delayed 18 months) would *not* be considered candidates for intervention, although they could be part of a "general language stimulation program."

The biggest problem with this approach to defining impairment is its assumption that asynchronous development across the various components of language is truly an abnormal pattern. As Chapman (1983) has argued, this assumption, at best, is not thoroughly tested and, at worst, appears not to be valid. That is, some normally developing children also seem to show patterns of strength in some areas and relative weaknesses in others. Another significant implication of this approach is that many children with synchronous but delayed patterns of development would *not* be considered significantly language impaired, and perhaps would not receive language intervention.

Regression Discrepancy. MA referencing has a disadvantage in that it requires standardized test scores or the results of observational procedures to be converted into age scores. Raw score to age-equivalent score conversions are based on techniques that result in an ordinal scale, not an interval scale, as is typically assumed. For example, on the *Test for Auditory Comprehension of Language* (Carrow, 1973), the difference between a score corresponding to an age equivalent of 3 years 0 months and a score with an age equivalent of 4 years 0 months is 21 items on the test. A 4 year old scoring at the 3 year level would be almost 2 standard deviations from the mean. In contrast, the difference between scores equivalent to the 4 and 5 year levels is only six items, a difference of only approximately ½ of a standard deviation. Thus, a 4 year old who is delayed 1 year would probably be viewed as having a significant impairment in the areas covered on this test. A 5 year old with a similar 1 year delay would be viewed as low average. This phenomenon is not specific to this test but is a characteristic of psychometric tests and the process used to compute age equivalencies. Interpretations based on age equivalencies may be highly misleading, especially when several test scores must be converted.

Snyder (1982) has focused attention on another method that controls for this type of error as well as the standard error of measurement that is characteristic of any test instrument. It also takes into account the fact that performance in areas such as intelligence is not perfectly correlated with language performance. This method is called regression discrepancy. The mathematical characteristics of this method are beyond the scope of this discussion, but details can be found in Salvia and Ysseldyke (1978) and Snyder (1982). Essentially, regression discrepancy would enable the clinician to take the child's ability scores (e.g., standard scores on some standardized test of nonverbal intelligence) and age and predict the child's expected standard scores on tests of language performance. This can be done by using data from the test publishers regarding the reliability of each test and how well the various tests are correlated. If the child's standard score on the language test is sufficiently below the predicted level, the child is viewed as language impaired.

With this procedure, the decision that a child is language impaired would be based on objective data with attested reliability and without the error introduced by all of the procedures already listed. There are some problems that should be pointed out, however. First, of the 13 frequently used standardized language measures examined by Snyder (1982), only five had sufficient reliablity measures *and* had been correlated with some measure of intelligence. Snyder concluded that, at present, many of our tests have not been sufficiently well tested to make this procedure possible. Efforts to produce better standardized tests should be increased to deal with this problem.

A second, and what I regard as a more serious, objection is that the procedure ties the clinician to the use of standardized tests to make the decision of whether language impairment is present. Although I believe that these tests are helpful when used and interpreted with caution, they cannot supplant a clinician's judgment of the child's overall communicative difficulties as determined through careful observation in various speaking contexts and detailed interviews with the child's caregivers and teachers. The advantages of this procedure would best be realized if the procedure is accompanied by a careful analysis of the child's communicative effectiveness in social situations.

What Is a Clinically Significant Discrepancy from Normal?

Once the clinician has decided on the ways in which the child's communicative performance is to be evaluated for comparative purposes, and once a decision with respect to the reference norm has been made, some criterion of what can be considered to be a *significant* deviation from the norm must be established. Identifications of impairment are commonly based on standardized test results. Typically, a figure such as 2 standard deviations below the mean (Bloom and Lahey, 1978) or below the 10th percentile (Lee, 1974; Rizzo and Stephens, 1981) is chosen. Unfortunately, this decision is arbitrary. A clinician cannot say with certainty that a child at the 1st percentile on a test of expressive language is experiencing general communicative difficulties, nor can she be confident that the child at the 15th percentile is free from problems in the transmission or comprehension of spoken messages. This arbitrariness will result from any approach that is based entirely on references to language performance with no accompanying appeal to the implications that deviations from the norm on language testing might have for more general life functions.

Although it is possible, it is more difficult to identify clinically significant deviations from the norm based on descriptions of the child's performance in naturalistic communicative contexts. Given the expected variability in development across normal children and the variability within the same child in different contexts, computing age equivalence on an observed level of communicative performance in social contexts is extremely difficult. Age- and stage-related behavioral profiles have been developed to make this process easier and somewhat more precise (Crystal, Fletcher, and Garman, 1976; Miller, 1981a), but several problems remain. For example, the Language Assessment, Remediation, and Screening Procedure (LARSP) (Crystal et al., 1976) enables the clinician to profile the syntactic structures used by the child and makes it possible to compare the child's performance with that of normally developing children. Deciding on what constitutes *significant* discrepancy from the norm is just as complex here as for the use of standardized tests, however. Crystal and associates suggest that deviations of greater than six months be considered indicative of potential problems. Even if the arbitrary nature of this suggestion can be overlooked, it is problematic, because a six month delay in a 4½ year old child is probably not as significant as the same six month delay in a 2½ year old child (Carrow-Woolfolk and Lynch, 1982; Kemp, 1983). Furthermore, to emphasize the point made earlier regarding individual variability among normally developing children, a six month "delay" on a profile such as the LARSP *may* not reflect a clinically significant delay at all.

CONCLUSION

Because the issues are so complex, it is not surprising that different experimenters and clinicians have adopted different solutions to the problem of identifying language impaired children. Clinicians should be aware of the many proposals that have been offered, and they should be especially cognizant of the implications of their own decisions. The acceptance of any one criterion as *the* answer to the problem of identifying language impaired children is, in my view, short-sighted and may lead us to complacency when more research and further discussion are what is really needed.

Clinicians must live with these issues as a part of their daily routines, however, and, to do their jobs they need some rational means of identifying language impaired children. To handle the practical aspects of this problem most effectively, the question "What is language impairment?" can and should be subdivided into the following three questions: (1) "Who can be viewed as language impaired?" (2) "Which language impaired children should receive priority for intervention?" and (3) "When should a child be dismissed from an intervention program?" Ultimately, the answers to these questions are personal and subjective, and each clinician will have to come to her own conclusions as to what is best. I offer the following as my own attempt to come to grips with these difficult matters.

Who Can Be Viewed as Language Impaired? I believe that the basic diagnostic decision concerning which children are language impaired should be dealt with from a normativist perspective. The following definition is a modification of that presented by Tomblin (1983):

> A child may be viewed as language impaired when the pattern of communicative performance exhibited enables a clinician to predict continued deficits in language development *and* in the social, cognitive, educational or emotional developments which rely heavily on language skills. Furthermore, infants who have biological or behavioral conditions that are commonly associated with future impairments in communicative functioning (e.g., Down's syndrome, profound hearing impairment, autistic symptoms) may be viewed as language impaired even before the age at which language forms typically begin to appear. The degree of confidence that a clinician can place in this prediction will determine the severity rating for the child's impairment.

This proposed definition has at least three significant advantages over other proposals. First, it requires the clinician to focus attention on the whole child, not just on the child's linguistic abilities per se. The clinician must probe into how the child is dealing with her everyday environment and then determine the extent to which problems in language may be contributing to the individual's overall level of functioning. This pragmatic perspective on diagnosis also has implications for intervention. From such a perspective, it seems to me that clinicians will be less likely simply to teach their language impaired children new things to say, and they will be more interested in helping children learn what they can *do* with their new linguistic attainments. I would regard this as a very positive shift in our attitudes toward language impairment and intervention.

Second, this definition makes it possible to identify children at all levels of the intelligence continuum. For example, most retarded individuals would be included in this definition. Some very bright children with language performance within the normal range based on CA could be included as well. These would be cases in which the child's verbal skills lagged so far behind abilities in other areas that excessive communication failure and frustration were the result.

Third, this definition makes it possible to identify children as language impaired at very early ages on the basis of nonlinguistic factors that frequently are associated with difficulties in language learning. Early intervention programs designed to minimize later linguistic deficiencies could be implemented at an early point in the child's development. The alternative, which I regard as unsatisfactory, is to wait until a significant difference has been detected between the child's actual level of language performance and the level expected for children of the same age. It is true that we presently do not have a great deal of information concerning those prelinguistic and early linguistic factors that reliably signal an increased risk for later language learning difficulties. However, a definition such as the one proposed should foster an intensification of research into the variables that might index later problems.

To put the proposed definition into practice, it is important to ask "On what bases can the necessary predictions be made?" When considering this question, it becomes evident that the methods used to enable clinicians to *predict* future difficulties in language and related areas of development will not differ significantly, at least at the present time, from the methods typically used to diagnose developmental delays in language functioning. This is because preschool children who have been diagnosed as being language impaired according to neutralist criteria (e.g., "clinical impressions" of delayed language functioning and below-normal performance on standardized language tests) typically have been found to encounter difficulties in language and language-related areas later in life. The results of several investigations (e.g., Aram et al., 1984; Aram and Nation, 1980; DeAjuriaguerra et al., 1976; Hall and Tomblin, 1978; King, Jones, and Lasky, 1982; Nippold and Fey, 1983; Weiner, 1974) have led investigators to the general conclusion that

> . . .children with language disorders generally do not present disorders confined only to oral language or present only during childhood. Rather, even when retarded children are eliminated, the majority continue to present broadly based language-learning problems with educational and social consequences for years to come. (Aram, Ekelman, and Nation, 1984, p. 243)

Much more research into specific factors that predict future problems is needed. For now, it appears reasonable to assume that the farther the child's performance on standardized and nonstandardized measures diverges from the level anticipated for children of the same CA or MA, the greater the clinician's confidence in her prediction of subsequent slow development in language and other areas that depend on linguistic knowledge.

The clinician can and should assess the child's use of language in conversational contexts. The child's performance in all areas of language content, form, and use can be compared to the clinician's expectations for a typical child of the same CA or MA. In addition, standardized language testing can be used to assist the clinician in making predictions. The more areas in which the child's performance diverges significantly from the norm and the greater the extent of these discrepancies, the greater the child's risk for persistent language, social, academic, and behavioral problems.

Let's take a brief look at how such a system might work. As a general guideline, we could suggest the 10th percentile on standardized measures as a cut-off point. So that children at all levels of intelligence could be included, the child's current level of language functioning would be compared with that of children of the same CA or MA, whichever was *higher*. By suggesting this as a guideline, I am asserting my belief that children functioning below this level on two or more language tests typically are at significant risk for future problems in language-related areas.

This is only a guideline, however, and this type of information should always be supplemented with other information regarding the child's typical social, cognitive, and linguistic performance. For example, a child who scores roughly at the 10th percentile on several language tests, but who is provided with a good linguistic environment at home and at school and appears to be functioning well in most social and conversational situations may be considered to be only mildly language impaired. The risk for future disvalue, although present, would appear not to be great. Another child who scores at the 10th percentile or perhaps even above (e.g., the 15th percentile) on the same battery of tests might well be considered to have a severe language impairment if other problems are present as well. Such a child might be experiencing behavioral problems, problems in social adaptation, or frustration as a result of faulty communication efforts. In addition, or alternatively, the child might use language to fulfill social functions very infrequently. A diagnosis of severe language impairment in this type of case would reflect the clinician's judgment that this child runs a high risk of suffering future handicaps in language-related areas as a result of her relatively low language performance. Finally (and perhaps least problematically), a child who performs two or more standard deviations below the mean would be considered to be moderately impaired at best because the risk for future difficulties would appear to be quite high.

Now consider an intellectually advanced child who performs at or below the 10th percentile on language tasks when MA is used as a reference, but whose performance is average, based on CA. If this child is not experiencing any difficulties with social, academic, or behavioral adjustment, I would not view the child as having a language impairment at all. If problems that appear to be the consequence of the child's relative difficulties in verbal expression and comprehension are present, however, the child could be considered to be moderately or severely impaired.

The clinician's diagnosis of impairment can be viewed as a hypothesis concerning the probability that the child will experience future academic, social, emotional, or behavioral problems that are at least partially a result of her level of communicative performance. The addition of a normativist perspective to the diagnostic process should motivate clinicians and researchers to begin to search for precise criteria that can enable them to predict more adequately which children with below average performance in language skills are consequently at high risk for lifelong difficulties in a broad range of life functions. To me, this seems like a very worthwhile and important objective.

Which Language Impaired Children Should Receive Priority for Intervention? One of the major consequences of implementing the definition of language impairment outlined earlier is that a large number of children will be diagnosed as mildly to severely language impaired. I believe that all language impaired children should be eligible for at least a trial period of language intervention. To deal with the large numbers of children identified as language impaired, however, clinicians must recognize that intervention cannot and should not always be conceived as a clinician and a child working together in the clinic. Other forms of intervention are possible and will be necessary for some children if the type of system I have suggested is to be used. For example, some children do not have the necessary cognitive abilities to support the functional use of linguistic symbols. Intervention with these and other children probably should involve consultations and training programs with the child's parents. The intent of this type of intervention would be to assist the family in their creation of an environment that is highly conducive to cognitive and linguistic growth in the child. The clinician's direct involvement with the child may be very limited. This issue is discussed more fully in Chapter 3 (see also Chapter 14).

It will also be important for clinicians to develop a system for setting caseload priorities. The system proposed here is predicated on two basic assumptions. First, it is assumed that children with moderate to severe impairments are in greater need of clinical attention than children who are only mildly impaired. Second, it is assumed that children who have language abilities (i.e., estimated language ages, or LAs) that are below expected levels based on their mental ages have more "room for growth" than do children who do not exhibit such a gap. Therefore, they may have more to gain from an intervention program. This assumption is based on my acceptance of the position that cognitive development and linguistic development are strongly correlated and that a child's language abilities are not likely to develop significantly in advance of the child's performance on nonlinguistic cognitive tasks. Children who are language impaired, but who exhibit no MA-LA gap may benefit from intervention, but their potential for dramatic changes in language that might significantly affect their performance in other life functions would appear to be less than that for children exhibiting a clear MA-LA discrepancy.

When these assumptions are applied to the entire group of language impaired children, the following list of priorities emerges:

1. Children with moderate and severe impairments who exhibit a marked gap between their estimated language age and either their MA or CA, whichever is *lower*. This group would include many retarded, deaf, autistic, specifically language impaired children and others, but would exclude children with above average intelligence who have language skills that are in line with expectations based on their CAs.
2. Children with moderate and severe impairments who have a marked MA-LA gap, but not a CA-LA gap. These children will have above average intelligence.
3. Children with moderate and severe impairments, but no MA-LA gap.
4. Children with mild impairments who exhibit a marked gap between their estimated language age and their MA or CA, whichever is lower.
5. Children with mild impairments and above-average intelligence, but no CA-LA gap.
6. Children with mild impairments, but no MA-LA gap.

Children falling in the higher priority brackets would be more likely to receive direct clinical contact from the speech-language pathologist and would be eligible for services at an earlier time than children falling in the lower priority groups. This set of priorities should be regarded only as a set of hypotheses concerning which children need intervention the most and which children can be expected to gain the most from an intervention program. With more research on these issues, some revisions, no doubt, will be necessary. In addition, as more thoroughly tested standardized assessment instruments become available, the use of estimated language and mental ages could conceivably give way to a regression discrepancy formula, such as that proposed by Snyder (1982). The formula would be used to establish caseload priorities, however, not as the basis for diagnosing language impairment.

When Should a Child Be Dismissed from an Intervention Program? Once the decision has been made to provide an intervention program to a language impaired child, it becomes important to think about the conditions under which termination of treatment would be warranted. For some language impaired children, acquisition of an adult-like linguistic system is not a realistic goal, and the clinician must have some basis for deciding when the cost of intervention significantly outweighs its benefit. Failure to set such criteria means that some children will require services for a lifetime even when the gains resulting from intervention are negligible.

Kemp (1983) stresses the importance of establishing criteria for termination before therapy begins (i.e., in a prospective rather than a retrospective fashion). I agree with the general thrust of this proposal. If realistic goals are established at the outset of the intervention program, one reasonable criterion for termination would be the attainment of these goals. However, adoption of this policy would often place the clinician in a difficult position. If the original goals of the program were met, on what basis could the clinician justifiably assume that more complex goals could not also be attained?

It appears that the answers to two questions are crucial in deciding whether or not to discontinue services to a child and the child's family. First, "Is the child improving and, if so, to what extent is intervention responsible?" And second, "Given the child's present level of functioning, can the child still be viewed as being language impaired?" On the basis of my consideration of these factors, I suggest that any of the following conditions would be necessary and sufficient reason for terminating a language intervention program for a particular child.

1. The child has reached all stated objectives and is no longer considered to be at risk for social disvalue (i.e., the child can no longer be viewed as language impaired).
2. The child's progress toward stated goals has plateaued and efforts made to modify the intervention plan, including goals, procedures, activities, and goal attack strategies (see Chapter 4) have not led to notable gains in the child's performance.
3. The child exhibits continued progress toward basic goals, but there is no evidence that the intervention program is responsible for these gains.

Ideally, children should be followed up after termination of treatment, and readmittance to an intervention program should be considered. This is especially important for children who have been dismissed on the basis of the first and third conditions above. For example, the clinician may have been wrong in her judgment that a child is no longer at risk for language and language-related problems. Children who seem to have overcome their early language and language-related problems should be monitored carefully and readmitted to an intervention program when this is warranted. Children who were dismissed on the basis of condition 3 would be expected to continue to make gains in language development even without further intervention. If, following a trial period of 6 months or so, the child does not demonstrate the anticipated gains, intervention should be reinitiated.

SUMMARY

In this chapter, I have presented a number of important and frequently overlooked problems associated with the identification of language impaired children. Several different approaches to diagnosis were presented. After a critical analysis of each of these proposals, I offered my own tentative solution to the problem. This solution involves addressing three related but conceptually distinct questions: (1) "Who can be viewed as language impaired?" (2) "Which language impaired children should receive priority for intervention?" and (3) "When should a child be dismissed from an intervention program?" My answers to these questions have been presented not as the final word on these important matters, but as hypotheses that are subject to modification as new and badly needed information about children with language learning problems becomes available.

Chapter 3

What Is Language Intervention?

As we discuss the numerous intervention approaches that have been proposed and implemented over the past two decades, it will become increasingly clear that what is referred to as intervention by one group of clinicians or researchers is markedly different from what is described as intervention by others. I have claimed that different theoretical positions of the developers and practitioners of intervention programs is a major reason for this fact. Johnston (1983) states her position on this point in no uncertain terms.

> . . .there is no prevailing similarity among the various approaches to language intervention. To assume that there is, or should be, is wrongheaded. There is no single answer to the question What is language intervention? not because authorities disagree, not because we lack the necessary facts, not because there are many equally good therapy strategies, but exactly because theoretic frameworks differ. (p. 53)

It is possible to handle this definitional problem in two ways. A clinician may have numerous definitions—presumably as many as any individual has theories. This may very well be the preference of many clinicians. Or the clinician can develop a definition that is sufficiently broad that it is not inconsistent with any particular theory. (Of course, this would include only those theories that admit the possibility that changes in the child's environment can have *some* impact on language learning.) Such a definition would encompass all types of intervention that have been proposed and that may be required under certain special circumstances. It is the latter task that I shall attempt here.

In my own view, language intervention occurs when some intervention agent (clinician, teacher, parent, sibling, etc.) stimulates or responds to a child in a manner that is consciously designed to facilitate development in areas of communication ability that are viewed as being at risk for impairment. There are two important parts to this definition: the agent must be doing something *consciously* designed to aid in development, and she must be doing this because the child is believed to be at risk for language impairment.

This includes as intervention a range of procedures and activities that some individuals will undoubtedly find to be too broad. For example, parents or teachers following up on clinician suggestions to use simpler language, to be highly responsive to the child, or to follow the child's lead would be engaging in intervention. This form of intervention is in rather stark contrast to more familiar situations, such as a child's producing sentences containing some linguistic form following an imitative stimulus and a presentation of a picture by a clinician.

This definition would also include individuals acting on their own initiative (i.e., without the directions of a speech-language pathologist) to help a child whom they feel is in jeopardy. For example, parents who tell their child to "stop being so lazy and talk correctly" would be engaged in intervention. Yet, the proposed definition would exclude as intervention all of the typical responses to young children by adults and older children that involve simplification of sentence content and structure, slowing of rate, pausing at syntactic boundaries, and so forth. All of these modifications occur naturally in adults' efforts to carry on conversations with young children; they are not employed for purposes of prevention or remediation of suspected learning problems.

The greatest advantage of this proposal is that it accepts as intervention the variety of approaches needed and used by clinicians operating under markedly different conditions (caseload content, caseload number, time, physical facilities, etc.) and with different theoretical orientations. In other words, what counts as intervention is not contingent on the particular theory or set of intervention principles to which a given clinician subscribes or the type of client receiving treatment. In some cases, the intervention process will consist primarily of consultative services—working with parents, teachers, and aides to help these individuals provide a more stimulating and responsive environment for a language impaired child. In other cases, the clinician will assume the role of primary intervention agent, with family members, teachers, and aides performing complementary or supplementary roles.

I find the breadth of this definition to be an asset rather than a liability. It simply requires that some distinction be made between intervention (including goals, procedures, and activities) that is well conceived, based on sound theoretically or empirically generated principles, and can be shown to be effective, and intervention that is based on guesswork, speculation, and convenience to the intervention agent. This places a heavy responsibility on clinicians to demonstrate that the intervention plans they design are having the predicted outcomes—that is, that the service provided is "good." I believe quite strongly that this is a responsibility that clinicians should be prepared to accept. Several of the remaining chapters in this book are designed specifically to assist clinicians in developing programs that will help them meet this objective.

Chapter 4

Developing Intervention Plans

Once the decision has been made to admit a language impaired child to intervention, steps must be taken to develop an intervention program or plan. Connell and associates (1977) pointed out that a clinician really has three options in planning an intervention program for an individual child. A program may be selected that has been developed by others from the list of well over 200 available programs (see Fristoe, 1975); a program may be selected from this list and modified in ways that are more consistent with the clinician's own theoretical position and the needs of clients; or the clinician may develop a program that is consistent with a particular theoretical position on language acquisition among language impaired children and that is designed to meet the specific needs of individual clients.

It might be expected that the first option of selecting an a priori intervention program would be the least experimental approach. Much as in the case of choosing a medicine, such as a headache remedy, selecting the tried and true method of treatment is usually the safest, if not always the most effective, course of action. Unfortunately, selection of an existing intervention program in no way assures the clinician that the program will work with her client. In fact, the clinician cannot even be certain that such a program has ever been put to any rigorous clinical test. Implementation of most available language intervention programs is every bit as much of an adventure into the unknown as choosing either of the other options. Furthermore, since these programs have not been designed to meet the needs of the clinician's specific client, it is quite likely that they will not sufficiently meet the client's needs. The clinician may be in the position of forcing children to fit the demands of her selected program rather than of modifying the program to fit the requirements of the child.

The second option, modifying an existing program, offers much more flexibility to the clinician but provides no more confidence that the program will be effective. In fact, even if a reasonably well tested program such as that proposed by Gray and Ryan (1973) is selected, any modification of the procedures would render accompanying data on the program's effectiveness meaningless. The clinician who selects an extant clinical program and then modifies it is not in error, unless she assumes that the modified program must necessarily have results at least as good as those observed by the developers of the original program. It might indeed be better than the original, but it also might not be as good. Therefore, the program is experimental and only careful experimentation can answer the question of its effectiveness.

The third option, of creating individual programs for each client, is, by its very nature, an experimental approach. This option gives the clinician maximum flexibility in designing the content of the program, the sequence of training, the specific procedures used, and so forth. Presumably, decisions regarding these aspects of the program would follow from the clinician's views on language learning and her knowledge of available procedures and the extent to which they have been tested in a controlled, experimental fashion. The only constraint placed on the clinician in implementing this individualized approach to language intervention is that she must demonstrate, through some reasonably objective means, that the programs she has developed and implemented effectively improve the communicative performance of specific clients in some meaningful and substantial way. Because this sole constraint is operative for all three of the program options outlined, this strategy would appear to offer the clinician greater flexibility and no less confidence in the potential effectiveness of the program than either of the other programming possibilities.

A highly personalized plan should be based on a comprehensive assessment of the child's social, cognitive, and linguistic abilities and an in-depth account of the child's daily routines—interactions with family members, teachers, friends, and so forth. Regardless of the theories underlying any approach to intervention, the planning stage can be broken down into four composite processes: (1) determining the goals of intervention; (2) selecting a set of procedures to be used to meet these goals; (3) selecting an approach for attacking the goals; and (4) developing activities so that these procedures may be optimally utilized. Figure 4–1 schematizes these processes and the manner in which they interact in the systematic development of an intervention plan.

DETERMINING INTERVENTION GOALS

The goals of intervention may be stated at a number of different levels of specificity. Figure 4–1 illustrates three levels that we have

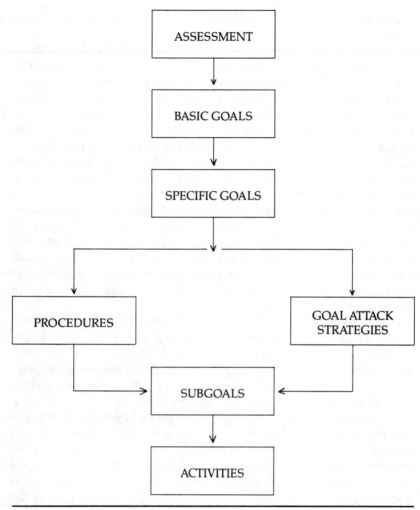

Figure 4-1.   The steps involved in developing an intervention plan.

found useful to set for our clients from the outset of the intervention program. Neither the levels represented in this figure nor the goals decided on for a particular child can be considered to be hard and fast. That is, a given clinician may find levels of specificity between those shown in the figure to be most useful; other clinicians may find that some of these levels are not necessary or that two or more of the levels represented can better be combined into single goal statements. Furthermore, for a given child, goals at any of the levels should come under periodic review and will probably need to be adjusted at various points of the program. This can only be done if assessment is an ongoing process that is viewed as an important part of intervention itself.

At the highest level, beneath *assessment* in Figure 4–1, is found *basic goals*. Determination of basic goals is discussed at length in Chapter 5 and criteria for their selection are presented there. Essentially, these goals are based on the child's pattern of social-interactional skills. Establishing basic goals helps the clinician to concentrate intervention efforts on the aspects of conversational skill that appear to present the greatest obstacles to effective communication. For some children, this is the form and content of the utterances they produce and have to understand. For others, establishment of the basic social skills on which communicative interaction rests is the priority. Children with the latter problem seem to have difficulties in communicating with other people at any level, verbal or otherwise. In many cases, a child will have several basic goals. For example, one goal may call for improvements in the child's general level of social-conversational interaction whereas another requires improvement in the use of language content-form interactions in the performance of existing speech acts.

Subordinate to basic goals are *specific goals*. This is the first level at which the specific behaviors that the child is expected to learn to understand and use actually become a part of the goal statement. Criteria that are useful in determining specific goals are presented in Chapter 6, as well as in Chapters 8 through 13. If the basic goal for a child is to teach new content-form interactions to fulfill available communicative functions, a relevant specific goal might be to get the child to use "where questions" to obtain information about the location of objects and to request action (e.g., "Where are my shoes?," expecting the adult to find them). Similarly, if the basic goal is to increase the child's use of assertive conversational behaviors, specific goals might be to encourage the child's use of assertions to describe novel aspects of the context without a prior question from an adult or to ask questions that request clarification of a conversational partner's inexplicit utterances.

Specific goals should also contain an objective statement indicating the criterion that must be reached before moving on to the next specific goal or set of specific goals. For example, I believe that it is critical that the child show some definite progress toward the use of present goals under reasonably typical communicative conditions before moving on to more advanced objectives. Lee, Koenigsknecht, and Mulhern (1975) base their decisions to terminate work on a goal on data from spontaneous language samples. They recommend that "Once a child is spontaneously formulating a language structure correctly 50 per cent of the time, it is no longer necessary to give primary emphasis to this structure in the remedial program" (p. 24). We typically set a criterion of 50 per cent correct use of a target behavior under reasonably naturalistic conditions, such as conversation during play or some activity of daily living (e.g., making popcorn or setting the table for dinner). After the child meets this criterion and new goals are established, we make provisions to sample the original behavior periodically to make sure that the trend toward mastery continues without further intervention. This procedure reflects my belief that, even with intervention, mastery of a new linguistic act will take place gradually, and that once the acquisition processes are set in motion through intervention, the child will continue to develop control over that feature without further intervention. This hypothesis is not always shown to be true, and more intervention is warranted under these conditions.

Other clinicians and researchers have adopted a criterion such as 80 or 90 per cent or even higher before new intervention goals are established (Connell, 1982; Culatta and Horn, 1982; Gray and Ryan, 1973; Guess, Sailor, and Baer, 1978; Leonard, 1975a,b; Mulac and Tomlinson, 1977; Zwitman and Sonderman, 1979). It is rare, however, that any arrangements are made at all for sampling the child's use of newly learned behaviors in communicative contexts.

The final set of goals, *subgoals*, is associated with steps along the way toward reaching the specific goal. It is often easier to decide on subgoals *after* a set of procedures and a goal attack strategy have been developed. These steps will be discussed later in this chapter.

For behaviorally oriented clinicians, subgoals may appear as highly programmed steps required to "shape" the target behavior from simpler behaviors that are less complex than the target. These goals are written operationally—that is, they state clearly what kind of stimuli will be presented and what kind of response is expected. Specific criteria are set to determine when to move to the next step in the behavioral program. A behaviorally written subgoal for training the use of "do" in questions might look like the following:

> The child will produce "do" in questions 9 out of 10 times in response to naturally occurring nonlinguistic stimuli in the preschool and following an imitative stimulus provided by the teacher.

Careful records must be kept by the clinician to verify that the child has actually met the prescribed criterion before advancing to the next level of difficulty.

For clinicians working outside the behavioral paradigm, there are not likely to be as many subgoals, and they will not be nearly so tightly programmed. Still, some checks on the child's progress on tasks that are less demanding than the specific goal are often helpful in informing the clinician that her procedures are having the desired effect. For example, in training "do" questions, one subgoal might be the child's regular use of the correct form in questions produced while playing the game "Go Fish" (e.g., "Do you have any eights? Do you have any twos?"). These questions in this game are highly routinized; therefore, they do not reflect the level of productivity required to use the form correctly under normal conversational circumstances. Nevertheless, progress on such a task may indicate that the general procedures being used are resulting in some gains.

Another subgoal that reflects an intermediate check on the child's progress toward achievement of a specific goal might be continued success in the use of "do" in a type of game in which the child must make guesses about the clinician or another child. For example, the task might be to guess what the clinician does every morning after the alarm clock rings (e.g., "Do you turn off the alarm clock?" "Do you get out of bed?" "Do you brush your teeth?"). Because these questions require much more cognitive and linguistic flexibility and creativity, they are likely to present more difficulty than the card game. In addition, because they are part of a planned activity that specifically requires their use in a highly repetitive manner, this type of task is not likely to be as taxing as the use of the correct form when it is required in a truly conversational context.

At the very least, subgoals should be set to ensure that the child has learned a general, abstract rule or concept that will enable her to generate target behaviors in a productive and creative manner. For example, if the clinician is training the use of the regular past tense morpheme "-ed," she may set aside 10 to 20 pictures or demonstrable actions which, if described, would call for the regular past tense. These stimuli could be presented on a regular basis as a formal check on the child's acquisition of the targeted rule. Under most circumstances, a subgoal of 80 to 100 per cent accuracy on this type of a task will be achieved well before the specific goal of 50 per cent correct usage in naturalistic conditions. This procedure of taking regular probes to assess progress toward subgoals is discussed in greater detail in Chapter 7.

SELECTING PROCEDURES

After selecting the specific goals, the procedures designed specifically to meet those objectives can be prescribed. Procedures are the methods or techniques used by the clinician that are expected to facilitate the child's understanding or use of a new target behavior. The decision regarding which procedures to use is based, to a very large extent, on the clinician's views on how children acquire language. Imitation and reinforcement will be the mainstay for clinicians with an operant view of learning; however, these procedures may not even occur to clinicians operating from within other theoretical frameworks.

We would like to be in a position to describe the child and her behavior and, on the basis of that information, select what we know to be the best procedures for that child. Unfortunately, this cannot yet be done. So we must formulate a hypothesis about what would be an effective procedure and test that hypothesis through our intervention program. Fortunately, we are not limited only to our theoretical notions of what should be effective. To make an informed decision, we must also use our knowledge of procedures that have already been reported in the experimental literature and the kinds of success that resulted. This type of information is examined in Chapters 8 through 14. We can add to this base our knowledge of the specific child with whom we are working and her learning style, general strengths, and weaknesses. Finally, the specific goals that we are addressing may influence our selection of procedures. It may be that a dramatically different orientation is needed when goals are as different as teaching the use of "is" as an auxiliary verb and getting the child to respond in a contingent fashion to the nonrequestive speech acts of a conversational partner.

When the clinician's own clinical experience is combined with a sound knowledge of theory and of the intervention literature, an awareness of the child's learning strengths and weaknesses, and a carefully selected specific goal, a reasonable hypothesis concerning the best procedure for a given child can be generated.

DEVELOPING GOAL ATTACK STRATEGIES

Once a set of specific goals has been decided on, the clinician must determine just how they are to be approached. For example, if five goals (A to E) have been selected, there are at least three ways in which the clinician can opt to proceed. These three goal attack strategies are illustrated in Figure 4–2.

First, in what may be called a vertically structured program (Steckol, 1983; Stremel and Waryas, 1974), one or two goals may be selected and trained to some criterion level before proceeding on to

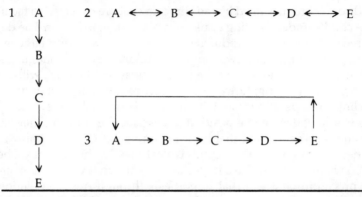

Figure 4–2. Three goal attack strategies: **1,** A vertical approach. **2,** A typical horizontal approach. **3,** A cyclical approach. A, B, C, D, and E represent predetermined specific goals.

other goals. This strategy of selecting only one goal at a time is used by Gray and Ryan (1973) and Guess, Sailor, and Baer (1974, 1978) and is highly consistent with the principles of behaviorism.

Two related strategies that are essentially vertical are recommended by Miller and Yoder (1974) and Lee and co-workers (1975). In their program for teaching early semantic relationships to retarded children, Miller and Yoder (1974) suggest that one relationship be trained at a time. Only when the child has attained mastery of a relation in a limited range of contexts should training on new targets begin. At the same time a new goal is added; however, the original goal should be emphasized in new contexts to encourage creative use of the structure. This makes it possible for the clinician to focus on more than one goal simultaneously. In their program for more intellectually and linguistically advanced children, Lee and colleagues (1975) recommend that each child have one primary goal, although it is possible to have two or more secondary goals as well. Models of the secondary target structures are provided to prepare the child for later stages in the program when these same goals have primary status. Once a primary goal has been attained, it may be reduced to secondary status. In these cases, responses may be required, but they will be evoked less frequently than the primary goal structure.

A second strategy for dealing with our five goals is shown in Figure 4–2, 2. Using this strategy, the clinician opts to work on all five goals at the same time. The amount of time needed to reach specific goals will vary considerably from target to target. New goals are added as the child meets the specific goal for each of the five original goals. Obviously, using this strategy, the amount of time spent on any one goal per session would be decreased. This strategy typically limits the high rates of repetition of a single target that are characteristic of many vertically structured programs. This is not necessarily a disadvantage, however. Muma (1978b) claimed that repetitiveness is not an important part of intervention and may even be undesirable. He regards variability as especially important and therefore would either select or, preferably, let the child select several goals at any given time.

It is possible to implement this second strategy using the techniques of behavior modification. For example, in the highly structured program of Stremel and Waryas (1974), two or three goals are worked on concurrently. Intervention is directed toward each goal for about 15 minutes per session. This strategy is essentially the same as the vertically structured design except that multiple goals are attacked in each session. Mulligan and Guess (1984) noted some advantages of alternating trials for different goals in some fashion. In this way, each targeted behavior is evoked only after some *other* targeted behavior has been produced. Dunlap and Koegel (1980) demonstrated that when the stimuli in discrimination tasks were varied so that no more than two successive presentations were administered before moving on to items for other tasks, the performance of their two autistic children was significantly better than in a condition in which the same task was drilled repeatedly.

Blank and Milewski (1981) presented a unique operant-based program in which several related targets are evoked in a random arrangement. Target sentences with related semantic content, but different syntactic structure, were presented in the following fashion: "Here is a boy. He is standing. Here is another boy. They are sitting. This is a truck. It can roll" (p. 71). Although each of these sentence types represented a specific goal, none of the targets were evoked in a successive, repetitive manner, at least in the early stages of the program.

Of the two general strategies already mentioned, vertical structuring is probably the most common, although less redundant, horizontally structured programs seem to be gaining favor (Steckol, 1983). A third possible strategy also exists. Although it is essentially a horizontal approach, it differs markedly from the strategy just discussed. In this approach, which has been borrowed from Hodson and Paden's (1983) plan for phonological intervention, the clinician would work on a number of specific goals in a cyclical fashion. As shown in Figure 4–2,3, for goals A to E, A would be the goal for week 1. Regardless of the child's progress (or lack of it), week 2 would be devoted to goal B. Goal C would be presented in week 3, goal D in week 4, and goal E in week 5. After the fifth week, cycle one would be completed. Cycle two would then proceed in essentially the same manner as cycle one.

Although in this example, each goal was targeted for one week, two or three weeks might just as easily have been chosen. The important difference between this and other strategies is that the clinician moves from one goal to another regardless of the amount of progress observed. As in the other horizontal approach, new goals could be added as specific goals were attained.

There are two rationales for this strategy. First, like the second strategy presented earlier, the fact that in normal language learning, progress on any one feature of language is gradual is taken into consideration. The child does not typically focus on only one aspect of language until it is completely mastered, and then move on to a single new target. Rather, the child is actively involved in the acquisition of many features of language at the same time. Second, it enables the clinician to present the child with brief but fairly concentrated "doses" of a given target behavior each week (or other designated treatment period). There is no evidence to suggest that a strategy of cycles is better (or worse) than the more commonly used vertical or horizontal strategies. Only adequately controlled experimentation will determine whether its use can be highly recommended in intervention programs.

Again, though, theory and experimental evidence are not the only important variables in selecting a goal attack strategy. The number of goals that can be addressed at one time is limited by factors intrinsic to the child, such as attentional skills, motivation, cooperation, and the rate of learning new communicative behaviors. Further restrictions are placed on the number of goals selected by practical extrinsic factors such as the amount of time actually allotted to intervention and the intervention procedures and agents selected. By having more than one goal, the clinician is more closely approximating a natural learning condition, since normally developing children typically show progression in a number of areas simultaneously. In these cases, the clinician must expect the child to show variable rates of learning due to factors such as readiness and need to use the behavior. With some children who require much repetition and many models, however, selection of several targets may reduce the probability that the child will show rapid progress in any one.

DEVELOPING INTERVENTION ACTIVITIES

Intervention activities provide the contexts in which procedures are implemented and in which learning takes place. Because of the manner in which language intervention was defined, activities can take on a number of different appearances. Essentially, they vary along what might be called a "continuum of naturalness." The factors influencing naturalness are (1) what the participants are actually doing (i.e., the activity itself); (2) where the activity takes place (i.e., the physical context); and (3) the individuals with whom the child is interacting (i.e., the social context).

Figure 4–3 provides an illustration of how these variables interact to influence the naturalness of a particular intervention activity. An *activity of daily living,* such as washing dishes, baking, getting dressed, or play that takes place at *home* with *family members* is shown to be most natural. A *drill*-like rehearsal of the target behavior in the *clinic* with the *clinician* is displayed as being at the low extreme of the continuum. Points toward the middle of the continuum reflect combinations of these factors; for example, free play in the clinic, involving family members and the clinician, would fall approximately in the middle. If the clinician alone were involved with the child in this same activity, it would be viewed as less natural, and if the session took place in the home with the clinician and family members, the activity would fall somewhere beyond the midline on the continuum. This scheme should not be taken seriously as an interval scale, but it clearly points out the relevant variables that add to and detract from the naturalness of an activity and may help clinicians to order activities according to their similarity to the everyday situations in which the child has frequent opportunities to communicate.

		organized	daily
	drill	games	activities
1. Activity	←		→
	0	+1	+2
	clinic	school	home
2. Physical	←		→
Context	0	+1	+2
	clinician	teacher	parents
3. Social	←		→
Context	0	+1	+2
	low		high
4. Overall	←		→
Naturalness	0	+3	+6

Figure 4–3.   A continuum of naturalness. The overall naturalness of an activity can be estimated by placing a value on the activity, the physical context, and the social context. The sum of these three values yields an estimate of the overall naturalness of the activity.

Craig (1983) pointed out that in some intervention approaches, the *behavior* that the child is expected to produce in the intervention session is essentially the same as the *activities* that are performed. She argued that this similarity is often the cause of a lack of generalization of training. For example, children often are required to practice their target behaviors while looking at pictures or observing the clinician's manipulations of objects. The child is not required to use her target behavior during the course of some broader social activity; the target behavior *is* the activity.

Intervention activities at the opposite extreme of the naturalness continuum differ markedly from the intervention objectives. Instead, they serve as ecologically valid contexts in which the need to communicate, using the target behaviors, arises naturally. For example, washing the dishes with father after dinner could serve as an ideal context for getting the child to request actions (e.g., "Give me the plate/cup/ spoon," "Wash this knife," "I need a dish towel"). Within this type of context, the intervention agent is free to intervene in whatever manner has been selected. The activity is the backdrop for the use of clinical procedures designed to help the child meet specific goals. Other common activities that are easily designed even in the clinic include playing with Play-Doh, playing house, dress-up and role-play, story-telling, making popcorn and juice, having parties, sorting clothes for a pretend washing, and so forth. The list is endless. Perhaps the best ideas for activities come from interviews with parents and teachers to determine the types of things that the children often enjoy doing at home and at school. The clinician's job is then to set up these activities in ways that make the child's goal behaviors necessary or at least highly useful.

This distinction between activities and goals is important. It is not likely that basic or specific goals or subgoals will be reached successfully unless, at some point in the intervention process, this distinction is manifested in the types of activities used. However, I believe that one of the greatest fallacies of current thinking about language intervention is the assumption that "natural is better." Any time that an activity falls high on the continuum of naturalness, it is viewed as a better activity. To my way of thinking, a more appropriate assumption could be stated as follows: "Natural is better *when the procedures that are employed within the activity are effective in reaching the child's goals.*" That is, *if* the procedures selected for the child can be implemented within an activity that is high on the naturalness continuum, and *if* they have the desired effect of getting the child to produce higher level communicative behaviors than was characteristic of her performance prior to intervention, the activity is more desirable than a less natural activity would be. For example, getting a child to produce a novel sentence containing a subject, verb, and object while using Play-Doh at home with her mother, where the need to communicate information has arisen naturally, can be viewed as much more significant than getting the child to produce the same type of sentence in the clinic in response to a picture.

This position seems hardly controversial. The real problem with the "natural is better" assumption is that on the basis of this assumption, some clinicians select activities that do not allow the implementation of effective procedures. Consequently, intervention sometimes provides little more than what the child would ordinarily get from the natural environment. History has demonstrated the extreme difficulties which many of these children have in extracting conventional patterns of communication from such natural contexts. For example, children who are reasonably good communicators but who have marked difficulties with language form often seem oblivious to many of the structural details of language. Since their own efforts to communicate are reasonably effective, the need to attend to and master the use of language form is often not readily apparent. In my experience, a clinician can often facilitate growth in the child's vocabulary and perhaps cognitive and pragmatic skills by providing highly natural and enriching experiences. The rate of development of syntax and morphology, however, often continues to lag.

To increase the salience of target behaviors and to encourage their spontaneous use, it is often necessary to develop activities that are fairly low on the naturalness continuum. The clinician has much greater control over the stimuli to which the child is exposed and over the child's attention and response to those stimuli under these cirucumstances. Even under these conditions, however, it is possible (and I think highly desirable) to create structured activities that illustrate to the child not only *what* should be said but also *when* and *for what purpose* it should be said. Some suggestions for modifying highly structured activities to heighten their functionality and naturalness are given in Chapter 8. Clearly, clinicians must be concerned with naturalness and ecological validity in developing activities. Failure to assess the child's performance in highly natural activities and to extend intervention to these activities when necessary is practically a guarantee that stated basic and specific goals will not be reached.

Chapter 5

Determining Basic Intervention Goals

Clinicians and researchers have often sought a useful system of classifying groups of language impaired children with unique identifying characteristics. These efforts typically have been predicated on the basic assumption that children exhibiting certain etiological or behavioral profiles are more likely to benefit from certain specific intervention approaches than others. A valid and reliable system of classification could lead to the development of goals and procedures that are tailored specifically to the needs of each particular group of children.

Several groups of language impaired children have been identified on the basis of causative factors (e.g., emotionally disturbed, mentally retarded, hearing impaired). Bloom and Lahey (1978) have argued quite convincingly that diagnostic classification of children is a problem in that professionals often disagree as to which label is best applied to an individual child. Even when such labels are agreed upon, the patterns of linguistic behavior among groups are not always unique. Therefore, attempts to categorize children by etiological factors do not lead to distinct sets of goals or procedures for children in different groups.

At some level, intervention with children from different etiologically based groups must differ. For example, hearing impaired children have identifiable sensory deficits that make them different from other groups of language impaired children. Because of these deficits, clinicians must use special techniques, such as amplification, speech-reading, cued speech, manual signing, or other methods, to enhance the reception of linguistic signals by these children. These same techniques are not necessary for many other language impaired children. Despite these differences in the mode of linguistic production and reception used, and despite their need for prosthetic management, the goals of language content, form, and use that are typically chosen for hearing impaired children and the procedures used to actually train these goals have been quite similar to those used for children reflecting markedly different etiological backgrounds.

A major reason for the failure to make clinically useful classifications of language impaired children is that the focus of assessment and intervention has always been children's language form: vocabulary, syntax, morphology, and phonology. Language impaired children's use of language form to capitalize on opportunities to communicate was not widely considered in language intervention until the middle and late 1970s (Bloom and Lahey, 1978; Holland, 1975; Mahoney, 1975; McLean and Snyder-McLean, 1978; Muma, 1978b). This is unfortunate because it is often along dimensions of language use that language impaired children differ most from one another and from children developing language normally. Bloom and Lahey concluded that

> the evidence that has been reported often points out the *commonalities* among children with different etiologies, as well as among the language behaviors that such children actually share with normal children who are first learning language, particularly with form. The qualitative differences reported so far predominate in the use component and are characteristic of *some* children who demonstrate severe impairment in social interactions. (p. 519)

Differences in the manner in which language impaired children put language to use often can be found even within a given diagnostic category. For example, following their review of the pragmatic abilities of children with specific language impairment, Fey and Leonard (1983) concluded that children in this group can be subdivided into three subgroups based on their levels of social-conversational activity. Some of these children can be described as conversationally active or even assertive. These highly verbal children tend to make functional use of the limited linguistic skills that they possess. Other language impaired children are responsive to their conversational partners but are essentially nonassertive. Children in the third group display general deficits in their patterns of social-conversational interaction. They are neither as assertive nor as responsive as children developing normally, and they exhibit a reduction in motivation to interact verbally with their social partners. It is possible for children in these three groups to have similar formal linguistic repertoires. Members of different groups are viewed as differing from one another primarily in their patterns of use of their available language skills.

Unlike traditional classification systems, this type of subgrouping of language impaired children according to their levels of social-conversational participation has some clear implications for the language interventionist. For example, children who become actively engaged in social interactions and participate readily in conversations create for themselves numerous opportunities to hear appropriate language models and to practice their use of existing language forms. Because they are highly motivated to communicate with their social partners, these children are likely to make at least occasional use of newly acquired content-form interactions (e.g., action–past, "played," "tackled," "washed"), thus increasing the probability that the new forms will develop into fully productive and highly automatized communicative behaviors. The clinician's task with such children would be to make more salient the relevant linguistic patterns that the child has failed to learn, to demonstrate to the child that these patterns are linguisticially significant, and to illustrate those naturalistic communicative circumstances in which these patterns are conventionally required.

In contrast, the child who exhibits reduced responsiveness to the conversational bids of others and who rarely initiates social interaction has limited opportunities to make use of any new language forms that the clinician may attempt to train. Even if such children can master new words and semantic and syntactic relationships trained by the clinician, these new forms will have no substantive impact on the child's ability to communicate. The ability to construct a complex sentence is of little use to a child who is relatively unmotivated to initiate and maintain social contact with others. Such a child may need assistance in developing more appropriate skills for establishing and managing social contact before goals of more complex language forms can be achieved and generalized into everyday speaking situations.

In this chapter, I will expand on the Fey and Leonard (1983) system of subcategorization to include a broader range of language impaired children. This system serves as the foundation for determining what I have referred to as *basic* goals of intervention.

A CLINICALLY USEFUL SCHEME FOR CLASSIFYING LANGUAGE IMPAIRED CHILDREN

Figure 5–1 illustrates the relevant dimensions of the classification scheme. Basically, it consists of two continua. One represents the child's *conversational assertiveness*—her ability or willingness (or both) to take a conversational turn when none has been solicited by a partner. The other continuum displays the child's level of *responsiveness* to the needs of her conversational partner. The intersection of the two continua shown in the figure results in the formation of four quadrants, each representing a group of children who exhibit different patterns of social-conversational activity: (1) assertive and responsive conversationalists (or *active conversationalists*); (2) responsive but non-assertive conversationalists (or *passive conversationalists*); (3) children who are neither responsive nor assertive in conversations (or *inactive communicators*); and (4) children who are verbally active but unresponsive to the conversational needs of their partners (or *verbal noncommunicators*).

It is important to stress the fact that the two variables of this scheme, assertiveness and responsiveness, lie on a continuum. Therefore, one child viewed as an inactive communicator could conceivably shun virtually all social advances and rarely or never make a social approach toward others. This would be a very extreme case, however. Other children fitting into this same category would be responsive in some cases and would also be expected to initiate communication under certain circumstances. Placement of a child in this category would reflect the clinician's judgment that, given the child's age, cognitive abilities, and formal linguistic skills, her willingness to be assertive and to respond to the initiatives of others is significantly below expected levels.

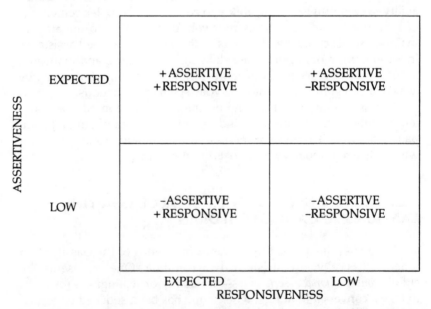

Figure 5–1.   A scheme for profiling children according to their levels of social-conversational participation.

It should also be emphasized that children within each of these four groups are not assumed to be identical with respect to their etiological classification or their profiles of formal linguistic capabilities. Children within each group are expected to differ markedly along dimensions that have been the focus of clinical attention in the past—lexical, semantic, syntactic, and phonological comprehension and expression, intelligence, and so forth. What is crucial is that two children exhibiting highly similar profiles along these traditional dimensions can fall into different groups based on their levels of social-conversational participation and that, as a result, different basic goals or at least different emphases on the same basic goals may be appropriate for each.

USING THE CLASSIFICATION SCHEME

Identifying children who exhibit different patterns of interaction requires language sampling, preferably in several contexts. Table 5-1 illustrates a taxonomy of conversational acts and utterance level discourse functions that conversational acts may serve in a conversation. I find this system useful in making determinations of a child's level of conversational assertiveness and responsivity to her partners, although many other systems are possible (see Chapman, 1981a, for a review). This analysis involves coding of each utterance at the conversational act level and at the discourse level.

The utterance level conversational acts in Table 5-1 are subdivided into four groups. There are two major groups, one representing assertive acts (i.e., those that typically are not overtly solicited by the partner) and one representing responsive acts (i.e., those that comply with the prior requestive acts or acknowledge and confirm prior non-requestive acts of the partner). Utterances coded as imitations are exact or partial replicas of prior utterances of the partner that add no new information to the conversation. The category "other" contains all acts that do not fit neatly into the first three categories. It should be noted that these utterance level conversational acts contain some level of discourse analysis since the coding for a particular utterance is at least partially dependent on the type of conversational act that precedes it.

As shown in the Table 5-1, there are four utterance level discourse functions, one of which will be assigned to every utterance. Coding the discourse function adds information to the analysis regarding the child's willingness and ability to initiate new topics when appropriate and to maintain and extend topics that are already established. Each

Table 5–1.   Proposed System of Coding Conversational Acts for Profiling Children's Levels of Social-Conversational Participation*

Utterance Level

Assertive Conversational Acts

1. Requestives: Solicit information or actions

   a. Requests for Information (RQIN): All forms of questions (including tags, e.g., "This is fun, isn't it?") designed to solicit new information from the conversational partner, e.g., "Why you sad?" "Where my mommy?" "You want you momma?" "Wanna say it?"

   b. Requests for Action (RQAC): Any forms that solicit the performance of some action by the partner, e.g., "Put blue," "Stick 'em in hard," "Gimme that," "You say it."

   c. Requests for Clarification (RQCL): All questions that seek clarification of some prior utterance, e.g., "What?" "Huh?" "No?" "A blue Play-Doh?"

   d. Requests for Attention (RQAT): Utterances that add no new information to the conversation but seek attention or acknowledgment from the partner, e.g., "Hey, look," "Now watch," "See this?" "Jason!" "Know what?" "Guess what."

2. Assertives: Label, report facts, state rules, explanations, and so forth

   a. Comments (ASCO): Identifications and descriptions of observable objects and events, e.g., "We go [went] our grandma's today," "Have birthday party," "That Vincey," "They hanged up."

   b. Statements (ASST): Reports of mental events, evaluations, statements of rules, explanations, and so forth, that are not directly observable, e.g., "Hafta squish it together," "You 'posed to blow it," "This don't go in here," "I wanna play that," "Better clean up," "Those not for play with."

   c. Disagreements (ASDA): Comments or statements that deny a proposition of some prior assertion, e.g., "No way, Jose," "I not silly," "That not mine," "No," or that indicate refusals to comply with requests, e.g., "I not telling you," "No."

3. Performatives (PERF): Claims, jokes, teasing, protests, and warnings that are accomplished just by being produced, e.g., "Look out!" "Don't step on it!" "Don't just breathe!" "That's mine!" "Hey, wanna play hide and see poop?" (laughs), "Can't catch me."

Responsive Conversational Acts: Provide information requested or acknowledge assertives and performatives

1. Responses to Requests for Information (RSIN): Attempts to provide new information requested by the partner.

2. Responses to Requests for Action (RSAC): Verbal accompaniments to the performance of an action requested by the partner.

3. Responses to Requests for Clarification (RSCL): Attempts to repeat or otherwise clarify a prior utterance following the partner's request for clarification.

4. Responses to Requests for Attention (RSAT): Responses to attentional requests that serve to acknowledge the partner and to indicate that the partner may continue, e.g., "What?" "Yeah."

5. Responses to Assertives and Performatives (RSAS): Simple acknowledgments of or agreements with prior partner utterances that add no new information to the prior utterance, e.g., "Oh," "Yeah," "Sure," "I know," "Okay," "Right." Utterances containing an RSAS plus some assertive act are coded under the appropriate assertive category.

Table 5–1   (continued)

Imitations (IMI): Utterances that repeat all or part of the previous utterance, including its intonation pattern, *and* that include no new information, e.g., RQIN: "What do you want?"; IMI: "What you want?"; ASST: "I like cookies." IMI: "Like cookies."

Other: Any utterances that do not fit clearly under the above categories

Discourse Level

Initiate Topic: Utterances that either do not follow a prior utterance or that introduce new information that is not related to information from a prior utterance

Maintain Topic: Utterances that are related to some prior utterance and that fulfill the speaker's obligations but that add no new, nonsolicited information

Extend Topic: Utterances that are related to a prior utterance and that extend the established topic by adding new semantic details or by shading appropriately to some related topic

Extend Topic—Tangential: Utterances that are related tangentially to some aspect of a prior utterance but do not seem to extend the topic in an adequate manner

---

*Each conversational act is coded at two levels of specificity: the utterance level and the level of discourse function.

Based on Dore (1979) and Chapman (1981a).

utterance, then, will be coded as a conversational act *and* for its discourse function to assist in determining the child's assertiveness and responsiveness in a variety of social contexts. In most cases, only one code for conversational acts and one code for discourse function will be required, although occasionally, exceptions will occur. A fairly common example is the case in which a child answers a question with a "yes" or "no" response and then, in the same utterance, produces a requestive act of her own (e.g., "Yeah, where you get yours?"). In these cases, we code the utterance as both RSIN and RQIN. As Chapman (1981a) points out, many other cases of multiple coding are possible. This is one typical case in which the added information provided by the multiple code is especially useful.

The Assertiveness Continuum

Children who are high on the assertiveness scale will exhibit frequent use of assertive conversational acts. Frequent usage of many requestive conversational acts is characteristic of children at the upper extreme on this continuum because these acts can be viewed not only as initiatory conversational bids but also as bids that place constraints on how the partner must respond to meet her social obligations. For example, a request for information requires the partner to respond in a manner that is consistent with the informational needs of the speaker, as explicitly expressed in the request (e.g., RQIN: "What are you doing?" RSIN: "Drawing a picture").

For children who are low on the assertiveness continuum, assertive conversational acts will be relatively infrequent. In addition, children described as low on the assertiveness continuum often produce high rates of acknowledgments and agreements (RSASs) (Fey, Leonard, and Wilcox, 1981; Stein, 1976; Watson, 1977). These are simple backchannel responses that allow the child to take a turn in the conversation without contributing any new information. Even though these responses are essential components of a smoothly flowing exchange of information, they can be used excessively by nonassertive children. The result is that these children routinely adopt the role of respondent rather than initiator in conversations. They may do very little to exercise their linguistic resources to communicate self-selected information to their partner.

The discourse level conversational acts are also helpful in determining a child's level of conversational assertiveness. Children who produce high rates of topic initiations and topic extensions will be placed higher on the scale than those children who rely more heavily on topic maintenance devices. An especially useful measure is to determine the proportion of responsives that the child produces that serve to extend the topic. These are cases in which the child is required only to provide specific information but opts to offer additional information as well. Frequent use of this type of conversational act will be characteristic only of children rated relatively high on the assertiveness continuum.

One quantitative measure that is very useful in determining the child's relative assertiveness is computed by dividing the number of assertive acts produced by the child by the total number of assertive conversational acts produced in the interaction by both participants. Proportions near 50 per cent indicate symmetry in the conversation with each participant contributing equal numbers of self-selected conversational acts. Proportions closer to 100 per cent indicate dominance of the child over her partner (i.e, high assertiveness), and proportions closer to 0 per cent indicate that the child was playing a more subordinate role in the conversation (i.e., low assertiveness).

Because there are so many critical variables that cannot be controlled in a language sampling situation, I am extremely reluctant to set quantitative criteria that might allow clinicians to make completely objective determinations of the child's position on either of the continua proposed in Figure 5-1. The data presented in Table 5-2 can be used as general guidelines that may be helpful as a part of a more complete analysis, but they should not be viewed as norms. The ultimate determination of a child's assertiveness must still be primarily

Table 5–2. Mean Proportions and Standard Deviations of the Total Number of Assertive Utterances Produced by Three Groups of Subjects in Three Social Contexts*

Partners	Subjects		
	LI	LN-Age	LN-MLU
Adults	33.5 (6.1)	24.2 (6.3)	21.0 (10.6)
Peers	52.0 (10.5)	45.5 (16.8)	56.7 (10.0)
Toddlers	76.8 (6.1)	65.8 (15.3)	49.7 (4.9)

*To compute the proportions, the number of assertive utterances produced by each subject in a free-play interaction was divided by the total number of assertive utterances produced by both partners. Proportions close to 100 indicate relative dominance on the part of the subject, whereas those closer to 0 indicate a more passive subject. Proportions near 50 indicate that the interaction was symmetrical, with each participant contributing similar numbers of nonsolicited, self-selected utterances.

The six language impaired (LI) children ranged in age from 4½ to 6 years. Six of the language normal children were matched to the LI children by age (LN-Age), and the remaining three (ages 3 to 3½) were matched to the LI children by MLU (LN-MLU).

Computed from Fey, M., and Leonard, L. (1984, pp. 420–421).

subjective. These data were taken from six specifically language impaired children, ages 4½ to 6 years old, six language normal children matched by age, and three language normal children matched by mean length of utterance (MLU), who were observed in interactions with an adult, a same-age peer, and a toddler (Fey and Leonard, 1984). All of the children were white and came from what were judged subjectively to be middle class homes. The children were unfamiliar with their listeners in each of the three interactions. The adults were mothers themselves, but none had had training in speech-language pathology.

A glance at these data reveals the crucial effect of the age and the cognitive and linguistic abilities of children's partners on their conversational performance. When they are with an unfamiliar adult, such as a clinician, children are likely to assume a more subordinate role in the conversation than when with a peer or a subordinate. It is imperative, then, that clinicians do not base their evaluations of high levels of assertiveness on a particular proportion, say 50 per cent. I have seen some children put on impressive displays of assertiveness but only produce 20 per cent of the nonsolicited productions in a conversation, owing to the highly verbal nature of their partners. *Initial impressions about a child's conversational assertiveness should be taken merely as clinical hypotheses that must await verification through further observation and through reports from parents or teachers, or both.*

The Responsiveness Continuum

Determination of the child's responsiveness to the partner's needs hinges on the answers to two major questions. First, the clinician must ask "How responsive is the child to the requestives of her partners?" Second, the clinician must determine "How responsive is the child to the nonrequestives of her partners?" Some provisions must be made in coding responses to account for the fact that many of the child's partners, especially adults, frequently cluster utterances together, giving a child little or no time to respond. A partner's utterance should be viewed as a stimulus requiring a response only when the child is given sufficient time to respond. In the system being presented here, 2 seconds is used as the cut-off time, and each utterance that is followed by a pause of 2 seconds or more is marked with " + ." Child utterances occurring within 2 seconds after a partner utterance are viewed as topic maintainers or extenders if they are indeed contingent on the previous utterance. Alternatively, they are coded as initiations if the topic is changed. A "no response" is counted only for those partner utterances that are followed by a " + ." In other words, if the partner produces another utterance within the 2 second period, the child is not viewed as having failed to respond to the original utterance.

The first question concerning responsiveness can be answered by determining the proportion of responsives that follow each of the types of requestives used by the partner. By definition, utterances coded as responsives are in some way contingent on a prior request. As an example of this type of analysis, let's take requests for information (RQINs) and requests for clarification (RQCLs). In normal development, contingent responding tends to occur earliest following questions (Bloom, Rocissano, and Hood, 1976). First, all of the partner's RQINs and RQCLs are located. Second, the number of utterances following such requests that are coded RSIN and RSCL are counted. Then, to compute a proportion, the number of the child's RSINs and RSCLs is divided by the number of the partner's RQINs and RQCLs.

To be coded as RSIN or RSCL, it is not necessary that the child's answer be correct in every way. We are attempting to analyze the child's functional conversational skills, not her semantic and syntactic abilities. For example, I showed a language impaired girl a picture of a fire and asked "Is fire hot?" The child responded "No." Even though this response was semantically incorrect, it indicates that this girl recognized the intent of my question and that she knew the appropriate form of response. Her response was contingent on my question, then, and it was scored as a responsive to a request for information that served to maintain the topic. With some children, however, the child's utterance will be unrelated to the stimulus, or, at best, only tangentially related. In the example just given, the child might have responded "You don't play with matches" or "Fire scares me." These utterances would be coded as ASSTs and, as such, would not be counted as responses to the stimulus. The discourse function of these utterances would be coded as "extend—tangential" to further document the fact that the child attended to some aspect of the stimulus but failed to respond to it in an adequate manner. The greater the child's proportion of appropriate responses, the higher she is rated on the responsivity continuum.

Because the situations in which language evaluations take place differ so markedly from one another and from the contexts typically found in studies of normal development, comparisons of assessment data with data collected in developmental investigations must be done with great caution. It is useful to have some developmental information as a general guide, however. Table 5–3 is presented as a very small and tentative data base to assist the clinician. This table contains the ranges of the proportions of contingent responses produced by four language normal children following adult questions (Bloom et al., 1976). This includes RSINs and all RSCLs except those that are responses to requests for repetition, such as "What?" or "Huh?" Contingent responses of all types, excluding imitations, are counted as responsives in this table. A clear developmental trend toward greater proportions of responsives following questions was observed for this group of children. Greater proportions of appropriate responding add support to initial hypotheses of a high level of responsivity.

Because responding to questions is one of the earliest aspects of conversational discourse to develop among language normal children, it is necessary to examine other instances of contingent speech as well. High levels of responsivity are associated with high proportions of child conversational acts that serve to maintain and extend the topic even when the child is under no obligation to do so. Therefore, it is useful to compute the proportion of the partner's nonquestion utterances (e.g., the partner's assertives, performatives, responsives) that are followed by the child's topic maintaining or extending utterances. Relatively large proportions of maintaining and extending utterances would indicate the child's willingness to attend to the details of her partner's conversational acts and to consider those details in formulating her own responses. A child who typically fails to respond to nonrequestives, who typically initiates new topics, or who extends topics with information only tangentially related to prior utterances is less

Table 5–3. Ranges for the Proportions of Contingent Utterances* that Followed Adult Questions (RSIN + RSCL) and Nonquestions (Maintain [M] + Extend [E])

Stage	Mean Age	RSIN + RSCL	M + E
1	21 mo	11–41	10–16
2	25 mo	41–70	18–28
5	36 mo	69–80	43–67

*The data in the table include utterances that Bloom and colleagues described as linguistically contingent, contextually contingent, and other. Imitations are not included in this adaptation.

The subjects were four language normal children at three developmental levels in dyadic interactions with an adult.

Computed from Bloom, L., Rocissano, L., and Hood, L. (1976, Table 4, p. 538).

aware of her responsibility to cooperate with a partner in the sharing of meaning and the creation of text. This latter child would be characterized as relatively less responsive on the responsivity continuum.

The ranges of the proportions of contingent responses to nonquestions produced by the subjects studied by Bloom and co-workers (1976) are provided in Table 5–3. Although the proportions are not as high as for the responses to questions and clarification requests, a very marked developmental increase can be seen in the table. As I cautioned before, these data should be used as guidelines, not as performance criteria.

LANGUAGE INTERVENTION AND PHONOLOGY

Before moving on to some examples of children in each of these groups and the basic goals that I view as being of central importance for each, I should comment on the role of phonology in a language intervention plan. The precise nature of the relationship between phonology and other components of language is, at present, unknown. It is an undeniable fact, however, that children with severely limited vocabularies and semantic-syntactic abilities are highly likely to have severely impaired phonological skills as well (see discussions in Aram and Kamhi, 1982; Panagos, 1982; Panagos and Prelock, 1982; Panagos, Quine, and Klich, 1979; Paul and Shriberg, 1982; Schwartz, Leonard, Folger, and Wilcox, 1980).

Clinicians cannot overlook the fact, however, that young children in the early stages of normal language development do not pronounce all of their sounds correctly. In fact, direct comparisons of the phonologies of language impaired children with the phonologies of younger, language normal children have yielded far more similarities than differences (Leonard, 1979; Schwartz et al., 1980). Therefore, in many examples of moderate to severe language impairment, improving the child's phonological skills will not be a priority basic goal. Rather, the focus will be on developing the child's lexical, syntactic, semantic, and pragmatic abilities. Perhaps because of the close relationship between phonology and other components of language, intervention that focuses on problems in these areas often results in positive changes in the child's speech pattern as well (Gray and Ryan, 1973; Matheny and Panagos, 1978).

In some cases, however, one of the child's greatest obstacles to effective communication is the inability to produce intelligible speech. Such children receive very little pleasure from speaking and are likely to be most successful when utterances are kept very short and firmly grounded in the nonlinguistic context. The child may be discouraged from exercising the extent of her linguistic knowledge and, in fact, may be encouraged to communicate in as simple a form as possible. I have seen passive conversationalists and inactive communicators who, following successful phonological intervention, made exceedingly rapid gains, particularly in lexical and conversational skills. These gains have been so rapid that I am convinced that these children's severe phonological difficulties were the greatest contributing factors in their nonassertive social-conversational profiles. Once their speech became understandable, they began to exhibit their previously available, but rarely used, formal and pragmatic linguistic abilities.

Work on phonology should not represent the only intervention provided even for children with this type of disorder, however. As a rule of thumb, if speech sound production is a significant component in the child's communication problem, and if the child has at least a 50 to 100 word expressive vocabulary, increasing intelligibility can be targeted as one basic goal in a more comprehensive intervention plan. It is likely that the need for this type of basic goal will cut across the boundaries between active conversationalists, passive conversationalists, inactive communicators, and verbal noncommunicators. That is, some children from each group may require a basic goal of improving intelligibility in conversational contexts.

CLASSIFYING CHILDREN AND DETERMINING BASIC GOALS

In the remainder of this chapter, I will present a detailed description of the characteristic features of children in each of the four groups depicted in Figure 5-1. Along with each description I will include one or more sample basic goals that would seem to be of primary concern in the remediation of the particular type of problem. Because no purely objective criteria for making classification decisions are available, I will present examples of cases taken from the professional literature or from my own files that I consider to be good examples of a particular group. This should assist the clinician in developing hypotheses regarding categorization for specific children.

Children Who Are Active Conversationalists

Quadrant 1 in Figure 5-1 represents a group of children whom I call active conversationalists. They are best characterized by their high levels of activity both as initiators of conversation and as respondents to the initiatives of their conversational partners. Furthermore, the initiations of these children tend to reflect an interest in their partners and a sincere desire to communicate information to those partners. These children may have severe impairments of language form, but this does not stop them from attempting to communicate with subordinates, peers, and even adults. Often they are effective communicators despite serious limitations in their expressive language skills. Typically, however, this communicative effectiveness is contingent on a good deal of effort being extended by the conversational partner, as is the case with young normally developing children. In sum, active conversationalists appear to recognize the reciprocal nature of social-conversational interaction. Given their cognitive or linguistic limitations, they display what are judged to be very acceptable levels of assertive and responsive conversational acts as well as concern for their partner's informational requirements.

Table 5-4 contains a dialogue between a 4 year 10 month old language impaired boy, Jason, and an adult woman whom he had never met prior to this session. On the basis of a previous language sample involving Jason and myself in Jason's home, Jason's MLU was found to be 3.98 morphemes, and he had a Developmental Sentence Score (DSS) (Lee, 1974) of 4.74. This placed him well below the 10th percentile for his mental age of 4 years 6 months (*Leiter International Performance Scale*) (Leiter, 1979). Language comprehension was a problem for Jason, as shown by a *Peabody Picture Vocabulary Test* (*PPVT*) (Dunn, 1965) performance at the 4th percentile and a *Test for Auditory Comprehension of Language* (*TACL*) (Carrow, 1973) score that placed him at the 11th percentile for his CA.

In the sample in Table 5-4, Jason and the adult were playing with a Candyland game, some soap bubbles, and some Play-Doh. Jason's problems with language form are manifested in this sample. His sentences are short, with numerous grammatical errors. Despite these problems, Jason exhibits the ability to play an active role in this very difficult social situation. Although no decisions should be based on such a small amount of data, we can examine this sample for evidence of Jason's assertiveness and responsiveness, as discussed in the previous section. First, Jason produced four different types of assertive acts in this brief interaction. Seventeen per cent of his total utterances were requests. Of his total utterances, 60 per cent served to initiate or extend topics. Importantly, 38 per cent of his responses to RQINs not only addressed the question but also extended the topic by adding unsolicited information. Finally, Jason produced 13 assertive conversational acts. This accounted for 32 per cent of the total produced by both speakers in this conversation. All of this information suggests that Jason should be rated well above the midline on the assertiveness continuum. This initial hypothesis was confirmed by observing Jason in subsequent interactions with an unfamiliar peer and with a toddler. He was the dominant participant in each of these two interactions.

The next task is to look for evidence of Jason's responsiveness. In the sample in Table 5-4, the adult produced 13 RQINs and Jason responded to 12, or 92 per cent of them. He responded appropriately to 100 per cent of the adult's four RQCLs. Finally, Jason produced both questions and assertives that served to extend the nonrequestive utterances of the adult. In all, he responded to 6 of 8 (75 per cent) of all adult nonrequestive stimuli. Based on this information, it could be hypothesized that Jason is highly responsive in conversations. This hypothesis was supported by our observations in the other contexts. In conclusion, then, Jason appreciated the fact that conversation depends on the give-and-take of information between participants, and he was willing and able to play an active role as both initiator and respondent. Therefore, he is an excellent example of an active conversationalist.

It should *not* be assumed that active conversationalists are completely free of pragmatic impairment. They may show deficits in any of the specific behaviors listed in Table 5-1 (e.g., production of requests for information, or production of statements), and they may not demonstrate flexible use of alternative lexical items and syntactic forms to perform certain conversational acts. For example, they may use imperative forms and need statements (e.g., "I need a drink") but fail to make use of interrogatives to express requests for action (e.g., "Can I have a drink?" or "Where my juice?). Nevertheless, the primary deficit in these children is in their production and comprehension of linguistic forms.

Although the *specific* goals for these children will differ depending

Table 5–4. A Sample Interaction Between an Active Conversationalist and an Unfamiliar Woman*

Adult	Jason (4 years 10 months)
(Picks up a card from game)	
1. Do you know what this is? [RQIN]	
	1. No. [RSIN—maintain]
2. That's candy. [ASCO]	
	2. Do we eat that? [RQIN—extend]
3. Uh huh. [RSIN]	
	3. Go buy one. [ASCO—extend]
	4. Store. [ASCO—extend]
4. You can buy 'em at the store. [ASCO]	
5. Mmhmm. [RSAS] +	
	(Picks up Play-Doh)
6. What's that? [RQIN]	
	5. I wanna make cookie. [RSIN—extend]
7. You wanna make some cookies? [RQCL]	
	6. Yeah. [RSCL—maintain]
8. Let's make a gingerbread man. [RQAC]	
9. Want to? [RQCL]	
	7. Yeah. [RSIN—maintain]
10. Let's move this back so we don't get it dirty. [ASST]	
11. Well, we'll just move it around a little bit, okay? [RQIN] +	
(Drops a piece of Play-Doh and reaches to pick it up)	
	8. What doin? [RQIN—initiate]
12. I dropped that on the floor. [RSIN]	
	9. Is it dead? [RQIN—extend]
13. It's okay. [RSIN]	
14. You gonna make some—What are you gonna make, a cookie? [RQIN]	
	10. Yeah. [RSIN—maintain]
	(Picks up jar of soap bubbles solution)
	11. This get wets with bubbles. [ASCO—initiate]
15. You like to blow bubbles? [RQIN]	
	12. Yeah. [RSIN—maintain]
16. Let's see. [OTHER]	
17. Let's do it. [OTHER]	
18. Will it stay like that? [RQIN]	
19. There. [OTHER]	
	13. Where mommy go? [RQIN—initiate]
20. I don't know. [RSIN]	
	14. Mommy's in the . . . [ASCO—extend]
21. Is your little brother here? [RQIN]	
	15. No, watching Judy. [RSIN—extend]
22. Do you have a baby brother? [RQIN]	
	16. Isaiah. [RSIN—extend]
23. Seven months old? [RQIN]	
	17. No, he's two months. [RSIN—extend]

Table 5–4 (continued)

Adult	Jason (4 years 10 months)
24. Two months? [RQCL]	
	18. Yeah. [RSCL—maintain]
25. Is he pretty big? [RQIN]	
	19. No. [RSIN—maintain]
26. Is he little? [RQIN]	
	20. No. [RSIN—maintain]
27. He's not? [RQCL]	
	21. He's little. [RSCL—maintain]
28. Does he cry a lot? [RQIN]	
	22. Yeah. [RSIN—maintain]
	(Picks up a game card)
	23. Hey, they got ice cream right here, right here. [ASCO—initiate]
29. They do. [RSAS]	
30. And what's this in her hand? [RQIN]	
	24. I don't know. [RSIN—maintain]
	25. Come from right . . . [ASCO—extend]
31. I think that's a cupcake. [ASST]	
	26. Cupcake right here. [ASCO—extend]
32. Yeah. [RSAS]	
33. Like those. [ASST]	
34. She got one of those to eat. [ASCO] +	
	(Picks up Play-Doh)
	27. Hey look! [RQAT—initiate]
	28. I wanna make mine cake. [ASST—extend]
35. That's a nice cookie, Jason. [ASST]	
	29. That Christmas. [ASCO—extend]
36. A Christmas cookie? [RQCL]	
	30. Yeah, Christmas. [RSCL—maintain]

*The session took place in a small room with only the two participants present. Significant nonlinguistic details are given in parentheses. Coding of Jason's conversational acts at two levels (see Table 5–1) is represented to the right of each of his utterances. Underlined segments indicate overlap between speakers. Pauses of greater than 2 seconds are indicated with " + ." Incomplete utterances are shown by ellipses (. . .).

on the nature of their production and comprehension deficits, there are two *basic* goals that seem to be appropriate for all children who fit into this basic pattern.

1. *Train new content-form interactions to perform available conversational acts.* This goal makes it clear that the focus of intervention for children with this type of problem is the training (or facilitation) of new linguistic forms to perform conversational acts that, by definition, have communicative intent. Specific goals will reflect this emphasis. For example, the child may ask "yes-no" questions requiring

the word "do" but omit or fail to front the auxiliary. The requisite conversational act is used, but the conventional form to fulfill that function is not. A specific goal in such cases that is consistent with this basic goal might be for the child to include the auxiliary "do" in sentence-initial position for these questions.

2. *Facilitate the use of old forms to fulfill alternative conversational acts.* In most cases, this goal will receive secondary emphasis and will be subordinate to the first goal. Specific goals underlying this basic goal will involve the selection of existing linguistic forms to be used to perform conversational acts for which they are not presently used. For example, the child may produce "yes-no" questions correctly but fail to use them to soften requests for action—that is, to make requests more polite (Prinz and Ferrier, 1983). The use of "yes-no" questions to perform requests for action could be a specific goal for this child. The procedures used to reach specific goals related to this basic goal are likely to be the same as those used to reach the first basic goal given earlier.

Regardless of the intervention approach taken, neither of these basic goals can be considered to be attained unless the child is making *functional* use of newly acquired language forms. Language form exists as an arbitrary, but conventional, means of transmitting information. The functional value of language form should be exemplified in every step of the intervention process.

Children Who Are Passive Conversationalists

Quadrant 2 of Figure 5-1 represents a group of children who are very aware of the social nature of conversation; they monitor and respond to the verbal and nonverbal initiatives of their partners. For example, they respond reliably (although not always accurately) to the requestives of their partners. These responsives are more likely to maintain than to extend the conversational topic, however. Furthermore, passive conversationalists often respond frequently and excessively to the nonrequestive conversational acts of their partners with RSASs. These responses may enable these children to participate without contributing substantive information to the developing text.

Unlike active conversationalists, children in this quadrant produce unsolicited conversational acts relatively infrequently. Despite having the linguistic means for producing requestive conversational acts, they do not use them often. In addition, assertives and performatives are infrequently produced. Therefore, the rates of topic initiations and extensions for these children are low as well. In addition, they are not likely to disagree when an obviously false assertion has been made by a partner. Thus, these children fall low on the assertiveness continuum and high on the continuum of responsiveness to the partner. Although they are willing to participate in social interactions, they are characterized by their adoption of the role of respondent and their relative neglect of their responsibilities as initiators of communicative exchanges.

Children who fit this basic behavioral profile have been reported frequently in the professional literature (Cunningham, Reuler, Blackwell, and Deck, 1981; MacDonald, 1985; see also Fey and Leonard, 1983, for a review). It is not necessary to look far among language impaired children to find those who seem to follow the conversational maxim "Speak only when spoken to." Although these children may have significant deficits in their knowledge and use of language form, it may be necessary to look beneath the structure of their utterances to fully understand the complexities of their impairment.

The dialogue given in Table 5–5 exemplifies the social-conversational style of a passive conversationalist. The child, Sean, was 4 years 7 months of age at the time of this interaction, and his Leiter MA was 4 years 6 months. Based on his CA, Sean's PPVT and TACL scores placed him at the 14th and 9th percentiles, respectively. These scores, along with Sean's conversational performance, indicated that comprehension was a significant component in his language impairment. Sean's expressive skills were even more significantly impaired, however. He had an MLU of 3.49 morphemes, but a DSS of only 2.98, well below the 10th percentile for his mental age. He was often frustrated by his inability to make others understand.

This example contrasts sharply with that given in Table 5–4. This comparison is especially useful because the two children involved are so similar in CA, MA, and formal linguistic ability. First we ask "How assertive is this child?" The results of several analyses suggest that Sean is reluctant to accept the role of initiator in this interaction. For example, only four, or 20 per cent, of his total utterances are assertive conversational acts. None of these are requestives or topic initiations of any type. Furthermore, only 15 per cent of his conversational acts extend the topic. None of these extensions occurs when he responds to his partner. His responses provide only the requisite information, not extensions to the topic initiated by the partner. Of all assertive acts produced in this interaction, only 11 per cent were produced by Sean, indicating that he was clearly subordinate to his partner in this situation.

Next, we turn to questions concerning Sean's responsiveness. In this area, he fares much better. Of the 12 RQINs and RQCLs produced by the adult that can be counted as stimuli, Sean responded to 11, or 92 per cent. Furthermore, he produced six responses to six adult non-

Table 5-5. A Sample Interaction Between a Child Who is a Passive Conversationalist and an Unfamiliar Woman*

Adult	Sean (4 years 7 months)
(Drops Play-Doh on the floor)	
1. Whoa, There's a little piece on the floor too. [ASCO]	
2. Do you have Play-Doh at home? [RQIN]	
	1. No. [RSIN—maintain]
3. No? [RQCL]	
4. It's kinda messy, isn't it? [RQIN]	
5. What're you gonna make first? [RQIN]	
	2. Gingerbread. [RSIN—maintain]
6. Do you use those? [RQIN]	
	3. Uh huh. [RSIN—maintain]
7. Oh. [RSAS]	
	(Gives Play-Doh to adult)
8. Oh, I get blue to match mine, huh? [RQIN]	
9. We better pull our sleeves up. [ASST]	
	4. Nah. [ASDA—extend]
10. 'Cause your sleeves are pretty long. [ASST] +	
11. Can you smash it? [RQIN]	
12. What can you make? [RQIN]	
	5. Gingerbread. [RSIN—maintain]
13. Gingerbread man? [RQCL]	
	6. Yeah. [RSCL—maintain]
14. Can you? [RQCL]	
	7. Yes. [RSIN—maintain]
15. Can you make a snowman? [RQIN]	
	8. Me not know. [RSIN—maintain]
	9. I want . . . [ASST—extend?]
16. Oh, it's real easy. [ASST]	
17. Just make some little balls. [ASCO]	
18. Can you make a snowman outside? [RQIN]	
	10. No. [RSIN—maintain]
19. In the snow? [RQIN]	
	11. Not XX snow. [RSIN— maintain]
20. We haven't had too much, have we? [RQIN] +	
(Illustrates rolling motion on Play-Doh)	
21. See, you just do like this. [ASCO]	
22. Make some ball. [ASCO] +	
	(Takes ball off of table)
23. Oops, you gonna put him to bed? [RQIN]	
	13. Nope. [RSIN—maintain]
24. Looks like a sandwich. (laughs) [ASST]	
25. Are you gonna make a a gingerbread sandwich? [RQIN]	

Table 5–5 (continued)

Adult	Sean (4 years 7 months)
	14. No. [RSIN—maintain]
	(Puts cover over Play-Doh)
26. He disappeared! [ASCO]	
	15. I want a nobodys to see it. [ASST—extend]
27. Nobody will see it. [ASST]	
	16. Yeah. [RSAS—maintain]
28. They even have bubbles in here. [ASCO]	
	17. Mmhmm. [RSAS—maintain]
29. Mm, I like bubbles. [ASST]	
	18. Oh. [RSAS—maintain]
	(Covers Play-Doh again)
30. I can hardly see him. [ASST]	
31. (You) cover him all up. [ASCO]	
	19. Yep. [RSAS—maintain]
32. Make him appear. [RQAC]	
	(Takes cover off Play-Doh)
	20. Back. [ASCO—extend]

*The session took place in a small room with only the two participants present. Significant nonlinguistic details are given in parentheses. Coding of Sean's conversational acts at two levels (see Table 5–1) is represented to the right of each of his utterances. Underlined segments indicate overlap between speakers. Pauses of greater than 2 seconds are indicated with "+." Incomplete utterances are shown as ellipses (. . .). Unintelligible syllables are represented as "X."

requestive stimuli. Of these responses, however, five (83 per cent) were RSASs and served only to maintain the topic. This is particularly strong evidence that Sean wants to participate in this interaction, but that he is unwilling to contribute actively to the development of text.

In sum, Sean's social-conversational profile, in contrast to Jason's, is characterized by low assertiveness and high responsiveness. As with Jason, we looked upon this characterization of Sean's conversational participation as an initial hypothesis that required further verification. This came when we watched him play a very subordinate role in an interaction with a peer. Parental reports of his play and conversation with other children at home were also highly supportive of our initial impressions. Sean's ability to play a lead role in an interaction was clear, however, when we had him interact in free play with a toddler. He demonstrated many assertive behaviors in this context that were produced only infrequently with adults and peers. This example suggests quite clearly that language impaired children may adopt a typical, restricted style of interaction even when they have the potential to perform in a much more socially appropriate manner.

It is doubtful that the problems with language form exhibited by children such as Sean are the sole result of their passive approach to conversational participation, although this certainly may be a contributing factor. It is much more likely that this style of interaction plays a significant role in the *maintenance* of the impairment. The relative failure of these children to initiate play and conversation with their peers and significant adults in their environments may effectively exclude them from many of the very types of social interactions in which language is typically learned. Helping them to become more active as initiators of conversations and conversational topics may place them in a better position to begin to learn language at a faster pace on their own. With this in mind, training new content-form interactions should be a lower priority for them, as is shown in the following suggested basic goals.

1. *Increase the frequency of use of available assertive conversational acts in a variety of social contexts.* In my experience, most children who are responsive but nonassertive have at least a small repertoire of what I have referred to as assertive conversational acts. The basic goal here is to encourage them to use these acts more frequently. Procedures would be selected that encourage the child to initiate communication, the form and content of that communication being subordinated to the act itself.

2. *Increase the child's repertoire of assertive conversational acts, using existing forms, when possible.* For some children, especially those functioning at relatively low linguistic and cognitive levels, efforts may need to be directed at facilitating the child's use of new assertive acts. For example, specific goals might be to increase the spontaneous use of protests in naturalistic contexts with peers (e.g., "no") or to request clarification from adults using the one-word response "What?" when a message has been unclear.

3. *Train new linguistic forms that are useful in performing available assertive acts.* As noted previously, most passive conversationalists are likely to use some forms of requestives and assertives. This basic goal simply suggests that efforts to facilitate the use of new language forms to the child should focus on assertive acts rather than responsive acts. Because the emphasis is on the production of assertive conversational acts, the procedures selected may differ significantly from those used for an active conversationalist. For example, the use of questions such as "What is the boy doing now?" to train a specific goal, action–object––place (e.g., "hiding frog under bed") may be appropriate in some circumstances for the active conversationalist. However, this stimulus would not be acceptable to meet this basic goal for the passive conversationalist, because the expected production is a responsive, not an

assertive. One of the clinician's charges would be to get the child to use the new structure without benefit of a requestive stimulus. This is a good example of a situation in which not only the goal but also the procedure is influenced by the child's basic social-conversational pattern.

Children Who Are Inactive Communicators

Quadrant 3 of Figure 5-1 represents a group of children who are low on both the assertiveness and the responsiveness continua. Some children in this group are severely socially isolated. The situation is not always so extreme, however, and the children are not necessarily autistic or schizophrenic. Some children who have severe problems with expressive language, including phonology, simply talk very little in comparison to their peers, although they often demonstrate in some contexts that they are capable of much more. These children can be pleasant, but they seem not to be too interested in conversation with at least some important members of their social environment. They initiate conversations very infrequently, especially given the fact that they have the ability to produce a number of initiatory behaviors. Furthermore, attempts to get them to respond often end in frustration (certainly for the clinician and parents and probably for the child as well). It has been my experience that children in this quadrant display greater comprehension deficits than children in the two groups discussed previously. My experience has been limited, however, and my impression has not always held true (see the example of Billy given later in this chapter). In any case, these children's lack of responsiveness always seems to go beyond an inability to understand prior utterances (i.e., even when language is kept quite simple, the basic unwillingness to respond persists). Further evidence for this impression is that the children often fail to respond to simple, nonspecific requests for repetition of their own utterances (e.g., "What?" or "Huh?"). When they do respond, the structure of their response is often shorter and less complex than they are capable of producing.

Inactive communicators are more likely than children in the first two groups to exhibit deficits in their range of conversational acts. These deficits usually involve, quite predictably, various types of requestives, such as requests for action, information, and clarification, as well as various types of assertives and performatives.

A conversation between a child identified as an inactive communicator and myself is presented in Table 5-6. The child, Billy, was 5 years 11 months at the time of this assessment. He had never been to our clinic and had never met me before. Unless a hearer was familiar

Table 5–6. A Sample Interaction Between an Inactive Communicator and the Author*

MEF	Billy (5 years 11 months)
(Both participants playing silently with Play-Doh)	
1. It's awful hard. [ASCO]	
2. I just bought this today. [ASCO] +	
3. It's awful hard. [ASCO] +	
4. I think it gets a little softer after you play with it. [ASST] +	
5. I bet I can guess how old you are. [PERF] +	
	(Still playing silently with Play-Doh)
6. Sixteen. [PERF]	
	(Shakes head)
7. No? [RQCL]	
	(Holds up five fingers—head still, looking down at Play-Doh)
8. How many is that? [RQIN]	
	1. Five. [RSIN—maintain]
9. Five, that's right. [ASST] +	
10. You're almost 6 years old though. [ASST]	
11. I know that. [ASST] +	
12. I bet you could never guess how old I am. [PERF] +	
	(Still playing with Play-Doh)
13. Do you think I'm 30 or 100? [RQIN]	
	2. Hundred. [RSIN—maintain]
14. You think I'm 100? [RQCL]	
	(Nods and smiles)
15. You do? [RQCL]	
16. No, I'm not 100? [ASDA] +	
17. I'm not 100 at all. [ASDA] +	
18. Your brother, Andrew, he's 16. [PERF] +	
	(Plays with Play-Doh)
19. It's very hard, isn't it, Billy? [ASCO] +	
20. I think I'm gonna make a dog. [ASST] +	
21. I have two dogs. [ASCO]	
22. I have two dogs at home. [ASCO] +	
23. One's named Basil and one is named Benny. [ASCO] +	
24. I think this guy's gonna hafta be Basil. [ASST]	
25. He's too fat for Benny. [ASST] +	
26. I hear you have a pet fish at home. [PERF] +	
	(Plays with Play-Doh)
27. Your pet fish, Max. [PERF] +	
	(Shakes head very slightly)
28. Right? [RQCL]	
29. No? [RQCL] +	
30. Max isn't a fish? [RQCL]	
	(Looks at MEF)
	(Shakes head)
31. A cat. [PERF]	
	3. No. [ASDA—extend]

Table 5–6 (continued)

MEF	Billy (5 years 11 months)
32. Yeah, I bet he's a cat. [PERF]	
	4. No! [ASDA—maintain]
33. No? [RQCL]	
	5. No, 's a dog. [RSCL—extend]
34. A teeny tiny little dog. [PERF]	
	6. No! [ASDA—extend]
35. Yeah, Max must be just a little tiny puppy. [ASDA]	
	7. Yeah. [RSAS—maintain]
36. Is he a little puppy or a big one? [RQCL]	
	8. Little. [RSIN—maintain]

*The session took place in a small room with the author, Billy, and Billy's parents present. The only props available were three cans of Play-Doh. Significant nonlinguistic details are given in parentheses. Coding of Billy's conversational acts at two levels (see Table 5-1) is represented to the right of each of his utterances. Pauses of greater than 2 seconds are indicated with " + ." Some discussion between Billy's parents and the author intervened between MEF 25 and 26.

with his patterns of phonological errors, Billy's connected speech was almost completely unintelligible. In fact, my charge in this assessment was to evaluate his phonological system. Administration of the *Northwestern Syntax Screening Test* (Lee, 1969) yielded a passing score in language comprehension and a failing score in expression. This finding of relatively good comprehension compared with poor expressive abilities was consistent with the information that was available prior to the assessment, so no further testing of formal linguistic abilities was done at this time. Billy's performance on the *Test of Nonverbal Intelligence* (TONI) (Brown, Sherbenou, and Dollar, 1983) placed him at the 64th percentile for his age, indicating normal nonverbal intelligence.

The sample in Table 5-6 contains far more utterances that are followed by a 2 second pause than in the previous two samples. The durations of some of these pauses were great, so it should be noted that this interaction was much longer than those transcribed in Tables 5-4 and 5-5. Still, although Billy rarely established and maintained eye contact during this interaction, he smiled and played readily in parallel and sometimes even associative fashion with me throughout the session. The willingness of this child to tolerate me, a stranger, and to interact at some level without overt fear and anxiety distinguishes him from some more severely disturbed children in this category, who are often identified as autistic or electively mute (cf. Kolvin and Fundudis, 1981).

The most important and obvious aspect of this interaction is Billy's reluctance to take a speaking turn. This low rate of utterance production occurred despite my efforts to talk about topics that I knew were of interest to Billy and to give him plenty of time to respond. Topic initiations were absent even from parts of the larger body of data from which this sample was extracted. Only three of his utterances (Nos. 3, 5, and 6) were topic extensions, and these involved only small contributions to the content of the conversation. Even though three of these responses (Nos. 3, 4, and 6) are ASDAs, Billy seems to have been unwilling to explain the source of his disagreement. In fact, Billy's responses Nos. 7 and 8 agree with my assertion that his dog is little. This was not a true assertion, however. In fact, his incorrect position contradicts the claim he made earlier in his utterance No. 6. Billy produced only three conversational acts that can be viewed as assertive compared to my 36 (8 per cent of the total). This measure, taken with all of the other evidence, suggests that Billy played a very nonassertive role in this interaction.

Unlike Sean, a passive conversationalist, Billy exhibited a level of responsiveness far below what would be expected based on his age and intellectual and language comprehension abilities. If we count only those adult utterances followed by long pauses as stimuli, Billy responded to most of my questions, but only four of eight questions received a verbal response. Importantly, all but one of these were single word responses, even though Billy was capable of producing long, if not structurally complex, utterances. Billy demonstrated that he understood the function of questions and even recognized that some response was required. His responses were limited, however, to the bare minimum required and generally did not further the development of conversational topics.

Billy's weaknesses in responding are especially clear when we examine his reaction to my nonrequestive conversational bids. It is important to note that the content of many of my performatives was especially designed to test Billy's willingness to disagree. Still, Billy responded to only 4 of 21 (19 per cent) of my initiatives. In sum, I viewed Billy's performance as being highly nonassertive and nonresponsive given his age and cognitive and formal linguistic abilities.

Billy's conversational performance with another unfamiliar adult during this same assessment yielded similar findings. We were unable to observe Billy with a younger child, but we did watch him in a free play session with his twin brother. Although both boys were virtually completely unintelligible, they each produced numerous conversational initiatives and appeared to be highly responsive to one another. Parental report assured us that with family members, Billy exhibited the ability to interact much more appropriately than he had in the assessment session. Thus, it was clear that his inactive pattern did not represent a general deficit in his *ability* to perform socially. The parents also reported, however, that Billy was quite shy at school and that our impressions correctly characterized his performance in many social contexts. Therefore, the basic goals discussed in the following paragraphs seemed highly appropriate in this case.

Attempts to get children with this type of problem to learn a new syntactic structure or new vocabulary items are typically unproductive. The children may, in fact, learn to imitate or even create novel sentences of a given syntactic pattern in therapy, but there is very little chance that this new acquisition will be put to functional use. The fundamental problem for these children seems to be more basic. They appear not to be highly motivated to initiate and sustain social contact. Since the primary function of language is communication, which is an inherently social act, children who show reduced willingness to participate in social interactions are at great risk for problems with language development, as well as with cognitive, educational, and psychosocial development. Therefore, even though goals of language form and content may be of some importance, they are viewed as secondary and receive less emphasis. The basic goals that will receive primary emphasis for these children include the following items.

1. *Increase the child's rate of positive social bids (verbal and nonverbal) in a variety of social contexts.* This goal differs only in degree from the first goal for passive conversationalists. Whereas the emphasis was on verbal productions for passive children, procedures for inactive communicators will be selected to facilitate social interaction of any kind. In addition, more emphasis will be placed on appropriate responding with an inactive child than with a passive conversationalist. Specific goals might include increasing the rate of positive social responses to partners (e.g., smiling, sharing, associative and cooperative play), more frequent assertive behaviors in particular social contexts (e.g., with the teacher, classmates, in "show and tell"), and more reliable responding to specific types of a partner's requestives and assertives. For this basic goal, it may not matter which specific conversational acts or linguistic forms are being used so long as the general frequencies of socially directed bids and appropriate assertive and responsive behaviors are increasing. Because of the high functional utility of requestives, however, facilitating these children's use of specific request types may be especially productive for them (Beisler and Tsai, 1983; Fay and Shuler, 1980).

When the child becomes more responsive and begins to initiate communication more frequently, real deficits in her conversational act repertoire and in lexical and syntactic abilities may become more apparent. At this point, the goals recommended for passive conversationalists will probably be highly appropriate.

Children Who Are Verbal Noncommunicators

Quadrant 4 in Figure 5-1 is occupied by children who are capable of assuming the role of initiator of conversations and conversational topics, but who fail to accommodate their own language to the needs of their partners. They appear to be assertive but highly unresponsive in social interactions. These children are typically quite verbal, often excessively so, and they frequently use a broad range of conversational acts. The semantic-syntactic relationships found within these children's utterances may be characteristic of language normal children of similar CA or MA. That is, in a clause-by-clause analysis of the child's sentences, semantic relations such as agent–action–object or location may be found. The weaknesses of these children are manifested in their production of high rates of utterances that are either unrelated or, at best, tangentially related to their own prior utterances or to the utterances of their partners. They seem to have specific deficiencies in their abilities to initiate appropriate topics and to maintain and extend the topics that have already been established.

The example in Table 5-7 illustrates this pattern of unresponsiveness in a verbal noncommunicator reported by Lucas (1980). The sentences produced by this child appear well-formed and appropriate when examined outside of the conversational context. Because no nonlinguistic contextual information is given in Lucas' example, I have made no attempt to code this sample using the coding system of Table 5-1. It is clear, however, that the child has no difficulty directing this interaction. The child produces 50 per cent of the total utterances, and most of his contributions are requestives and assertives. Yet, throughout this brief interchange, the adult is struggling, without much success, to follow the child's inexplicit communication efforts. None of the adult RQCLs in Nos. 1, 2, or 6 receives a satisfactory response. The child's questions in Nos. 6 through 9 appear to have been asked just for the sake of asking, because the information from one, when the adult can answer, does not lead logically into the other (Nos. 7 and 8 may be exceptions). The child's response in No. 10, as well as his general unresponsiveness to adult requestives, suggests that he may have significant language comprehension difficulties.

For some verbal noncommunicators, the neglect of the partner's utterances is almost complete. For example, Blank, Gessner, and Esposito (1979) reported a child, aged 3 years 3 months, who had formal linguistic skills that were well within the normal range and who in other respects appeared normal. Blank and co-workers described this child's use of language as follows.

The general picture that emerges is one of noncommunication. John spoke a great deal, but his utterances, whether as responses or initia-

Table 5–7. An Example of an Attempted Conversation Between a 4 Year Old Child Best Described as a Verbal Noncommunicator and an Adult*

Child	Adult
1. Give me that.	
	1. Which one do you want?
2. I have that.	
	2. What do you have?
3. No more glue, please.	
	3. Okay, I have the glue.
4. I don't have any of that yellow glue, see?	
	4. Yes, I see.
5. See, I need more yellow glue.	
	5. Yes, I see that you need more yellow glue.
6. When did you go?	
	6. What do you mean?
7. Where do you live?	
	7. In Jonesborough.
8. Do you have a house?	
	8. Well, I do own my house.
9. What is your name?	
	9. You know what my name is!
10. Jimmy.	
	10. No, that is your name.

*From Lucas, E. (1980). *Semantic and pragmatic language disorders: Assessment and remediation* (p. 53). Rockville, MD: Aspen Systems Corporation. Reprinted with permission.

tions, were rarely appropriate to the utterances of the other participant. He did not follow a theme in any coherent manner and he seemed basically uninterested in the content of the participant's verbalizations. (p. 346)

John's parents responded consistently and adequately to his assertive acts, thus enhancing the likelihood of a smooth, coherent dialogue. Even under these ideal conditions, however, John responded in a semantically appropriate manner to only 24 per cent of the parents' requestives and to 27 per cent of their assertives. The system used by Blank and co-workers (1979) to code the child's utterances was more semantically based than the one presented in this chapter, so it is likely that these percentages would be slightly higher using the proposed system. Nevertheless, Blank and associates concluded that "At the time when he was capable of initiating almost any type of exchange, he paid little attention to the language directed towards him" (p. 344), and this typifies the performance of children I refer to as verbal noncommunicators.

Within the coding system provided in Table 5-1, then, the primary characteristics of verbal noncommunicators will be high rates of no responses or initiations following partner requestives. In addition, verbal noncommunicators are likely to produce large proportions of tangential topic extensions. High rates of imitation may also be observed. The frequency of tangential topic extensions and imitations suggests that these children attend to their partners and may be interested in maintaining social contact with them, but they do not accommodate their actions, verbal or otherwise, to meet their partners' needs. Language seems to occur for its own sake rather than to serve a number of primarily social functions.

For some verbal noncommunicators, viewing the problem as one of insensitivity to the conversational partner is only partially adequate. There are two reasons for this. First, some of these children are prone to plunging into lengthy narratives that are also characterized by very weak coherency between utterances or between clauses within the same utterance. The following example, taken from Schwartz (1974), illustrates this type of intraturn semantic difficulty. The child, aged 6 years 2 months, was asked to tell all she could about a button.

> You can roll it and throw it, but you never smash a window, because if you have a button or a shape that goes on the wall or if you take it and hang it on the dress that would be very nice. (pp. 466–467)

Schwartz (1974) refers to this incoherent speech as "cocktail-party speech" and suggests that it is characteristic of many children who are hydrocephalic. Whether the incoherency found within these children's own speaking turns is due to the same factors responsible for their high rates of tangential and unrelated responses to the utterances of their partners is not known at this time. Second, some researchers have suggested that the reason for many of these children's inappropriate productions is that they have significant deficits in their knowledge of the ways in which topics can be initiated and maintained. Thus, some highly verbal autistic children who make frequent use of inappropriate questions may do so in an effort to maintain the interaction at those times when they lack the knowledge of more appropriate ways to initiate and extend the topic (Hurtig, Ensrud, and Tomblin, 1982). Philips and Dyer (1977) as well as Prizant and Duchan (1981) have taken similar positions with respect to the immediate echolalic responses in autistic children.

There is an important implication of the hypothesis that much "noncommunicative" behavior represents the child's efforts to sustain contact. At least for some children, these inappropriate behaviors should not be extinguished in a direct manner. Rather, more appropriate behaviors need to be taught so that the inappropriate responses are no longer needed.

Clearly, the needs of verbal noncommunicators are different from those of children exhibiting the other three patterns discussed earlier. They may need assistance with the form of their utterances at some point during the intervention program, but this type of traditional goal must be subordinated to other basic goals, such as the following ones.

1. *Increase the relatedness of the child's responses to the assertive acts (e.g., requestives, assertives, performatives) of the partner.* I suggested earlier that the use of questions as stimuli might be contraindicated when working with children who are passive conversationalists. Unlike passive conversationalists, verbal noncommunicators produce an overabundance of divergent speech and have difficulty planning utterances that converge on the semantic and syntactic constraints of prior utterances. Therefore, questions and other requestives that place easily identifiable constraints on the manner in which the child can respond appropriately will be highly suitable for these children. As for the other groups of children, however, the focus of intervention should be on the functional utility of social-linguistic responses. Therefore, this basic goal could not be viewed as having been attained until the child responds to a variety of naturally occurring conversational acts in a meaningful, rather than a highly contrived, way. Reaching this goal is likely to require a careful inquiry into the child's comprehension skills, which may be significantly impaired, and the careful tailoring of partner speech patterns to reflect an awareness of the child's comprehension limitations.

2. *Facilitate the child's production of sequences of utterances that are topically related to one another.* If the tendency to produce tangential or off-topic responses following the conversational partner is related to the child's off-topic responding within speaking turns, little direct work may be required on this basic goal. This relationship has not been established by empirical methods, however. Work on specific goals subordinate to basic goal No. 1 could proceed successfully without having any effect on the child's ability to produce strings of related utterances within a speaking turn. To test this possibility, the clinician could monitor the child's use of within-turn sequences of related utterances throughout training on goal No. 1. Using this type of experimental design the clinician could test her hypotheses regarding the relatedness of these two types of behavior and would be in a strong position to demonstrate the effectiveness and efficiency of the clinical program (see Chapter 7 for more details on this type of experimental design).

3. *Encourage the child to establish referents in a clear and unambiguous fashion.* Since the verbal noncommunicator does not adequately consider the listener in planning utterances, many pronouns and nonspecific nominals (e.g., "thing," "stuff") are likely to appear in the child's speech

when their referents have not clearly been established in prior discourse. This basic goal requires the child to reduce her usage of these unspecified terms and to communicate in a more explicit fashion that takes the listener's needs into consideration. A specific goal that might be subordinated to this basic goal might be to get the child to respond correctly to requests for clarification that request specification of these referents. For example:

Child:　I watched last night.
Adult:　You watched what last night?
Child:　Sleep in my bed.
Adult:　No, tell me! What did you watch last night?
Child:　Dukes of Hazzard.
Adult:　Oh, I didn't see it last night.

Obviously, this specific goal also ties in nicely with and would be appropriate for basic goal No. 1 as well.

SUMMARY AND CONCLUSION

Language impaired children are typically diagnosed and described behaviorally on the basis of their ability to use and understand lexical and grammatical forms. Thus, we read about children who have expressive language delays, delays in receptive as well as expressive language, vocabulary deficits, grammatical deficits, and so forth.

My claim in presenting a different means of profiling language impaired children's abilities does not contradict the existence or the utility of these more traditional descriptions. An evaluation of a child's language that does not include a careful analysis and description of the child's lexicogrammatical skills in both comprehension and expression would be painfully incomplete. The system that I have proposed in this chapter, however, acknowledges what I perceive to be an incontrovertible fact—children who display similar profiles of the comprehension and production of language form can differ dramatically in their ability to communicate and to participate effectively in the exchange of information through discourse. The hypothesis that I have developed in this chapter and will continue to develop throughout the rest of this book is that these differences warrant close clinical attention. More specifically, I am suggesting that because of basic differences in their social-conversational styles, children with similar formal linguistic profiles have different needs. The basic goals that are selected for language impaired children should reflect the clinician's awareness of these differences. A summary of the four different patterns of conversational participation that I have discussed and the

Table 5–8. A Summary of Primary Basic Goals Recommended for Children Who Exhibit Different Patterns of Social-Conversational Participation

ACTIVE CONVERSATIONALISTS

1. Train new content-form interactions to perform available conversational acts.
2. Facilitate the use of old forms to fulfill alternative conversational acts.

PASSIVE CONVERSATIONALISTS

1. Increase the frequency of use of available assertive conversational acts in a variety of social contexts.
2. Increase the child's repertoire of requestive conversational acts, using existing forms, when possible.
3. Train new linguistic forms that are useful in performing available assertive acts.

INACTIVE COMMUNICATORS

1. Increase the child's frequency of social bids (verbal *and* nonverbal) in a variety of social contexts.

VERBAL NONCOMMUNICATORS

1. Increase the relatedness of the child's responses to the assertive acts (e.g., requestives, assertives, performatives) of the partner.
2. Facilitate the child's production of sequences of utterances that are topically related to one another.
3. Encourage the child to establish referents in a clear and unambiguous fashion.

basic goals that I view as highly suitable for each is provided in Table 5–8.

There is nothing sacred about these particular goals. This list is meant to be instructive, not exhaustive. Furthermore, it is quite possible that a child who exhibits characteristics of a given pattern will require assistance typically required by children who exhibit a different pattern. For example, an active conversationalist may need intervention directed toward responding appropriately to certain types of questions or toward clearly establishing referents in discourse. In most cases, however, if goals for a child who clearly fits one pattern are selected from the set of goals associated with another group, these goals are likely to be accorded lower priority than the goals for the child's own group. Of course, it should be recognized that the patterns of conversational activity produced by a given child will change as the result of intervention, maturation, experience, and so forth. As such changes occur, the child's intervention plan must be adjusted accordingly.

A final word of caution regarding the use of this classification scheme is warranted. There is little question that some children will not fit neatly into any one of the proposed categories. Rather than exhibiting the extreme patterns represented by the four corners of the system, many or perhaps most children will regress toward the center; that is, many children will not seem highly assertive or highly responsive; however, these same children may not appear to be especially nonassertive or unresponsive when compared with other children of similar linguistic and intellectual ability. In other words, as with any classification system presented to date, many children are likely to "fall through the cracks" of the proposed system. Given the fact that assertiveness and responsiveness are assumed to vary from child to child (and even within children) along continua, this is expected. *There should be no effort to force children into a group just for the sake of categorization.* The degree of confidence that can be placed on a child's classification in the scheme and on the basic goals that are recommended for each group depends entirely on the degree to which the child's observed patterns of communicative interaction match the pattern that has been described and was illustrated by example. If a child's performance seems to border on two or more of the four groups described, it is likely that attention to the basic goals for each of the groups will lead to the development of the most effective intervention program possible.

I believe that this scheme is useful because it ensures that new linguistic forms will not be viewed as goals in and of themselves, as has often been the case in the past. Instead, attention is directed toward the child's use of language to communicate more effectively or efficiently. Sometimes this will involve training new language forms, and other times it will not. Ultimately, it is improvement in communicative ability, not simply the ability to say new words and sentences, that will have a positive and lasting effect on the child's performance in social contexts and on society's assessment of the child.

Chapter 6

Determining the Content and Sequence of Specific Goals: Developmental Versus Remedial Logic

Many authors and analysts of intervention programs and procedures from a number of different theoretical persuasions have argued that the normal sequence of development should serve as the basis for specific goal selection (Bloom and Lahey, 1978; Bricker and Bricker, 1974; Cole, 1982; Gray and Ryan, 1973; Groht, 1958; Lee et al., 1975; Miller and Yoder, 1974; Rees, 1972; Stremel and Waryas, 1974). This position has been termed *developmental logic* by Guess and co-workers (1978). Using developmental logic, the clinician selects as goals (1) expressible content, (2) language forms needed to express that content, and (3) in some cases, factors governing the use of those forms in the same order as they would appear in the developmental course of a child learning language normally. It is assumed that since this order for learning these particular aspects of language occurs naturally for children learning language normally, it must also be the easiest and, therefore, the best course to follow in teaching language impaired children.

Especially for clinicians who believe in the principles of social learning theory, interactionism, or the transformational account of acquisition, following some account of the normal pattern of development may be essential. Since learning is believed to depend to a large degree on the child's present state of knowledge of the physical, social, and linguistic worlds, and on her present social and physical environments, the child may not be ready to learn and employ certain language concepts and behaviors in any general or generally useful way. Patterns of normal development would seem to be the most reliable guide to determine those aspects of language that the child is best equipped to learn.

Guess and co-workers (1974, 1978), who have worked almost exclusively with severely and profoundly retarded children and adults, are ardent supporters of a different and sometimes conflicting position, which they term *remedial logic*. These investigators operate within the operant paradigm, which holds that by careful manipulation of stimuli and contingencies of reinforcement, individuals can be taught a variety of skills regardless of their prior behavioral and psychological histories. They claim that

> Remedial logic, by contrast, supposes that children being taught language relatively late in their lives, because they have failed to acquire it adequately in their earlier experiences, no longer possess the same collection of abilities and deficits that normal children have when they begin to acquire language. . . .
>
> Remedial logic, then, will not ask in what order the retarded child needs to learn language, but rather in what order the language taught most quickly will accomplish some improvement in the child's communication. (1978, p. 106)

As was pointed out in Chapter 1, adoption of operant learning theory does not commit the clinician to training any particular language forms or to selecting any particular sequence in which these forms must be trained. These decisions are based on the clinician's analysis of each individual's specific physical and social situations and the outcome of clinical experimentation with various training sequences. In other words, the issue of what to train and in what sequence is an empirical matter.

Guess and colleagues (1978) present an excellent example of this approach. First, they carefully recorded the number of sessions that it took each of their clients to reach criterion in each of the steps in their program. They then modified the procedures used to reach the objective for a given step when that step appeared to be relatively difficult compared to neighboring steps. They also modified the original order so that there was either a general trend toward smaller numbers of sessions to criterion for steps later in the sequence or relative stability in the number of sessions required from step to step. Such trends might suggest that earlier programs in some way prepare the child for later programs. At least it could be claimed that an order following such a pattern was reasonable.

Unfortunately, although this information can be valuable for planning sequences, it does not deal with the question of which language forms actually will help the child to communicate more effectively. This is because the criteria used in the program of Guess and associates (1978) do not involve the child's functional use of new language forms in natural speaking contexts. The number of sessions to criterion really tells us nothing of the extent to which the subjects studied by Guess and co-workers actually used their newly trained language abilities in their everyday settings. It seems to me that if improvement in functional communication is to be the basis for making clinical decisions concerning the content and sequence of a language program, the functional use of trained behaviors must be the variable of concern, not the mean number of sessions to criterion, based on clinic performance.

At present, there is really no experimental evidence to suggest that the content and sequence for any one nondevelopmental training program leads to improved communication more quickly than another. The unfortunate consequence of this fact is that the use of remedial logic often leads to very questionable goals and procedures based on the clinician's intuitions about what will be most functional for a given child. For example, step 7 of Guess and co-workers' program (1978) is to train the child to respond appropriately to yes-no questions with a yes or no response. On the surface, this would seem to be a highly useful goal. Furthermore, based strictly on the results of the careful program testing done by Guess and colleagues, the step appears to be well placed.

The problem lies in the subgoals that follow. To reach this goal, children are asked to respond correctly with 80 per cent accuracy to questions such as "Is this a cup?" as a cup is clearly displayed by the clinician. I have considered this and other steps in these programs for ten years now, and I am still at a loss as to how such a response to such an unlikely question can be considered functional in the child's naturalistic interactions with the environment. If at least some attention had been given to the normal sequence of development, yes-no questions that require a child to deny propositions such as "this is a cup" would have been dismissed in favor of questions that query the child's needs and desires (e.g., "Do you want a cup?"). Responses to these latter types of questions that either accept or reject an offer would seem to meet the needs of most children and caregivers more adequately than the type actually programmed by Guess and co-workers. (This more appropriate type of question-response sequence was described as an *alternative* step in the program by Guess and associates [1974], but it was to be used only if the child failed to perform unsatisfactorily on the basic step.) It seems that the "remedial logic" of even the best intentioned and thoughtful clinician sometimes can lead to goals that are of questionable utility to the child. Therefore, the normal developmental sequence would seem at least to be less arbitrary and, perhaps, more valid as the determiner of program content and sequence.

DEVELOPMENTAL LOGIC: RATIONALE

The foregoing situation being the case, a closer look at developmental logic, its rationale and its implications, is warranted. Developmental logic is based on several principles of normal language learning and on the general theoretical assumption that learning something new depends to a large extent on the child's present level of knowledge of the physical, social, and linguistic worlds, as well as her current environmental conditions. First, despite numerous reports of variation among normally developing children's strategies of language development (Bloom, Lightbown, and Hood, 1975; Braine, 1976; Dore, 1974; Horgan, 1977; Nelson, 1973; Weiss, Leonard, Rowan, and Chapman, 1983), general patterns in the sequence of development have been observed. This finding no doubt reflects to some extent the fact that certain linguistic structures are incorporated within more complex structures and, therefore, may be developmental prerequisites to these later achievements. For example, it is unlikely that verb–noun constructions would develop prior to understanding or use of the isolated verbs and nouns of which they are composed. Similarly, it is not likely that auxiliary verbs (*is, can, may, will*, and so forth) and verbal inflections (e.g., past and present tense suffixes) would develop before simple, unmodulated verb forms.

Second, there are strong parallels in normal development between many cognitive and linguistic achievements, such that one is not likely to be far in advance of the other. This implies that later-developing linguistic structures not only are more complex linguistically than earlier developing forms, but they also encode concepts and relations among concepts that are more complex. It follows, then, that earlier developing language forms should be the easiest on both cognitive and linguistic grounds for language impaired children to learn.

A third reason for selecting a developmental sequence for a training model, which is often overlooked, is that from the very early stages of development, children combine words with gestures and other contextual elements so that they are quite functional, if not particularly explicit, communicators (Bloom, 1970, 1973; Brown, 1973; Greenfield and Smith, 1976; Halliday, 1975; Leonard, 1976). The early developments of normal language learners seem to be the result of children adapting rapidly to their physical and, especially, their social conditions; children seem to learn language forms that are most useful in their communicative interactions with their social environment (Bates and MacWhinney, 1979, 1982).

Miller and Yoder (1974) selected the normal developmental sequence as a model for their training program, reasoning that "regardless of the level of language at which the child ceases learning, he will be able to communicate in his environment to some extent" (pp. 518–519). In other words, a language impaired child who learns language in the same sequence as normally developing children will have a maximally functional communicative system, given the limited linguistic and cognitive resources available. If the communicative potential of very young, normally developing language users with very limited lexicogrammatical skills is kept in mind, and if functional communication is the basic goal of early intervention, developmental logic should lead to the selection of goals in a sequence that is consistent with the basic intent of remedial logic: to facilitate communicative effectiveness as rapidly as possible.

DEVELOPMENTAL LOGIC: POTENTIAL PROBLEMS

There are several facts that warrant the clinician's concern in adhering strictly to developmental taxonomies for goal selection. First, the clinician must recognize that an individual's theory of development influences dramatically the type of normal profile that is developed. The profiles described by Crystal and colleagues (1976), Lee (1974), Miller (1981a), and Tyack and Gottsleben (1974) are based almost entirely on syntactic and morphological categorization. Goals selected on the basis of these profiles will involve the teaching of grammatical form (e.g., subject–verb–object, verb–noun–adverb, article–noun, preposition–article–noun). In contrast, the sequences of Bloom and Lahey (1978), MacDonald and Blott (1974), and Miller and Yoder (1974) have a distinctly more semantic basis. A clinician following one of these sequences would select for training what Bloom and Lahey have called content-form interactions (agent–action–object, "Doggie catch Frisbee"; attribute–object, "Dirty water," and so forth) rather than strictly grammatically based forms.

Because grammatical structures, such as subject–verb–object encompass a number of different content-form interactions, such as agent or instrument–action–object (e.g., "Rock break window") and experiencer–experience–object (e.g., "Popeye need spinach"), and these different content-form interactions tend to be learned at different developmental stages (Bloom et al.; 1975; Braine, 1976; Leonard, 1976; Wells, 1974), users of these two developmental profiles could generate markedly different goals and stimuli for clients at essentially the same developmental level. Bloom and Lahey (1978, pp. 447–488) have demonstrated the differences in goal selection resulting from their own analysis procedures and those of Lee (1974), Tyack and Gottsleben (1974), and Muma (1973). Clinicians should be aware that the particular profile of development that they select will reflect the theoretical assumptions of the developer of that profile.

A second caution is even more significant than the first. As noted above, the use of taxonomies of normal development for goal selection assumes to some extent that the acquisition of later developing structures *depends* on the prior mastery of earlier developing structures. That is, if the child has developed a form early in development, this acquisition places her in a better position to acquire forms typically learned later in development. As Johnston (1982a) has pointed out, however, language learning does not depend solely on the child's present linguistic knowledge. A host of cognitive, social, motivational, and emotional factors also impinge on the child and influence which new content-form interactions will be most useful at a given point in development. Therefore, for any two linguistic achievements, one may be dependent on another, or no relationship at all may exist between the two forms. Johnston states:

> For any two language patterns, Form B may normally be learned after Form A for linguistic reasons, e.g., because B incorporates A, or for nonlinguistic reasons, e.g., because B requires an understanding of perspective and A doesn't. In the latter case, learning A may in no way prepare the child for learning B, and in fact may be quite unnecessary. . . .
>
> If the typical language disordered child is indeed still mastering the plural -s while acquiring catenative verbs like *gonna*, this would indicate that although the plural -s is normally learned prior to *gonna* there is no direct dependency between the two patterns. For these forms, the therapist may comfortably violate normal guidelines, setting higher-level phrase structure/lexical goals simultaneously with lower-level morphological goals. Adherence to the normal course of acquisition could in this case deprive the child of appropriate learning opportunities. (p. 790)

A related problem with the use of taxonomies of normal development is that, despite careful attempts by authors to avoid the problem (e.g., Crystal et al., 1976), these profiles can give the erroneous impression that the different phases or stages of development are discrete, with development at each phase being completed before acquisition of features from subsequent phases are begun. For example, the third person singular, present progressive form "is [verb]ing" is placed at Level III by Tyack and Gottsleben (1974). The corresponding plural form "are [verb]ing" is classed as a Level IV behavior. Of these two forms, many language clinicians would select "is [verb]ing" as a target to be trained at an earlier point in time than the plural form. This step is in line with the developmental point of view.

In many cases, however, clinicians opt for a vertical goal attack strategy and would train the first target to very high rates of accuracy, say 80 or 90 per cent, before moving on to the later development. As was pointed out in Chapter 4, this approach (training forms at a given developmental level to some very high criterion before moving on to goals at a later stage) does *not* conform to what we know of development. In fact, many children may begin to use "are" before the word "is" is used consistently in all obligatory contexts (Brown, 1973). This occurs because linguistic forms are typically learned gradually, over a considerable period of time. While forms at one level of complexity are being mastered, acquisition of later-developing forms is already beginning. There are very few proposals for language intervention that acknowledge this aspect of development and incorporate it into the intervention procedures (see Bloom and Lahey, 1978; Crystal et al., 1976; Hodson and Paden, 1983; Winitz, 1983).

A fourth concern to clinicians adopting developmental logic as the basis for program planning is most applicable to language impaired children with normal or near-normal intelligence. For example, despite frequently noted deficits in certain areas of cognition, specifically language impaired children often have cognitive skills in advance of what might be predicted based on their estimated language ages (Camarata, Newhoff, and Rugg, 1981; Kamhi, 1981; Terrell, Schwartz, Prelock, and Messick, 1984). Therefore, when it is determined that the later-developing target may be of particular importance to the child, it may indeed be possible to begin training at levels significantly higher than might be indicated on a profile of language development. At least the cognitive demands of these later-developing structures would not appear to be a significant obstacle to their acquisition by some language impaired children.

Fifth, among language impaired children, comprehension skills frequently outstrip expressive language skills (Rizzo and Stephens, 1981; Stark and Tallal, 1981). This pattern suggests that at least some language impaired children may be ready to learn language forms that would not be attainable for normally developing children at similar levels of expressive ability. It may be that training could be made more efficient by carefully assessing the comprehension skills of each child and choosing to train the use of language forms at developmental levels commensurate with these higher levels. The rationale for this procedure is that, since the child can understand certain types of sentences, the expressive use of these forms may be learnable. Furthermore, earlier-developing forms on which the trained form is based may then develop spontaneously without further training. The possibility that prior knowledge of a structure may enhance the language impaired child's ability to learn and generalize the use of that structure has also been noted by Leonard (1974, 1981) and Johnston (1982a).

A final important caution is that with few exceptions (e.g., Leonard, 1975b), the developmental approach to goal selection has not been shown through appropriate experimental means to be better than any other model. This is not because attempts to demonstrate the effectiveness of the applications have failed, but because no such attempts have been made. Therefore, regardless of the method used by the clinician to select and sequence training goals, the clinician again finds herself in the role of clinical researcher. That is, since we do not really know which training sequence will have the most rapid, positive effect on the child's communicative abilities, any route taken by the clinician will be a partially experimental one.

In this chapter, a few instances in which it may be advisable to diverge from the normal sequence have been pointed out. Several other such instances will be described in Chapter 8. Nevertheless, at least as a starting point, the normal sequence of development seems to provide the least arbitrary and most theoretically sound basis for programming intervention content.

Chapter 7

Evaluating the Success of Language Intervention

The very future of our clinical profession hinges on our ability to demonstrate to the consumers of our services (or their parents), administrators of health- and education-related programs, federal and state (or provincial) policy makers, insurance companies, and the general public, who often directly or indirectly subsidize our services, that our clinical efforts have the results that we claim they will have. Given this fact, it is surprising that so little has been done to ensure that the treatments we use actually foster improved communication abilities in our clients. Only recently have serious discussions concerning program evaluations emerged (see, for example, Connell et al., 1977; Costello, 1983; McReynolds, 1983; Muma, 1978a; Prelock and Panagos, 1981; Schery and Lipsey, 1983).

I claimed in Chapter 4 that if the clinician is truly aware of the experimental nature of her work and acts accordingly, she will spend a good deal of time developing highly individualized intervention plans. I also claimed that this is likely to be a highly effective means of reaching stated objectives. To substantiate this latter claim, the clinician must learn ways to demonstrate that her services have been effective in reaching the child's program goals. This can be done, but it requires a good deal of planning from the outset of training.

The experimental methods that are most accessible and most realistic for language clinicians are single-subject research designs in which the client serves as her own control. For our present purposes, I will describe only the "multiple baseline" procedure. This procedure is adequate to demonstrate the effectiveness of intervention procedures with an individual client, and it does not require the clinician to withhold treatment from a client or reverse the effects of treatment by using the same procedures to return the child's performance to original baseline levels. Readers interested in more detailed information on this and a host of other procedures should consult McReynolds and Kearns (1982).

To make use of multiple baseline procedures, the clinician must follow a number of steps before any treatment begins. These steps are outlined in Figure 7–1. First, the child's performance must be assessed, preferably in several communicative contexts, and the child's communicative abilities and weaknesses must be carefully described.

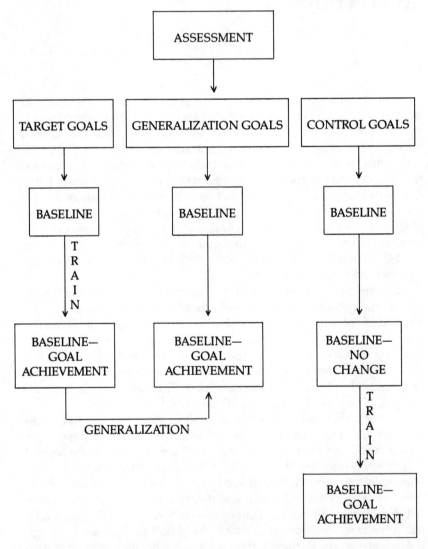

Figure 7–1. The proposed steps in a multiple baseline intervention design.

These efforts should enable the clinician to form hypotheses about the nature of the child's problem. Second, goals must be established based on the results of the assessment. Criteria for developing basic goals were presented in Chapter 5, and some general suggestions for determining specific goals were given in Chapter 6. More elaborate guidelines for specific goals are provided in Chapters 8, 11, 12, and 13. Ideally, three types of goals focusing on specific linguistic behaviors should be selected: (1) behaviors that will be the direct *targets* of the intervention program; (2) behaviors that are similar to the target behaviors in some ways, but will not be targeted directly *(generalization goals)*; and (3) behaviors that are developmentally and functionally appropriate but which are sufficiently different from target behaviors that they are not likely to be influenced by training on target behaviors *(control goals)*.

For various theoretical and empirical reasons, the clinician might expect that, upon successful completion of training on target goals, generalization goals might be attained with no further training. For example, training the child to produce "is" as an auxiliary verb (e.g., "The lady is working") may not be necessary after training "is" as a copula (e.g., "The doggie is sick"). This process is often called response generalization and is discussed more fully in Chapter 8. Control goals reflect deficits that are likely to be the focus of intervention at some point in time, but they are not a priority, and no immediate steps will be taken to facilitate their development. Some possible target, generalization, and control goals are presented in Table 7–1.

The third step in the procedure involves collecting baseline data on all of the target, generalization, and control behaviors. This is not a difficult step, but it is an expensive one in terms of utilization of the clinician's time. It requires the clinician to observe and measure the child's use of the behaviors of interest. These observations should take place over at least two and preferably more sessions to ensure that the child's use of the behaviors is stable. The general rule to follow in determining the ideal number of baseline measurements to take is "the more, the better." The clinician must balance this control on the child's initial knowledge and use of the language behaviors of interest prior to intervention against the cost of her own and the child's time. In my own view, the advantages of a procedure that offers the benefit of objective demonstration of progress in a carefully controlled manner far outweigh the costs of the three or four clinical sessions typically required to obtain the necessary baseline information. It should be added that, in most cases, collecting baseline information on several goals does *not* take up a whole intervention session.

What, then, constitutes a valid baseline measurement? It is not

Table 7–1. A Sample of the Specific Goals Designed for a Language Impaired Girl*

Target goals:

1. *The appropriate use of the copula "is" in yes-no questions ("Is the doggie sick?") to obtain information that is not clearly specified in context.* This form is typically omitted in all obligatory contexts, but the child uses this syntactic device to determine whether an utterance directed to her is a question or an assertion (i.e., she seems to understand its syntactic function).

2. *The appropriate use of "he" and "she" in assertions to refer to previously specified animate antecedents (e.g., "That boy," "The mother").* The child always replaces nominative case pronouns "he" and "she" with the accusative pronouns "him" and "her," respectively. When the clinician uses the accusative forms incorrectly in subject position, the child often reacts by laughing and saying "You silly."

Generalization goals:

1. *The appropriate use of the auxiliary "is" in yes-no questions ("Is the lady working?") to obtain information not clearly specified from the context.*

2. *The appropriate use of copular and auxiliary forms of "is" in statements to describe objects, persons, and ongoing actions.*

3. *The appropriate use of the pronouns "he" and "she" in subject position in questions about previously specified antecedents.*

Control goals:

1. *The appropriate use of "will" to indicate intention or to describe some future event in statements and questions.* This form is always omitted when required, although the child makes occasional use of "gonna" and frequently refers to predicted events and outcomes. The child also responds appropriately to the clinician's utterances containing "will" (e.g., by answering "yes" to questions like "Will the bus fall?" as a bus is pushed toward the edge of a table).

*Criterion for moving on to generalization or control goals is 50 per cent use on each of the target goals in a play activity.

uncommon for investigators and clinicians to assess the child's use of a structure by means of some form of self-devised, structure-specific language test that is typically administered in the clinic and involves the description of pictures or actions by the clinician. When pictures, objects, and actions that were *not* used in training are selected, this practice is extremely useful as a measure of the child's ability to produce novel forms of the target structure. For example, in training the pronoun "they" in sentences such as "They are running," Courtright and Courtright (1976) kept aside a set of 20 generalization pictures that portrayed events that could be described using the target structure. These pictures were never used in training. Following a set of training trials, the children in this study were required to respond to the generalization pictures using the target structure. No feedback regarding the accuracy of the children's responses was provided during these probes. Improvement on this type of test demonstrates to the clinician that the child has gained productive control over the structure being trained. In other words, the clinician can be certain that the child has learned more than simple imitative responses. Johnston (1982) has noted that such a demonstration really does not reflect generalization of a rule, as is often claimed, but rather constitutes the child's instantiation of a rule that has been trained. This performance is expected if the goal of training a rule has been reached. We routinely use this evaluation procedure and set a criterion of 80 per cent or higher as a subgoal of our intervention plan.

Importantly, these tests usually are similar to the types of activities carried out in the intervention context. Therefore, they may tell us very little about the child's knowledge of how the structure can be used for communicative purposes. It is possible for a child to demonstrate forms of progress that have little or no bearing on the way the child actually uses language in typical social interactions (see especially Cullata and Horn, 1982; Mulac and Tomlinson, 1977). Connell (1982) has pointed out that improvements on this type of task typically precede improvements in naturalistic contexts when therapy has taken place in a traditional clinic-type setting. Therefore, it is essential that the child's use of target forms be evaluated in naturally occurring social contexts both before intervention is begun and at various stages throughout intervention to assess the child's progress toward attainment of the basic goal.

Insisting that the child's performance be observed in naturalistic contexts does *not* mean that the clinician cannot exercise control over the physical, social, and linguistic parameters of the setting. Since many targeted forms do not occur frequently, the clinician will have to plan specific activities and situations in which the target form is believed to be highly likely to occur. The specific verbal and nonverbal stimuli used to evoke the target structure should differ from the stimuli used in training, however, and the context should be similar in many ways to the types of activities in which the child frequently engages. Several of the principles for enhancing the naturalness of trainer-oriented approaches to training language forms presented in Chapter 8 are useful in helping clinicians design these types of activities.

Figure 7-2 illustrates a child's use of target, generalization, and control behaviors over four baseline sessions. Note that the target and control behaviors were sometimes used correctly. This exemplifies the need for taking baseline measurements over several sessions. If intervention had proceeded after session 1, the clinician would have been operating under the faulty assumption that the child sometimes produced "will" correctly, but always omitted "is" in all contexts.

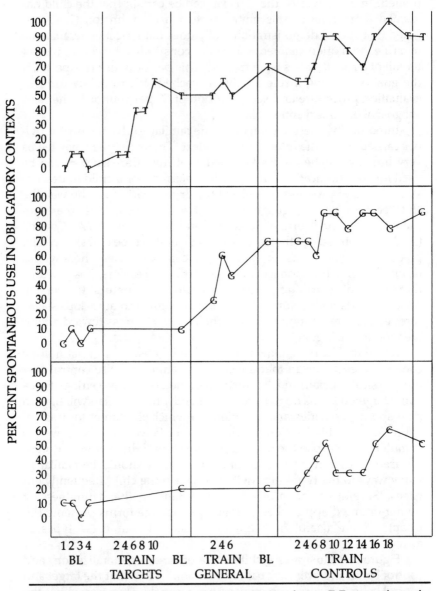

Figure 7–2. Results of a multiple baseline intervention design. *T,* Target goal, copular "is" in questions. *G,* Generalization goal, copular "is" in assertions. *C,* Control goal, "will" in assertions. *BL,* Baseline sessions. Training segments are shown in weeks of intervention.

Following careful analysis of the child's performance prior to intervention, intervention procedures are then administered for the target behaviors only. This treatment portion of the design will continue until criterion for the target goals has been reached. Regular baselines must be determined throughout the treatment phase of intervention, at least for the target behaviors. Depending on the nature and the number of the goals selected, weekly or biweekly administrations of the subgoal-related tasks are typically realistic. Monthly samples collected in more naturalistic contexts are also quite practical. The clinician does not need to transcribe and analyze all aspects of these samples. Rather, the emphasis should be on contexts in which the target, generalization, and control behaviors are obligated.

Once criterion has been met for the target goals, new baselines of all of the original goals are determined. To demonstrate that a child has actually improved in targeted areas and that improvement was the result of intervention and not some other factors external to intervention, training should result in large gains on the target goals that are stable over time. These results should be observable in naturally occurring communicative contexts that differ from the conditions under which intervention took place. At the same time, much smaller gains or no gains at all should be observed for the control targets. Because no effort is directed toward improving the child's use of control behaviors, improvements in use of these language behaviors would suggest that factors other than intervention, such as maturation, might have been responsible for gains on the target goals as well.

The child's post-intervention performance on generalization goals has no bearing on the demonstration of intervention effectiveness. Clearly, then, selection of generalization goals is not critical to the use of a multiple baseline design. However, improvement in the use of these behaviors when no improvement on control goals is observed suggests that the program designed by the clinician was highly efficient; that is, significant gains were made in related areas that received no direct clinical attention, as was predicted. This also indicates that the basis for predicting gains on generalization goals following training on target goals has merit; the theory receives support from such a finding.

The results reported in Figure 7–2 indicate that intervention was effective in fostering the child's appropriate use of "is" in yes-no questions, but that this did not result in the predicted pattern of generalization. When this pattern of results occurs, one fruitful option for the clinician is to initiate treatment on these goals while continuing to provide no treatment for control goals. The steps to follow are identical to those stated earlier: collect baselines, treat new target goals to criterion, then collect baselines on target and control goals.

There is one more step that the clinician can take to strengthen further the claim that intervention was responsible for the observed gains. This step involves training on the existing control goals. Note that the child's use of control behaviors will have remained relatively stable over the same period in which significant gains have been made on target and generalization goals. Should gains on control behaviors appear following the initiation of treatment procedures on these goals, the clinician has extremely strong evidence that the child has made gains and that these gains were the direct result of intervention activities and procedures. In other words, the clinician has strong evidence that her efforts have been effective.

This method of changing old control goals to new target goals has practical as well as methodological advantages over other procedures. When intervention begins for old control goals, new control goals (and generalization goals) can and should be selected as well. Lengthy baseline periods are not required for the new targets, however, because they have already been monitored over many sessions. It is true that some part of a few sessions must be designated for collecting baseline data on new generalization and control goals. But still, as long as a good set of basic and potential specific goals is developed at the outset of intervention, the clinician can move effectively and efficiently into the next phase of language facilitation.

It should be noted that not all authorities agree on the use of baseline procedures. For example, Muma (1978a) objected that dependency on baselines, which require quantification of the child's communicative behavior, may reduce the complex systems and processes of language and language acquisition to numbers. The consequence of this "numbers game," as Muma calls it, is a distortion of the language system that the clinician is trying to enrich through the use of intervention techniques.

I am in basic agreement with Muma when he confines his arguments to discussions of standardized tests that yield numbers such as language ages or mental ages rather than descriptions of how the child communicates in natural settings. I would also agree that, unless a clinician has adopted an underlying behavioral approach to intervention, careful recording of every stimulus presented by the clinician and every response produced by the child may not be necessary (see Hodson and Paden, 1983, for an example in phonological intervention). The *quantity* of responses produced by the child may not be nearly as important as the *quality* (i.e., the use of a target form in a relevant and meaningful social context). Yet I am unfamiliar with descriptive approaches to language analysis that do not involve counting of the relevant behaviors and of the contexts in which the relevant behaviors should have occurred. The consistency of application and breadth of a child's newly acquired rule can be determined in no other way, to my knowledge. Consequently, I believe that the clinician must take regular baselines of the type described earlier, and this includes counting the instances in which a behavior is obligated and the number of times the relevant behavior was used appropriately and inappropriately.

The clinician must show great caution in the determination of what constitutes an obligatory context for a behavior. For example, I have observed many cases in which the clinician described a child's behavior as 50 per cent correct on agent–action utterances, 35 per cent correct on subject–verb–prepositional phrase sentences, and so forth. Such statements are difficult to interpret. How is it determined that an agent–action or a subject–verb–prepositional phrase utterance was obligated by the context? If a child pushes a car across the room, does this constitute an obligatory context for an action–object utterance? It is not difficult to see that such a procedure would lead to highly unreliable and probably invalid observational records. Many such actions are observed daily, but we do not always feel obligated to communicate information about these events to those around us.

The clinician should claim that an obligatory context for a behavior selected as a specific goal has occurred only when both of the following conditions have been met: (1) a relevant nonlinguistic event or state that could call for use of the behavior has occurred or is expected to occur; and (2) the child performs a communicative act that is consistent with the goal, but this act omits some essential aspect of the goal behavior or uses that aspect in an inappropriate fashion. In other words, the child must produce some part of the relevant linguistic act but make an error on the part that has been specified as a goal.

A few examples should be helpful. The response "playing" should not be viewed as an inappropriate response to the question "What is the boy doing?", and this should not be viewed as an obligatory context for agent–action. The question has presupposed the agent of the action, "boy," and to repeat it is redundant. In contrast, if the child is playing with a model of a boy, then makes the boy run and says "boy," the clinician has some justification for viewing this as an obligatory context for agent–action. In this case, the child has expressed a desire to communicate relevant information about the event, the agent, but has omitted a critical element, the action. Such a decision is not made without some risk. For example, the child may have been intending to say something like "This is a boy" (Howe,

1976). Nevertheless, in some cases, such rich interpretations are necessary.

As a final example, suppose the specific goal involves getting the child to use available words to request desired objects in situations in which she typically reaches and grunts while looking at the adult. If a context is created in which a highly desirable object is held out of the child's reach, only the first of our two conditions would have been met. An obligatory context for the use of the word would be counted only in those cases in which the child actually made some communicative attempt to obtain the object as well.

It should be clear that the clinician must be closely in touch with the pragmatic factors involved in the given speaking context to come to a reasonable determination that the child should have encoded more information than she actually did. More details on some of these pragmatic factors are presented in Chapters 8 through 13.

One final point should be made here. Multiple baseline designs are commonly associated with applied behavior analysis, which is closely allied with operant learning theory. I do not believe, however, that use of this procedure commits a clinician to a behavioristic approach to treatment. Indeed, the procedures used to reach the goals in Table 7–1 could be focused on the child rather than oriented on the trainer. For example, the clinician could play with the child in a very nonintrusive manner, giving the child control over what is said. No requests to use the target structures would be needed at all. Whenever the child produced an utterance containing an obligatory context for any of the target forms, the clinician might expand that utterance, emphasizing the correct target form. The following example should clarify this expansion approach (see Chapter 10 for a more extensive treatment of these procedures).

Child: That a ball?
Adult: *Is* that a ball? I don't know. *Is* it?
Child: Yeah, a football. Daddy like a play football. Him play good.
Adult: Oh, *he* plays well. *Is* Daddy the quarterback?

Note that no efforts are made to supply the child with reinforcement, although it could be argued that the expansion or contingent adult attention serves as a reinforcer. Furthermore, the clinician does not impose any particular constraints on what the child says. She is a respondor to, not a stimulator of, specific overt responses by the child (Weiss, 1981). This procedure is not derived from operant principles, although it is not necessarily inconsistent with those principles.

Importantly, a clinician operating from within this type of framework is perfectly capable of devising picture description or guessing game tasks that can be used to measure the child's progress toward reaching subgoals. Similarly, data on the child's use and misuse of target behaviors can be collected during play activities. As long as the procedures are directed toward a set of target goals, the same sorts of generalization goals and control goals as are shown in Table 7–1 might be selected. If these procedures are effective, improvements should be noted on target behaviors and possibly generalization behaviors, but not control behaviors.

It might be claimed that such broadly based procedures could conceivably have a general effect on the child, resulting in improvements on control goals as well as target and generalization goals. I would agree in principle with this claim. Nevertheless, the fact remains that if control behaviors show gains commensurate with target and generalization behaviors, the clinician can be very happy for the child, but she must be cautious in assuming that her procedures were directly responsible for those general gains. The specific procedures may indeed have been responsible for a general surge in the child's development, but this would not have been clearly demonstrated. Of course, having good stable baseline information prior to intervention strengthens the claim that general improvements were indeed the result of the intervention and not other uncontrolled factors.

The bottom line to this discussion is that multiple baseline procedures can be adapted so that they are compatible with most theories from which clinicians draw their basic assumptions about learning. With a little imagination (and a lot of hard work), intervention plans can be developed so that the clinician can use whatever clinical procedures best fit the child's needs and her own theoretical persuasions, and it can be demonstrated clearly whether the intervention is having a significant effect on the child's communicative behavior.

Chapter 8

Training Content-Form Interactions: Trainer-Oriented Approaches

Unlike normal children, who seem to treat language form itself as a type of problem to be solved (Cromer, 1981; Karmiloff-Smith, 1979), many language impaired children seem content with the bare necessities of communication—they do not actively process linguistic input in an effort to induce its structure. Therefore, their rates of development in language form, especially syntax and morphology, are slowed dramatically. Regardless of the social-conversational profile exhibited by a particular language impaired child, it is likely that at some point in the intervention program clinical attention must be focused on the two basic goals stated below. For children displaying an active conversational style, these basic goals of intervention will be the priority from the outset of the intervention program:

1. To train content-form interactions to fulfill existing conversational acts; and
2. To facilitate the use of existing forms for use in alternative conversational acts.

It is important that each of these goals makes reference to the *functions* of trained content-form interactions. Regardless of the intervention approach taken, neither of these basic goals can be considered to have been achieved unless the child is making functional use of newly acquired language forms in meaningful contexts. This criterion has not typically been used by researchers or clinicians working with language impaired children. It is my belief that this fact is at the heart of many of the difficulties we have confronted in designing truly effective intervention procedures.

CONSIDERATIONS INFLUENCING SPECIFIC GOAL SELECTION

In Chapter 6, the pattern of normal development was evaluated as the basis for selecting specific goals. It was concluded that, at present, this pattern provides the least arbitrary and the most valid sequence for intervention. By using developmental logic, the clinician is most likely to select goals containing content that the child is capable of co-ordinating conceptually and is highly motivated to commmunicate. These would seem to be the behaviors that the child is "ready to learn." By focusing intervention on this type of goal, learning should be optimally rapid and generalization of the behaviors to nonclinic contexts should be most complete.

However, it was also pointed out that there are a number of problems associated with the wholesale adoption of a developmental approach to intervention. In this section, I will present seven factors that should be considered once several possible goals have been uncovered on the basis of developmental logic. These include (1) the child's current level of functioning on the structure; (2) the potential effect of the new forms on the child's communicative effectiveness; (3) response generalization; (4) teachability; (5) perceptual saliency; (6) the child's comprehension skills; and (7) the child's phonological abilities. Final decisions on which goals to select can be made on the basis of these factors. On some occasions, this will result in a violation of what is typically considered to be the normal path of development.

The Child's Current Level of Functioning on the Structure

If normal development is to be used as a guide for choosing the goals of intervention, some performance criteria must be developed to determine those structures in the sequence that will require attention and those that will not. In most analysis procedures (Bloom and Lahey, 1978; Crystal et al., 1976; Lee, 1974; Miller, 1981a; Tyack and Gottsleben, 1974), some method is first used to place the child at a particular stage or level of development. For example, Miller and Tyack and Gottsleben use mean length of utterance (MLU) to ascertain the child's developmental stage. Those forms that are expected to have been learned by normal children before this stage of development but have not yet reached the performance criterion are considered to be primary candidates for specific goals. Those forms that are expected to develop during or shortly following the child's present stage are considered potential goals.

At present, two performance criteria are most popular among researchers and clinicians: productivity and mastery. A form may be regarded as productive when evidence exists that the form is a part of the child's linguistic system, not just a patterned sequence learned by rote and used in highly restricted contexts. Although what can be taken as evidence of productivity is debatable (see Ingram, 1981; Leonard, Steckol, and Panther, 1983), Bloom and Lahey (1978) regard a form as being productive when it appears at least four times in a 1 hour language sample. There should be at least some variablility in the words used in each of the four examples of the form noted. In other words, four repetitions of the same utterance would not constitute attainment of the criterion level.

If productivity is the criterion adopted, those content-form interactions at and below the child's level of functioning that were not yet productive would be selected as goals. This criterion has the advantage of not being overly rigid. As I have noted in previous chapters, children developing normally achieve mastery of a structure over time. The criterion of productivity takes this fact into consideration. Once the child has developed productive control over a new language form, intervention energies would be focused on new forms, thus enabling the child to complete the progression toward mastery on her own. The disadvantage of such a criterion is that it is conceivable that a child could achieve a performance criterion and still be functioning at a very low level of performance, say 25 per cent in obligatory contexts. A language impaired child functioning at this low level may need some help to master the structure in a relatively quick and efficient manner.

Typically, mastery is defined operationally as 90 per cent correct usage of the form in contexts that obligate its use. The arbitrariness of the 90 per cent criterion should also be acknowledged. However, this figure seems reasonable—it is high enough to indicate a near-adult level of use of the form, but it is sensitive to the fact that, under certain cognitive, linguistic, social, or emotional pressures, a child developing a new linguistic structure will occasionally make an error. Yet, if a 90 per cent criterion is selected, and all forms below the child's stage of development that do not meet this criterion are selected as goals, there are two unfortunate results. First, too many goals are likely to be selected. The sheer number of goals that this procedure generates is very cumbersome and, in fact, overwhelming for many children (and clinicians!). A much more important implication of the 90 per cent criterion is that each goal that is selected presumably must be trained to the 90 per cent correct level before the goal is reached. This procedure requires the clinician to continue training beyond the point at which the child is potentially capable of mastering the structure on her own.

Some set of criteria intermediate to productivity and mastery may be most desirable. The following proposal, which is summarized in Table 8-1, is based on some suggestions made by Lee and co-workers (1975). Content-form interactions that are required on at least five occasions during one or more language samples and which the child uses with 10 to 50 per cent accuracy are selected as priority goals. Success on these goals is likely to be rapid because they reflect content-form interactions that the child is already beginning to acquire and for which the child has a demonstrated need. The child does not need to make a new acquisition, but to extend the breadth of the existing semantic-syntactic rule and to automatize the application of that rule in a variety of appropriate communicative contexts (Johnston, 1982b).

Goals of secondary priority are those content-form interactions that are attempted but never used correctly. That is, the child produces utterances that obligate the use of these forms, but omits them or substitutes an inappropriate form. For example, in stating her intention to perform an act, the child might say "I (is gonna) write on chalkboard." The selection of the auxiliary form "am" ("am gonna") or, alternatively, "will," would be appropriate under these circumstances. Because the child *never* uses these forms correctly, progress may be a bit slower than for the first set of targets. However, observation of how and under what circumstances the child attempts a structure provides important cues for designing ideal intervention activities. For example, we recently observed a 4 year old boy in a group of three children. The children and the clinician were engaged in a cookie baking activity. At the start of the activity, the materials were placed out of reach, but visible to the children. When asked "Where's the cookie mix?", all of the children began searching for the mix. Upon discovering the box of cookie mix, the boy said "I find it" as he pointed to a shelf well beyond his outstretched arm. The clinician promptly directed him to "Get it for us." After a brief pause, the child shook his head to indicate negation and said "I have wings." He had found a nonconventional way of communicating this information involving both lexicogrammatical form and gesture (as well as a bit of self-styled humor).

Based on this type of information, "don't" and "not" used to deny complete propositions containing subject–verb–(object) structure were viewed as high priorities for specific goals for this child, even though several other goals might have taken priority according to accounts of normal development. Progress on goals selected in this

Table 8-1. Performance Criteria*

First Priority Goals	The child uses the structure in 10 to 50 per cent of at least five obligatory contexts.
Second Priority Goals	The child uses the structure in 0 to 10 per cent of at least five obligatory contexts.
Third Priority Goals	The child uses no sentences that obligate the use of the form.
Do Not Consider As Goals	The child uses the structure in greater than 50 per cent of at least five obligatory contexts (or 3 of 3 or 3 of 4 correct uses).

*Performance criteria for determining when a potential specific goal should be selected for intervention and for determining when intervention on a goal is no longer needed. Potential goals are those content-form interactions that typically develop before or during the phase of language learning at which the child is currently functioning.

manner are often reached more quickly than expected because of the ease with which activities can be developed. In essence, the child shows the clinician the types of activities in which she is highly motivated to use language that obligates the target forms. These are ideal language-learning contexts.

Third priority goals are those content-form interactions that are expected, given the child's general level of linguistic functioning, but that are *never* attempted. For example, based on a given child's overall level of functioning, it might be expected that she would be producing sentences containing the semi-modal "gonna." However, samples of the child's language may indicate that she never makes reference to events that have not yet taken place. Thus, no utterances obligating the use of "gonna" would have occurred. Such a form would receive third priority in the proposed scheme. In these cases, it is possible that the child does not possess the underlying conceptual basis (content) for the use of the form. In our example with "gonna," the child may have difficulty representing mentally the outcome of ongoing events and states. If this is the case, it is not likely that the need to communicate such information will arise. Progress is likely to be slower on these goals than on first or second priority goals in which the child has demonstrated some degree of control over the concepts involved in the target form as well as the need to communicate this underlying conceptual information.

Finally, content-form interactions that are produced with greater than 50 per cent accuracy in obligatory contexts are monitored carefully to make sure that the development that is predicted to occur without intervention does, in fact, occur. They are *not* targeted for intervention, however. A goal can be said to have been reached when the child produces at least five *different* utterances that require the structure in a reasonably natural communicative context and uses it appropriately with greater than 50 per cent accuracy.

The Potential Effect of the New Forms on the Child's Communicative Effectiveness

If some combination of normal developmental profiles and the child's present level of functioning with respect to a new language form is used, the clinician will usually consider several possible goals. On the basis of their own analysis procedure, Bloom and Lahey (1978) identified 15 immediate training goals for their demonstration client, Tommy. Regardless of the goal attack strategy selected and the type of multiple baseline approach designed, the list of potential goals will typically need to be pared down, and there should be some systematic means for selecting one possible goal over another.

One way of doing this that is highly consistent with an emphasis on facilitating communication in everyday contexts is to ask the question, "Which of the forms that *could* be selected are likely to have the most significant impact on the child's communicative capabilities when this phase of training has been completed?" Unfortunately, the answer to this question is not simple, and it raises an important issue.

This issue involves decisions to teach certain grammatical inflections. Before reaching MLUs of around 2.0, children's new acquisitions typically add significant semantic content to the linguistic expression. Either a new semantic relation is learned or one relation is coordinated with others in a manner that was not previously part of the child's linguistic system. For example, in phase 3 of Bloom and Lahey's (1978) plan for developing goals, stative relationships are introduced, first in two-constituent utterances (e.g., "like cookie"). At the same time, action relations may incorporate agents and objects into three-constituent strings, such as "Daddy play piano."

Beyond this point, children begin to modulate the meanings of earlier semantic relationships by adding inflectional morphemes, such as plural and possessive markers on nouns and present progressive and third person present singular markings on verbs. They also begin to use a host of function words, such as copular and auxiliary forms of "be," articles, and prepositions. These structures are grammatical in nature and, in many cases, the semantic information that they add to a linguistic expression is redundant. For example, adding "'s" to "John" in the phrase "John's book" may *clarify* the relationship between "John" and "book," but this relationship has already been *established* by the juxtaposition of the two words. The absence of this morpheme in many forms of English is evidence that syntax alone

(along with presupposed contextual information) is adequate to sig-
nify the possessive relationship. This same argument may be raised
with respect to many other morphological inflections and function words.

The redundancy in linguistic systems is not unimportant—it provides multiple cues to meaning that make the speech signal much easier to process. The fact that very little new information is contained in
these forms, however, raises some question about their suitability as
specific training objectives for some children, especially when a decision must be made to train either a new grammatical morpheme (say,
the article "a") or a new coordination of semantic-syntactic relations
(say, the embedding of attributive relations into action relations expressed with two clausal constituents—e.g., "throw dirty sock").

The prognosis for some language impaired children to obtain a
complete adult-like linguistic system is poor, at best. Are these children better served by being trained to produce all of the conventional
details of their language, or by being trained to produce utterances
that encode more complex semantic-syntactic relationships? Surely,
when a child has the cognitive capability to coordinate several semantic relationships, giving that child the ability to *express* those relationships in a single utterance gives her more communicative power than
would the training of a function word or inflectional morpheme that
adds no new semantic detail.

This position can be disputed on several different grounds. Gray
and Ryan (1973) state that

> The neglect of function words and grammar will result in a child who
> responds to certain situations with a predictable and stereotyped verbal
> response often described as telegraphic speech. The result is not propo-
> sitional speech. . . . (p. 12)

But "telegraphic speech" is highly propositional! Furthermore, it
is rule-governed (although the rules are simpler than those of the
adult language), and, if intervention is thoughtfully planned and implemented, it need not be either unduly predictable or stereotyped.
Training goals that overlook, at least temporarily, function words and
grammatical morphemes do *not* neglect grammar, since the order of
clausal constituents and elements of phrase structure, such as adjectives, possessives, modal verbs, and prepositions that carry a heavy
informational load, would follow the adult pattern. The linguistic
product of an intervention program that trains a child to produce this
type of "telegraphic" system *should* be highly propositional and functional, although it would *not* contain many of the fine points of the
adult language.

Another objection concerns the cognitive abilities of the child for whom goals are being selected. Ingram (cited in Leonard, 1973) pointed out that some language impaired children seem to have communicative difficulties that are at least partially due to problems in the mental representation of objects, events, and relations. Ingram recommended a strategy in which the child is first taught to increase utterance length by adding grammatical detail but without adding semantic (cognitive) detail. For example, sentences like "that *is* mommy" (demonstrative–entity) would be taught before sentences like "that *Suzy* mommy" (demonstrative–possessor–possessed). That is, there may be some clinical advantage to selecting grammatical morphemes as training objectives. Since these morphemes serve largely a grammatical rather than a semantic function in sentences, their use may pose fewer constraints on the child's *cognitive* system than the use of a new semantic relation or the addition of a semantic relation to existing semantic-syntactic rules.

It is conceivable that children are, at certain times in development, more capable of learning purely grammatical devices than they are of learning more complex semantic-syntactic relations. For example, adding "-ing" to verbs that already represent ongoing actions requires only that the child associate a new form with existing meanings and intentions. Adding a semantic relation such as location to an agent-action–object construction, however, means that the child must now coordinate an extra semantic relationship along with those typically produced under similar circumstances. This involves added syntactic *and* semantic complexity, and, therefore, may be more difficult for the child to acquire.

At present, we do not have enough information to resolve this issue completely. My current view is that there are circumstances under which it is highly appropriate to train new semantic-syntactic relationships, even when the normal pattern of development would be better served by training a new morphological inflection or function word. The appropriate circumstances arise when (1) the clinician believes that this strategy will more significantly enhance the child's communicative capabilities; (2) when a complete adult grammatical system does not appear to be a realistic objective for the child in question; and (3) when the child produces utterances with relevant semantic content omitted, indicating that she has a real need to produce more semantically complex structures.

Response Generalization

In language intervention, response generalization can be said to have occurred when the training of one form for a particular function results in improved performance on other related forms or functions without specific training. There has been some clinical research in this area, and it should be useful to clinicians planning target and generalization goals. Leonard (1974) reported a study in which he tested to see if training "is" as an auxiliary in statements (e.g., "The man is fishing") to preschool aged language impaired children would have any effect on the children's use of "is" in questions or "is" when used as a copula (e.g., "This meat *is* tough"). He found that following successful training on copular "is," improved performance was also observed in all of these other contexts. Training only the auxiliary form of "is" generalized equally well to untrained forms using this word. Since there are other forms of the auxiliary "be" ("are," "were," etc.), Leonard also asked if training the "is" form would influence the child's use of "are." Unfortunately, it did not. Virtually these same results for "is" and "are" have been observed by Gray and Fygetakis (1968b), Hegde (1980), Hegde and McConn (1981), Hegde, Noll, and Pecora (1979), and Ruder (1978), using subjects at a wide range of ages and levels of cognitive abilities.

In a similar type of experiment, Wilcox and Leonard (1978) trained question forms containing a wh-word (either "who," "what," or "where") and an auxiliary (either "is" or "does") to a group of specifically language impaired children (e.g., "Where is the boy going?" "Where does the boy live?" "What is the dog chasing?"). Most of the children in the study used wh-questions prior to the experiment, but all made consistent errors in their use of "is" and "does" in these types of questions. Each child was trained on only one combination of wh-word–auxiliary. After training in only one context, the children were able to generalize the appropriate use of the auxiliary to other wh-forms. However, they did not show much generalization across auxiliaries. In other words, training "is" in one context significantly influenced the use of "is" in other contexts but had virtually no impact on the use of "does." Training "does" in one context resulted in generalized "does" usage, but in very little improvement in the use of "is."

There are a number of significant clinical implications of this body of research. First, at least for the forms that have been subjected to clinical investigation to date, response generalization can be expected to occur for clients at a number of different ages and developmental stages. Second, what seems to be generalized is the specific form that is trained, not the linguistic category to which that form belongs. In other words, if "are" is trained as an auxiliary in statements, generalization to the other uses of "are" may be expected to occur. Changes in the child's use of other forms of the copula or other auxiliaries are not likely to result from this training, however. Third, it follows from these first two conclusions that specific forms that appear in a number of different speech acts may be preferable as intervention targets to other candidate forms that are more limited in their potential uses. Selection of these multipurpose forms may lead to greater efficiency in reaching basic goals.

An example of how this increased efficiency might be achieved should be helpful here. Suppose that the child has begun making reference to future events but omits the modal verb in all cases. One of the first forms of modality expressed by young children is the catenative "gonna." Most developmental profiles (e.g., Lee [1974], Miller [1981a], Tyack and Gottsleben [1974]) place this form at an earlier developmental level than the true modal auxiliary "will." Therefore, using the normal developmental model, when it comes time to teach a form to express the child's intentions to perform acts, "gonna" is the likely choice. Our present knowledge of the pattern of response generalization resulting from training suggests that an alternative to this selection based on normal development should at least be considered.

"Gonna" is a very frequently occurring verb form in colloquial speech and in speech to children, but it is used in a relatively limited number of syntactic constructions to assist in the performance of a limited number of speech acts. More specifically, "gonna" is used to state intentions and to make predictions in declarative syntactic forms. It *does* occur in question forms, but in these forms it does not act like other auxiliary verbs. For example, we might say "Are you gonna go to the game?" but never "Gonna you go to the game?" On the other hand, "will" occurs in the same declarative forms as "gonna" to express essentially the same meaning. In addition, it appears *before the main verb* in all types of questions. In this respect, it is like all other English auxiliaries—it is part of the syntactic operation used in English to form interrogatives. Unlike "gonna," "will" may *also* be used to soften request forms (i.e., to make them more polite — e.g., contrast "Will you help me?" with "Help me!"). It is true that a sentence like "Are you gonna help me?" is possible, but this form will occur under different and more restrictive conditions. Finally, "will" occurs readily in elliptical utterances. These are typically responses to questions (e.g., Adult: "Who will help me clean the table?" Child: "I will"). The fact that "will" occurs in utterance final position with full stress actually makes this a rather ideal training context. "Gonna" *never* appears in such an elliptical form; rather, the response to a question such as "Who's gonna help me clean the table?" may be "I am," but not "I gonna."

I am well aware that these various uses of "will" often occur at different developmental stages. The claim here is that if "will" is trained, the clinician *might* expect greater response generalization than if "gonna" is trained. This would make the intervention process more efficient. As was pointed out in Chapter 7, it is often the case that language impaired children "know" much more about language than they actually put to use (Leonard, 1974). What intervention may do for these children is teach them that forms such as "is," "do," and "the" are truly significant and that they *must* be used at certain times. When "is" or "are" is trained as a copula, for example, the child may recognize that this form is important. She then falls back on previous knowledge of its use and begins to use it appropriately in nontrained as well as trained contexts.

Much more research is needed to confirm previous findings on response generalization and to determine whether similar results will occur when different structures are trained. Furthermore, we desperately need research on patterns of generalization that might be predicted based on what the child *knows* about target forms prior to intervention. For example, if the hypothetical child discussed in this section can comprehend the distinction between sentences like "John will play," "John plays," and "John played," she would seem to be in an ideal position to learn to produce "will" in limited contexts and to generalize it rapidly to nontrained contexts. Some experimentation such as that described in Chapter 7, which is based on the clinician's existing knowledge about response generalization and about the child's knowledge of the target goal prior to intervention, should assist in the development of more efficient intervention programs.

Teachability

Teachability may play an important role in helping the clinician to reduce the size of a list of goals that has been developed on the basis of other factors. This notion was discussed by Lahey and Bloom (1977) with respect to developing an early lexicon for nonverbal children. It can be of practical importance in the selection of *all* goals, however. Basically, a highly teachable goal will yield an affirmative response to each of the following questions.

1. Are the stimuli demonstrable or picturable?
2. Can the stimulus materials be organized easily?
3. Are target forms evokable with meaningful questions and comments?
4. Do occasions for use of the structure occur frequently and naturally in activities in which the child is frequently engaged?

The assumption is that, all other things being equal, goals that are more "teachable" will be learned more quickly by the child. If all four of these questions are addressed, it is difficult to argue with this assumption. Teachable forms are likely to be heard by the child frequently, and opportunities for their use will occur often. These are optimal conditions for instituting intervention procedures. The greatest danger in using teachability in the goal selection process is that it can be accorded entirely too much weight. Goals may be selected on the basis of the materials that the clinician has available or can obtain easily rather than on the child's real needs. *This practice should be avoided at all costs.* Teachability is most important over the short term—when the clinician believes that the child must experience immediate success and the speed of acquisition is at a premium.

Perceptual Saliency

The issue of perceptual saliency is complex because saliency is not something that can be measured objectively by an adult observer. What young children find to be highly noticeable may not match perfectly with an adult's intuitions on which aspects of the speech signal are most likely to attract attention. To date, studies of the forms that normal children are most likely to attend to, imitate, and learn seem to be those that are stressed (Blasdell and Jensen, 1970; DuPreez, 1974) and those that occur at the ends of phrases and sentences (see Chapman, 1981b, for an interesting discussion). These same items are typically those that carry the most new information, so it is not always clear whether children are especially sensitive to the greater intensity and duration and the higher fundamental frequency that are characteristic of stressed forms or whether they are actively seeking those particular forms that carry the heaviest informational load. In any case, it does not seem unreasonable to speculate that forms that bear a large share of the informational content of a linguistic expression and that carry primary or secondary stress are most likely to be processed and learned quickly by language impaired children.

In selecting specific goals for intervention, the factor of perceptual salience may be of some practical utility. For example, consider the example of "will" that was discussed earlier. Once a clinician has decided that "will," used to express intention and prediction, is to be a goal, she must decide on the contexts in which the form will be used. When auxiliaries appear in complete declarative sentences and in wh-questions, they typically receive very little stress. In fact, "will" is frequently represented in contracted form in declarative sentences. It might be argued on this basis that training in declarative forms should appear later in training, after other uses of "will" have been established. Although some auxiliaries, such as "do," frequently are weakened considerably in utterance-initial position for yes-no questions, other auxiliaries, such as "will," receive greater than normal stress at the beginning of a question. This may make the question form a better target than the declarative. The final possibility is to train "will" in elliptical forms in response to questions such as "Who will go first today?" As mentioned previously, in the response "[noun] will," "will" is in utterance-final position and it receives at least secondary stress—more than is typical in many other contexts.

When we begin intervention on any form, we consider perceptual saliency very carefully. The training of auxiliaries seems to be an area in which saliency could be a very critical factor in intervention program development. For "will" and other auxiliaries, we often select as target goals the elliptical and yes-no question contexts. Here, the form seems to be optimally salient. The clinician can provide many stressed models of the form in these contexts without adding very unnatural sounding stress to the form in declarative constructions (e.g., "I *will* be back tomorrow morning"). These other contexts are suitable as generalization targets.

Comprehension

There is a long-standing debate over whether it is appropriate to focus intervention efforts on the child's comprehension or production abilities. The answer to this question would be very simple if it were *always* true that training a content-form interaction in comprehension led to the child's use of the new form in her spontaneous language or that such training *never* resulted in correct use of the new form. Unfortunately, the experimental results on this issue are mixed. Although there is some evidence that successful teaching of language forms in comprehension does, in fact, result in improvements in production (Leonard et al., 1982; Willbrand, 1977; Winitz, 1976), this has not always been the case (Guess, 1969; Guess and Baer, 1973). The training of new language forms in production has sometimes resulted in improvements in comprehension (Gray and Ryan, 1973; Guess, 1969), but this finding has not been universal, either (Guess and Baer, 1973).

There is a great deal of evidence that a child's spontaneous use of a language form does not ensure that the child can always comprehend the same form (see reviews in Bloom and Lahey, 1978; Chapman, 1978). On the basis of this fact, we test comprehension of potential target forms as carefully as possible. If all of the other factors that have been discussed can be considered equal, those forms for which the child shows clear evidence of comprehension are given priority as intervention targets. The child could certainly be viewed as "ready" to learn to produce these forms.

When a target is selected that the child appears not to comprehend, the success of the intervention is judged on the basis of the child's ability to *produce* the target in natural communicative contexts. Once this goal is achieved, the form is tested in comprehension. In some instances, intervention focusing on the comprehension of the target in everyday communicative contexts will be required even after goals for production have been attained. This is essentially the procedure used by Guess and co-workers (1978). The reader is referred to Chapter 10 on "hybrid" procedures for some ways to facilitate comprehension in natural communicative environments.

The Child's Phonological Abilities

For children in the early phases of language development, new lexical items will often be selected as specific goals. There now exists some rather compelling evidence that both language normal and language impaired children are likely to learn to use new words more readily when the target words contain initial consonants that are already part of the child's sound system (Leonard et al., 1982; Schwartz and Leonard, 1982). This appears to influence the child's *use* of new words, not their comprehension. These findings have significant implications for goal selection. For example, a word such as "pop" would probably make a better target than "juice" for a child who produces no syllable initial fricatives or affricates. This factor must be balanced against all of the others that have been discussed.

To sum up this section on specific goal selection, it should be clear that there are numerous factors to consider, each of which may be of considerable importance. After consideration of each of these factors, along with the child's special needs, the clinician can develop a reasonable number of goals that will have a significant impact on how the child communicates. Deciding on which goals are *best* has always been a personal matter that is, to some extent, a function of the clinician's beliefs about what language is and how it is learned. Clinicians should become comfortable with this fact because, as long as individualized program development is viewed as desirable, disagreement from clinician to clinician about what is most important is inevitable.

INTERVENTION APPROACHES

The basic goal of facilitating children's development of new content-form interactions has received far more clinical and research attention than has any other area of language intervention. It is understandable, then, that more procedures have been developed to treat deficits in language form than any other type of language impairment.

In this and the next two chapters, I will present the basic characteristics of a number of existing trainer-oriented, child-oriented, and hybrid approaches to intervention. The procedures characteristic of each approach will be discussed in what I hope to be sufficient detail to enable a clinician or student not previously acquainted with any one procedure to be able to grasp its finer points and, conceivably, put it into practice. Where it is possible, representative examples of each general approach will be presented at several different developmental levels (e.g., training vocabulary, early multiword constructions, and later syntactic and morphological developments). This should enable the reader to see how theoretical principles are transformed into clinical procedures. It is hoped that this will provide the background necessary to help clinicians see how they can create new, different, and possibly more effective procedures than have been developed to date.

Trainer-Oriented Approaches

Trainer-oriented approaches to intervention all have several characteristics in common: the clinician determines the goals of intervention and dictates when and where intervention will occur, the type and rate of presentation of stimuli, the type and frequency of presentation of reinforcement, and the particular topography of responses judged to be correct. The structure of a trainer-oriented session is predetermined by the clinician so that nonverbal and verbal stimuli that are relevant to the teaching goal can be accentuated and irrelevant stimuli can be carefully controlled. Although these approaches vary in terms of what I have called naturalness, they tend to fall lower on the naturalness continuum than child-oriented or hybrid approaches because of their inherent structure. I use the term trainer-oriented rather than clinician-oriented because even though the clinician typically selects goals and prescribes times for intervention, other professionals such as teachers and teachers' aides as well as family members will frequently have occasion to implement the procedures. In the following discussion of trainer-oriented approaches, we will examine operant procedures, modeling procedures, and some modifications of these practices that are designed to enhance their naturalness.

Operant Procedures

Many procedures making use of operant technology have appeared, and they are, without question, the most thoroughly tested of all procedures available to the language clinician. All of the procedures are explicit in their control of the verbal and nonverbal *stimuli* preceding the child's response, the precise nature of the child's *response* (i.e., what can be considered a correct response and what cannot be so considered), and the contingencies of *reinforcement.* Most, but not all, procedures make use of *prompts,* which are instruction-bearing or imitative stimuli that help ensure that the child will respond correctly. When these prompts are used, they must gradually be eliminated or *faded* in a carefully controlled fashion.

In some cases, production of the complete response is too difficult for the child in the early stages of training. In these cases, the correct response is *shaped* by reinforcing the child's productions of components of the complete response, then gradually increasing the complexity of the task by reinforcing only those responses that are in some way closer approximations to the target.

Operant techniques are often placed into a highly structured organizational framework to facilitate the acquisition of new behaviors, in this case language. In this type of operant conditioning program, every step of the program is carefully planned out in some predetermined fashion. The sequence of training objectives is developed so as to maximize the probablity of correct responding. High rates of success lead to high rates of reinforcing and, theoretically, to a maximally efficient route to acquisition of the target behavior.

Gray and Ryan's (1973) program for "is interrogative" is an excellent example of virtually all of the operant conditioning procedures just discussed. The specific goal for this program is the child's use of "is" as a copula and as an auxiliary in forming five different question patterns. The nine major subgoals of this program are listed in Table 8–2. This general outline of steps illustrates quite clearly the increase in complexity from the beginning of the program to the end. Small plastic tokens are administered immediately after a correct response. At a later point these tokens can be redeemed for small prizes. Criterion for advancement to each successive step in the program is 10 in 10 in group contexts and 20 in 20 when working with individuals.

Unlike many operant programs in which only a few specific responses are trained, in this program each response produced by the child is evoked by a new picture or a new aspect of the same picture. Therefore, a large set of pictures is necessary. Before completing the program, the child will have responded to possibly hundreds of different nonverbal stimuli and will have produced just as many different sentences, each following the target sentence pattern.

Let's consider how a clinician might train the use of "is" in questions in this type of behavioral program. In the first series of the Gray

Table 8–2. The Major Subgoals of Gray and Ryan's Program (1973) for Training "Is" in Interrogative Sentences

1. Imitation of "Is [subject] [noun/adjective]?" (e.g., "Is [the] man [a] teacher?" "Is [the] lady funny?").

2. Imitation of "Is [subject] [verb]ing?" (e.g., "Is [the] boy working?").

3. Imitation of "Is [subject] [preposition] [noun]?" (e.g., "Is [the] dog on [the] bed?").

4. Imitation of "Is [subject] [verb]ing [noun/adverb]?" (e.g., "Is [the] squirrel climbing [a] tree?" "Is [the] girl working hard?").

5. Imitation of "Is [subject] [verb]ing [preposition] [noun]?" (e.g., Is [the] dog playing on [the] swing?").

6. Imitation of all of the foregoing types of sentences combined in an alternating fashion.

7. Spontaneous production of a question of types 1 to 6 following a verbal stimulus and a request to guess (e.g., "In this picture, I see a cat. Guess if the cat is jumping over the fence or playing in the water"). The picture is provided *after* the child guesses correctly.

8. Spontaneous production of questions of types 1 to 6 following requests to guess during a story-telling activity.

9. Spontaneous production of questions during conversation.

*In all steps, verbal stimuli are paired with picture stimuli.

and Ryan program (1973), the clinician first shows the child a picture and asks a question of the target form that is in some way related to the picture (e.g., "Is the baby tall?"). Next, the clinician says the child's name. This prepares the child to listen carefully to the imitative model "is" which is presented next. Finally, the child responds, in this case, with the word "is." Following is an illustration of this type of teaching episode:

(The clinician shows the child a picture of a baby smiling)
Clinician: Is the baby happy? Richard, say "Is."
Richard: Is.
Clinician: (presents a token) Very good!

Step 2 is virtually identical to step 1, except that the model to be imitated by the child is made more complex by adding one word, the subject of the complete sentence (e.g., "Is baby"). In step 3, one more word is chained to the model so that the child is required to respond with the complete target response following an imitative model (e.g., "Is baby little?").

In the remaining steps of this series, the child's task is made more complex by gradually fading the model. In step 4, for example, the model is presented *before* the child's name. This enables the clinician to insert a brief delay between the model and the child's response.

(The clinician shows the child a picture of a fire station)
Clinician: Is the truck red? Is truck red? . . . Richard?
Richard: Is truck red?

In step 5, a reduced model "is" is presented *after* the child's name, but the child is required to produce the complete response (e.g., "Is the truck red? Richard? Is. . ."). Step 6 is identical to step 5 except that the same procedure used in step 4 is also used here to delay the child's response. Finally, step 7 involves the presentation of a stimulus and no model. Therefore, the child must imitate the verbal stimulus with no added assistance.

One other important aspect of this and most behavioral programs is that the reinforcement schedule is gradually reduced. This procedure is motivated by a principle of operant conditioning that suggests that high levels of performance can be maintained only if the contingencies of reinforcement become less discernible (i.e., the child can no longer be certain when she will be reinforced so she works hard to receive what little reinforcement she can get).

I have presented this program as an exemplary model of an operant conditioning program. Each step is carefully calculated and controlled by the clinician. In the discussion that follows, several applications of these basic procedures are presented to illustrate the range of approaches that can be used to teach language form within the basic operant paradigm.

Some Representative Operant Approaches. As part of a comprehensive language program, Stremel and Waryas (1974) trained their clients to produce at least 15 verbs before combining nouns and verbs into simple multiword constructions. There are four major steps used for all of the verbs, although more basic steps even lower in complexity are programmed for the first few verbs taught. Step 1 is a comprehension task in response to the mand "Show me girl jump/ride/look/ play." If the child correctly manipulates the doll, she is rewarded with a redeemable token and social praise. If the child is incorrect, reinforcement is withheld, and the correct response is modeled. Then a new trial is initiated.

Step 2 is the same as step 1 except that, as the child correctly manipulates the doll, the clinician presents an echoic stimulus (e.g., "You say 'jump.'" The child must imitate the verb to receive reinforcement. In step 3, a picture of an action is presented along with the echoic stimulus "Say 'girl *look*.'" The child must imitate the verb correctly to receive reinforcement. Finally, in step 4, a picture is presented along with a question stimulus, "What [noun] doing?" In this final step, the child must generate the appropriate verb with no prompt.

Throughout training, two or more verbs are trained simultaneously by alternating from one to the next in a quasi-random fashion. If the child has difficulty with these steps, other intermediate or "branching" steps are also preplanned. Stremel and Waryas (1974) do not present specific data on this part of their program, but they note that, in general, trained structures often were not used consistently outside of the clinic until 2 months after reaching criterion.

A less programmed approach was taken by Jeffree, Wheldall, and Mittler (1973) in their efforts to train a simple two-word construction, "[noun]–gone," to express disappearance or nonexistence. Their clients were two 4 year old boys with Down's syndrome, each of whom had approximately 30 words in his expressive lexicons as well as a few unanalyzed phrases (e.g., "here y'are"). Neither of these boys appeared to be very active verbally at the outset of the investigation. Intervention took place during what was referred to as contextual play. In this procedure, "[noun]–gone" constructions were modeled by the clinician throughout the sessions, following the hiding of objects and pictures. The target nouns were five words that the child used prior to training. The child was reinforced socially and through the presentation of special toys when one of these constructions was imitated. In addition, a special box was used into which objects could be dropped. The child was allowed to pull a lever causing the reappearance of the object following appropriate imitation of the model. As can be seen, although operant procedures were used in this study, the amount of control imposed by the clinician is much less than that used in the Gray and Ryan (1973) or Stremel and Waryas (1974) procedures.

While the procedures were provided to one child, the other served as a control. He played with the same objects and heard the same words modeled by the clinician, but the target construction was never modeled and the child's productions were not reinforced.

The results of this investigation are somewhat mixed. Across the first 30 play sessions, the verbalizations of both children increased dramatically. Two-word constructions of the type trained were used only by the experimental subject, however. Furthermore, following five sessions of training subsequently initiated for the control subject, he also began to produce the target structures spontaneously in the clinical context. These results rather convincingly suggest that the procedures were effective. Unfortunately, data collected in the classroom do not support this conclusion. Analysis of these data indicates that, although the experimental subject made substantial gains that transferred to the classroom, similar gains were also made by the control subject who had received no intervention for multiword constructions. In fact, the control subject's use of language actually decreased in the classroom following intervention. Thus, even though the authors of this study concluded that the procedures were effective, the results seem to show only that the procedures effectively modified the children's performance within the clinical context. Changes made outside the clinical context could have been the result of a number of factors unrelated to intervention.

Zwitman and Sonderman (1979) presented an operant intervention approach that differs significantly from those discussed previously. Their program was used to meet a number of different specific goals, including new words and a variety of syntactic constructions. Their subjects were 11 specifically language impaired children with normal comprehension abilities. These children were described as demonstrating "limited conversation," indicating that they may not have been normally assertive or, perhaps, even responsive. The program lasted for approximately 5 months, during which time 25 sessions of 45 minutes each took place. In addition, the program was described to the children's parents, who were to administer the program for 10 to 15 minutes daily at home.

In this procedure, cards representing each grammatical or semantic notion in the target structure are color coded and placed in a sequence for the child to label. Thus, a picture of a boy, followed by a picture of a neutral figure eating from a spoon, followed by a picture of candy would be used to represent the sentence "Boy eats candy." There are seven basic steps to training a particular structure. At each step in the program, if the child responds correctly, redeemable tokens are administered. When the child is incorrect, the same stimuli are repeated. Correct responses following such stimulus repetitions are socially reinforced, but no token is administered.

In the first step, the cards for the target are arranged in order and an imitative model is presented (e.g., "Dog bites bone"). The second step is identical to the first, but no imitative model is presented. The child must generate the complete response by labeling each of the pictures in the sequence. Third, the child is presented with the cards in a random order along with a model of the sentence. The child's task is to arrange the cards correctly and imitate the sentence. The fourth step is the same as step 3, except that the cards are presented and the child is instructed to "make something." The task here is to arrange the cards and produce a sentence without a model. Step 5 is the same as step 3, but in this step, only the first card is color coded. The child must rely on her understanding of the model sentence rather than the color codes to sequence the cards appropriately. Step 6 is the same as step 5, but the child is asked to "make something." The basic pattern of the steps should now be clear. First, pictures, color codes, and imitative prompts are used to foster correct productions. Then, these prompts are gradually faded. Finally, in step 7, the child is required to produce the target structure in response to a picture (i.e., all of the cues and prompts of previous steps are removed).

Based on a delayed imitation type of task, following the period of intervention, the children receiving training made gains that were statistically greater than a group of 11 specifically language impaired children of similar ages and impairments who had received no training. Results from spontaneous language samples collected following training suggested that gains had been made by most children; however, two children who completed training on "is" and passed the imitative posttest failed to use the structure in their spontaneous speech. Three children who had been trained to use articles successfully similarly failed to use them in their spontaneous speech.

Schumaker and Sherman (1970) used a combination of imitation, fading, and reinforcement to reach the specific goal of production of the past tense allomorphs /t/, /d/, and /əd/ as well as the present progressive inflection "-ing." Their subjects were three moderately retarded subjects, aged 14 to 18 years with mental ages of 3 to 7 years. Several verbs requiring each allomorph to form the past tense were selected. In condition 1, the clinician said "Now, the man is painting. Yesterday, he _____, say 'painted.' " The reverse order of these cues was used to evoke the present tense, progressive aspect verb form. Correct responses were reinforced with redeemable tokens. Incorrect responses were punished with the statement "No, that's wrong" followed by 5 seconds of silence. Gradually the imitative stimulus was faded. After the client reached criterion for both inflections on one verb, a new verb requiring the same type of inflection was presented. In condition 2, a second class of verbs requiring a different past tense allomorph (e.g., /d/) was trained in the same manner. Condition 3 involved the combination of the verb classes trained in the first two conditions (e.g., Now, the man is painting. Yesterday, he _____." Now, the man is playing. Yesterday, he _____"). In conditions 4 and 5, the third allomorph, /t/ was trained and then all three forms were combined.

All three subjects in this study learned to respond correctly to all of the verbs used as training stimuli. They also learned to produce correct responses for verbs that were not used in training.

In a slightly different procedure, Hester and Hendrickson (1977) trained three specifically language impaired children, aged 3 years 6 months to 5 years 0 months to produce sentences of the form "[Subject] is [verb]ing the [noun]" (e.g., "The boy is washing the car.") to express the relations agent–action–object. In their procedure, an action was enacted before the child, who was then asked, "What's happening?" If the child's response contained all of the target features, she was reinforced. If the child responded incorrectly, the clinician reenacted the action and an imitative model was provided. This procedure was successful in getting the children to produce the target structure correctly in the training context, while looking at filmed rather than live enactments of actions, and in spontaneous samples collected during free play in the children's classroom.

In the procedures presented thus far, the orientations of the investigators have been primarily behavioristic, even though the goals were occasionally selected on the basis of psycholinguistic principles (e.g., Gray and Ryan, 1973; Hester and Hendrickson, 1977; Stremel and Waryas, 1974). The following examples, although operant in nature, are different in that they incorporate psycholinguistic principles into the general procedural framework.

Blank and Milewski (1981) designed a program for training simple sentences using the hypothesis that children develop syntactic knowledge on the basis of a "distributional semantic analysis" (Maratsos and Chalkley, 1980). For example, verbs do not just represent semantic categories such as actions and states, but in addition they are more clearly defined by their privileges of occurrence in sentences before -ed, -s, and -ing, and after do, will, is and so forth. Blank and Milewski argued that if this is the case, general properties of verbs are most likely to be learned when the myriad operations which they undergo are presented explicitly to the child.

This program was designed for a 4½ year old autistic child with limited functional language and frequent echolalia. The program had numerous specific goals, including seven simple sentence types and a number of variants produced by alternating nouns and pronouns, verb number, and so forth. Some examples of these basic sentence types are "Here/This/That is a [noun]" (e.g., "This is a bike"), "The [noun] is [verb]ing" (e.g., "The boy is pedaling"), "The [noun] has a [noun]" (e.g., "The boy has a friend"), and "The [noun] can/wants to/ likes to [verb]" ("The boy likes to ride").

In the first phase of the program, the subgoal was the fluent and complete imitation of these sentence types when presented with clear perceptual referents and a verbal stimulus. The stimuli for each goal were alternated in a quasi-random fashion—for example, "Here is a man. He has a hat. He is wearing a coat." The second set of subgoals required the child to generate one of the target behaviors following a nonverbal representation and a relevant question. First, an imitative stimulus followed the question. For example,

Clinician: Where is the boy? Here is the boy.
Child: Here is the boy.

The imitative prompt was then removed, requiring the child to comprehend the question and respond appropriately. At this stage of the program, each specific target behavior was addressed separately. Once the child responded reliably to each new question type, the new structure was mixed with other structures already learned. This made it possible for the clinician to vary the syntactic form of each successive response while keeping the semantic content fairly stable. For example, after a doll was placed in a sitting position, the child was asked, "What is the doll doing?" Then the doll was removed and the child was asked "What was the doll doing?" At each stage of the program, the child was reinforced with hugging.

The results of this program are reported descriptively. Because no methods were used to control for the effects of maturation, it is difficult to determine the extent to which improved performance was due to this particular form of intervention. Nevertheless, the sentences that this child was using 12 months after the program was initiated were impressively well-formed and appropriately contingent to the questions of the adult. Unfortunately, but not surprisingly, he "still did not speak extensively without being questioned" (p. 79).

In Schumaker and Sherman's method (1970) for training past tense and present tense, progressive aspect verb inflections, both forms were trained simultaneously, one form contrasting with the other. However, no nonverbal stimuli were used. Therefore, the responses of the subjects were controlled by a very restricted set of verbal stimuli (e.g., "now" and "yesterday"). Connell (1982) claimed that, if the objective of intervention is to facilitate acquisition of linguistic rules, the relationship between form and meaning must be made explicit to the child. This can be done, he argued, by contrasting the meanings of two forms trained simultaneously.

Connell (1982) illustrated this principle of contrastive meanings in intervention by outlining an eight-step program designed to teach the use of the auxiliary "is" in response to questions. Criterion for moving from one step to the next is 90 per cent. In step 1, the clinician shows the child pictures and asks questions such as "What is the girl doing?" An imitative stimulus is then provided (e.g., "The girl is swinging"). In step 2, a picture is shown to the child and then taken away. The clinician parallels this demonstration with a verbal commentary (e.g., "The man is smoking. Now the man is done. What did the man do? Say 'The man smoked' "). In other words, step 2 requires the child to imitate a past tense verb form. Steps 3 and 4 are identical to steps 1 and 2, except that the imitative stimulus is dropped. In step 5, the two different types of stimuli are combined in an alternating fashion. The child must make a discriminating response based on pictorial stimuli alone.

Steps 6 to 8 are designed to facilitate generalization and may not be necessary. Step 6 is identical to step 5, but a different set of 25 to 50 pictures is used. Step 7 is a repetition of 6, except that a different trainer administers the stimuli. Finally, in step 8, the procedures are moved to some new environment outside of the typical clinical context.

Connell (1982) offered no evidence regarding the effectiveness of this procedure. It stands, however, as an excellent example of how theoretical principles can be used to generate novel intervention procedures. Connell's basic theoretical orientation is operant, but his views on language structure have clearly been shaped by current psycholinguistic thinking.

Evaluation of the Procedures. There is absolutely no question that operant procedures are effective in getting children to produce new utterances that are more complex in structure than utterances produced by those same children prior to intervention. This conclusion is supported by the successful training of many different linguistic structures. This includes words (Garcia, Guess, and Byrnes, 1973; Olswang, Bain, Dunn, and Cooper, 1983; Stremel and Waryas, 1974; Welch and Pear, 1980; Zwitman and Sonderman, 1979), simple two- and three-constituent clausal constructions (Hester and Hendrickson, 1977; Jeffree et al., 1973; Lutzker and Sherman, 1974; Zwitman and Sonderman, 1979), elements of verb phrase structure, such as auxiliaries (Gray and Fygetakis, 1968b; Hegde, 1980; Hegde and Geirut, 1979; Hegde and McConn, 1981; Hegde et al., 1979; Hughes and Carpenter, 1983; Wheeler and Sulzer, 1970; Zwitman and Sonderman, 1979), elements of noun phrase structure such as articles, adjectives, possessives, and pronouns (Gray and Ryan, 1973; Hegde and Geirut, 1979; McReynolds and Engmann, 1974; Smeets and Streifel, 1976; Zwitman and Sonderman, 1979), noun and verb inflections, such as plural and possessive -s and present and past tense inflections -s and -ed (Baer and Guess, 1973; Gottsleben, Tyack, and Buschini, 1974; Guess, 1969; Guess and Baer, 1973; Hegde et al., 1979; Schumaker and Sherman, 1970). A number of studies have demonstrated the utility of operant procedures in training slightly more complex structures such as auxiliary-subject reversals in questions (Gray and Fygetakis, 1968b; Gray and Ryan, 1973; Mulac and Tomlinson, 1977) and complex sentences (Stevens-Long and Rasmussen, 1974; Tyack, 1981). These encouraging reports are even more impressive when we consider that the same procedures have been successful in training children and adolescents from a variety of etiological groups, including severely or profoundly retarded and autistic as well as specifically language impaired children.

One of the major strengths of most of these reports is that care was taken to ensure that the children who were trained did not simply learn the mechanical reproduction of certain words or combinations of words in response to the same stimuli that were present during training. Although in most cases a very limited number of sentences and phrases were actually trained, following training the subjects typically were required to respond to certain stimuli on which no training had been provided. This procedure was discussed in detail in Chapter 7. Almost without exception, the subjects of these studies have developed some generative use of the target structure as evidenced by their ability to produce nontrained sentences in response to novel stimuli.

Unfortunately, there are problems with using this method of post-testing as the sole basis for determining intervention success. First, in most of these studies, untrained probes are presented in succession. This procedure makes it possible for the child to develop a type of mental set; the child can focus her attention completely on the desired language form. To continue playing the clinician's game, the child simply maintains this mental set and responds to new stimuli in like fashion. This situation differs markedly from normal communicative contexts in which a given linguistic form may be required only occasionally under sometimes emotional circumstances in which the child is motivated to communicate meaning. Although the performance of children in these studies is an impressive indication that they are aware of some *pattern* and not just the specific forms, it is in no way indicative of how children will respond when they are not "mentally set" to respond in this fashion.

Second, the stimuli being used as probes are highly similar to the stimuli used in training. For example, even though new pictures are used, the basic characteristics of the pictures remain identical to training stimuli. The mode of presentation, including the verbal stimulus, is identical to training presentations. Thus, even though it can be said that the child has learned a rule, it is not at all clear that the rule that has been learned is governed by relevant characteristics of potential speaking situations that arise in naturally occurring contexts. Connell (1982) has noted that a child trained to use "is" with traditional operant procedures could perform successfully on this type of post-test even if a highly idiosyncratic rule had been learned.

> The child could learn that *is* is used after the subject noun of every sentence. Alternatively, the child could learn that every verb which can be pictured has *be* preceding it. Either of these inappropriate controlling elements will result in some apparently correct responses, but neither of them adequately represents the adult rule. (p. 232)

In other words, the results of this type of generalization testing do not tell us very much about whether the basic goal of training—facilitating the use of new language forms to serve real communicative functions—has been reached.

It is rather remarkable that so few studies have attempted to measure children's use of targeted language forms in communicative contexts that differ in some substantial ways from the training setting. Of those studies that have assessed the child's posttraining gains under substantially different circumstances than those present during training, the results have been mixed.

Several studies have failed to obtain the desired generalization to natural speaking environments despite high levels of accurate responding within the clinic. As noted previously, Jeffree and co-workers (1973) failed to demonstrate that their preschool subjects with Down's syndrome generalized the use of simple two-word constructions expressing the semantic relation "disappearance" to classroom situations. Zwitman and Sonderman (1979) reported several cases in which children reached training criteria and passed specially designed tests but failed to use trained structures in spontaneous conversations with their mothers. Mulac and Tomlinson (1977) reported that despite demonstrations of learning on tasks administered within the clinic, their specifically language impaired subjects who received training on the use of "is" in yes-no questions failed to exhibit use of this structure when it was required in extra-clinic situations.

Hughes and Carpenter (1983) performed one of the most rigorous tests of extra-clinic generalization to date. Their four subjects, 4 to 6 years old, who were specifically language impaired, were trained to very high levels of within-clinic use of the auxiliaries "is" and "are" using a highly structured operant approach. Throughout and following training, the children were also observed at home with their mothers, who had not participated in training. Thus, the stimuli, the setting, and the communicative partner were different from the training setting. Following four weeks of training, the children were responding with the target structures at high levels of accuracy. Unfortunately, virtually no gains were observed from pretraining baselines to posttraining baselines in the extraclinic context.

The results of several other studies are slightly less unsettling. For example, Hester and Hendrickson (1977) were successful in helping their subjects to produce their target form "[Subject] is [verb]ing the [noun]" in spontaneous language samples with stimuli that differed from those used in training. This positive finding may be related to the fact that live enactments were used as stimuli in this study rather than pictures, as is typically the case. Welch and Pear (1980) offer some qualified support for this hypothesis. They trained words to four retarded children between the ages of 5 and 14, using objects, pictures, and line drawings. For three of the four subjects, training on objects led to the most successful generalization to correct naming in the natural context. The fourth child, who was more advanced at the beginning of the study than the other subjects, generalized to labeling in her residence regardless of the stimulus type used. In the Welch and Pear study, however, the clinician was with the child during generalization testing. This weakens interpretations of the results.

Hegde (1980) tested the effects of training "is" to his two 5 year old subjects in three contexts: in the therapy room with the clinician; in a different room with the child's mother, a student clinician, and the clinician; and at home with the child's parents. The results of these reasonably naturalistic probes indicated that intervention had been highly successful. A minimum of 30 obligatory contexts was produced in each setting with a minimum of 89 per cent correct uses of "is." Significant numbers of the sentences produced had never been produced during training, suggesting that the children had indeed developed productive control over a linguistic rule.

Positive results for generalization of training on a variety of different language structures have been reported by Gray and his colleagues (Gray and Fygetakis, 1968a,b; Gray and Ryan, 1973). These studies involved primarily 3 to 7 year old specifically language impaired children, most of whom appeared to have some receptive as well as expressive language deficits. These children made significant gains that were reported to transfer to school and home activities in which the clinician was not involved. Of the several cases cited by Gray and his colleagues, the most specific and detailed report of this success was cited by Gray and Ryan (1973). In this study, 10 specifically language impaired children made novel use of trained structures in the home with the parents who (1) reportedly did not engage in any overt teaching; (2) did not correct the children's ungrammatical efforts; and (3) reinforced all utterances produced by the children (i.e., whether they were grammatically well formed or not). Although these studies are extremely encouraging, they are reported in a rather anecdotal fashion and lack the necessary experimental rigor to enable us to conclude with confidence that the basic goal of improved communication was actually reached. This caution seems warranted, given the negative results reported by Mulac and Tomlinson (1977) cited earlier.

The types of intervention procedures presented in this section have had only limited success in achieving generalization of trained structures to naturalistic contexts. The most commonly used operant procedure to facilitate generalization has been called *sequential modification* by Costello (1983). "Sequential modification occurs when the treatment environment is systematically extended from one location to another and until spontaneous generalization to nontreatment environments has occurred" (Costello, 1983, p. 290). Several investigators have shown that helping the child to generalize depends to a large extent on the addition of training steps that require the child to use trained language forms in different social and physical environments (e.g., Garcia, 1974; Handleman, 1979; Hegde and McConn, 1981; Mulac and Tomlinson, 1977; Rubin and Stolz, 1974).

For example, Mulac and Tomlinson (1977) trained two groups of specifically language impaired children, aged 4 years 4 months to 6 years 3 months to produce well-formed questions involving the inversion of "is" and the subject of the sentence (e.g., "Is daddy sleeping?"). The Gray and Ryan (1973) procedures were used with one exception. For one group, a new sequence designed to facilitate a transfer of learning from the clinic to other settings was added to the basic procedures, which include a structured home-based carryover program with parents as intervention agents. In this phase of the program, the clinician, the child, and the child's parent walked to various locations on a university campus. Stories were read to the child and questions were asked at various points in the story to evoke target responses from the child. After two such sessions, two additional sessions were held in which the same participants simply walked around campus and conversed. Again questions were asked to evoke target responses. In these four 20 to 30 minute sessions, the clinician evoked the first 20 responses. Then the child's parent evoked 10 more responses in the same manner as the clinician. Over the next eight days, the parents were required to conduct four more similarly structured sessions in different rooms in their homes.

To measure the children's progress, six different tests, varying in their degree of structure from imitation to spontaneous conversational samples, were administered by the child's clinician, by another clinician in a different room, and by the child's parent at home. The results revealed that only the group receiving additional transfer training improved significantly from pretest to posttest on the extraclinic tasks even though both showed significant within-clinic gains. Two factors weaken the authors' conclusion that additional training in extraclinic contexts will bring about successful transfer of training. First, the children who received extraclinic training obtained approximately 2 hours more training than the remaining subjects. It is not entirely clear whether the differences between groups were due to the nature of the added training or to the fact that one group simply received additional training trials. Second, it should be noted that the greatest improvements of the group that received sequential modification were on the tasks that were most similar to training (e.g., guessing games and imitation). It is not clear that any improvements were obtained on the least structured tasks, including spontaneous conversation with the parent at home.

Garcia (1974) trained what was euphemistically termed a "conversational" sequence to two profoundly retarded individuals, aged 12 and 18 years. They were trained to respond to a picture in the following manner:

> (a picture is presented by the clinician)
> Client: What is that?
> Clinician: What do you see?
> Client: It's a _____.
> Clinician: Do you want the _____?
> Client: Yes, I do.

Use of this trained sequence was not observed with adults other than the clinician until training procedures involving the other adults with the clients were implemented. As Bloom and Lahey (1978) pointed out, the failure of these children to generalize their learning may be related to the fact that the specific behaviors involved were far in advance of these children's current levels of functioning.

To sum up, operant methodologies have a long history in language intervention. They have been used to treat many diverse language forms, varying from very simple to very complex. These procedures generally have been successful in developing generative rules in the children who, prior to intervention, exhibited little or no ability to use them. With only a few exceptions, however, children trained using these procedures do not automatically begin using their new language forms as a medium for communication. Some techniques, such as sequential modification, have merit and are likely to prove useful in the future. Yet, as Spradlin and Siegel (1982) claim, ". . .the problem is how to incorporate procedures into the *initial training* that will actively induce generalization" (p. 3, italics added). If our procedures are to be effective in reaching our stated basic goals, we must show our clients from the outset of intervention that the new forms they are learning are not simply parts of games to be played in therapy but crucial parts of the communication game that is played all day, day in and day out.

Social Learning Approaches—Modeling

Approaches to language intervention that are based on learning theory are not limited to operant principles and procedures. Social learning theory, although similar in many respects to operant theory, has some very basic differences, which are manifested in the intervention procedures that it has spawned.

The modeling procedures used by Leonard (1975a), which are modifications of those developed by Bandura and Harris (1966), are presented in Table 8-3. These procedures, designed to train subject-verb constructions to children presently not making use of this structure, illustrate the basic principles of the social learning approach.

Several similarities between operant and modeling approaches can be seen from this example. For example, as in many operant approaches, modeling sessions typically take place in a traditional clinical context and are rather formal in design. Furthermore, extrinsic reinforcement typically is used to reward correct productions.

Despite these surface similarities, several fundamental differences can be seen between the procedure presented in Table 8-3 and the operant procedures discussed previously. First, the child's most important task is to listen. No responses are required until 10 to 20 models have been presented. In fact, steps should be taken to make sure that the models are presented in an uninterrupted fashion. Although the child is quiet, learning should be occurring through the child's active processing of the training stimuli.

Second, the child listens to *many* different stimuli that exemplify the language structure being trained. It is the underlying structure that the child is required to induce and later replicate, not the topographical pattern of a particular sentence. Generally, the pictures used to model a structure are not used again in training and the entire set of pictures representing a structure is large.

Third, the child is never required to imitate a sentence immediately following the model. There is some evidence that such imitation is contraindicated (Courtright and Courtright, 1976, 1979). Using strictly operant procedures, the child's task is to mimic correctly the stimulus presented by the clinician. In modeling, the child's immediate task is to solve the problem of language structure—to determine the pattern that cuts across *all* of the stimuli presented.

Fourth, reinforcement has different properties in this case than in the operant procedures. It is initially vicarious—the child should be

Table 8–3. The Modeling Procedure of Leonard*

1. The child, the clinician, and a confederate of the clinician, the model, are seated at a table.

2. A pretest is administered by showing the child action pictures or by performing actions and requesting the child to "Tell me what's happening here."

3. The clinician tells the child to listen to the model, who is going to talk in a special way when a picture is presented or an action is performed. The child is told that the model will earn chips (redeemable tokens) only when she talks in the special way (e.g., subject–verb constructions).

4. The clinician gives a picture to the model and asks "What's happening here?" Pretest stimuli are *not* included in training. Tokens are provided on a continuous schedule when the model correctly produces the target structure (e.g., "Boy drink").

5. To enhance the child's awareness of the pattern underlying the models, intentional errors are made on 20 percent of the model's utterances (e.g., "boy" or "drink"). These utterances receive no reinforcement. This procedure is sometimes referred to as developing an attentional set.

6. This procedure is followed until 10 models have been presented.

7. The child is then encouraged to talk like the model in response to the same types of verbal and nonverbal stimuli. The pictures or actions themselves differ from the modeled stimuli, however.

8. The model and the child alternate productions until the child produces three consecutive correct subject–verb sentences. Then the child continues on her own until criterion of 10 consecutive novel sentences containing the target structure is reached.

9. The pretest stimuli are then re-presented to the child without models to determine the extent of the child's acquisition of the structure.

*Based on Leonard, L. (1975a).

motivated to attend to the sentence presentations because *the model* is being reinforced. This vicarious reinforcement is used to help establish an attentional set (i.e., to help the child focus attention on the critical apects shared by all of the modeled sentences). Thus, reinforcement as a strengthener of responses is not a crucial concept in this theory or within this paradigm. Finally, there is typically much greater flexibility allowed in the child's response. If the target is subject–verb constructions, the clinician will likely accept any of the following: "boy drink," "the boy drink," "boy drinking," "the boy is drinking," and so forth. In imitation-based approaches exact replication of the stimulus is often required.

Representative Examples of the Use of Modeling. Although the potential exists to vary the basic modeling procedure in many ways, most studies to date have used designs quite similar to that described in Table 8–3 (cf. Leonard, 1974, 1975a,b,c,d). A few interesting modifications of this basic approach have appeared, however. Leonard (1975b) demonstrated that shaping may be incorporated into the basic modeling procedures. He trained the auxiliary forms "don't" and "is" to eight specifically language impaired children, aged 5 to 9 years old, who did not use these structures prior to training. Two different shaping sequences were employed, one that followed the normal developmental sequence and the other an additive sequence. This sequence began with the critical target form ("is" or "don't") and added subsequent elements to this form. These sequences are shown in Table 8–4.

The procedures for "is" training were nearly identical to those of Leonard (1975a) in every other respect. For each step in the sequence, 10 to 20 models reflecting the level of complexity characteristic of that step were presented. The models were then followed by the child's attempts. Criterion for moving to each successive step in the sequence was 10 consecutive appropriate responses.

To train "don't," Bellugi's method (1967) of testing negation was used. One card containing two pictures was presented. One picture involved an action and the other involved similar persons and objects in an inactive state. Each model, which involved a description of the *second* picture, was preceded by reference to the first picture (e.g., "Here, cars go, but here, *no go/ they no go/ they don't go"*). All 10 to 20 models were presented in this fashion at each step in the sequence, with the models reflecting the varying levels of complexity of each step.

These methods of shaping within a modeling framework were effective in getting the children to use the target structures in response to nontrained stimuli following approximately 75 minutes of training over a 2½ week period. The developmental sequence required significantly fewer trials to reach criterion and resulted in significantly greater numbers of correct responses than did the additive sequence.

Wilcox and Leonard (1978) used modeling to train the use of questions of the form what/where/who–is/does–subject–verb (e.g., "Where does the lady sleep?") to a group of specifically language impaired children, aged 3 years 8 months to 8 years 2 months. Most of the children demonstrated some limited use of wh- words and auxiliaries prior to training, but none appropriately inverted the order of the subject and auxiliary in any type of question in spontaneous speaking. The model in this study was a toy bear with a speaker mounted in its chest. The clinician presented a picture to the bear so that the child could easily see it and requested a question (e.g., "Ask me where the lady sleeps"). A footswitch was then tripped so that the bear could provide models that had been preprogrammed on an audio recorder. Another important modification was employed in this investigation. When the child produced a question incorrectly, the clinician responded by saying, "No, you should have said _____ ." Thus,

Table 8–4. The Developmental and Additive Shaping Sequences Used by Leonard*

Developmental Sequence	Additive Sequence
"Is"	"Is"
1. Daddy work.	1. Is.
2. Daddy working.	2. Is working.
3. Daddy is working.	3. Daddy is working.
"Don't"	"Don't"
1. No throw.	1. Don't.
2. They no throw.	2. Don't throw.
3. They don't throw.	3. They don't throw.

*Based on Leonard, L. (1975b).

not only was the child informed that her response was incorrect, but, in addition, the correct form was modeled. Imitation was not required, however. Finally, the model and the child alternated responses throughout the entire training period rather than only until the child produced three correct responses. After each child reached criterion, probes containing new pictures and requiring questions not used in training were administered. Based on the children's performance on this type of posttest, these procedures were highly successful.

The success of the Wilcox and Leonard procedures (1978) suggests that the model does not need to be another person. This is an important finding for clinicians whose access to supportive personnel is limited. Even more encouraging evidence in this regard is provided by the studies of Courtright and Courtright (1976, 1979). In the first of these studies, modeling was used to train the subjective case pronoun "they" to eight specifically language impaired children between the ages of 5 and 10. These children typically used the objective case form, "them," in subject position. The clinician served as the model simply by showing the child 20 pictures and producing a sentence containing "they" to describe each one. Following this presentation, the child was requested to describe the same 20 pictures following the prompt "Tell me about them." In this procedure, no reinforcement was used, nor was any effort made to establish an attentional set by erring on 20 to 30 per cent of the model's sentences. Furthermore, no alternating between model and child was used at any point in training. Only three 20 minute sessions, each separated by 3 to 4 days, were provided. A probe using a different set of 20 pictures was given after each training block and again 1 week after the termination of training. The children were observed to make consistent gains in their use of "they" across the three sessions. These gains were still notable 1 week after training.

The second Courtright and Courtright (1979) study examined more closely the need for a third party model by comparing the progress of a group of children trained using a third party model and a group of children trained with the clinician as model. The children in this study were specifically language impaired and ranged in age from 4 to 7. The structure being trained was the artificial form "[Noun] means to [verb]ing," which was used to describe pictures ordinarily requiring present progressive verb forms (e.g., "The boy is playing" would be modeled as "The boy means to playing"). The experimental design of Courtright and Courtright also enabled them to assess the effects on learning of presenting tokens following correct responses. The procedures were identical to those of the previous study with the exception that following the models, a new set of pictures was provided as stimuli for the children. The results of posttraining probes with novel stimuli indicated that modeling was successful, that the clinician and a third party were equally successful as models, and that the use of response-contingent tokens did not improve the children's performance.

Evaluation of the Procedures. Modeling, in its various forms, has been used successfully to train vocabulary (Leonard 1975c), subject–verb constructions (Leonard, 1975a,c), verb–object constructions (Leonard, 1975d), agent–action–object constructions (Prelock and Panagos, 1980), use of the auxiliaries "is" and "don't" (Leonard, 1974, 1975c), appropriate use of subjective case pronouns ("he" versus "him," Leonard, 1975d; "they" versus "them," Courtright and Courtright, 1976), artificial constructions to describe ongoing actions (Courtright and Courtright, 1979), and wh- questions (Wilcox and Leonard, 1978). Most of the subjects in these studies have been young children, some of whom were normal, some specifically language impaired, and some moderately developmentally delayed, ranging in age from 2 to 10 years; however, the procedures seem applicable for older, more severely cognitively impaired individuals as well (Prelock and Panagos, 1980).

I am aware of only one report of negative results with the use of modeling procedures. Connell, Gardner-Gletty, Dejewski, and Parks-Reinick (1981) attempted to replicate the investigation of Courtright and Courtright (1979) using procedures that they claimed were virtually identical to those in the original study. The children that they attempted to train were reported to be similar to those of Courtright and

Courtright, and the target was the same artificial sentence structure. Not only did the children fail to improve on posttesting, but in addition only one child ever used the structure, and this occurred only one time! Courtright and Courtright (1981) responded that Connell and associates must have misused the procedures. Given the range of variation in the procedures that have been used successfully by other investigators with both normal and language impaired children, however, this seems highly unlikely. In our own experiences with modeling, we too have found children for whom the procedures simply were not effective. In many of these cases, we resorted to a brief period of imitation training to heighten the salience of the target form. Upon returning to the modeling procedures, performance typically, but not always, has improved. The extreme differences in the results of Courtright and Courtright (1979) and Connell and associates are unexpected, and they remain unexplained.

The significant client variables that determine whether modeling will or will not be effective are completely unknown at present. It has always interested me that no mention is ever made in research reports of difficulties in getting children to sit and listen quietly to models. We often see children who are not at all willing to do this, and they tend to be the ones for whom the procedures are least effective. The hypothesis that these procedures will be most effective for those children who sit quietly and willingly listen to the models must await experimental verification. It seems plausible, however, given the theoretical justification for the procedures.

In three independent studies, modeling has been shown to be more effective than imitation procedures. For example, Courtright and Courtright (1976, 1979) observed that performance on structured posttests containing items not used in training was significantly higher for the children receiving modeling than for those who received operant training. Prelock and Panagos (1980) demonstrated that their retarded subjects who were trained to use agent–action–object utterances using modeling made much more flexible and creative use of the trained structure than did a group of matched subjects who were trained using imitation and reinforcement procedures.

Some cautions should be made before accepting this conclusion, however. In the original Courtright and Courtright (1976) investigation, each subject in the "mimicry" condition was required to look at pictures and mimic the sentences produced by the clinician. No reinforcement, shaping, changing of reinforcement schedules, or any other operant procedures were employed. Thus, it cannot be concluded on the basis of the results of this study that modeling procedures are more effective than operant procedures, in general.

This problem was resolved to some extent by the second Courtright and Courtright (1979) study. In this investigation, tokens and praise were used in both a mimicry (immediate imitation of each stimulus) and a modeling condition and were found to have no significant impact on the children's correct responding. No effort was made to determine whether the tokens and verbal praise used in this study were reinforcing in any way, however. This makes it difficult to interpret the pattern of results observed (Connell et al., 1981).

Another potential problem with the Courtright and Courtright (1976) investigation is that the children receiving mimicry training had much higher scores on the baseline test than did the subjects who were trained with modeling procedures. This problem was controlled statistically in an appropriate fashion; however, it may be that the higher baseline scores of these children made mimicry training a poor choice of intervention procedures. Friedman and Friedman (1980, see the next section) observed that rigid operant procedures were most effective with low functioning children. This hypothesis deserves experimental attention because the answer to this problem may lead to a determination that some procedures are more effective than others with certain types of children or with children at certain stages of development.

As was the case for studies of operant procedures, investigations of the modeling approach have consistently tested the results of training using stimuli that were not used in training. Thus, there is no question that the children in these studies learned some rule that enabled them to create novel utterances of the target form. However, the same criticisms marshaled against using this type of probe as the only form of posttraining assessment in the foregoing section are relevant in the case of modeling studies as well. The nature of the rules learned (e.g., the scope of the rules and their extent of application in naturally occurring communicative contexts) is still very much open to question.

In fact, the study by Prelock and Panagos (1980) is the only modeling study of which I am aware in which posttesting was done in a language sampling situation. Based on this testing, modeling led to greater usage of the target structure in spontaneous speaking than did operant techniques; however, each of the subjects in this study used some agent–action–object constructions prior to the investigation. Thus, Prelock and Panagos seem to have shown only that modeling is more effective than their mimicry procedure in increasing subjects' usage of target forms. They did not facilitate the acquisition of a new structure. Furthermore, details of the sampling procedure are not presented, so a cautious interpretation of their observed pattern of results seems warranted.

Modeling procedures, like social learning theory in general, are intuitively very appealing to me. The clinician's task is to carefully arrange stimuli so that the underlying abstract rule is made more transparent for the language impaired child. In addition, the clinician must arrange the learning context in such a way that the child is highly motivated to attend to the target linguistic variable. The problem that the child must solve in this training paradigm, and the manner in which she must solve it, is not unlike that which is characteristic of normal language learning. Therefore, this approach has the potential value of preparing the child to attend more closely to grammatical detail. As a result, whatever cognitive resources the child has available may be rendered operative to induce language structure from less ideally structured models present in the natural environment. This possible virtue has never been tested, however, so it remains an hypothesis very much open to question.

The basic question that must be asked of modeling procedures is exactly the same as that for operant procedures. Do they help to facilitate the growth of functional communication skills among children whose development in these areas is markedly delayed? Results so far are encouraging, but the truth is, we really do not know. This is not because the procedures have been shown not to be effective, but because the crucial testing of the procedures' effects on language use in natural situations has not been done. I believe that Connell's conservative approach (1982) is prudent here and elsewhere.

> Regardless of the approach used, clinicians would be well advised to remember the tentative nature of their selection and monitor their assessment and training procedures as if the procedures were not effective. That is, clinicians should hold a healthy skepticism towards their selection since they do not have the privilege of confidence which empirical evidence might afford. (Connell, 1982, p. 236)

Ecological Validity and Trainer-Oriented Approaches

It is clear from the discussions of the operant and modeling approaches that trainer-oriented approaches have had limited success in getting children to make use of new lexical and grammatical forms outside the clinic context. Given the highly restricted contexts in which these types of training typically take place, this unfortunate result is, perhaps, not too surprising. Many investigators (e.g., Hubbell, 1981; Mahoney, 1975; Muma, 1978b) have argued that one of the reasons these procedures have not had lasting impact on children's communicative performance is that they are not *ecologically valid*. In other words, the clinical contexts in which these new forms are used bear virtually no relationship to actual communicative situations.

There is a clear need to develop procedures that may be employed in contexts more directly representative of the child's typical language-learning and language-using environments. Two trainer-oriented intervention approaches, Interactive Language Development Teaching (ILDT) (Lee et al., 1975) and the Environmental Language Intervention Strategy (ELIS) (MacDonald, 1978; MacDonald and Blott, 1974; MacDonald, Blott, Gordon, Spiegel, and Hartmann, 1974) were developed with this express purpose in mind.

Interactive Language Development Teaching. ILDT (Lee et al., 1975) was developed as an alternative to what are considered to be two opposing extreme approaches: highly structured, operant programs and relatively unstructured language stimulation techniques (see Chapter 9 for more complete information on these procedures and the rationale for their use). Recognizing the difficulties inherent in training a specific language form in an uncontrolled conversational context, the authors developed a story-based teaching strategy and claim that it "approximates as closely as possible the conversational setting of normal language development" (p. 7). Although the lessons used in this approach are developmentally sequenced and a list of preplanned stories following the pattern of Lee's Developmental Sentence Scoring procedure (1974) is presented, this is not a highly inflexible set of programmed steps and procedures. The clinician is encouraged to be creative by designing new stories and adapting the procedures to her own and her clients' specific needs. Furthermore, the clinician is encouraged to interact with the children in a way that fosters their own creative thinking and verbal responding.

Each lesson, which lasts approximately 50 minutes and typically involves a clinician and three to six children, consists of two basic parts. The first 30 to 35 minute segment involves the presentation of a story especially designed for the children in the group. Lee and co-workers (1975) make several suggestions for planning stories that will be maximally effective in training grammatical structure. First, the theme of the story, its characters, and events in which they play a role should be familiar to the children. This makes the content of the stories easier for the children to identify with and enables them to attend more closely to the grammatical targets. Second, story narrative should be designed so that important events are repeated and restated, giving the children maximum opportunity to hear models of target structures and facilitating comprehension of the story line. Third, target responses should be required from the children only after sufficient information is provided to make the informational content of the response clear and relevant. Although relevant, nontarget responses are encouraged from the children, production of target responses should not require the child to infer the correct answer from incomplete information presented in the story. Fourth, new structures should be modeled by the clinician several times in several stories before requiring production of that structure in an effort to facilitate comprehension of these forms. Fifth, stories should provide many opportunities for the child to hear and produce target forms.

It is suggested that the primary target for a given child be presented at least five times per story. Secondary targets, including those that have recently been acquired and those that will become primary targets in upcoming sessions, should be presented three or four times per story. Finally, on occasion, the clinician should ask questions that require the children to think about details relevant to the story that are not explicitly presented. The clinician is free to elaborate on or modify the planned story at any time. Often, spontaneous responses of the children make ad hoc modification or some digression from the story line desirable. Taking advantage of these opportunities enhances the naturalness of the procedures. An example of each of these aspects of story construction is provided in the model story presented in Table 8-5.

Various props should be used to provide a nonlinguistic backdrop for the events described in the story. Felt boards and either commercially available or homemade materials designed to stick on a vertically oriented board are extremely useful in this regard. It is stressed that these materials need not detail every aspect of the story, but should assist in holding the children's attention on the story.

The clinician presents the narrative and occasionally calls on the children to answer questions relevant to the story. Although some children may be working on identical structures, goals are likely to vary from child to child. This makes it necessary for the clinician to present different types of stimuli to different children in the group.

When the child's response matches the target form, the clinician acknowledges its accuracy. If the child's response does not include the target structure, one of several "interchange techniques" is used to get the child to expand on the original response. These techniques, presented in Table 8-6, should seem familiar. Despite the emphasis on the differences between this and the operant approaches discussed, the basic procedures of this approach are immediate imitation and social reinforcement. Thus, its basic pedagogic principles are operant in nature. It is the context in which these procedures are used and the opportunities that children have for spontaneous contributions to the story that really make ILDT different from other operant approaches. The list of techniques in Table 8-6 reflects a hierarchy of complexity. Children at more advanced stages of training on a particular form

Table 8–5. A Part of a Sample Story for Interactive Language Development Teaching*

Narrative	Target Response
Cookie dough is soft and flat.	
What is it?	It is soft and flat.
Here are some cookie cutters.	
Karen is cutting out cookies.	
And so is Susan.	
Susan is cutting out cookies, too.	
What is she doing?	She is cutting out cookies.
There are two kinds of cookies.	
This one is round.	
This one looks like a star.	
This cookie is a star.	
And this is a round cookie.	
What kind is this?	This is a round cookie.
What kind is that one?	That one is a star.
Mommy says:	
I'm gonna bake them.	
Let's put them in the oven.	
The oven is for baking.	
The cookies go in the oven.	
Let's bake them.	
What does Mommy say?	Let's bake them.

*Primary targets stressed include "is," the conjunction "and," and the contracted form "let's."

From Lee, L., Koenigsknecht, R., and Mulhern, S. (1975). *Interactive language development teaching* (p. 129). Evanston, IL: Northwestern University Press. Reprinted with permission.

should have to deal with less explicit prompts that are lower on the list than should children who are just beginning training on a new structure. Although it is desirable to evoke a correct response in some way each time a child is called on to respond, when an interchange becomes lengthy, the target child becomes frustrated and other children become disinterested. This problem can be avoided by reducing the demands on the child and modifying goals when necessary.

Following the story and a short break, the children take part in some group activity that focuses on the theme, characters, concepts, vocabulary, or grammatical forms contained in the story. These may be artistic (e.g., drawing, tracing, cutting and pasting), dramatic (e.g., role play, dressing up, taking pretend picnics or other trips), or real-life activities (e.g., washing windows or clothes, popping corn, baking cookies, playing hide-and-seek). The clinician takes whatever opportunities that occur within this less structured part of the approach to collect language samples to assess the children's progress, to provide models of target structures in meaningful contexts, and to evoke target responses from the children. No specific techniques are sug-

Table 8–6.   The Interchange Techniques Used in Reacting to Incorrect Responses in the ILDT Procedure*

1. *Complete model:* a verbal prompt which the child must imitate.

   Clinician: Are they helping?

2. *Reduced model:* an imitative prompt that contains only part of the target response.

   Clinician: Are. . .

3. *Expansion request:* the clinician requests an expansion but presents no model.

   Clinician: Tell me the whole thing, or
   Tell me more.

4. *Repetition request:* the clinician requests a repetition from the child, but presents no model.

   Clinician: Tell me that again, or
   What did you say?

5. *Repetition of error:* the clinician repeats the child's error as if to illustrate the inappropriateness of the response.

   Clinician: They helping?

6. *Self-correction request:* the clinician asks the child to consider the accuracy of her response.

   Clinician: Did you say that right? or
   Is that right?

*Techniques are ordered from the most to the least helpful to the child. All examples refer to the child's response "They helping?" In each case the target sentence to be elicited is "Are they helping?"

Based on Lee, Koenigsknecht, and Mulhern (1975).

gested for this part of the session, although the hierarchy of interchange techniques should prove useful here as well.

I am aware of only six published clinical reports on the use of ILDT. The first is a report of a 3 year investigation presented by Lee and co-workers (1975). Twenty-five specifically language impaired children, aged 3 years 2 months to 5 years 9 months, participated in approximately 96 sessions spread over an 8 month period. These children exhibited pretreatment delays in expressive syntax averaging 21 months according to estimates based on Developmental Sentence Scoring (Lee, 1974). Some deficits in comprehension were also noted, although these were not nearly as great as the expressive impairments. The description of subjects used in this investigation is exemplary.

Lee and co-workers (1975) reasoned that, for children showing a delayed pattern of language growth, normal gains over the period of treatment could be considered strong support for the success of the procedures. Therefore, their experimental design involved making comparisons between estimates of language development, in months, with the time spent in treatment. Their pre- and posttreatment measures were age-equivalency estimates taken from the children's DSS scores. The language samples on which the scores were based were collected by individuals who did not take part in training.

The average DSS gain was 10.8 months compared to an average treatment duration of 8.3 months. Thus, ILDT was supported as an effective procedure for specifically language impaired children performing in the average range of intelligence. On the basis of these data, it appears that not only were the children not losing any more ground to children developing normally, they were actually catching up.

A more thorough analysis of the children's scores within each DSS category showed that they were using significantly more grammatically appropriate personal pronouns and main verbs following intervention. Furthermore, the average score for entries within the main verb, negative, and wh-question categories was greater than before training. The total scores in the personal pronoun, main verb, secondary verb, and sentence point categories were all significantly greater following intervention than before. Although the procedure of converting DSS scores to age equivalents to make the type of comparison made by Lee and co-workers (1975) is suspect on statistical grounds (see the discussion in Chapter 2), this pattern of results is encouraging, especially since the dependent measures reflect performance in a conversation with an adult who was not part of the training program.

Friedman and Friedman (1980) augmented the data presented by Lee and co-workers (1975) with data collected from a similar group of children who were exposed to a highly structured operant program for the same number of sessions over a similar 8 month span. Their intent was to determine whether ILDT was more effective than the operant training program, as would have been predicted by Lee and co-workers. The same pretreatment measures were taken, and comparisons indicated no statistically significant differences between the two treatment groups on any measure. Statistical analyses of the gains made on the DSS from pretest to posttest also exhibited no differences between the treatments; both types of treatment resulted in statistically significant gains.

Upon closer examination, however, Friedman and Friedman (1980) noted several interesting patterns of performance based on pre-experimental differences between the individual children. Specifically, their results enabled them to predict that children with higher Stanford-Binet intelligence quotients (> 112) will make optimal gains on the ILDT procedures. Similarly, children with high DSS entry levels (> 5.5) can be expected to make greater gains following ILDT than following a highly programmed approach. On the other hand, children with pretreatment DSS scores of less than 1.6 are likely to benefit more from the programmed procedures. Finally, the ILDT can be expected to yield optimal gains for children with high visual-motor abilities. In sum, children with higher intellectual and language abilities prior to treatment appear more likely to benefit from the less structured, more natural ILDT procedures. These general conclusions are supported by Simon (1976), who reported on the basis of her own clinical experiences that ILDT was not successful with three low-functioning autistic and retarded children.

It should not be concluded, however, that ILDT is, in principle, appropriate only for children who are functioning at normal intellectual levels and who already possess basic syntactic structure. McGivern, Rieff, and Vender (1978) modified the procedure for use with 5 to 15 year old children with intelligence quotients of 28 to 66. These children were all using two- to three-word utterances prior to training. Unlike in the original description of the procedure, these investigators used token reinforcement and food to reward both attention and correct responding. Furthermore, instead of using a new story with a different theme for each session, the same story was used for each of four 30-minute sessions held weekly. In the first session of the week, the story was read and relevant vocabulary and syntax were tested. No productions were evoked from the children at this stage. On the second day, time was spent teaching vocabulary and related concepts, but no story was told. On the final two days, the story completed on the first day in the week was re-presented in a fashion resembling the procedure as described by Lee and co-workers (1975). Short vocabulary and imitative syntax quizzes were administered after these sessions.

New stories were presented each week for a period of 7 months. The 28 children (mean age = 10 years 4 months) who received this treatment in the classroom from their teachers demonstrated significantly greater DSS gains than did a control group of 28 children (mean age = 10 years 2 months) who received similar amounts of training using activities based on the Illinois Test of Psycholinguistic Abilities (Kirk, McCarthy, and Kirk, 1968), Peabody Language Development Kits (Dunn and Smith, 1965), and other materials designed for training expressive syntax. There was also some evidence that the children receiving ILDT were attempting sentences requiring more complex structures, even though these attempts were not yet grammatically well formed.

Although these results are encouraging, some of the DSS analyses were performed on samples as small as five utterances. These small samples undoubtedly led to some highly unreliable analyses. Furthermore, it is not possible to discern who collected the language samples and in what manner they were collected. The extent to which these problems might have affected the results cannot be determined from the published report of the study.

Ratusnik and Ratusnik (1976) presented a report of the successful use of ILDT with four psychotic children, ranging in age from 5 years 11 months to 7 years 5 months and with Stanford-Binet IQs ranging from 50 to 83. On the basis of careful descriptions that were provided, they could all be described as displaying a pattern characteristic of either inactive communicators or passive conversationalists (see Chapter 5 for detailed descriptions of these patterns). None of the children initiated much meaningful speech. They all displayed aberrant and negative patterns of interpersonal behavior. In addition, they had substantial deficits in their use of sentence form.

The ILDT procedure was one part of an intensive therapeutic milieu involving regular individual speech and language lessons, family therapy, and participation by parents, counselors, and educators at the health center attended by the children. ILDT was used in the recommended group format, two times weekly for one hour over a 6 month period. As in the study by McGivern and colleagues (1978), tokens were used to reward correct responses. One other significant modification of the procedure was used with these children. Following the clinician's story, the children were asked "Who wants to tell the story?" All children who so desired were then given an opportunity to manipulate the props and tell their own version of the story. All of the interchange techniques in Table 8–6 were used during this story retelling activity. This procedure gave the children an opportunity to *initiate* meaningful language to communicate with their peers. Such opportunities make it difficult for nonassertive children to stay in a responsive, noninitiatory mode of interaction throughout the entire session. Reportedly, the children in the study enjoyed this part of the procedure. They clapped for one another on completion of their stories.

After 6 months, all four of the children exhibited marked gains in their meaningful use of syntactic structure. They all engaged in dialogue with the examiner about their everyday experiences. Just as importantly, delayed and immediate echolalia, jargon, and inappropriate prosodic patterns were virtually extinguished. The children also made notable gains in visual-motor functioning and eye-hand coordination as well as in their concept of body image. Finally, the negative behaviors characteristic of their preintervention behavior were reduced dramatically.

Although Ratusnik and Ratusnik believed that the ILDT procedure was largely responsible for the observed improvements, it is difficult to determine precisely how much or what aspects of the progress were actually due to the procedure. Nevertheless, the observed gains were impressive and suggest that the procedure has merit even with emotionally disturbed children.

In a study previously discussed in part in the section on operant procedures, Hughes and Carpenter (1983) presented results that were not nearly as encouraging as those just reported. Each of the four specifically language impaired subjects in the study by Hughes and Carpenter was trained to produce either "is" or "are" using ILDT. Following four weeks of training, each of the subjects demonstrated significant gains on tasks within the training setting. Unfortunately, no gains were observed in the children's language usage at home with their mothers. Although the reasons for this failure to generalize to contexts outside the clinic are not clear, it may be important that Hughes and Carpenter did not provide their subjects with theme-related activities following each of the stories, as recommended by Lee and colleagues (1975). Furthermore, even though each subject was performing at much higher levels within the training sessions following 4 weeks of training, none of the subjects had reached levels of performance typically viewed as sufficiently high to warrant moving on to higher levels of training. It may be that ILDT takes longer to establish correct responding in some children. Such a finding would not be a liability, however, if the ultimate result was a significant gain in usage of the target structure in spontaneous speaking contexts.

Reported results on the use of ILDT are sufficiently encouraging to warrant further use and more intensive testing of this intervention approach. Because of its demands on the child's attention and comprehension abilities, it appears to be most useful for children who have already developed base syntactic structure and who have average or above average intellectual abilities. With sufficient modification, however, the procedures may also be effective with moderately and mildly developmentally delayed children and even some emotionally disturbed children.

A major advantage of this procedure is that the verbal stimuli presented in the stories are all topically related to one another. The result is a coherent (if not particularly dramatic) semantic whole. Children exposed to this procedure have the opportunity to learn about the structure of stories, the contingent nature of successive utterances, and the cohesive devices that effectively tie the semantic information in one sentence to that in other sentences (e.g., anaphoric pronouns, specific articles, conjunctions). Whether or not children make use of this opportunity and learn these aspects of language through this procedure is unknown. Nevertheless, it is an opportunity that is totally absent from the procedures presented thus far.

The Environmental Language Intervention Strategy (ELIS). The ELIS was designed to assist young children who produce primarily single-word utterances in their acquisition of multi-word semantic relations. The emphasis in this program, the functional use of these early relational structures, is discernible at virtually every level of training.

The procedures used in this program are operant in nature, but there are two critical features that distinguish it from the operant programs discussed previously. Each of these modifications enhances the "naturalness" of the procedures and makes them more ecologically valid than would otherwise be the case. First, the trainer can be a significant person or persons in the child's everyday environment and the procedures can be used in the home. For example, MacDonald and co-workers (1974) successfully trained parents to employ these procedures as the primary agents of their children's intervention programs (see Chapter 14 for a discussion of the parent training procedures). Second, from the very outset of intervention, the child is exposed to target stimuli and is required to produce the target form not only in imitation in a traditional clinic setting, but also in conversation and in play.

The differences in stimulus conditions for the imitation, conversation, and play phases of training are outlined in Table 8–7. A nonlinguistic event precedes some linguistic stimulus in each phase. In the imitation and conversation phases, these events are set up by the clinician and are rather contrived, but in play, the nonlinguistic event should occur as a part of the activity itself. For imitation, the linguistic stimulus is an imitative prompt, whereas a question typically is used to evoke a response in the other two conditions. Finally, the consequences for correct and inadequate responses are highly similar for imitation and conversation. Note, however, that the response to the child during play takes on a much more natural, conversational tone (e.g., the clinician responds appropriately to the content of the child's requests and comments and, where possible, expands the child's utterance by filling in grammatical details).

In a typical session, the trainer would work on the same goal for approximately 15 minutes in each of the three conditions. These sessions take place at least three times a week in the home. Parent trainers have monthly contacts with the language clinician to review the child's progress and make any necessary changes in the child's program. New semantic relations are trained as the child develops control over existing targets.

MacDonald and colleagues (1974) used these procedures with six children with Down's syndrome, aged 3 to 5 years. All of the children were using primarily single-word utterances prior to intervention, but

Table 8–7. An Outline of the Three Phases of the Environmental Language Intervention Strategy*

I. *Imitation*

   A. A nonlinguistic and a linguistic cue are paired and a cue is given for a verbal imitation (e.g., the adult gives a cookie to a doll and says, "Feed dolly").

   B. If the child responds correctly, the adult repeats the verbal stimulus, and gives social and token reinforcement (e.g., "Feed dolly. Good talking" and presentation of a redeemable plastic token.)

   C. If the child responds incorrectly or does not respond, the adult looks away from the child for 3 seconds and repeats the stimuli one or two times.

II. *Conversation*

   A. The nonlinguistic stimuli are the same as those for imitation.

   B. The linguistic stimuli are questions rather than imitative prompts (e.g., "What am I doing?").

   C. The adult's response to correct productions is the same as for imitation.

   D. If the child responds incorrectly or does not respond to the question stimulus, an imitative cue is provided followed by a repetition of the stimuli (e.g., "Say, 'Feed dolly.' What am I doing?''). This may be repeated one or two times.

III. *Play*

   A. As the child is at play, the adult asks for a conversational response by asking a question that is appropriate in the context. For example, the child and adult might be playing with dolls. If the child picks up a brush to brush the doll's hair, the adult might ask, "What are you doing?" Alternatively, the adult might pick up the brush and ask something like, "What should I do?"

   B. If the child provides a correct response containing the target semantic relation(s), some confirming response is given (e.g., "Yeah, you're brushing dolly's hair" or "You want me to brush dolly's hair. Okay." A request might be made for a more complex response on certain occasions. For example, if the child says, "Brush hair," the adult might respond "Yeah, say, 'Brush dolly's hair.' "

   C. If the child does not respond or responds incorrectly, the adult does not confirm the child's response or comply with the child's request. Instead, a 3 second pause is followed by a prompt for imitation, as above.

*Each phase is administered during a single intervention session.
Based on MacDonald, Blott, Gordon, Spiegel, and Hartmann (1974).

they showed comprehension of all of the trained structures and even used them on reportedly rare occasions. After 2 months of training, three of the children showed greater gains in MLU and in use of various semantic relations than the other three children who were not involved in therapy from the outset. Their greatest gains were on the semantic relations that had been selected for training (action–object and [word]–locative). The same children were retested after 3 months and were observed to have made gains in MLU judged to be as great as those reported for normal children (Brown, 1973). A similar program was then administered to the remaining three children. These children showed rapid gains in MLU following only 1 month of training. Similarly encouraging results were observed by Manolson (cited in MacDonald, 1978) in further applications of essentially this same approach with children with Down's syndrome, aged 4 to 8.

Other reports on the use of ELIS have also been positive. Kemper (1980) trained five parents of language impaired children to use ELIS and instructed them to administer two sessions of at least 15 minutes' duration at least three times per week. Parents were also encouraged to use the procedures when occasions arose spontaneously throughout the day. The children all had large comprehension-expression gaps. They each had 10 to 50 word lexicons, but reportedly used no multiword utterances.

Following the 12 week program, the children exhibited significant increases in their use of all six semantic relations that had been trained. No details are provided on how the posttreatment testing was done, and no information is provided on the specific progress of individual children. Nevertheless, these results converge nicely with those of MacDonald and colleagues (1974) and suggest that ELIS is effective in training the expression of semantic relations to preschool-aged children whose comprehension exceeds their expressive abilities.

The report of Simon (1976) confirms the positive outcomes of these investigations and indicates that the population for whom the strategy is effective may be quite broad. Simon reported success with low-functioning autistic-like children for whom ILDT procedures had proved ineffective. These children were not clearly described in Simon's brief letter, but her report of success with children functioning at low levels of cognitive ability suggests the possibility that ELIS may be a viable approach for children who fit several of the four social-conversational patterns described in Chapter 5.

Enhancing the Naturalness of Trainer-Oriented Procedures and Activities

To date, the most ubiquitous problem with language intervention programs has involved getting the child to use trained behaviors in everyday contexts for the purpose of interaction with the social environment. This is typically referred to as a generalization or "carryover" problem. Despite the fact that this problem has plagued interventionists from the very outset of their efforts to help language impaired individuals, it has received serious attention only in the last few years and remains a black mark on the record of our clinical profession (see Costello, 1983; Guess, Keogh, and Sailor, 1978; Harris,

1975; Johnston, 1982b; Leonard, 1981; Spradlin and Siegel, 1982; Stokes and Baer, 1977).

There is no question that the most commonly used trainer-oriented procedures are implemented in very unnatural activities (see Figure 4–3). We can be equally certain that this lack of naturalness is at least partially responsible for problems in generalizing new acquisitions to everyday communicative contexts. In most cases, trainer-oriented activities involve drills in the clinic, administered by the clinician. There are some notable exceptions to this general pattern. For example, sequential modification techniques by their very nature take place outside of the original clinic context. Even when using these techniques though, a clinician is frequently the administrator of the procedures. In addition, despite efforts to make the activity seem more realistic, there is very little that is natural about a clinician following a child around and asking questions with answers that are clear from the nonlinguistic context. Even in these extraclinic environments, then, the clinician typically views the child's goal as being the appropriate use of the target form, not the use of the appropriate form to communicate relevant information under conditions in which the child is highly motivated to share that information.

Interactive Language Development Teaching (Lee et al., 1975) and the Environmental Language Intervention Strategy (MacDonald and Blott, 1974; MacDonald et al., 1974) are excellent examples of modifications of the classical intervention techniques that effectively enhance naturalness. The procedures that are used within these two intervention approaches are not new. The activities in which the procedures are implemented differ significantly from traditional intervention approaches, however.

In this section several suggestions on how a clinician can modify the activities in which trainer-oriented procedures are implemented will be presented. These suggestions are really no more than hypotheses about how available procedures can be rendered more effective. They are based on interactionist principles of language use as well as on research reports and observations from within an interactionist framework (see Chapters 9 and 10). I have no doubt that making use of such modifications makes trainer-oriented activities more natural; the question of whether they result in greater generalization remains unanswered. A summary list of these principles is provided in Table 8–8.

Make Informativeness a Clinical Principle

Greenfield and Smith (1976) presented evidence that the particular aspect of an event that young, normally developing children at the

Table 8–8.   Principles for Enhancing the Naturalness of Trainer-Oriented Intervention Procedures and Activities

1. Make informativeness a clinical principle.
2. Create training contexts in which the motivation to communicate is present and real.
3. Help the child to use the target form to express both responsive and assertive conversational acts.
4. Present multiple exemplars of the target language form.
5. Organize patterned stimuli so that the child listens to and is ultimately required to create cohesive text.
6. Introduce "distractor items" into the activity.
7. Encourage the child to converse about things not present in the immediate context.

single-word stage of development are most likely to encode linguistically is the aspect that is most novel, dynamic, salient, or otherwise uncertain. For example, a child who notices a ball on the floor may say "ball" as she goes to retrieve it. After examining the ball for a few seconds, the child may throw the ball across the room. At this point in time, the ball itself is no longer a new object; therefore, the child is less likely to label it than before. Now it is the child's action of throwing that is most novel, and she would be more likely to say something like "throw," if such a word were available.

Greenfield and Smith's observation (1976) led to the proposal of a general hypothesis that has come to be called the *informativeness principle*. The principle makes no claims about *when* the child will talk or which specific words the child will select to encode an event; it merely suggests that *if* the child opts to communicate, that aspect of the event that is represented in the child's utterance will be the most informative aspect.

Several experiments have shown that for normally developing children and for some language impaired children, the informativeness principle is operative and may be used to predict successfully which aspects of an event a child at the single-word stage of development will encode when she decides to talk (Greenfield and Smith, 1976; Leonard, Cole, and Steckol, 1979; Rowan, Leonard, Chapman, and Weiss, 1983; Snyder, 1978). Furthermore, both normal and language impaired children appear to be most likely to imitate words when they represent these same uncertain contextual elements (Greenfield and Zukow, 1978; Leonard, Cole, and Steckol, 1979; Leonard, Schwartz, Folger, Newhoff, and Wilcox, 1979).

These findings suggest that many of our attempts to train new words to young children have been poorly conceived. The most common technique has been simply to select one object from an array of objects placed before the child and ask "What's this?" or "What do you see?" The object is in plain view of both the child and the clinician, and it has undergone no new transformations. Therefore, it is not new or dynamic and would not be likely to be labeled by most children under ordinary circumstances. Repeated presentations of the same object and verbal stimulus further decrease their informativeness.

Table 8–9 illustrates several ways in which the clinician can manipulate the context to increase the informativeness of words that are being either tested or trained. The activities for nouns, and verbs are adapted from Snyder (1978). Many other activities are possible. The essential features of these activities are an initial redundant pattern, followed by some change either in the action performed on a static object or in the object that is playing a role in some repetitive action.

With a little imagination, similar procedures can be developed to assist in the teaching of words reflecting possessors, locations, attributes of objects, and so forth. For example, suppose that one of the words to be trained is "pretty," used to describe an attribute of an object. One way to evoke the use of this word might be to look at a series of black and white drawings in a coloring book. After viewing several pictures in this fashion, the page would be turned to a drawing in full color. Following a pause to see if the child responds communicatively in some way, the clinician could employ the procedures of her choice. For example, a request for imitation (e.g., " 'Pretty,' say 'pretty' ") would be likely from a clinician operating within an operant framework. A clinician who holds the assumptions of social learning theory or an interactionist viewpoint would be more likely to model the response (e.g., "pretty") and then respond appropriately should the child imitate spontaneously (e.g., "Yeah, this picture is *pretty*").

A variation on this type of activity might include the block game shown in Table 8–9 for nouns. In this variation, the child could be given plain, uncolored blocks to put in a container. After several such transactions, the child would be given a colored block. The color of the blocks on successive presentations should be varied to ensure that the word "pretty" is not associated with a specific color.

A horizontal goal attack strategy (see Chapter 4) would assist in creating informative contexts for stimulus presentations and would probably be advisable in teaching an early lexicon, based on this principle. This strategy avoids the repetitious stimulus presentations characteristic of most approaches.

I see at least two important advantages to the procedures in the table over those typically used to train new lexical items. First, under these circumstances, the chances are great that the child is attending

Table 8–9. Examples of Activities Designed to Enhance the Informativeness of Target Words*

Nouns

1. The clinician shows the child how blocks can be tossed into a pail. She hands several blocks to the child, one by one, and then gives the child an exemplar of the target word (e.g., a doll).

2. The clinician rolls a ball to the child. They roll the ball back and forth several times. Then the clinician rolls to the child an exemplar of the target word (e.g., a car, bus, truck).

3. The clinician shows the child how blocks can be stacked. She gives the child several blocks to put on a pile and then gives her an exemplar of the target word (e.g., a cup, ball).

Verbs

1. The clinician and child roll a ball back and forth as in No. 2 above. Then the clinician throws or bounces the same ball.

2. The clinician and child stack blocks together. While the child continues to stack, the clinician pushes the stack over so that it falls down.

Adjectives

1. The clinician hands the child several simple line drawings to examine. Then, the child is given a drawing in full color as the clinician says "pretty."

2. Several pieces of clean white clothing such as socks and T-shirts are given to the child to put in a box. Then a dirty item is given to the child. The clinician says, "dirty," and gives the item to the child to put in the "washing machine."

3. Several identical pictures of an animal are given to the child for examination. Then the clinician gives the child a picture with the animal dressed in a hat or in some other unusual circumstance and says, "funny."

Possessives

1. The child and clinician sort clothes brought from home. At first all of the clothes are the same (e.g., Daddy's). Then an item of the child's mother's is passed to the child. Repeat for "Mommy's," "Ernie's," and so forth.

*Based on Snyder (1978).

to the aspect of the event being lexicalized. Presenting a verbal stimulus on occasions such as this should facilitate the child's acquisition of the relevant sound-meaning relationship. Often, imitation does not need to be evoked with a request; the child will imitate spontaneously. Second, by modeling uses of target words or requiring the child to imitate the words under these circumstances, or by using both methods, the clinician is helping the child to learn not only *what* to say, but *when* it is appropriate to say it. Especially for children who are not active conversationalists, this would seem to be an ideal alternative to the common clinical procedure of having the child respond to questions. It may encourage the spontaneous use of words in response to relevant nonverbal stimuli among children who are typically not likely to verbalize unless a response is requested.

Greenfield and Smith (1976) and Bates (1976) both claimed that young children's tendencies to lexicalize informative aspects of their environments is an early example of their developing presuppositional abilities. In normal discourse, speakers must ascertain which of the relevant aspects of the information they wish to communicate are already known by the listener. In other words, they must determine what information is given, and what information is new. Typically, "given" or "old" information is somehow reduced in the speaker's expressions, whereas new information is expressed explicitly. For example, when a question such as "Where is the boy sitting?" is asked, the most likely response is a prepositional phrase (e.g., "on the roof"). This is a perfectly comprehensible and, in fact, a perfectly grammatically well-formed response. This is because the information that is omitted from the response (e.g., "The boy is sitting") can be *presupposed* by the participants in the conversation—it is recoverable from prior linguistic context and, therefore, may be considered as "old information." This process of omitting old information that can be recovered from the linguistic context is called *ellipsis*.

Another means of reducing redundancy in our expressions is *pronominalization*. When we first make reference to a person or an object in a conversation, we must label it by name. On future references, the same individual or object may be referred to with an *anaphoric pronoun*, such as "he," "she," "it." Anaphora occurs when a pronoun's referent can be determined by referring back to some prior point in the discourse.

Ellipsis and anaphora are two of several processes of *cohesion* used by speakers to tie related sentences together into a semantic whole or *text* (Halliday and Hasan, 1976). Each of these processes is related to our notion of informativeness and each can be exploited in clinical contexts. Unfortunately, most intervention procedures ignore this crucial aspect of discourse. The result is that children are often required to talk about noninformative events or to encode aspects of events that most normal conversationalists would often find unworthy of comment or would omit from expression because of their redundancy in the speaking context. The following episode, in which the goal is the use of "is" as an auxiliary verb in present progressive verb forms, will be quite familiar (e.g., see the technique of expansion requests in Table 8–6 and the stimuli used to evoke complete sentences in Table 8–5).

(The clinician turns over a picture of a boy sitting on the roof of a house)
Clinician: "Where is the boy sitting?"
Child: "On the roof."
Clinician: "Say the whole thing." Or "No, use 'is.' " Or "The boy. . . ," etc.
Child: "The boy is sitting on the roof."
Clinician: "Very good."

There are really two problems with this very familiar type of clinical example. First, since both the clinician and the child can see the picture, there is really nothing in the picture that can be considered very informative. The motivation to communicate anything at all about the picture may not be very great. Second, by forcing the child to produce a complete response when an elliptical response is acceptable, the clinician may be teaching the child a very unnatural way of responding to questions which runs counter to the tendency of languages to reduce redundancy when possible. The child may learn to use "is" in contexts in which its use is questionable. If this is the case, training of conversationally appropriate elliptical responses will have to be instituted at some later point in training.

This added training of ellipsis can be obviated by adopting informativeness as a clinical principle that is operative in all phases of intervention. In the foregoing example, the clinician wanted the child to include the subject, the verb, and the prepositional phrase in the response. The problem was that part of the desired response was presupposed by the stimulus, making that part of the response less informative and less likely to be included. The clinician's goal in planning intervention contexts should be to set up situations in which the critical portions of the child's response are not presupposed and, therefore, are highly informative.

Let's look at a couple of ways this could have been done using the same "is [verb]ing" example. Instead of using pictures, movable objects would probably be more appropriate for this objective. This procedure can be implemented easily within a play activity. The clinician might place various "animate beings" in various locations, describing each situation in turn. For example, "These guys are sitting in funny places. Look, the girl is sitting in the tree. The bear is sitting on the stove. The daddy is sitting under the table." After several examples such as this, a *new* animate being would be placed in a *new* location (e.g., the boy might be placed on the roof). This new placement could be accented with interjections like "Ah oh!," or "Now look!" Rather than describing this herself, the clinician would simply pause, waiting for the child to initiate a response.

In my experience with active conversationalists, these children often beat the clinician to the punch and place *their own* objects in new locations, describing the situation after they have performed the movement. If this does not happen, and the child does not respond, the clinician may just move on, preparing a new situation that may be more successful. Alternatively, she may be a bit more direct by asking the child something like "What now?", which requires a response from the child, or an imitative stimulus could be provided. Note that, because of the way in which this event has been structured, the response "on the roof" seems incomplete.

Another method that is often successful, especially with active conversationalists, is the use of what I call "false assertions." To the best of my knowledge this technique was introduced by Crystal and associates (1976). Using the example just described, the clinician might place the boy on the roof and say "Oh look, the dog is jumping on the roof!" Children who are passive conversationalists and children who are inactive communicators will typically let these obviously inaccurate statements pass uncorrected. Some procedures, such as imitation or modeling, may be needed to encourage these children to respond. On the other hand, active conversationalists are often prompt in registering an objection and a correction to these assertions. Again note that because the subject and the verb were incorrectly labeled, a new subject and verb are highly likely to appear in the child's corrective response—for example—"No, the *boy* is *sitting* (on the roof)."

We have had great success with false assertions by letting the child be the "teacher." The child's job is to correct a puppet who "sometimes gets all mixed up." The puppet then describes several related aspects of a story and the child's task is to correct the puppet.

By structuring the activity in these ways, the clinician sets up a context in which a response that does not contain the target structure will be incomplete. If the response does not contain an appropriate use of the target structure, any of the interchange techniques in Table 8–6 could be appropriate. Such an activity has excellent potential for children who seldom make spontaneous use of their linguistic knowledge. It creates situations in which the child's task is not simply to use a target form, but to use it to fulfill some communicative purpose, in this case to describe a novel event or to correct the clinician or puppet.

As a final example of how informativeness can be used to modify traditional procedures, I offer the case of teaching pronouns. It should be clear from the foregoing discussion that pronouns cannot occur at the whim of the speaker. They typically occur when the referent for the pronoun is clear from the context or has been explicitly pointed out in prior discourse. That is, they often serve an anaphoric function. To teach pronouns, then, it would seem advisable to create situations in which the pronoun was required only after a referent had been clearly identifed. The name of the referent would no longer be informative, making pronominalization highly appropriate. A sample sequence of this type of stimulus organization, taken from Skarakis and

Greenfield (1982), is presented below.

> (A ball is shown on top of a hill)
> Clinician: Here is a ball on top of the hill.
> (The ball is shown rolling down the hill)
> Clinician: Now, the ball is rolling, rolling down the hill.
> (A boy is shown picking up the ball at the bottom of the hill.)
> Clinician: And what happened here? (p. 463).

At this point, the clinician can intervene in whatever way deemed appropriate (e.g., by providing an imitative stimulus, "A boy is picking *it* up," by providing a whole series of such sequences with a model providing the answers, by letting the child attempt a response and then correcting it, if necessary, and so forth). The real advantages of this procedure are that the child receives not just an example of the relationship between "it" and an inanimate referent but also an example of the use of "it" when it is conversationally appropriate. The form of the pronoun and the content that it represents are explicit, as are the conditions in which a pronoun is likely to be used.

Create Training Contexts in Which the Motivation to Communicate is Present and Real

The desired outcome of intervention is for the child to use conventional linguistic forms to express meaning when the need for such expression arises. Although this need originates from within the child, it is typically induced by events occurring in the environment that make social interaction necessary and desirable. A clinician can exploit this fact by manipulating the environment in very significant ways to intensify the child's need to communicate.

Whereas the informativeness principle may be exploited to influence the *content* of the child's utterances, this principle suggests that through careful control over certain characteristics of the environment, the clinician can exert some influence over *when* the child initiates communication. It is also suggested that new content-form interactions are most likely to be learned and used appropriately if the clinical context provides opportunities to use the new forms under conditions of real communicative need.

One problem with traditional types of intervention programs is that children are trained to attend to and produce new language forms, but no effort is made to ensure that they use those forms meaningfully with some real communicative intent. Wilcox and Leonard's question training paradigm (1978) is a good example of this kind of oversight. The children in this study looked at pictures and asked questions such as "Where does the boy live?" They learned the forms of the response, but what did they learn about asking questions? Pictures of common events that are explicitly portrayed and that are in plain view of both the child and her partner are not likely to motivate questions. This is precisely because the need for most questions, a lack of information, is absent from the context.

We have made highly successful use of modeling to teach question forms using structured activities that created the need for questions. For example, placing an opaque barrier between the child and the clinician makes it possible for the clinician to examine pictures and perform actions that the child cannot see. When the clinician laughs at or makes comments about these pictures or activities, many children want to find out what's going on. For children who are not active in conversations, these are contexts in which requiring them to use questions is most appropriate. In this type of activity the child receives very naturalistic reinforcement (an informative answer) for each question that is asked.

Table 8–10 illustrates an activity that we used to teach a 6 year old girl to use "is" as an auxiliary in questions. She typically omitted "is" in all contexts. She was an active conversationalist, so cues to get her to ask questions were not needed. The fact that she often tried to peek around the barrier to see what was so interesting made it clear that we had been successful in creating the motivation for the performance of a question.

The use of a barrier to induce the motivation to speak is not limited to teaching questions (see also Chapter 13). Something as mundane as using the present progressive "is-[verb]ing" can be worked easily into this type of communicative task. One way this can be done is to give the child a set of pictures involving actions performed by a given individual or group of individuals. The clinician will have the same set of pictures but in a different order. The child's task is to arrange her pictures in whatever order desired and to describe each one so that the clinician can sequence her set of pictures in an identical fashion. The child must use the target form appropriately. If she does not, the clinician may intervene in whatever manner is deemed appropriate. The aspect of this type of activity that differs from traditional trainer-oriented procedures is that the child must not only use the target form correctly, she must also communicate information regarding the events and their sequence to the listener. In other words, in this activity, the need to communicate underlies the performance of all of the child's speech acts.

Table 8–10.   A Training Sequence Using the Modeling Procedure*

Clinician:	This doll is the father. This is the mother. This is the boy, and this is the girl. They are going to get up and get ready to go to work and school. The doll, Harlan, is going to try to guess what they're doing. He's going to talk in a special way. You listen to Harlan's questions. Later, you'll get a chance to guess just like Harlan.

(The barrier is placed between the child and the materials which will be manipulated by the clinician. Harlan takes a position *on the child's side.)*

Clinician:	Ding-a-ling-a-ling.
Harlan:	Is the alarm going off?
Clinician:	Yes, it is. (Makes a yawning sound).
Harlan:	Is the mother waking up?
Clinician:	Nope.
Harlan:	The boy waking up?
Clinician:	Use your special talk.
Harlan:	Is the boy waking up?
Clinician:	No, he isn't.
Harlan:	Is the father getting up?
Clinician:	Yes, he is. (Removes barrier and shows father getting out of bed). I wonder what he is gonna do now? (Makes a sound like flowing water).
Harlan:	He turning on the water?
Clinician:	I didn't hear your special talk.
Harlan:	Is he turning on the water?
Clinician:	Yes, he is. Do you know why?
Harlan:	Is he taking a bath/ taking a shower/ brushing his teeth?
Clinician:	Yes, he is. Mother is doing something now.
Harlan:	Is she getting up?, etc.

Next, the child gets a turn to ask questions using "special talk."

*This procedure exemplifies a way in which a realistic need to communicate can be created in a structured setting. The target structure is the use of auxiliary "is" in questions. Materials include several dolls representing family members, toy bedroom, bathroom, and kitchen furniture, and a large doll or puppet to be used as a model.

Help the Child to Use the Form to Express Both Responsive and Assertive Conversational Acts

One of the simplest methods of evoking a specific response from a child in a clinical context is to ask a question. It is understandable, then, that many intervention paradigms make extensive use of questions to supplement nonverbal stimuli in evoking the production of target forms. With some children, however, the unfortunate consequence of this type of training is that the child will use the new form only to respond to the requests of others, not to initiate communicative acts (cf. Blank and Milewski, 1981). In these cases, training may have a relatively small effect on the child's communicative potential.

This problem can be handled by making sure that the child is us-ing the form in contexts other than responses to requests before termi-nating training on that particular goal. If such usage does not occur spontaneously, intervention should be continued to encourage its de-velopment. The suggestions made earlier regarding the informative-ness principle and the principle of creating the need to communicate should be useful in this regard.

We used imitation and modeling procedures to establish the use of the past tense morpheme in the 6 year old girl referred to earlier in Table 8–10. Unfortunately, her use of each of the three allomorphs of this morpheme was confined primarily to answering questions. Even in these cases her use of the morpheme was inconsistent in conversa-tional situations. To hasten the generalization process, we decided to help this child use the target form in questions.

Our specific goal was the use of the past tense in questions of the form "Who–[verb]ed–the [noun]." One activity we designed involved the child playing the role of a mother who had gone shopping. While she was away, her children had helped her around the house. We placed pictures on the table to serve as reminders for each event. We also modeled the correct past tense form as we described what the children had done. For example, "Oh look! Someone *cleaned* off the ta-ble. Somebody *washed* the dishes. Someone *picked* up their clothes."

The child's task was to guess which of three children, represented by three small dolls, had done each task. That is, she was to ask ques-tions such as "Who washed the dishes?" As expected, she made sev-eral errors on this task, and we responded by using many of the inter-change techniques recommended by Lee et al. (1975) (see Table 8–6).

Again, this child provided us with evidence that we had designed a task that appropriately considered the two principles stated earlier. On one occasion, following the child's correct use of the form, the cli-nician triumphantly recorded the correct response on a score sheet and failed to answer the question. Our subject responded in a rather perturbed fashion, "Well, which one?!" She was clearly asking these questions with the intent of getting an answer. In such cases, there is *no* better reinforcement than fulfillment of this intent.

Present Multiple Exemplars of the Language Form Being Trained

Language is by its very nature flexible, allowing users to make highly creative use of its components: words, phrases, sentences, sto-ries, and so forth. Thus, a word will typically apply not just to one specific exemplar, but to many exemplars belonging to the same con-ceptual class. A sentence form such as agent–action–object or subject–verb–object applies not just to a handful of meanings specifically trained in the clinic but to an almost unlimited range of meanings that can be expressed using these linguistic patterns or rules.

It is not difficult to teach children to use specific words in highly contextualized situations by using a great deal of repetition and a vertical goal attack strategy. Imitative prompts can be used until the child responds with the same word consistently; then the prompts are dropped. The uses of words learned in this fashion can even be highly functional, such as the case where a child indicates her toileting needs by saying "pee" or "poop." However, when these productions are learned by rote and their use remains limited to the heavily restricted contexts in which they were learned, the child is still not using language per se.

It is also true that language forms can be taught using only a small handful of exemplars (e.g., Hegde, 1980; Hegde and McConn, 1981; Hegde et al., 1979). In these procedures, the same sentence is repeated over and over until some criterion (e.g., 10 in 10) is reached. Then, if the child does not demonstrate the learning of a rule by responding correctly to nontrained items, a new sentence can be trained in the same fashion.

There are two significant limitations with such a procedure. First, it is likely that the rule that is developed under these circumstances will be limited in scope. To ensure that the child develops a lexical concept or a syntactic rule that is as broadly based as those of adults, many examples of each rule should be presented. This furnishes the child with ample opportunity to develop and test hypotheses regarding the nature of the rule governing the use of modeled sentences. Second, failure to provide the child with many examples of the target makes it impossible to implement any of the proposed principles for enhancing naturalness. A highly repetitious procedure concentrates solely on the form of the utterance. The child cannot really be expected to learn anything about the situations in which a new form is likely to be used in an activity that requires nothing but meaningless repetition. There is nothing in this type of task that tells the child to use the new form when she is trying to communicate. Some children seem capable of making this quantum leap from concentrated repetition of a few exemplars to use of the concept or rule outside the clinic. In my experience, and judging from the reports in the literature, most cannot.

Organize Patterned Stimuli so that the Child Listens to and is Required to Produce Cohesive Text

One of the most unnatural characteristics of typical intervention contexts is that the stimuli presented to and the responses expected from the child are completely unrelated to prior discourse. For example, pictures are often used as training stimuli. The child looks at one picture and responds to a question relating to the picture. Then another picture, which is usually totally unrelated to the first picture, is shown. A new question, topically unrelated to the first, is presented, and the child is expected to respond. This procedure bears only a vague resemblance to typical social interaction, whether verbal or not.

Interactive Language Development Teaching (Lee et al., 1975) is one of few procedures that follows the principle of presenting stimuli in such a manner that they have some broad semantic coherency. I believe that this is one of the reasons for its success. Ratusnik and Ratusnik (1976) exploited the potential of this aspect of ILDT fully by having the children retell the story in their own fashion following the clinician's presentation.

There are relatively simple and inexpensive ways to present pictorial or other stimuli in such a way that the verbal models of the clinician and productions of the child follow a theme. For example, consider a child being trained to use the modal auxiliary "will." Instead of showing this child a set of unrelated pictures for description, the clinician could show the child a sequence of pictures, each one depicting a highly predictable step in a highly familiar activity, such as popping corn.

A modeling procedure that exemplifies this principle for enhancing naturalness is given in Table 8–11. This example follows the sequence of pictures related to popping corn in Simon's (1980) package of stimulus materials. It illustrates how the clinician can "tell a story" while being highly selective in the models that are presented to the child.

Following the clinician's story, the child gets a turn. At least at first, we typically have the child retell the same story that was modeled. The information present in such a story is obviously not new. The informativeness of the story can be enhanced by bringing in a peer, the child's parent, or even a doll or puppet. The child's task would be to tell this naive person what will have to be done to make the popcorn. On a structure like "will," for which a prediction must be made without benefit of a picture, it is likely that many aspects of the story will be omitted. Because of the meaningfulness of the child's responses, this is of little consequence. There are ways that have already been discussed to help the child, though. For example, false assertions are quite useful in this case. To get the child started on the popcorn story, the following episode might occur.

Clinician: Okay, there is a girl and she will make some popcorn. First, she will get some soap.

Table 8–11. Modeling that Illustrates the Principle of Organizing Stimuli so that the Child Will Use the Target Structure to Create Cohesive Text*

Clinician:	Today, we're going to pop some popcorn. These pictures tell a story about a little girl who will fix some popcorn too. You listen and I will try to think of all of the things that she will do. I'm going to talk in a special way. Then, you will get a chance to use your special way of talking when you tell the story.

(The picture sequence is then presented to the child, but all of the pictures are covered. As each statement of intention is made, the appropriate picture is uncovered, thus clarifying the temporal relationship between the statement and the activity.)

> First, the girl will get the popcorn.
>
> Next, she will get the popper.
>
> Oh yeah, she will need some oil.
>
> Then, she will plug in the popper.
>
> Next, she put some oil in the popper. Ah oh. I forgot to use special talk. She will put some oil in the popper.
>
> Then, she will pour the popcorn in a cup.
>
> Next, the popcorn will go in the popper and the girl put on the cover. Oh no. I forgot my special way of talking again. She will put on the cover.
>
> Then, she will wait. The corn will make a lot of noise as it pops.
>
> Finally, it stop popping. I mean, it will stop popping.
>
> Then, the girl will take off the lid.
>
> She will pour the corn in a bowl.
>
> And then she will salt it.
>
> Finally, she will eat the corn.

*The specific goal is the use of "will" to state intentions or to predict outcomes.
Based on a set of pictures taken from Simon (1980).

Child:	No!
Clinician:	No, what?
Child:	Popcorn.
Clinician:	What about it?
Child:	She will get some.
Clinician:	Oh, she will get some popcorn. Yes, she will. Then what?

Following the retelling of this narrative, the steps in the popcorn-making procedures actually can be carried out. Comments like "I wonder what will happen now" or false assertions like "This popcorn won't pop" that the child can refute (e.g., "Yes, it will" can be used to create opportunities for the spontaneous use of the target form.

There are several advantages to this procedure. First, when the child is finished with a block of trials, she will have told (or at least will have been a coparticipant in telling) a meaningful story. That is, her use of the new content-form interactions will have resulted in something more than a set of sentences. The child can be praised for making sense, not just for making use of new structures. Second, this procedure is more like a naturalistic language learning context in that the child is required to process discourse (i.e., to extract meaning from a sequence of topically and syntactically related sentences). At the same time, the child must notice the structural similarity of each successive sentence. Of course, this might also be viewed as a liability since it increases the complexity of the task.

A third advantage is that this procedure creates a format for the clinician to model a variety of cohesive devices. If Table 8–11 is examined carefully, a number of uses of anaphoric pronouns, definite articles, and conjunctions can be found that serve to tie each utterance to preceding utterances. Whether the child actually profits from these examples of cohesive devices and the opportunities that the procedure provides to produce them is unknown. These models and opportunities are simply not present in other procedures in which successive stimuli are not topically related, however.

Introduce Distractor Items Into the Activity

In most of the activities and procedures discussed thus far, the clinician tries to make the target form explicit by producing a number of sentences that contain the desired structure with few interruptions by potentially distracting stimuli. Then, when the child has the opportunity to produce sentences containing the structure, they are often produced one after the other. As I pointed out earlier in this chapter, such dense concentrations of a given sentence structure are not common in discourse. When the child establishes a mental set on the target structure, she may be able to produce it correctly with great consistency, only to falter in more realistic situations in which the structure is called on only occasionally amid a number of potentially distracting stimuli.

To prepare the child for this more naturalistic type of speaking situation after consistently high rates of accuracy in typical clinical contexts, we begin to insert topically relevant comments following the child's utterances. Our objective is to make the child process our verbal contributions and to get her to produce at least one nontarget utterance of her own before proceeding to a new target production. The following episode, involving the specific goal of "is" as an auxiliary in questions (see Table 8–10), should give a good idea of this principle.

Child: *Is* the man waking up?
Clinician: Yes, he is. I got up late today. Boy, I was really tired.
Child: Not me. I got up early.

Clinician: And you're not tired?
Child: No.
Clinician: Well, this man is tired. I wonder what he's going to do next?
            (Makes a noise to simulate the flow of running water—
            "shhh")
Child: He taking a bath?
Clinician: What?
Child: Is he taking a bath?
Clinician: He sure is. Boy, I bet that will wake him up.

Under these slightly more naturalistic conditions, we almost always see an initial drop in performance levels. When this is the case, we establish a new subgoal of 80 to 90 per cent correct and work to reach it in activities based on the principles presented in this section. Distractor items are introduced regularly and with increasingly greater frequency until questions are being asked at a rate that more closely approximates natural conversation. This procedure is not unlike the generalization procedure of Culatta and Horn (1982), which will be discussed in Chapter 10.

Encourage the Child to Converse About Things Not Present in the Immediate Context

Up to 2½ or 3 years, most of what children talk about is directly related to the immediate, perceptible context. As their cognitive and linguistic skills develop, however, they become increasingly capable of talking about objects, events, and relations displaced from the speaking context. Spradlin and Siegel (1982) pointed out that one factor in our failure to help children to generalize target language forms outside the clinic is that we rarely offer them the opportunity to use new forms to communicate about important events that are divorced from the immediate context.

One method of providing such opportunities is simply to sit down and talk with the child with few or no props. In other words, strike up a conversation about a topic in which the child is interested. False assertions are especially effective in these situations in getting the child to produce a particular type of structure in a spontaneous fashion. Various interchange techniques can be used to help the child correct any errors in the use of the target forms. Using this method requires the clinician to give up a great deal of control, however, and particularly if the child is just beginning to acquire a new structure, this may not be desirable. More importantly, in this type of situation, unless the child is a fairly active conversationalist, she may not talk very much in this context.

The ILDT (Lee et al., 1975) procedure makes use of two techniques that are helpful in getting the child to use language in a less contextualized fashion. First, the props that are used are nothing more than that—props used to hold the story line together. No effort is made to picture or enact every detail of the story. The child is required to process the story by relating verbally transmitted details to previously stored information. Since this is what is done in normal discourse processing, requiring children to do this in therapy activities makes the activity more like an everyday task.

Many language impaired children would be unable to perform this task were it not for another important procedural detail of ILDT. Recall that the stories designed for this procedure are based on activities with which the child has some familiarity. When stories focus on events to which the child can easily relate, the child is likely to have a mental scheme or script that includes the materials and events typically associated with this event. If some details that are represented verbally in the story are not represented visually through the props, the child can rely heavily on this script in determining the meaning of the sentences presented.

The activity recommended in Table 8–10 for working on questions requires the same reliance on schemes for familiar events. This activity involves "getting up in the morning," one with which the child is very familiar. When cues designed to motivate the need for questions are presented, they relate to these everyday events (e.g., the alarm goes off, the water is turned on, the table is set for breakfast). Had some idiosyncratic event been selected for this activity, the child would probably not have generated questions on her own, and perceptible props such as pictures would have been needed.

Another example of how the clinician can encourage the child to use decontextualized language is by taking turns describing the routine actions of family members, friends, and so forth, in very familiar activities like getting ready for school, helping with the dishes, or attending a birthday party. Many of the same procedures discussed earlier can be incorporated into this type of activity. The example in Table 8–12 illustrates an activity designed to evoke the third person, present singular morpheme on a variety of different words to describe familiar events that are not present. This same format can be modified easily to get the child to predict events (e.g., "What will our moms do tomorrow morning after the alarm goes off?") or to recall past events (e.g., "Let's talk about what we did to get ready for school this morning").

In this activity, the child hears frequent models of the target structure from the clinician. Memory of relevant events is facilitated by talking about common circumstances for which the child has a well-formed script. Furthermore, the clinician's contributions serve to remind the child of possible activities in which the characters might get

Table 8–12.   A Technique Designed to Get the Child to Use the Target Structure (the Third Person Present Singular Morpheme) to Describe Events Not Represented in the Speaking Context

Let's talk about all of the things that happen every day in the morning. I'll tell you something that happens at our house, and then you can tell me what happens at your house.

Clinician:	My dad gets up first.
Child:	My *mom* gets up first.
Clinician:	My dad does. Then, he puts on his robe.
Child:	My mom put on her clothes.
Clinician:	She what?
Child:	She put on her clothes.
Clinician:	Oh, she puts them on. My dad puts on his robe. Then, he brushes his teeth. How 'bout your mom?
Child:	No.
Clinician:	No what?
Child:	She don't brush her teeth. She wakes me up.
Clinician:	Oh, she wakes you up. My *dad* wakes me up. Then, he makes breakfast for me.
Child:	Your dad?
Clinician:	Yeah.
Child:	My *mom* make breakfast for *me*.
Clinician:	She *buys* breakfast for you?
Child:	No, she makes it.
Clinician:	Oh, she *makes* your breakfast.
Child:	Yeah. She makes cereal and sometime eggs.

involved. By providing these supports, we have found that many children are capable of talking at length on topics that require the use of target structures in a highly decontextualized fashion. Such activities may enhance not only the child's command of language as a tool for communication of nonpresent events but also the child's use of language as a tool of thought.

Finally, there are some language forms that simply are not appropriate for describing events that are ongoing or that have taken place in the immediate past. A particularly difficult form is the use of the perfective aspect (e.g., has eaten, have taken, had stolen). It is unlikely that a clinician will deal with this structure unless the child is fairly mildly impaired and is at least five years of age. I have chosen the past perfect as an example of the many structures that must be targeted for some children, but that are not particularly frequent in the language and cannot be readily pictured or acted out. A method that we have used with some success on this and other infrequently occurring structures involves the creation of simple miniproblems that the child must solve. The problems are presented linguistically with limited or no assistance from pictures or other props. A sample of this type of story is given in Table 8–13. Note that, even though a number of different main verbs could be selected for the solution, the past perfect form is highly appropriate, if not obligatory. Furthermore, each of the principles for increasing naturalness discussed in this section is realized in this task. The information contained in the child's response is new. Therefore, the child is typically motivated to communicate that information. Each response may follow a question, although other types of eliciting stimuli are possible, as the table illustrates. Even though all of the child's responses contain the past perfect, there is a great deal of discourse between each response, and more can be added with little difficulty. Many exemplars of the target form can be illustrated and, perhaps most importantly, the child must process text to be able to infer the answer. The child's response is an important contribution to the generation of text.

This type of activity can be used with either operant or modeling procedures. Our efforts have involved modeling exclusively. Several stories are told as the child listens. Only after hearing numerous models is the child given a chance to "solve the mysteries." Regardless of the procedures selected, the activity is markedly different from those typically used for such structures. For example, contrast this activity with a situation in which the clinician provides the child with a picture of a girl with a cookie sheet full of burned cookies. A question stimulus might be used, such as "Had the girl burned cookies or cake?" The expected response would be "The girl/she had burned the cookies." The child may learn the form in this manner, but she will have no idea of when perfective verb forms are called for rather than past tense forms. The picture in this case might have been appropriate for either structure. Although some appropriate pictures may well be available, the clinician will have to be very selective. If the child can follow stories such as those presented in Table 8–13 based solely on linguistic stimuli and inference, the task is more natural and the use of the form is likely to be more appropriate.

CONCLUSION

The literature on trainer-oriented procedures makes two points quite clear. First, the procedures are highly effective in getting young children to produce new language forms. The generally positive out-

Table 8–13. A Method for Evoking the Use of Past Perfect Constructions in Contexts in Which the Use of the Perfective is Obligatory

Clinician:	Suzy liked to bake chocolate chip cookies. One day, she decided to make some. She mixed the batter and spread the cookies on the sheet. Then she put them in the oven and turned on the timer. When the timer went off, Suzy got a big surprise. There was smoke everywhere and the cookies were black! What had happened?
Child (or model):	She had set the timer wrong. She had left the cookies in too long. They had burned.
Clinician:	Basil, the dog, loved chicken. One day Karen decided that she would surprise the family with fried chicken for dinner. She laid the chicken on the table. Then, she remembered that she had no flour. She rushed off to the store in her car. When she returned, she was surprised to find that her chicken was gone. Can you guess what had happened?
Child (or model):	Basil had been hungry. He had jumped on the table and had eaten all of the chicken.
Clinician:	Mother gave Kathy and Cheryl some money to go to MacDonald's for lunch. She said, "Remember, eat what you want, but don't eat too much! And don't eat too quickly!" Kathy and Cheryl spent every bit of the money they had. Soon, they were back home. Later, that day, Kathy and Cheryl went to their mother and said, "We don't feel good. Our stomachs hurt." I wonder what had caused their stomach aches.
Child (or model):	They had not listened to their mom. They had eaten too much. They had eaten too quickly.
Clinician:	Amy loved dogs and cats and all animals. One day, she was driving in her car. Suddenly, something small and black was in the way. Amy turned the car quickly and crashed into a tree. Do you know what had happened?
Child (or model):	Maybe she had seen a cat. Maybe a dog had run into the street. Maybe she had seen a skunk!

comes resulting from these procedures makes me quite reluctant to give them up completely. Second, children who perform well in highly unnatural traditional clinic contexts often fail to use their target forms in realistic communicative situations. This finding makes it clear that we cannot remain content with the trainer-oriented procedures that are currently available.

Some modifications in the procedures must be made so that the activities in which children use the target forms in the clinic do not differ so dramatically from the functional communicative contexts in which the forms are required. I have presented seven principles that, if carefully attended to, would seem to help us achieve this goal. If these principles are applied, there is a cost: The number of responses that a child produces in the types of activities I have suggested is not nearly as great as the number that can be evoked in traditional operant or modeling training paradigms. It is at this point that theory becomes very important. If a clinician believes that language learning is a function of practice and reinforcement, application of these principles may not be too appealing. If a clinician believes that learning is likely to be the result of observing language in action, doing the job it is meant to do (i.e., transmit meaning), applying these principles to existing procedures would seem to have considerable promise. Only time and careful experimentation will enable us to know this for sure.

Chapter 9

Training Content-Form Interactions: Child-Oriented Procedures

In trainer-oriented approaches, the trainer is in virtually complete control of the language learning situation. She has established notions about what the child should learn, how it should be learned, and where it should be learned. She controls the stimuli that the child must attend to, how the child must respond, and the specific contingencies that follow correct and incorrect responses. In at least some sense, the mechanisms of learning are placed in the hands of the trainer, not the child.

All of the trainer-oriented methods involve attempts to make *direct* and *specific* changes in the child's language abilities. This attitude toward intervention is at least partly a reflection of our traditionally neutralist view of language impairment. That is, the *child* has a problem with specific aspects of *language* and, therefore, it is these *specific language behaviors* that must be affected directly through intervention. This viewpoint is highly intuitive, and trainer-oriented methods, which are highly compatible with it, represent what Watzlawick, Weakland, and Fisch (1974; cited in Hubbell, 1977, 1981) call attempts at a *first-order change.* If our attempts at training a particular language form through trainer-oriented methods fail, we may modify our intervention plan, but our conviction to the theoretical notions underlying the procedures we are using (i.e., operant theory or social learning theory) remains firm and our general approach to such problems remains unchanged. For example, the modifications that we make might involve simplification of the stimuli presented, production of more models of the form for the child to hear, more careful patterning of the models we present, simplification of the target response, modification of the response contingencies, more frequent reinforcement of models for producing the correct targets, and so forth. In each of these cases, the relationship between child and trainer remains the same—the trainer is in control, and the child must comply.

By examining language impairment from a broader, normativist perspective, it can be seen that the child's difficulties with language do not exist in isolation. Indeed, they can only be manifested within a broader social framework that includes not only the child's behavior, but also the child's influence on the behavior of others. As others react to the child's behavior patterns, the child responds in turn. Through mutual adaptation, stable patterns of interaction between the child, her caregivers, teachers, friends, and so forth, are established. In discussing the social organization of the problems of a learning disabled child named Adam, Hood, McDermott, and Cole (1980) commented that

> Adam's learning disability is [as] much in the world as in his head, not just in the sense that the world is passively there as a medium of expression for the disability, but because the world can be described as a field of forces which organize Adam as a display board for the weaknesses of the system in which he is immersed. (p. 159)

The child's language trainers, family, and other significant individuals in her life, then, do not simply provide the social context within which the child's language impairment is exhibited; through their accommodation of their own behaviors to those of the child, they become a part of the child's problem itself. For example, Wellen and Broen (1982) observed that the older siblings of language impaired children were far more likely to answer questions that were addressed to their siblings than were the older siblings of two groups of language normal children. This finding does not indicate that the siblings of the language impaired children were wrong or bad; it is merely an illustration of one way in which members of the family tend to adapt to language impaired children. To the extent that these adaptations reduce the language impaired child's need to process information presented linguistically and to generate meaningful responses, such behavior may be a hindrance to rapid linguistic growth.

When a language impaired child is unassertive and produces relatively few initiatory conversational acts, and particularly if they are relatively unresponsive as well, adults seem to respond naturally in two different ways. In the case of Conti-Ramsden and Friel-Patti (1983), Marshal, Hegrenes, and Goldstein (1973), and Siegel, Cunningham, and Van der Spuy (1979), the parents tended to fill in the gaps, often with questions and commands, apparently in an effort to maintain some type of positive interpersonal contact with the child. When this happens, the child adopts the role of a junior partner in social interactions and her lack of assertiveness may be perpetuated. Another reaction to a child's relative lack of responsiveness that has even more alarming implications is the adult's reduction in stimulation and responsiveness to the child (Wulbert, Inglis, Kriegsman, and Mills,

1975). Without frequent positive interpersonal contact with significant members of the child's social environment, notable gains in language growth among children with language impairments are not likely to ensue.

Language clinicians are not immune to the natural tendency to make accommodations to the child's problem. In fact, the clinician who uses trainer-oriented methods exclusively (especially without some of the modifications suggested in Chapter 8) may cast the child into her familiar role as the responder and unwittingly nurture the child's tendency to perform in a passive or inactive manner.

If this account of language impairment as a complex transaction between the child and her environment (Bloom and Lahey, 1978; Hubbell, 1981; McLean and Snyder-McLean, 1978) is accurate, the social-conversational behaviors of the child's clinician, family, and significant others may play a role in sustaining the child's language difficulties. Fortunately, this account also suggests that these same individuals, by modifying their means of interacting with the child, can be positive influences in the child's language development processes. The objective of this type of *second order change* is not to teach specific language behaviors but to modify the relationship between the adult and child to one in which the child is viewed as an equal. As Hubbell (1981) puts it, "We change how we attempt to make change" (p. 254).

Through successful adjustments in the relationships between the child and significant members of her social environment, the frequency of positive, reciprocal communicative interactions between the child and her partners might be expected to increase. These positive interactions increase the number of opportunities for communication and provide the framework through which language development can proceed at an optimal pace (Hart and Risley, 1980). Importantly, taking this attitude toward intervention means that what is learned, when it is learned, and how it is learned is left in the hands of the child—hence, I refer to the procedures that result from this rationale as *child-oriented*. These procedures, which can be implemented during the routine daily activities of the child and family, fall at the opposite extreme from many trainer-oriented procedures on the naturalness continuum (see Chapter 4). In the next sections, I will discuss these procedures and evaluate the experimental efforts designed to test their effects on children's formal language growth.

FACILITATIVE PLAY

The most immediate objective of child-oriented intervention is to create a highly accepting and responsive environment in which the child is motivated to communicate spontaneously with her social partner. Facilitative play, in which the child is free to select the materials and the manner in which they are used, is usually chosen as the context in which child-oriented procedures are used. A description of the specific procedures used to facilitate interaction and, ultimately, language growth are described below.

Following the Child's Lead

The three fundamental steps in child-oriented approaches are to *wait* for the child to initiate some behavior, to *interpret* that behavior as meaningful and communicative even if it was not so intended, and to *respond* to the behavior in some communicative manner that is assumed to facilitate language development. Materials that are useful in activities believed to be appealing to the child should be available. The child is free to choose from among these alternatives. The activities in this type of intervention context are *autotelic*, or self-reinforcing, making extrinsic reinforcement unnecessary. The adult's role is one of a skilled observer, waiting for the child to initiate actions and presenting simple linguistic stimuli that are meaningfully associated with the child's actions and objects of attention. "The specialist does not manipulate the situation to elicit predetermined utterances from the child but rather enters into the learning situation by reacting to the child's freely chosen communicative and linguistic repertoire" (Weiss, 1981, p. 41).

Self-Talk and Parallel-Talk

Two verbal techniques that can be used during facilitative play with the child are *self-talk* and *parallel talk*. Van Riper (1963) described self-talk as "talk[ing] aloud to ourselves, verbalizing what we are seeing, hearing, doing, or feeling" (p. 146). This type of speech is useful for children who are extremely reluctant to interact, because it provides some model of the act of speaking, while making no demands on the child even to listen. The clinician's enthusiastic self-talk during highly animated play is often very effective in establishing interactive play between the clinician and the child. The potential of self- talk as a language facilitating procedure can be enhanced by observing what the child is doing, and then performing similar activities with similar materials. Self-talk under these conditions will refer to objects, actions, and relations that are highly similar to those on which the child has focused her attention. By paralleling the child's play in this fashion, the clinician can also communicate to the child that her selection of activities and active involvement with the available toys is acceptable and is viewed as positive from the clinician's perspective.

It is parallel talk, however, that has real potential to assist the child's language growth. In parallel talk, the clinician shifts from her own thoughts and actions to assertions about the actions and objects of attention of the child. There is little need for concern about getting the child to attend to intervention stimuli, because it is the child, not the clinician, who determines what those stimuli will be. Again, no demands are placed on the child to respond. By pairing language that is simple in grammatical and semantic detail with the child's actions, the clinician may assist the child in developing associations between words and their referents. Just as importantly, this procedure may stimulate the child's formulation and testing of hypotheses about the association between word combinations and the relations between objects, states, and relations in the nonlinguistic world. Perhaps the most vivid example of this technique that I have seen was reported by Belkin (1983) in her work with a 5 year old autistic boy who was functioning at the single-word level of production.

> Each time we went back to his classroom, David...put his eyes next to a crack in the wall and slowly moved along the wall, keeping close attention to the length of the crack. I also touched the crack, named it, and showed him other cracks, which I coded with the content categories *existence* and *recurrence,* as in "another crack," and *action,* as in "touch crack," respectively. In this manner, David's preoccupation with perceptual configurations, such as lines and lights, became a vehicle for demonstrating that I appreciated what was of interest to him and for helping him associate these figural preoccupations with linguistic form. (p. 138)

A further advantage of parallel talk is that by producing utterances highly related to the child's own interests, the clinician may be increasing the probability that the child will produce a spontaneous verbal response. Once the child is producing self-initiated utterances in this fashion, the clinician can make use of contingent verbal responses. By responding verbally to the child's self-selected verbalizations, the clinician may not only be helping to sustain the positive interaction between the child and herself; she may be exploiting an ideal language learning opportunity.

Expansions

Expansions are contingent verbal responses that repeat the child's prior utterance while adding relevant grammatical and, sometimes, semantic details. For example, the child might say "baby" or "sleep" or "baby sleep" after placing a doll in a crib. Examples of expansions to these utterances would be "The baby is sleeping," "The baby is asleep," or "You put the baby to sleep." The basic semantic intent of the child's utterance is repeated, and relevant details are added to transform the utterance into a semantically complete, grammatically well-formed utterance. Because the adult's utterance so closely matches the child's intents and interests, it should be easy for the child to comprehend. Under these circumstances, the child may be able to attend more completely to the semantic and grammatical details not found in her own utterance. Which of these details will be attended to most carefully will depend on a number of factors, most of which are internal to the child. The child may focus her cognitive resources on aspects of the content and form of the adult input that she is "ready to learn."

At the very least, expansions indicate to the child that the adult is listening intently and that the child's turns at speaking are worthy of consideration and acknowledgment. There is an interesting feature of expansions that may have important implications for language intervention. Young children with normal language are more likely to produce spontaneous imitations following adult utterances that are expansions of their own productions than following any other type of adult conversational act (Folger and Chapman, 1978; Scherer and Olswang, 1984). Thus, the use of expansions may also play a role in the child's development of appropriate ways of responding in a contingent fashion to partner verbalizations.

Expatiations

Expatiations are contingent responses to the child's utterances that extend some aspect of the child's meaning by contributing some new, but relevant, information. To illustrate the difference between expansions and expatiations, we can examine some possible expatiations to the "baby sleep" example used earlier. The clinician might say, "She is very sleepy/tired," "She needs a nap," "It's time for baby to go to bed" or any number of related sentences. The characteristic that is common to these responses is that each one presupposes the information provided in the child's production and then extends the topic in some meaningful way.

Such interactive episodes may have value for the child in at least two ways. First, the fact that the semantic features of the expatiation are closely related to the child's utterance may make it easier for the child to comprehend the words and relationships in the adult's sentence. If the child does not understand an aspect of the sentence, she may be highly motivated to search for a reasonable interpretation.

Thus, this method of responding to the child may foster an active search by the child for relationships between the adult's utterance (form) and meaning (content). Second, like expansions, this type of interaction may facilitate the child's awareness and appreciation of the reciprocal nature of conversation. By talking, the child gets other people to talk about topics that are of particular interest. In this way, expatiations give the child a sampling of discourse through the contributions of both social partners. In observational investigations of mothers and their children with normal language, expansions and expatiations are typically among the features of adult input that are most strongly correlated with indices of linguistic growth in children (Barnes, Gutfreund, Satterly, and Wells, 1983; Cross, 1978).

Recast Sentences

Recast sentences are really just a specific form of expansion. Instead of repeating the child's own sentence and filling in missing semantic and grammatical details, however, recast sentences change the basic sentence modality or voice of the original. For example, the child's utterance, cast as an affirmative, declarative sentence (e.g., "This dolly is sick"), might be recast as an interrogative (e.g., "Is she sick?") or even a negative interrogative (e.g., "Isn't she sick?"). In a similar fashion, active sentences (e.g., "The dog is eating the weenie") can be recast into the passive voice (e.g., "The weenie is being eaten by the dog"). The rationale for the use of these procedures is similar to those for expansions and expatiations.

Simplifying the Linguistic Complexity of Speech to the Child

There is little question that the adult's speech should be simplified along semantic and grammatical parameters to meet the child's communication needs. The key to such simplifications appears to be an honest attempt by the adult to communicate with the child (i.e., to carry on a conversation). If the adult attends closely to the child's nonlinguistic and linguistic behavior and responds to each in the ways described earlier, the result will be speech that is semantically and grammatically much simpler than would be characteristic of speech to older children and adults.

At this time, there is very little evidence to suggest whether talk to language impaired children should consist of very short, simple utterances that lack certain grammatical details (e.g., "the baby sleep," "sleep in bed," "baby tired") or whether simple but grammatically well-formed utterances should be used. For two reasons, my own preference is to produce simple but grammatically complete phrases and sentences in speech to young children. First, the child's comprehension may well be greater than her production capabilities, and she may even *expect* to hear function words (auxiliary verbs, copulas, articles, etc.) in the adult's speech (Duchan and Erickson, 1976). Second, children who have no knowledge of certain grammatical functors are likely simply to filter them out, attending only to those parts of the sentence that have meaning for them (Snow, 1979). In other words, grammatical functors may be of use to some children in comprehending utterances. These children should not be short-changed. By the same token, these grammatical devices, when produced in simple sentences, are not likely to interfere with comprehension for children who have no knowledge of their meaning or use.

Build-ups and Breakdowns

Two simple techniques that can be used to heighten the saliency of grammatical classes (noun phrase, verb phrase, prepositional phrase, etc.) and the boundaries between classes, as well as to facilitate the child's comprehension of adult sentences, are called *build-ups* and *breakdowns* (Weir, 1962). Using these methods, the clinician takes the child's utterance, expands it (i.e., "builds it up"), then breaks it down into its individual constituents and builds it up again in a highly repetitive fashion. The following verbal interaction is an illustration of how the clinician can respond to the child using semantically and grammatically complete constructions and simultaneously "put the internal structure of the sentence on display."

Child: Baby sleep.
Adult: Yeah, the baby is sleeping.
        She is sleeping in the bed.
        Sleeping in the bed.
        In the bed.
        The baby is sleeping in the bed.
Child: Sleep in bed.

This technique will not be effective for a child whose attention is drifting rapidly from one activity to another. Fortunately, most young children enjoy the repetition of actions that they find interesting, and they will attend to favorite objects for periods of at least several seconds, especially when an important adult shows an interest. The occasional use of build-ups and breakdowns provides a potentially powerful means of exposing the child to new linguistic forms that are closely related to their own objects of attention and self-selected topics of conversation. Cross (1978) found that maternal partial repetitions (i.e., breakdowns) of their own utterances were significantly associated with accelerated growth among young language normal children.

EVALUATION OF THE PROCEDURES

A number of authors have described and recommended the use of child-oriented procedures as I have presented them in this section with language impaired children (DeMaio, 1984; Fey, Newhoff, and Cole, 1978; Hubbell, 1981; Nelson, Carskadden, and Bonvillian, 1973; Seitz and Hoekenga, 1974; Seitz and Marcus, 1976; Seitz and Riedell, 1974; Van Riper, 1963; Weiss, 1981). Unfortunately, the empirical foundation on which the use of the procedures rests is painfully weak.

Of the reports just cited, only those of Seitz and Hoekenga (1974), Seitz and Marcus (1976), Seitz and Riedell (1974), Nelson and co-workers (1973), and Weiss (1981) have been in any sense experimental. Only the results of the use of these procedures on children's language form will be discussed in this chapter. More details on the changes in social-communicative behaviors resulting from these procedures are reported in Chapter 11.

Seitz and Hoekenga (1974) trained the procedures to the parents of three retarded children, at least two of whom also presented behavior problems (see Chapter 14 for more details on parent training). They also included in their study one child of normal intelligence whose parents believed that the child was retarded. The children and parents were seen 3 days per week for 8 weeks. All of the children showed increases in MLU at the posttest. The increases ranged from 0.45 to 2.26, with a mean of .9 morphemes.

Gains in utterance length have not always resulted from this form of treatment. Seitz and Riedell (1974) used identical procedures with a severely retarded child and her parents. Following the 8 week program, this child demonstrated no gains on the only dependent measure of linguistic form, MLU. At a second posttest, 3 months after program completion, the child's MLU was actually lower than on the pretest and first posttest by nearly 50 per cent. The child's mother claimed that the child's performance on the second posttest did not capture the child's gains in language skills, however. More importantly, it appeared that by the time of the second posttest, the mother had dropped many of her facilitative behaviors in favor of her original constraining style of interaction. Seitz and Marcus (1976) investigated the use of facilitative play procedures with the mother of a 20 month old, multiply handicapped child. As a result of treatment, this child exhibited minimal gains in language form, although some notable gains were observed in the child's amount of talking and in overall responsiveness to the parent.

The subjects who participated in the investigation by Nelson and co-workers (1973) were children with normal language between 32 and 40 months of age. These children were seen in 20 minute sessions for a period of 13 weeks. The average amount of time in intervention was 425 minutes. In the sessions, the children were free to play with and talk about a variety of different play materials. One group of children received no other treatment. Expatiations that were contingent on the children's utterances were presented to the children in a second group. The third group of children received contingent expansions and recast sentences. The results on posttesting indicated that the children in this latter group produced significantly more verbs and more auxiliaries than the children in the control group. They also performed significantly better on a sentence imitation test than the controls. No other significant differences were observed. Because these language normal children were already at fairly high levels of language development, it can only be speculated how effective the procedures might be with older, language impaired children.

In the Weiss investigation (1981), language clinicians used child-oriented procedures in the classroom for one-half day, on a daily basis. Although children described as "language handicapped" were included, it is impossible to tell how many were involved and what their problems were from this report. The procedures were administered to all children, including those who were linguistically normal. There is no report of the pre- or posttreatment performance of the language impaired children on the dependent variable, an adaption of the Fluharty Screening Test for Preschool Children (Fluharty, 1974), so there is no way to determine that the language impaired children made any significant gains at all. The children in classrooms who received treatment had significantly higher Fluharty scores than the children in control classrooms at posttesting, however. Furthermore, a longitudinal investigation suggested that fewer children in the experimental classrooms required special services for language-related problems over the next 3 year period. This report indicates that child-oriented procedures may be useful as a preventive measure when applied indiscriminately to large groups of young children. However, the extraordinarily high rates in the control group of children who required speech-language services (22 to 33 per cent over the 3 year period) suggests that some sampling error might be responsible for these differences. Several methodological problems make it difficult to draw any meaningful conclusions from this study regarding the efficacy of these procedures with language impaired children.

In sum, child-oriented procedures have not been put to an adequate test to determine their effectiveness in facilitating children's development of content-form interactions. The results of reports that are available are mixed. In addition, reports of successful interventions are fraught with methodological problems. For example, in the successful interventions of Seitz and Hoekenga (1974), pre- and postintervention evaluations involved only one brief interaction between parent and child. This type of design is not adequate to test the effectiveness of the procedures. We have observed an enormous amount of inter-session variability in the measures we select to assess the interactive behaviors of parents. The variability of measures such as MLU for children has been well documented. It is possible then, that the measurable changes in parent and child behavior following treatment represent not reliable and durable patterns of growth but spurious variability or simply the effects of the fact that, with practice, parents often begin to feel more comfortable in the clinic while being videotaped. Studies that use large subject populations or that make use of appropriate baseline procedures are needed badly. For example, a replication of the investigation by Nelson and colleagues (1973) using language impaired children would be especially informative.

It is generally expected that gains made in spontaneous talking and utterance complexity resulting from these nonconstraining types of treatments in naturalistic contexts will be generalized to a number of social contexts. Similarly, it might be anticipated that new behaviors acquired in naturalistic contexts will be durable and that children in this type of program will continue to develop over long periods of time. However, I am not aware of any study that has sampled the child's postintervention behavior in sufficient detail to conclude that either of these assumptions is true. Even for those cases in which positive results were obtained, it is not illogical to suspect that the child's gains will be specific to those persons who make frequent use of facilitative play procedures and deal with the child on a more equal interpersonal level. Continued growth would seem to depend on the stability of the child's use of more assertive conversational behaviors and on the parents' continuation of the facilitative play procedures.

CONCLUSION

Because there is only weak empirical support for the efficacy of child-oriented procedures as facilitators of the acquisition of new content-form interactions, some clinicians may wish to dismiss the procedures entirely for the purpose of attaining basic goals dealing with language form. Others, such as myself, may be willing to hang on to the procedures on the grounds that even though they have not been shown to be effective, neither have they been shown *not* to be effective.

Those who find the procedures to be of some potential use and those who do not probably hold markedly different theoretical positions on the nature of language learning. For example, child-oriented procedures free the child from adult constraints on the child's learning and allow the child to direct available resources toward features of the adult linguistic input that she may be ready to learn. The procedures are highly compatible with the views that the child is an active participant in language learning and that learning processes within the child are responsible for language growth. Therefore, overt responses produced by the child are not required to assume that learning processes are operative. Because the adult's language is closely matched to the child's self-selected actions, objects of attention, and conversational topics, the relevant content–form–use interactions presented in the adult input should be maximally transparent and, therefore, learnable for the language learning child. These are the basic assumptions of the interactionist position presented in Chapter 1. The procedures are also easily rationalized with the principles of social learning theory and transformational generative grammar. In fact, Weiss (1981) claims that her child-oriented intervention model is "based on the innatist theory of language learning" (p. 40).

There is no question that behaviorists would have an explanation from within operant theory if these procedures were shown to be successful. After all, the adult presents stimuli, the child responds, sometimes imitatively, and the adult provides contingencies in the form of attention and topic relevant utterances that may serve to reinforce the child's productions. But I don't believe that a behaviorist would ever have designed these procedures, nor do I believe that the procedures would be highly recommended as an effective and efficient teaching strategy. We really have a theoretical clash here, and clinicians who are well ensconced in operant procedures are likely to have great difficulty with the idea that no specific language structures are selected as goals. Furthermore, they will probably be very uncomfortable with the notion of refraining from demanding responses from the child and from providing tangible reinforcement for "correct" responses (see, for example, the discussion of incidental teaching and the mand-model procedure in Chapter 10). Since responses and their consequences represent major mechanisms of learning, under what other conditions could learning be assumed to be occurring? This is a good example of how our theoretical positions regarding learning influence not only what we do in intervention contexts but also how we evaluate the intervention efforts of others.

To sum up, I believe—largely on theoretical rather than empirical grounds—that child-oriented procedures belong in the language clinician's armamentarium for the purpose of training content-form interactions. They may be especially useful when general gains in language comprehension are the focus of the intervention program. It is interesting that of all of the studies that have examined the use of child-oriented procedures, only the investigation of Weiss (1981) has used a measure of comprehension to evaluate the results.

This type of approach is not for every child, however. For example, we have used these procedures with many active conversationalists. In my experience, when these children are already communicating successfully without using the grammatical detail expected for children their age and their level of cognitive abilities, they need more carefully patterned stimuli and more direct teaching to acquire rapidly the knowledge that grammatical details are important in communication and must be used. This is not to say that these children cannot learn through a child-oriented approach. It is simply a suggestion that they may learn more quickly through other teaching methods (cf. also Hubbell, 1977). Second, in many cases parents and family members are already interacting with the child in a nonconstraining and highly responsive manner. In other words, the child is already being exposed to what might be viewed as ideal language models and contingent responses. It is difficult to see how an intervention plan based on these procedures will add significantly to the language facilitation that the child has been receiving and to which she has not responded adequately (Leonard, 1973).

On the other hand, if the acquisition of language content-form interactions is a basic goal for children who are moderately passive or inactive in conversations, these procedures might have a greater and more durable impact than most types of trainer-oriented procedures. These children often profit from experience in contexts in which they can assert themselves without fear of reprisal. The learning context becomes not only a place where the child is exposed to meaningful stimuli to facilitate learning but also a place where newly acquired language forms can be attempted and practiced. Perhaps even more importantly, because these procedures can be used easily in a variety of contexts, caregivers and siblings trained in their use can take the role of interventionist throughout the child's day. *Every* context becomes a learning context.

I am in agreement with Hubbell (1981), who suggests that the environment created by a clinician and family who use child-oriented procedures may be helpful as a milieu in which children can practice new content-form interactions recently trained through other clinical methods. That is, it is possible to train a specific goal using some trainer-oriented approach and then provide a less structured context in which the child is free to use the new form. As Craig (1983) notes, however, the theoretical clash alluded to earlier exists in this situation. Because of their basic theoretical assumptions, some clinicians are simply not comfortable with waiting for the child to use a new structure in a truly meaningful context, and they hasten to evoke the target response from the child, designing activities and using prompts that are not compatible with the naturalistic design of a child-oriented approach.

Because no specific goals of language content and form are addressed with child-oriented procedures, it is difficult to document progress and demonstrate conclusively that progress is the result of the training procedures. That is, if specific target, generalization, and control goals of language form are not selected, and if broad changes across a number of areas of linguistic performance are expected, a multiple baseline design such as that described in Chapter 7 cannot be implemented. This should not preclude use of the procedures with the intent of facilitating the child's comprehension and use of new language forms. It should make the clinician reasonably cautious in claiming that her program was responsible for the child's language gains, however. To offset this problem somewhat, it is absolutely essential that fully adequate pre- and posttreatment baselines on the child's behavior (and on the parents' behavior if they are being trained as interventionists) are collected. It is also helpful if individuals who do not participate in intervention are responsible for obtaining the baseline information. These steps help the clinician to document the claims that the child's posttreatment gains are actually the result of intervention.

Chapter 10

Training Content-Form Interactions: Hybrid Intervention Approaches

One of the most readily identifiable problems with most trainer-oriented approaches is that they are not ecologically valid (i.e., activities in which the procedures are used are typically very low on the naturalness continuum). The result has been that content-form interactions that are acquired in clinical contexts too frequently are not generalized to social contexts outside the clinic. Child-oriented approaches reflect a quantum leap in naturalness from many trainer-oriented approaches, and they occupy the opposite extreme on the continuum in Figure 4-3. New language forms acquired within these learning situations are probably more likely to be used by the child in functional communicative contexts. As pointed out in Chapter 4, however, naturalness is a positive aspect of an activity only to the extent that procedures implemented within the activity are successful in helping the child reach stated goals. For at least some children, the lack of focus on a set of specific goals within child-oriented approaches may reduce the overall effectiveness of the procedures. In these cases, intervention approaches that fall somewhere between the two extremes may be most beneficial.

What I refer to as *hybrid approaches* are attempts by clinicians to develop intervention activities that are highly natural and, at the same time, provide the clinician with opportunities to make use of procedures that will maximize the speed, durability, and generalizability of language learning. There are three characteristics common to most of the hybrid approaches to be discussed in this section. First, the clinician will have at least one and, typically, several specific goals (e.g., agent–action, action–object, attribute–object, object–place). These goals will be selected through a careful consideration of the same factors discussed in detail in Chapters 7 and 8. Second, the clinician will select activities and materials that appear to be highly conducive to the spontaneous use of utterances containing the content-form interactions identified as goals. Third, the clinician will modify her own language not just to reflect the communicative needs of the child but also to emphasize the use of the child's target forms.

PLANNING ACTIVITIES—MODIFYING THE ENVIRONMENT TO MOTIVATE THE CHILD TO USE SPECIFIC TARGET FORMS

Before discussing individual hybrid approaches, some elaboration on the ways in which the clinician can manipulate the environment to her own and the child's advantage is in order. All manipulations are designed to encourage the child's use of language that obligates a specific target form.

In the example below, the specific goal for one child, Kate, is the use of "where" questions to request action from the partner (e.g., "Where is my paint brush?"). Note how the clinician arranges both the linguistic and nonlinguistic contexts to create a naturalistic situation in which a "where" question would be highly appropriate. The clinician has already told the group of four children that they are supposed to "draw a pretty picture for Daddy."

Adult:	Erin, here is your paper.
	Jeanette, here is your paper.
	Kate, here is your paper.
	That's all I have. Erin, where is Kerry's paper?
Erin:	(Looking for paper) Don't know.
Adult:	Jeanette, where is it? Where is Kerry's paper?
Jeanette:	I can't see it.
Adult:	Where could it be? (Gestures to Kate, indicating that the paper is on an adjacent table) Kate, where is it?
Kate:	(going to get paper) On the table.
Adult:	Oh, thanks, Kate. Okay, here's a red crayon for Kerry. Here's one for Erin. Here's a red one for Jeanette. (Looks at Kate, empty-handed)

The child is likely to be highly motivated in this type of context to initiate a communicative bid (e.g., "Where's my crayon?")—and this is the moment at which the clinician steps in with the procedures of her choice. It is important to note that the targeted language that is required in this situation is not needed just for its own sake; it is language used during the course of attaining some higher goal—in the example given, drawing a picture.

Planning this type of activity and taking advantage of every possible opportunity to make meaningful use of a target structure is not an easy task, and it requires a good deal of skill that comes with practice and lots of "hit and miss" efforts. The success of hybrid procedures really hinges on the clinician's ability to create real needs to communicate in naturalistic contexts, however. Lucas (1980) describes the clinician in this role as a "saboteur."

> The adult becomes a saboteur rather than a doer for the child. As a saboteur, the adult changes the nice, organized environment into one that needs constant verbal interaction. Only possible verbal solutions provide pleasant consequences. The following items and events suggest ways to develop an environment of problems that need verbal solution: taped together scissors, plugged glue bottles, empty or dried-up pens, broken pencil leads, coat sleeves turned inside-out by the morning aide when the children aren't watching, not enough chairs, not enough snacks, cups with holes in the bottom, missing toys, flat balls, short jump ropes, missing colors or paints, not enough paper, no tacks for hanging pictures, tables with missing legs, water faucets turned off tightly, baseballs without bats or bats without baseballs, etc. (p. 213)

Constable (1983) notes the importance of selecting activities with which the child is familiar. In these activities, the child will have a *script* (Nelson and Gruendel, 1979; Nelson, 1982). As discussed in Chapter 8, scripts are mental representations of events and the temporally and spatially related acts that typically characterize such events. For example, at birthday parties, there is a host and guests, certain games are played, the guests bring presents which are opened by the host, songs are sung, and most importantly, everyone gorges on cake and ice cream. If intervention activities for which the children and adults share a common script are selected, many manipulations of the script can be performed, creating the need for functional language. Constable (pp. 109–112) breaks down the activities such as those suggested by Lucas (1980) into four guiding strategies that can be used to manipulate the nonlinguistic environment.

Violation of Routine Events. In this strategy, a familiar step in an activity is omitted or performed incorrectly. For example, popcorn is placed in a popper that contains no oil and has not been plugged in, and the clinician says, "Now let's watch it pop!" Another example might involve trying to make a cookie mix without water or pouring a bit of the mix on the table with no bowl. It takes a very passive or inactive child not to take issue in some way to these actions.

Withholding Objects and Turns. The example given earlier involving the missing crayons to evoke a "where" request is a good example of this strategy. The child must perform some type of conversational act (request for attention, action, information, statement, etc.) to get a turn or an object that is crucial to completing some larger task.

Violation of Object Function or Manipulation. Using this strategy, the clinician may have difficulty drawing because she is using the wrong end of the pencil. Or the bowl may be upside down as the clinician directs the child to pour in the cookie mix. A variation might be to say, "We need something to put the mix in." The clinician might then remove a shoe as if she had struck on a convenient solution to the problem.

Hiding Objects. We have found that we can hide many objects that are needed to complete a task, such as making juice or preparing for snack, with excellent results. If a withheld object is hidden, and the clinician acts as if she does not know the location, guessing games requiring highly functional use of question forms are fun and useful (e.g., "Where is the juice?" "Is it in the drawer?" "Did you look in the refrigerator?") For children at higher stages of development, guessing can take on more complex forms (e.g., "I think it's in the cupboard," "I wonder if it could be in that bag").

The reader is referred to Chapter 8 (pages 168 to 187) for other strategies involving manipulation of the linguistic (e.g., false assertions) and nonlinguistic context that should prove useful in planning naturalistic activities for hybrid procedures. Only one of these techniques warrants further elaboration here. In a reasonably naturalistic context that has been designed so that the need for the child's target structures arises frequently, the child is likely to produce many utterances that either contain the target form or obligate its use. The clinician can respond to these utterances by picking up materials similar to those of the child and recreating an event similar to that originally encoded linguistically by the child. This new event then sets the stage for either another, similar response by the child, a model of the correct response by the clinician, or both. In the following example, responsive and assertive acts encoding stative relations were targeted for a 4 year old mildly mentally retarded child who was producing two-word constructions with considerable regularity.

(Juice is in plain view on the table)
Child: Want juice.
Adult: Oh, you want juice.   (gives juice to child)
        I want some juice too.   (drinks juice and picks up a toy bear)
        Look, *bear* wants juice.   (gives juice to bear and picks up a toy lamb)
        Oh, the *lamb* wants juice. (picks up a doll and cup)
        Ah oh!   (waits for child response)
Child: Girl juice.

This technique provided the child with several models closely related to her own and then set up a situation in which it could be expected that she would comment using the target structure. Even when the child does not respond to this type of manipulation with the target form, the models may be of some value in helping the child to learn to comprehend and use the structure. At this point in the episode, the clinician can intervene with any of the procedures to be discussed in the remainder of this chapter.

Despite the similarities among hybrid approaches, they differ from one another in the procedures used to facilitate the acquisition of content-form interactions and in the extent to which the clinician uses controlling behaviors. In other words, some approaches are more child-oriented than others. As we will see in the following discussion of several hybrid approaches, these differences result primarily from the developers' theoretical positions on learning.

FOCUSED STIMULATION

There are two key elements in what I refer to as *focused stimulation* approaches (see Leonard, 1981, for a slightly different definition). First, the child is not asked to respond at any time, although the clinician works diligently to arrange the verbal and nonverbal context in such a way that the child is motivated to produce utterances that obligate the use of the target forms. Second, the clinician produces a high density of the child's target forms in meaningful and highly functional contexts. The clinician's talk may focus on the environment (e.g., self-talk or parallel talk), it may be contingent on the child's utterances (e.g., expansions, expatiations, recast sentences), or the target form can be emphasized prior to *and* following the child's utterances.

The interaction in Table 10–1 exemplifies all aspects of this approach. The child's mother is used as a confederate in this particular example. The child receives frequent models and contingent responses that are focused on the topic that the child acknowledges in her first speaking turn. These responses are similar in form and content to the child's own utterance. The target form "can't" is presented in several word positions, which demonstrates its flexibility (as with other English auxiliaries), and the clinician takes advantage of sentence initial position to heighten the saliency of the target. All of these steps may help to direct the child's attention to the form of the adult's utterance.

This basic approach really concentrates more on comprehension than production, even though its success is often measured by the child's ability to make use of target forms following treatment. Winitz (1983) has called this intervention strategy *language facilitation through comprehension* and believes that this and other procedures that emphasize comprehension (Winitz, 1973) are likely to be more successful

Table 10–1. An Example of a Focused Stimulation Approach to the Teaching of the Use of "Can't" to Deny Propositions

Clinician:	I have a dog that can fly.—*False Assertion*
Child:	Doggie not fly.
Mother:	Doggies can't fly.—*Expansion*
Clinician:	Can't doggies fly?—*Recast*
Child:	No.
Clinician:	I think they can.
Child:	Nope. Bird fly.
Mother:	Doggies can't fly. Birds can fly.—*Expansion*
Clinician:	Oh, that's right. Doggies can't fly. They don't have wings

than other approaches. This is because they focus on the child's internal processing of meaningful linguistic stimuli, not just the spoken products of this processing.

Because the child is never required to respond, and because the activity used is typically play or some other autotelic activity, focused stimulation would appear to be highly ecologically valid. In other words, when the child makes use of the target form during the course of this form of intervention, she will do so while performing a self-selected conversational act in a highly functional communicative context. The basic difference between these and child-oriented procedures is the emphasis on a small set of preselected specific goals.

Leonard and co-workers (1982) used prototypical focused stimulation procedures to train words to 14 specifically language impaired and 14 language normal children, ages 2 years 8 months to 4 years 2 months and 1 year 5 months to 1 year 10 months, respectively. In addition to these experimental subjects, eight language impaired and eight language normal children were used as controls. These children were all using only one word at a time in their spoken communicative efforts, and they had vocabularies ranging from 25 to 75 words.

The intervention, which was provided only to the experimental subjects, consisted of a total of ten 45 minute sessions held three times per week. All sessions took place in the children's homes in an informal play context. Each child had a total of 16 target words, which were trained simultaneously, using a horizontal goal attack strategy. That is, there was no effort to give the child successive models of the same word. For each child, eight of the words represented objects and eight represented actions that were demonstrated by the interventionist. During the course of play with many toys, the interventionist presented the target object to the child and produced the appropriate label in final position of a sentence (e.g., "Here's the *shell*" or "Watch the baby *kneel"*). Each word was produced in this manner five times for a total of 80 (16 × 5) presentations per session.

As might have been expected, more words were comprehended ($\overline{X}$ = 7.14) than were produced spontaneously ($\overline{X}$ = 3.50) by the experimental subjects. The control subjects showed virtually no gains in comprehension or production over the intervention period, indicating that the gains of the experimental children were a result of the treatment. Somewhat surprisingly, the language impaired children acquired the same number of words as the language normal children in both comprehension and production. Furthermore, when the number of times that each word was produced spontaneously during the sessions was examined, it was found that the language impaired children used the target words as frequently as did the language normal children.

It is important that the children in both experimental groups comprehended and produced significantly more object words than action words. This suggested to Leonard and co-workers (1982) that, if speed of learning is a clinical priority, it may be more efficient to teach object words than action words, at least in the early stages of intervention. Another important finding of this study is that both the language impaired and the language normal children acquired more words made up of sounds that were present in their existing phonologies than words containing sounds not observed in their spontaneous speech prior to intervention. This observation indicates that clinicians who are planning goals for an early lexicon should focus on words containing sounds that the children already produce, when possible. On the basis of results obtained by Leonard and colleagues (1982), learning can be expected to proceed most rapidly on these items.

Willbrand (1977) used a focused stimulation approach to teach early two-word combinations to 10 preschool children, all but one of whom was specifically language impaired. Willbrand notes that these children "meaningfully responded to and related to objects and people in the environment similar to other children of their age level" (p. 39). This suggests that the children were reasonably active conversationalists. They were primarily single-word users at the start of the program and had at least 15 words. Each child received treatment for only one target at a time (vertical goal attack), and concentration on this target was continued until the child spontaneously used the target construction 10 times. Then new targets were added. The individual sessions lasted 45 minutes. During the sessions, the clinician produced frequent models of the child's target in a telegraphic fashion ("See book," "See Jimmy," "See Pookie," etc.). The child's spontaneous production of single words were expanded into the target structure (e.g., Child: "apple," Clinician: "See apple"). Uses of the target form were responded to with a smile and the word "Good."

Willbrand (1977) presents data from five individual children, each of whom made impressive gains in the spontaneous use of a handful of simple constructions. She also provides some descriptive information on all 10 children as a group. Although this information is limited, it appears that all 10 children made some progress using these procedures. This study lacks the extremely careful experimental control of the investigation by Leonard and associates (1982), however.

The children in the investigations by Leonard and co-workers (1982) and Willbrand (1977) investigations had normal hearing and, with the apparent exception of one of Willbrand's subjects, were of normal intelligence. However, the results of three other investigations indicate that early language learning in hearing impaired and mentally retarded children can also be facilitated using focused stimulation.

Culatta and Horn (1981) taught the mothers of four hearing impaired children, ages 18 to 26 months, to present their children with multiple exemplars for target words and to label each exemplar several times. For example, to teach "open," various containers with lids, drawers, and doors were presented. As each object was opened, the word, "open" was used in isolation (i.e., with no surrounding linguistic context). Six 5 minute intervention sessions, consisting only of this type of high density exposure to a word and its referents, were held daily in the home. The parents were also instructed to use the same procedures throughout the day in more naturalistic contexts. After the first week, all four children exhibited significant gains in the spontaneous use of the first target. None of the children made any spontaneous uses during probes for the second target word. The second target word was trained during the second week. Performance on the first word remained high after the second week, and spontaneous usage of the second target increased markedly for all of the children. This simple multiple baseline experimental manipulation enabled Culatta and Horn to claim, with justification, that their intervention was responsible for the children's gains. Just as importantly, each of the children learned numerous other words not assigned for teaching during the intervention period. For 96 per cent of these nonassigned words, the mothers reported that they trained the words using the focused stimulation procedure during their routine daily activities. This finding suggests that the new acquisitions were also the result of the intervention procedures.

McConkey, Jeffree, and Hewson (1979) trained parents to use focused stimulation with 10 preschool-aged children with developmental delays ranging in severity from mild to moderate. A specific goal (e.g., five vocabulary items or a particular two-word combination) was selected for each child. Simple activities, designed to be fun for the parent and the child, were demonstrated to the parents at each clinic visit. Each simple activity (mailing letters in a cardboard box, playing with dolls, hiding objects) required use of the child's specific language targets (e.g., "gone–[noun]," for the letter game; "here–[noun]" for the hiding game). Following the collection of baseline data in several play sessions in their homes, parents were instructed to use the target form in comments about the game and to follow the children's lead rather than using questions and commands to direct their attention and actions. A written outline of the goals and procedures was given to the parents and they were instructed to play the games for 10 minutes or so each day. Parents were encouraged to audiotape these sessions whenever possible. Follow-up contacts were arranged in the clinic every two weeks. Feedback on the parents' use of procedures was provided, and new activities were described at these times.

All of the children exhibited gains, and for seven of the children these improvements were dramatic. The greatest gains occurred in those situations in which both parents and, in one case, even a sibling played the games. The least significant progress occurred in one child who was the most significantly language impaired and in another child whose parents reportedly failed to play the games regularly and eventually dropped out of the program.

To assess more completely the influence of parental behaviors on the children's learning, McConkey and co-workers (1979) monitored the number of statements versus questions, commands, and other types of constraining verbalizations during the intervention sessions. Seven of the 10 parents whose language was analyzed exhibited significant increases in the use of statements (and, therefore, decreases in questions and commands) over the course of treatment. Thus, there is reasonable evidence to suggest that the parents implemented the procedures appropriately and that the children's improvements in their targeted verbal behaviors were the result of the parents' concentrated exposures of the target forms and of their new, less constraining style of play with their children. Two of the three parents whose rates of statements remained low took part in a special training session. Following this session, the parents' use of statements in the activities went up by roughly 60 per cent of their original usage as averaged across 10 home sessions. The authors claim that the children's use of language also improved during this time, although there is no clear evidence to support this claim presented in the report.

In a study of 4 to 6 year old children with Down's syndrome representing this same general type of hybrid approach, Cheseldine and McConkey (1979) simply provided parents with toys and other play materials and with a set of specific goals, such as a small set of verbs and simple word combinations involving these verbs. No formal instructions or demonstrations were given. Mothers and fathers were each asked to carry out and tape record at least four play sessions in the home over a period of 1 to 2 weeks. For three of seven children, large increases in the use of target verbs occurred during the four sessions. No changes were observed for the other four children. Interestingly, although the successful and unsuccessful parents used equivalent numbers of the target words during the sessions, the successful parents were far more likely to use them in short statements, whereas the unsuccessful parents tended to use the words in questions and demands for a nonverbal response. This finding suggested the possibility that simply exposing children to target forms was not enough; rather, successful intervention may depend on presenting examples of the target in nondirective forms of conversational acts.

Following their initial experiment, Cheseldine and McConkey (1979) involved one pair of unsuccessful parents in a 30 minute discussion with the clinician. The parents were provided with written and oral instructions to use the target forms in a nonconstraining, facilitative manner. Over four more sessions, these parents increased their use of statements dramatically and made commensurate reductions in their use of demands. Their child made a 300 per cent increase in the spontaneous use of the target words over these same sessions. The parents of two other children, who received no further training, exhibited no changes in their use of statements and demands over the four sessions. Their children made limited or no gains in their use of the target verbs. These results provide limited but encouraging support for the hypothesis that at least part of the effectiveness of focused stimulation is due to the nonconstraining conversational role adopted by the interventionist.

The studies presented above that have made use of focused stimulation represent efforts to facilitate acquisition of early developing language forms. In the two remaining approaches to be presented in this section, more complex language structures were targeted.

Culatta and Horn (1982) designed a focused stimulation procedure as a means of achieving generalization of forms already trained to a 100 per cent criterion using trainer-oriented procedures. The four specifically language impaired children who received treatment ranged in age from 4 years 6 months to 9 years 4 months. Each child had two different specific goals (copula "is," "will," "he," etc.). Performance in spontaneous speech on these goals varied from 20 per cent to 80 per cent correct in obligatory contexts.

Intervention was based on what might be called "scripted play." The clinician described a context and assigned the child a role to play within that situation. For example, the location might be a grocery store with the child as a clerk, or a plane crash, involving a toy plane and a number of toy passengers. Many of the techniques described at the beginning of this chapter were used to arrange for specific situations in which the child's target was obligated. For example, to evoke the copula "is," the child, playing the role of store clerk, might be handed the wrong item to put on the shelf (e.g., "This is not candy. This is a jar of pickles"). At another point, the clinician, acting as customer, might indirectly request information (e.g., Clinician: "I need the soap." Child: "It's on the last shelf"). Or the clinician might violate some part of the script (e.g., Clinician: "I have to stack these things correctly." Child: "This is not right. The cereal is upside down"). A sample transcript including these and other techniques taken from Culatta and Horn (1982) is provided in Table 10–2.

One other evoking strategy that appears in the table in the clinician's fourth turn diverges a bit from the notion that focused stimulation involves no direct requests for responses. Here, the clinician uses a direct request for a target response. I include Culatta and Horn's procedure as focused stimulation because (1) this strategy is used sparingly, (2) the requests are part of the activity, not simply requests for imitation, and (3) in every other respect, this approach to evoking responses is identical to other focused stimulation approaches.

One unique aspect of Culatta and Horn's approach (1982) deserves attention. At the beginning of intervention (Step 1), the clinician works assiduously to provide stimuli that will create a need for the target in 75 to 100 per cent of the child's productions. Similarly, the clinician models the target form in 75 to 100 per cent of her utterances. When the child omits the target or uses it incorrectly, expansions and expatiations containing the target are used. Thus, both linguistic and nonlinguistic contexts are focused almost exclusively on a single target response (vertical goal attack). Table 10–2 is an illustration of the clinician's behavior at Step 1. At Step 2, the clinician reduces the frequency of her models to about 50 per cent and arranges to evoke target utterances from the child in 50 to 75 per cent of the child's total utterances in the activity. Step 3 involves reduction of clinician models to roughly 25 per cent and decreases in the evocation of the child's target to 25 to 50 per cent of the child's responses. Finally, in Step 4, the clinician uses the target only as the need for it occurs naturally, and she creates the need for the child to use the target less than 25 per cent of the time. Thus, the child is gradually required to produce utterances containing the target form amid more and more distraction from other linguistic and nonlinguistic stimuli. Step 4 approaches a naturalistic conversational context in which the need for any particular language form will arise fairly infrequently.

Table 10–2. An Example of a "Focused Stimulation" Intervention Approach*

A recreated plane crash was used to evoke the copula in this session. The props included a toy plane and truck and an assortment of dolls and animals. The clinician initially asked the child to identify which of the dolls were passengers and which were airline workers. After the passengers boarded, the clinician made the plane crash during takeoff, which required the child to identify the injured passengers and locate first aid equipment.

Clinician	Child
1. We're operating an airplane. Some of these people are passengers. Some are workers. It's time for the passengers to get on the plane. Is Mickey Mouse a passenger or a worker? Mickey *is* a passenger. Elephant *is* a worker. This girl *is* a passenger. This boy *is* a worker. He *is* the ticket taker. What about the giraffe?	
	1. Giraffe is a passenger. Here monkey. . . . Monkey is a passenger. Tommy a worker, my worker.
2. Tommy *is* your worker. Oh good. He can serve coffee and pop to the passengers. Here, Mommy *is* a passenger. She *is* going to Florida. Dog *is* a passenger too.	
	2. Cat is a passenger. This is a passenger. This dog is a passenger. This dog is an airplane worker. He's gonna take tickets.
3. Everybody's on the plane. The plane *is* taking off. (The clinician makes the plane crash and scatters the passengers around the room.) Some of these passengers may be hurt. We gotta find the hurt ones. Oh no, elephant *is* hurt.	
	3. Mickey hurt.
4. Mickey *is* hurt, too? Tell the pilot. Mickey *is* hurt.	

*Step 1 from Culatta, B., and Horn, D. (1982). A program for achieving generalization of grammatical rules to spontaneous discourse. *Journal of Speech and Hearing Disorders, 2*, pp. 174–181. Reprinted with permission.

Intervention sessions in Culatta and Horn's program (1982) were held twice weekly for 45 minutes each. The criterion for moving from step to step was 9 correct out of the first 10 responses for two consecutive sessions. This criterion was reached at Step 4 for all four children on both targets in 19 to 28 sessions. Furthermore, samples of the children's spontaneous speech that were collected during play following treatment indicated that the children maintained these high rates of accuracy in an even more naturalistic situation.

It should be kept in mind that the children used in the Culatta and Horn investigation (1982) were already producing their target forms at fairly high rates of accuracy. Although the use of a multiple baseline procedure provides some assurance that the rapid progress observed would not have resulted without some generalization treatment, it is not clear whether the children would have mastered these particular targets on their own over a slightly longer period of time. What is of major importance to us here is that this intervention approach does indeed appear to speed *mastery* of individual language targets.

The last investigation to be reported in this section warrants mention because it relates to the issue of focused stimulation as an approach to training the acquisition of complex language forms. Unlike the other studies, however, Nelson (1977) included only language normal children (aged 28 to 29 months) in his attempts to facilitate acquisition of complex verb forms and complex questions. The verb forms were the auxiliary "will," the use of conditional verb forms (e.g., "could," "would"), and the use of the past tense in sentences containing two main verbs (e.g., "You ran the race and won"). Question forms included tag questions (e.g., "He's silly, isn't he?"), wh-negative questions (e.g., "Who doesn't want one?"), and other negative questions (e.g., "Can't you get it?"). Six children were assigned to the verb group and received stimulation only on the verb targets. Another six children received stimulation only on target question forms. Only five 1 hour intervention sessions were employed over a 2 month period. All sessions took place in the children's homes. The interventionist modeled target utterances with extremely high frequencies (well over 100 per session) and responded to the children's productions with recast sentences, where possible. The results, based on the children's nonimitative productions during the fourth and fifth intervention sessions, indicated that all six children in the verb group had learned one or more verbal targets and only one child had acquired one of the question forms. The findings for the children in the question group paralleled these results. All of these children acquired spontaneous use of at least one question target and only one child acquired any of the nonstimulated verb forms. It is not clear from this report how productive any of the new verb forms were for the children, however. It is possible that these gains represented the acquisition only of highly restricted context-specific language forms. Nevertheless, the observed pattern of results is a rather compelling demonstration of the potential of these methods for facilitating the acquisition of complex language forms.

Focused stimulation, as defined here, seems to have a very broad application in terms of both the content-form interactions that can be facilitated and the types of children who may be able to benefit from the procedures. It has been used to facilitate the acquisition and mastery of lexical, early relational, and more complex syntactic forms to normal, specifically language impaired, mentally retarded, and hearing impaired children across a broad age range. Belkin (1983) reports successful use of the approach with emotionally disturbed children, as well, although she presents no quantification of her clients' improvements. There is little question that the gains in complex language structures observed by Nelson (1977) would not occur as rapidly among populations of language impaired children. Notwithstanding this fact, the existing experimental support for stimulation techniques with language impaired children indicates that their use in attempts to facilitate the development of highly complex language forms among language impaired children is very much in order.

The approach is strongly focused on comprehension, and because the language stimulation is carefully structured to occur in meaningful contexts, facilitation of functional comprehension skills is a likely outcome of this form of intervention (Leonard et al., 1982). Even when no demands are placed on the child to respond, however, at least some language impaired children seem to use their new acquisitions with frequencies as great as those of language normal children with similar formal linguistic abilities (Leonard et al., 1982).

VERTICAL STRUCTURING AND EXPANSION

In focused stimulation approaches, the clinician interacts with the child in an activity that, although contrived, is still high on the naturalness continuum. Furthermore, there are no efforts to get the child to respond verbally to questions and other directives. The procedures presented in this section are similar to those used in focused stimulation, but the clinician presents the stimuli under less natural conditions and produces requests routinely to get the child to make some initial response to those stimuli. Importantly, no effort is ever made to actually produce the *complete* target response.

Although *vertical structuring* of discourse occurs even in highly sophisticated conversations, it typically has been discussed as a language learning strategy at the early stages of learning (e.g., during the transition from single-word to two-word utterances). In these examples, the child produces a single-word utterance that is semantically incomplete. The adult then produces a contingent question requiring the child to fill in added information. When the child supplies this information, she has, in effect, produced a sequence of two semantically related words. The entire episode would look like the following:

Child: (pointing at a ball) Ball ⎯⎯⎯⎯⎯⎤
Adult: Yeah, where?   │
Child: Table. ◄⎯⎯⎯⎯⎯⎯⎯⎯⎯⎯⎯⎯⎯⎯⎯⎯⎯⎯⎯┘
Adult: Uh huh, the ball is under the table.

It is not clear that the child is actually aware of this relation at the time of her original utterance (i.e., she may be attending to the two objects and not the spatial relationship between the two). It should also be noted that this is a far cry from syntactic performance. But it is possible that this type of interaction between adult and child can foster the child's attention to semantic and syntactic relationships. Scollon (1976) speculated that these vertical discourse structures might provide a bootstrap for the child to begin producing multiword combinations to express semantic relations.

In the last line of the foregoing example, the adult adds another turn that may also have some influence on development. In this turn, the child's productions are combined under one intonation contour in a well-formed *expansion*.

Schwartz, Chapman, Prelock, Terrell, and Rowan (1985) designed an experimental investigation to test the influence of vertical structuring and expansion on the development of multiword combinations. Their subjects were six language normal children, aged 1 year 5 months to 2 years 1 month. The children had 26 to 79 words in their vocabularies, but careful testing indicated that they rarely or never used successive single-word productions (e.g., "ball", "go") or multiword productions.

The intervention period extended over approximately 3 weeks, during which 10 sessions were carried out. The target goals for the children were noun–noun constructions expressing several different semantic relations (e.g., agent–object—"baby cookie"). A total of 16 stimuli were presented in each session, eight using pictures depicting the target semantic relationships and eight that were enacted by an adult. The interesting approach used by these investigators is outlined in Table 10-3.

Schwartz and co-workers (1985) observed that children receiving this treatment performed significantly better on a 24 item posttest involving nontrained combinations ($\overline{X}$ = 3.0) than they had when the test was administered pre-experimentally. All but one of the children used more two-word constructions on the posttest than they had on the pretest. A control group of 11 children at the same stage of development who did not receive the treatment exhibited no significant differences in multiword performance on the posttest after the same time period. This suggests that gains in the experimental group were the consequence of the intervention procedures. Gains were small, but the intervention was brief and took very little time to administer.

Table 10–3. The Vertical Structuring (Plus Expansion) Procedure Designed to Facilitate the Development of Multiword Combinations*

1. The child is shown a picture depicting a semantic relationship or a relationship is demonstrated using objects.

2. The clinician directs the child's attention to the stimulus, if necessary (e.g., "Look" or "Look at this").

3. The clinician asks the child "What's happening?" or "What's this?" and waits for a response.

4. If the child produces the multiword target, another stimulus that may or may not reflect the same semantic relation is presented.

5. If the child does not respond or produces an unrelated utterance, the clinician asks "What's this?" or "Who's this?" while pointing at the referent for the first noun in the construction, and waits for a response. If the child responds correctly, the clinician confirms the response (e.g., "yeah," "yes," or "uh huh").

6. Regardless of the accuracy of the child's response, the clinician points to the referent for the second noun in the construction and asks a question designed to evoke this noun, (e.g., "Where's the ball?" or "What's the dog wearing?"). Again the clinician waits for a response.

7. The clinician acknowledges the child's response, if correct, and then expands the child's production into a well-formed utterance containing the semantic-syntactic relationship encoded vertically by the child (e.g., "Yeah, the ball is under the table" or "The dog is wearing a hat.")

*Based on Schwartz, R., Chapman, K., Prelock, P., Terrell, B., and Rowan, L. (1985).

The real question, of course, is whether the same procedures are effective with language impaired children. Fortunately, Schwartz, Chapman, Terrell, Prelock, and Rowan (1985) also viewed this question as important and sought to answer it in another investigation. The experimental subjects in this study were eight specifically language impaired children between the ages of 2 years 8 months and 3 years 4 months. These children had vocabularies ranging from 25 to 54 words and no multiword combinations in their spontaneous speech. Two language normal children at the same language level were used as controls. The procedures were identical to those shown in Table 10–3 and used by Schwartz and co-workers (1985). The results of this study were in the same direction as the original study, but the effects of training were even more pronounced for the language impaired children in this investigation than they were for the language normal children who received intervention in the first study! Although there was a good deal of variability among subjects, all but two subjects exhibited gains on the posttest of five or more multiword combinations, when compared to pretest performance. Interestingly, the only subject who produced no combinations on either test had the smallest vocabulary, consisting of only 25 words.

The methods of Schwartz and his colleagues include both vertical structuring and expansions. Therefore, it is impossible to determine which, if either, of these procedures was primarily responsible for the gains observed among the experimental subjects. There is some evidence that the investigators' expansions might have been the most significant aspect of the intervention design. For example, Hovell, Schumaker, and Sherman (1978) used a procedure highly similar to that of Schwartz, Chapman, Prelock, Terrell, and Rowan (1985), but no effort was made to establish a vertical structure from the child. As soon as the child produced the first word of a multiword target, the interventionist (the child's own mother) produced an expansion (e.g., Adult: "What's this?" Child: "Dog." Adult: "Big dog"). Verbal praise was offered if the child used the target word combination or if any part of the adult expansion was imitated. In other words, some overt attempt at reinforcement was made, but this was contingent on any response, not just the target. This procedure was successful in increasing the use of adjective–noun combinations by four 22 to 24 month old language normal children in response to pictures and the question "What is this?" Unfortunately, when the mother's use of expansions was terminated (i.e., during baseline), correct responding to probes returned essentially to zero. Furthermore, no instances of adjective–noun combinations were observed in the taped spontaneous conversations of these children with their mothers following treatment; however, each mother reported hearing an appropriate usage of the expanded combinations during nonrecorded spontaneous interactions. Although these results demonstrate the power of expansions, the extent to which they contribute to stable learning can be questioned.

A more clear-cut demonstration of the utility of expansions in language learning was presented by Scherer and Olswang (1984). These investigators first collected spontaneous speech samples from four 23 to 24 month old language normal children and their mothers. From these data, they established that spontaneous imitations of the children were more likely to occur following their mothers' expansions of the children's own utterances than under other conditions. This finding replicated the results of an earlier investigation of Folger and Chapman (1978). In other words, children are more likely to imitate adult expansions of their own utterances than other types of adult conversational acts.

Based on the results of the observational study, mothers were trained to use procedures that were similar to those of Schwartz, Chapman, Prelock, Terrell, and Rowan (1985) (see Table 10–3) with the exception that no attempt was made to establish a vertical structure.

Instead, the mothers presented the child with a picture, asked a question (e.g., "Who/What is that?"), expanded the child's response in a manner consistent with the child's multiword target, and waited for the child to imitate. Following imitations, the mothers said "yeah" or repeated the child's imitative production.

Each child had two targets that included two- or three-word semantic relations. It may be important that the children showed evidence of comprehension of all of their target structures even though they rarely or never produced them. Each target was worked on separately to make use of a multiple baseline experimental design. Treatment was administered in the home at least five times per week. The results of this carefully controlled study were that (1) spontaneous imitations were highly likely to occur following the mothers' expansions; (2) the onset of imitations of the targets occurred before the onset of spontaneous productions; (3) the children learned to use the targets spontaneously after as few as six sessions; (4) the use of imitation decreased following the onset of spontaneous productions; (5) generalization of the target semantic relations to nontrained stimuli occurred in most cases without additional training, and in other cases with minimal training; and (6) learning was a result of the intervention procedures.

Finally, there is some evidence that expansions may be effective in a more naturalistic format to facilitate the acquisition of early semantic and syntactic relations to language impaired children. Branston (1979, cited in Chapman, 1981b) used an expansion-based procedure to train a semantic relation to each of five developmentally delayed children who exhibited no use of their target prior to intervention. The procedure used was similar to that of Scherer and Olswang (1984) except that, instead of using pictures, the children were involved in activities in which the target semantic relations could be exemplified using objects and actions. The student teachers who participated in the training sessions manipulated the nonlinguistic context and asked questions requiring the use of one of the elements of a two-word relation. Then they expanded the child's production. After only 4 weeks of daily 20 minute sessions, the children showed significant increases in their spontaneous and imitative use of the target structures.

Wilcox (1984) used expansions in a very informal and nonconstraining play context to train "subject–verb–object" forms (e.g., "Monkey eat cookie") to a 3 year 8 month old language impaired boy. Using a multiple baseline design, the same procedures were then used to facilitate the child's use of "-ing" in the same types of constructions. Significant increases in the use of these behaviors were observed over a 7 week period.

Orazi and Wilcox (1982) used expansions in a successful effort to facilitate the use of subject-auxiliary (or copula) inversion in yes-no questions in plural and singular forms (e.g., "Is Stevie sick?" "Are the dogs hungry?"). The subjects were four children ranging in age from 3 years 5 months to 4 years 7 months. They were seen three times weekly in half-hour sessions. Following a maximum of 8 weeks of intervention, large gains were observed in these children's use of the auxiliary in both yes-no questions (target goals) and declaratives (generalization goals) in spontaneous speaking contexts. The greatest gains were noted for the inversion of subject and copula in yes-no questions. Only very small changes were noted in the use of the copula and auxiliary forms in wh- questions (e.g., "Where are they going?").

Taken together, the studies presented on vertical structuring and expansion indicate that these procedures can be highly effective, even when production of the complete target response is never required. Furthermore, with the exception of the study by Hovell and co-workers (1978), the only contingent feedback to the children was an expansion, an imitation, or a confirmation (e.g., "yes," "uh huh," or "yeah"). Although most of the procedures used in these studies called for special materials that were presented in fairly contrived contexts (e.g., pictures), the Branston (1979), Wilcox (1983), and Orazi and Wilcox (1982) investigations illustrate the utility of expansions in naturalistic contexts.

To date, vertical discourse structuring and expansion have been used effectively primarily to train early developing content-form interactions. Determination of the utility of these approaches in facilitating the acquisition of more complex forms must await further investigation. Certainly, the evidence presently available documenting the usefulness of recast sentences and expansions in training complex structures (Nelson, 1977; Nelson et al., 1973), along with the evidence on expansions for facilitation of early developing content-form interactions more than justifies these future clinical-experimental efforts.

INCIDENTAL TEACHING—THE MILIEU TEACHING MODEL

The next two approaches to be presented, *incidental teaching* and the *mand-model* procedure, are both based on operant principles of learning. They warrant careful attention by clinicians not only for their potential value as intervention approaches, but also as evidence that there is nothing about operant theory that obligates language clinicians to the use of highly unnatural and highly rigid drill-type activities. Although applied operant theorists are committed to procedures such as the use of imitative prompts and cues as well as some form of reinforcement, incidental teaching and the mand-model procedure make it clear that prompting and cuing can be done during the course of highly natural activities in which the child's reinforcement is a natural outcome of the communicative situation (see also Meline, 1980).

In the view of Hart and Rogers-Warren (1978), incidental teaching "integrates the best features of the training and talking environment. It structures the learning of language forms within the context of social communications. In this way, milieu teaching provides opportunities for the child to learn both 'what to say' and 'how to say it' " (p. 200). The approach was developed to provide a link between highly formalized, individual sessions and naturalistic communicative situations. The success of early implementations of the approach in facilitating generalization of language forms acquired through formal operant training programs led to attempts to use the same methods as a primary form of intervention.

The procedures, which are outlined in Table 10-4, are essentially the same as those used in the operant programs discussed in Chapter 8. According to Hart and Rogers-Warren (1978), the only mandatory components are found in the first five steps of the table. The following example illustrates this part of the approach.

(The teacher arranges the room so that paints, paper, and other desirable play materials are out of the children's reach but clearly visible.)

Child: (gesturing to the teacher to get the paint)

        (teacher walks to child and raises hands in a questioning way)—*Focused Attention*

Child: (looking at teacher) Paint.

Teacher: What kind?—*Question*

Child: Red paint.

Teacher: (giving paint to child) That's right. You want the red paint.—*Confirmation*

The remaining steps are optional, and they often have been reported to be required only in a limited way (Hart and Risley, 1974, 1975, 1980). These prompts virtually always will be necessary at least for a short period of time, however, if the intervention target is not a part of the child's current repertoire of language forms or if the child is not a highly active conversationalist. An example of the use of these prompts, in which the goal is a complex sentence containing an adverbial clause of purpose, is given below.

(The child reaches for blocks, then looks at the teacher, signalling for her to get the blocks.)

Table 10–4.   The Incidental Teaching Procedures of Hart and Risley

1. The clinician arranges the classroom or other context so that various objects that are desirable to the children are visible but out of reach.

2. The *child* selects the topic stimulus and initiates the interaction verbally or nonverbally.

3. If the situation is deemed appropriate, the clinician decides what language response to obtain from the child.

4. The clinician uses a cue to get an elaborated response containing the target form.
   a. The first approach used is always *focused attention,* which consists a physical approach toward the child, eye contact, or a questioning look. The clinician then waits briefly for a response.
   b. If no response is given to the focused attention, a general question is asked (e.g., "What do you want?" "What is that?" or "Why do you want that?").

5. If the child's response to the clinician's cues appropriately includes the target form, a *confirmation* of the child's response is provided. This confirmation will typically contain a *model* of the child's target form (e.g., "Oh, I see, you want the paint so you can make a picture").

6. If the child does not respond to the clinician's cues, or the response does not include an appropriate use of the target form, some form of prompt is provided.
   a. *A request for the target response* (e.g., "You need to tell me" or "Say the whole thing").
   b. *A request for a partial imitation* (e.g., "Say 'I want the paint so _____.' " Child: "I want the paint so I can make a picture").
   c. *A request for a complete imitation,* (e.g., "Say, 'I want the paint so I can make a picture' ").

7. If the child fails to respond correctly to the prompt, one more prompt is administered.

8. If the child responds appropriately, a confirmation is provided.

9. If the child still fails to respond, the clinician gives her what is wanted and tries to determine what cue is best for the next teaching situation.

Teacher: (looking at child)—*Focused Attention*
          What?—*Question*
Child: Want the blocks.
Teacher: What for?—*Question*
Child: Blocks.
Teacher: Say "I want the blocks so. . ."—*Request for Partial Imitation*
Child: So I can build.
Teacher: Say the whole thing.—*Request for Target Response*
Child: I want the blocks so I can build.
Teacher: Very good. You want the blocks so you can build. Here they are.—*Confirmation*

The greatest differences between incidental teaching and trainer-oriented operant approaches pertain to the locus of teaching. First, incidental teaching takes place in the child's classroom or home, during the course of everyday activities, not in the "sterile" clinic. The modeling of target stimuli and reinforcement of target behaviors occurs amidst a number of irrelevant stimuli (e.g., desks, chairs, the teacher, the room, etc.), as is the case in any speaking situation. This situation can be viewed as ideal, even from within operant theory. In operant terms, because irrelevant stimuli are free to vary under these more naturalistic conditions, no irrelevant stimulus is likely to gain stimulus control. Therefore, the child's use of a target behavior (say, agent–action–object) should be more apt to occur in the presence of relevant stimuli (e.g., the child sees a boy throwing a ball and says "Boy throw ball") and will not depend on the presence of stimuli that are irrelevant to the use of the target form.

Second, it is the *child*, not the clinician, who determines when a teaching episode will begin and what the consequences for the child's correct production will be. In the operant terms of the developers of the approach,

> . . .when a child initiates language use, he or she identifies what is, for him or her at the moment, a pre-potent reinforcer. The power of incidental teaching arises from its capitalization on this moment when a particular reinforcer . . . happens to be the strongest one in the context of the child because the child has chosen it in preference to everything else currently in the environment. (Hart and Risley, 1980, p. 430)

Problems with choosing an appropriate form of reinforcement for a particular child are solved by allowing the child to select the topics of her communicative attempts. Following production of an elaborated form, the child-selected reinforcer is provided.

Step 9 of the procedure, as outlined in Table 10–4, also represents a departure from traditional operant procedures. Unlike more formalized operant procedures that require a correct response before a reinforcer is administered, in incidental teaching, only two different prompts are attempted on any single teaching occasion. Following the second unsuccessful prompt, the child is given the object of her request, whether or not the target form has been produced correctly. Repeated efforts to get the child to use a specific target response are likely to reduce the moment's considerable value as a locus for learning and may even decrease the likelihood that the child will initiate future communicative efforts. Actually, this procedure is more in line with the functional basis of operant theory than more traditional operant-based approaches; that is, more attention is placed on the function of the child's communicative efforts than the linguistic form selected by the child.

The effectiveness of incidental teaching was first demonstrated by Hart and Risley (1968). The subjects were 15 preschool children, aged 4 to 5, from very low income families. Their receptive language skills were depressed slightly as judged from their mean Peabody Picture Vocabulary Test score of 79. The goal in this study was to teach the children the use of color adjectives during free play. The playroom was designed as described previously so that toys and materials could only be obtained through adult mediation. The use of the incidental procedures during two 30 minute free play sessions for a 19 day period led to dramatic increases from baseline performance in all of the children's use of color adjectives and color–noun combinations. More importantly, when the contingencies were changed so that the use of a color adjective was no longer required to obtain play materials, the use of color names and color–noun combinations did not return to baseline levels. According to Hart and Risley, this suggests that the contingencies in the natural environment were strong enough to maintain the behaviors developed through incidental teaching.

Hart and Risley (1974) replicated and extended the results of their earlier investigation. The subjects were 12 children from low-income families. In this study, children were first required to produce only a noun to obtain their desired play materials. Then procedures were implemented to get the children to elaborate on this nominal response. For example, following the child's production of a noun, the teacher might have asked, "What kind?" or an alternative might have been presented requiring the child to produce the entire noun phrase (e.g., "I have a blue crayon and a red crayon"). In the third phase of the experiment, children were required to explain the reason for their requests (e.g., "I want a car so I can play with it"). These responses were prompted with questions (e.g., "Why?" "What for?") and with requests for the target (e.g., "Say the whole thing"). These steps were spread over a 148 day school term. The results paralleled the first study. With each new contingency, the rate of production of target forms increased dramatically from baseline across all or most of the group involved. Importantly, these productions of targets were often new, previously unheard word combinations, indicating that some degree of creative usage of the target structures had been facilitated. These results for compound sentences were replicated in a study by Hart and Risley (1975).

Campbell and Stremel-Campbell (1982) provided evidence that incidental teaching can be used to facilitate the use of language forms by moderately mentally retarded children. Their two subjects were 10 and 12 years of age, and their target goals were the use of "is" and "are," first in wh- questions (e.g., "Where is my book?"), then in yes-no questions (e.g., "Is it time for math?"), then in statements (e.g., "That is fine with me"). All intervention took place in the classroom. One 15 minute session was performed daily during an academic task and another took place during a self-help task. Details on these tasks are very sketchily reported. The procedure was highly similar to that of Hart and Risley (1968, 1974, 1975) with the major exception being that, if the child used the target correctly, confirmation was presented in the form of verbal praise, repetition of the question, the answer to the question, and a token. If the child's attempt did not contain an appropriate use of the target, the child's question was expanded. If this expansion was correctly imitated, the child was given social praise, but no token. Otherwise, the clinician prepared for another teaching context.

As a result of this program, both boys showed rapid improvements in the use of "is" and "are" in wh- questions in the training contexts. In a nontraining free play context, however, production of the forms stabilized above 50 per cent only after 45 sessions for one boy and approximately 25 sessions for the other. Following training on wh-questions, neither child showed substantial and highly stable response generalization to the use of the target forms in yes-no questions or statements. Training of the forms in yes-no questions moved more quickly than wh- question training for both children, however. Only one child received training on statements, and the targets generalized to this context in free play more quickly than they did for either wh-questions or yes-no questions. The fact that structures trained in the classroom did not generalize quickly and completely to free play contexts calls to question the assumption made by some that generalization is not a crucial issue when using "naturalistic" teaching approaches.

Although systematic incidental teaching procedures have not been widely tested, the results of attempts to use this form of intervention have been uniformly positive thus far. They appear to be useful for children from low income backgrounds whose language skills are only mildly or moderately delayed with respect to middle-class norms. It is unclear whether the procedures actually led to the acquisition of new language content-form interactions by these children from lower socioeconomic classes or whether the procedures simply facilitated their frequent use. More carefully controlled investigations are needed to answer this important question. In at least one study (Campbell and Stremel-Campbell, 1982), however, the approach was effective in teaching forms ("is" and "are") that had been attempted by the children prior to intervention but were rarely used correctly. McGee, Krantz, Mason, and McClannahan (1983) have used a modification of Hart and Risley's approach to teach the recognition of object labels to autistic individuals.

We have used incidental teaching successfully to train new language forms to specifically language impaired and mildly mentally retarded preschool children in a small group preschool program. In all of our successful attempts, however, the children were already able and usually willing to imitate the target during a functional communicative attempt. Hart and Rogers-Warren (1978) and Hart and Risley (1980) believe that, in order for these procedures to be effective, the child must be able to imitate the clinician. If the child does not respond easily to such prompts and cues, Hart and Risley (1980) claim that

> One-to-one training may be needed in order to establish a basic communicative repertoire of pointing, asking, identifying, and/or attending to contextual cues for language use. Children may have to be trained to discriminate and respond to the adult cues and prompts that will enable incidental teaching to work. But even while such training is in progress, children need an environment expressly designed and continuously adjusted to produce exploration and initiation, such that the children's behaviors come under the control of increasingly varied aspects of the environment. (p. 431)

A fairly broad range of language forms has been facilitated through the use of these procedures. In general, development of target forms may occur a bit more slowly than when using more highly constraining trainer-oriented approaches, but from all indications, use of target forms and, sometimes, nontrained generalization forms, is generalized spontaneously to contexts in which the use of those forms is no longer required. In at least some cases, however, this generalization is not complete—that is, the child may not use the structure spontaneously 100 per cent of the time without some further training or without allowing some time for the child to master the form spontaneously (Campbell and Stremel-Campbell, 1982).

One of the most important findings of research on incidental teaching is that the children tend to talk more to teachers and to one another as a result. Furthermore, when the children speak more frequently, they make use of more diverse and complex language forms. Hart and Risley (1980) point out that "appropriate talk in more different conditions means the use of correspondingly more different words and sentence types in order for language to be functional in those more varied stimulus contexts" (p. 430). In a nutshell, the use of language begets the acquisition and use of more complex language. Hart and Risley's explanation for this finding is distinctly operant. It is interesting, however, that this assumption is the very foundation of child-oriented procedures. Regardless of a clinician's preferred explanation, it is clear that increases in the child's attempts to communicate meanings to others leads to a greater need for the child to find more elaborate ways of encoding those meanings linguistically.

THE MAND-MODEL PROCEDURE

The *mand-model* approach is like incidental teaching in every respect with the exception that the child is not required to initiate communication before teaching begins. Instead, the clinician observes the child carefully and, when the child moves toward an object or shows an interest in some aspect of the environment, the clinician *mands* a verbal response (e.g., "Tell me what that is," "Tell me what you need"). If the response is correct, the child is reinforced verbally (e.g., "Great! You asked for the big ball so here it is") and through presentation of the object of the child's request. If the child does not respond or produces an incomplete form of the target, prompts such as those used in incidental teaching are employed. For example, the clinician can *model* the correct response and request the child to imitate it. Occasionally, the clinician calls upon the child to respond with a description or a statement about what she is doing or what she sees (e.g., "Tell me what you are making"). In this approach, then, the clinician takes greater control over when the child will talk and what the child will say.

Rogers-Warren and Warren (1980) used the mand-model approach with three preschool children, aged 3 years 4 months, 3 years 7 months, and 4 years 5 months at the outset of the investigation. All three children were receiving individual language intervention using trainer-oriented operant procedures throughout the training period. Two of the children exhibited significant discrepancies from the norm in language as well as in academic and social skills. The third child was mildly impaired and was described as being similar to the subjects of Hart and Risley (1968, 1974, 1975).

The mand-model procedures were used by classroom teachers during typical preschool activities. Children had a great deal of freedom to select activities and play objects. Although each child had specific intervention goals for individual sessions, the teachers made no efforts to evoke these specific targets. Instead, reinforcement was contingent on rather loosely defined goals, such as one-word responses for one child and two- and three-word responses for another. For the least significantly impaired child, complete sentences with at least three words were targeted.

This form of intervention led to marked increases in the rates with which the children verbalized and in their responsiveness to the teacher's mands during free play (see Chapters 11 and 12 for more details). Careful examination of the data indicates that most of the children's verbalizations were in response to teacher's mands, however. Each child's transcripts were examined for instances of use of language forms that were being targeted in the individual sessions. The two most severely impaired children showed clear gains in their use of target vocabulary and noun–verb–noun (e.g., "Me draw a picture") constructions, respectively. Gains made by the third child were observed, but they could not be viewed so easily as the result of intervention.

The results of an investigation by Warren, McQuarter, and Rogers-Warren (1984) paralleled those of Rogers-Warren and Warren (1980) (see Chapter 11 for more details on this study). The mand-model procedure can be used successfully with moderately to severely language impaired children. When the situation calls for a hybrid procedure in which the clinician can still exert a great deal of control over the nonlinguistic as well as the linguistic context, this may well be the procedure of choice. Although Warren and colleagues found increases in the spontaneous use of language resulting from the use of this technique, the clinician must keep a watchful eye on the possibility that the child is making gains in the use of target language forms but is rarely using those forms except as responses to questions and requests to talk.

CONCLUSION

Hybrid approaches of all types appear to have a great deal to offer language clinicians and their clients. Like child-oriented approaches, their greatest advantage over most trainer-oriented approaches is that they can be used throughout the day by teachers and parents without disrupting daily routines. Even the more contrived types of activities such as the picture description tasks used by Schwartz, Chapman, Prelock, Terrell, and Rowan (1985) and by Scherer and Olswang (1984) are not unlike everyday activities involving parents and their children (e.g., the "reading" of picture books). Branston (1979), Orazi and Wilcox (1982), and Wilcox (1984) have shown that these procedures need not be limited to a set of pre-established stimulus materials.

With very little adaptation, all of these approaches could be used in a group setting or even in the classroom. Because there is greater emphasis on the presentation of target forms in meaningful, naturally occurring contexts than in most trainer-oriented approaches, intervention might be maximally effective in groups. Not only can a given child's target forms be modeled by peers in group contexts, but in addition, the presence of several children in a given activity probably increases the number of opportunities for the child to use target responses. If the child does not respond with the desired target form, the clinician can capitalize on these same opportunities to model the target structure for the child.

The classroom is the standard setting for incidental teaching and the mand-model procedure. The clinician, teacher, or parent must simply be prepared to use the prescribed procedures in those situations in which the child's use of a target content-form interaction is appropriate and meaningful. It is possible that, in many cases, the clinician can have the greatest impact on a child's communicative potential by training parents, teachers, and other significant members of the child's social environment in the use of these procedures. In Chapter 14, the available options for involving the family are discussed in greater detail.

Because hybrid procedures can be implemented in everyday contexts, it is likely that more complete learning and generalization of target forms will occur than in more commonly used trainer-oriented procedures. Unfortunately, there is not much hard evidence at this time to show that this is the case. The only real attempts to test this hypothesis have involved incidental teaching and the mand-model procedure. Hart and Risley (1975, 1980) observed stimulus and response generalization in free play both indoors and outdoors following incidental teaching of complex sentences. These improvements were maintained even when reinforcement was no longer made contingent on the target language form. Rogers-Warren and Warren (1980) observed maintenance of high rates of verbalization that resulted from their use of mand- model procedures as late as 7 months following the termination of intervention. Unfortunately, these investigators did not report on the children's use of trained content-form interactions during these follow-up observations. Warren and colleagues (1984) observed increases in MLU in their subjects that were reasonably stable over a generalization period during which mands and models were no longer being used. During this period, however, the teachers used very high rates of questions. Therefore, the children were still being required to respond by the teachers at rates comparable to the intervention period. Whether longer utterances would have been used under less constraining circumstances is not known.

The investigation by Campbell and Stremel-Campbell (1980) employed the most stringent test of generalization in that observations were made during free play, a context in which teaching *never* took place. Although generalization did occur, it lagged well behind the very high and stable performances characteristic of the teaching contexts. Furthermore, once performance stabilized above 50 per cent in free play, it did not increase rapidly with additional intervention in the training contexts. This finding suggests that some extra intervention may be required to help children use newly acquired structures consistently in a variety of social and physical contexts. This conclusion must be tempered by the fact that Campbell and Stremel-Campbell used token reinforcement throughout the training and maintenance phases of intervention rather than relying on the answers to the children's questions as reinforcement. Had they not relied on token reinforcement, it is possible that attainment of the training criterion would have been delayed somewhat, but generalization conceivably might have proceeded more rapidly.

It is also possible that language impaired children, like language normal children, require a period of time after the establishment of a new language structure to master it completely. After acquiring a new language form and learning *how* and *when* it should be used through hybrid teaching approaches, language impaired children may master newly acquired structures with reasonable speed and spontaneity without extra training. Studies should be undertaken to determine whether mastery of a new content-form interaction is more likely to occur spontaneously following more naturalistic hybrid training approaches than traditional trainer-oriented approaches once a certain criterion, say 50 per cent in generalization contexts, has been reached.

In sum, the process of experimental validation of the use of hybrid procedures is still in its infancy. The results to date give reason to be optimistic, however. It seems fair to conclude that the approaches presented in this chapter all have considerable promise in training children to make use of new content-form interactions. Furthermore, the fact that models of the target forms can be presented in a concentrated fashion in meaningful contexts that arise naturally makes hybrid approaches (such as focused stimulation, vertical structuring, and expansion) ideal for the facilitation of comprehension skills of language impaired children.

Chapter 11

Facilitating Spontaneous Talking

In the last three chapters, approaches that can be used to facilitate children's acquisition of new language forms were discussed. These same approaches can be used to help children use already-acquired language forms to perform alternative conversational acts. These are the basic goals that will receive primary emphasis for children viewed as active conversationalists. For other children who are less assertive in conversations, however, these same goals probably should be subordinated to goals directed toward the children's inability or unwillingness to initiate communicative bids with expected frequency. In this chapter, clinical approaches designed to help children attain the following basic goals will be discussed:

1. Increase the frequency of use of available assertive conversational acts in a variety of social contexts.
2. Increase the child's repertoire of assertive conversational acts, using existing forms, when possible.

These are the primary goals for children that I have identified as passive conversationalists. They will also be appropriate for many children who are inactive communicators. A third goal for passive conversationalists was also suggested in Chapter 5: Train new linguistic forms that are useful in performing available assertive acts. This goal can be reached using the clinician's choice of procedures discussed in Chapters 8, 9, and 10 and will not be discussed further here. It is important, however, that when new content-form interactions are emphasized in work with passive conversationalists and inactive communicators, careful attention must be paid to the stimuli to which the child responds verbally. Unless procedures are implemented to ensure that the child is using target forms to perform *assertive* conversational acts, it is not likely that the new forms will be used by the child in a spontaneous fashion outside the clinic setting.

SELECTING SPECIFIC GOALS

For the first of the two basic goals to be discussed in this chapter, specific goals can be addressed at two different levels. At the first level, the clinician's specific goal would be essentially the same as the basic goal. In other words, the emphasis would be on increasing the frequency of conversational initiations and extensions, regardless of the specific type of conversational acts performed or of the form and content of the child's contributions. If this basic goal is further specified at all, the clinician might decide on some number of assertive conversational acts to be produced per session that would be acceptable and establish this as a criterion. For example, the goal could be stated as "the production of at least 50 assertive conversational acts that serve to initiate or extend a conversational topic in a half-hour free play interaction with the child's parents." Other specific goals would be similar, but should involve different partners in different locations (e.g., the mother, father, or brother in the home or at the grandparents' home). The actual numbers selected can be based on data such as those presented in Chapter 5, but ultimately, such criteria are fairly arbitrary. The rate of child initiations and extensions will always be a function of the particular context in which the conversation occurs, the topic being discussed, how the conversational partner performs, and so forth. Subgoals reflecting slightly lower frequencies could also be established to help the clinician monitor the child's progress toward the specific goal.

It is not clear how generalization and control behaviors could be determined using this type of goal. Therefore, the multiple baseline procedures presented in Chapter 7 probably could not be used. Careful baselines over several sessions before, during, and following intervention are very important under these circumstances. Audiotaped samples collected by the parents in the home can be very effective and efficient in this regard (see Chapter 14).

Specific goals designed to assist the child in reaching the basic goal of increasing the frequency of available assertive conversational acts can also be established at a second level. For example, the clinician might observe that the child produces most or all expected acts but that certain ones crucial to communicative effectiveness are produced with very low frequencies. For a child with this type of problem, the clinician's specific goals would involve attempts to facilitate the child's use of one or more particular types of conversational acts. To select a reasonable set of such goals, the clinician should attend to essentially the same factors as those discussed in Chapters 6 and 8. For example, establishing goal priorities should involve at least an evaluation of (1) the order of the potential targets in a normal developmental sequence (e.g., comments typically develop before statements and disagreements); (2) the potential effect of each of the possible target acts on the child's communicative effectiveness (e.g., requests for action and protests may have a more significant social impact than requests for information in the early stages of development); (3) response generalization (e.g., increasing the use of requests for information might result in increased usage of requests for attention, clarification, and possibly even action without further specific training); and (4) teachability (e.g., it may be easier to train the use of requestives than assertives because the clinician can demonstrate to the child the appropriateness of a request simply by providing the object or information that was requested). Assessment of these factors should assist the clinician in determining which specific conversational acts would be of the greatest benefit to the child. These acts would then be targeted.

Generalization and control goals could then be selected and a multiple baseline experimental design (see Chapter 7) could be used. For example, a target goal might be to get the child to increase her use of all types of requests for information. Whether or not the child used the appropriate syntactic form would not be important; the emphasis would be on production of the requestive act itself. Because requests for clarification are a specific type of information request, their use might be selected as a generalization goal. That is, as the child's use of information requests increased as a direct result of intervention, the clinician reasonably might expect to observe a spontaneous increase in the child's use of requests for clarification. It is also possible that attempts to facilitate the use of questions could enhance the child's use of specific language forms conventionally required in the production of questions. For example, the child might fail to invert the subject and auxiliary in the formation of questions. If this were the case, one generalization goal might be to increase the use of appropriate subject-auxiliary inversions in the formation of questions of all types (e.g., "Where *is the boy* going?").

Another type of generalization goal might involve the child's use of target conversational acts in new physical and social contexts. For example, baselines could be taken with the clinician and parents in the clinic and also with the parents in the home. If intervention concentrates on in-clinic activities, the increased use of targets in non-training contexts could be viewed as attainment of generalization goals. However, if the parents are involved in the intervention program, as they often will be, these increased rates of assertive acts at home must be viewed as target goals rather than generalization goals.

Because emphasis on the use of questions could conceivably have a general influence on a child's level of assertiveness, it is possible that increases in the use of requests for information could also influence the child's use of nonrequestive acts, such as comments, statements, and disagreements. Still, it seems that these changes, if they occurred at all, would be likely to lag significantly behind increases in the use of requests for information. Therefore, any of these types of assertions that could be viewed as potential targets might be used as a control goal. Another alternative for control goals would be to select some specific language form that is developmentally appropriate for the child, but is rarely or never used correctly. For example, it is not likely that intervention designed to get the child to use more questions would play a direct role in facilitating the child's acquisition of particular language forms, such as articles, inflectional morphemes, and prepositions.

Following a careful assessment of the child's social-conversational behavior, the clinician might observe that the child fails to produce one or more particular assertive acts that are expected, given the child's present level of cognitive and formal linguistic functioning. Because some acts occur relatively infrequently even among normally developing children, it is essential that careful baselines be obtained to be certain that sampling error is not the reason for the child's failure to produce a particular act. If no evidence for that act is obtained, the clinician may adopt the basic goal of increasing the child's repertoire of assertive conversational acts. That is, new conversational acts will be taught to the child. This goal will be appropriate for many passive conversationalists and inactive communicators, especially if they are in the early stages of language development.

The forms of a target conversational act that typically are earliest to develop should be selected as the first targets in most cases. For example, if requests for clarification are trained, a form of nonspecific request for repetition (e.g., "What?" or "Huh?") would probably be the best place to start. If disagreements are chosen as targets, the form "no" or "not–X" (e.g., "not red," "not your cookie") would probably be the simplest and most generally applicable form possible. Once these forms are acquired and are being used effectively and spontaneously, more complex forms could be targeted. At this point, the basic goal would shift from training a new conversational act to training a new form of an existing act (i.e., basic goal No. 3 for passive conversationalists). Control goals most likely would be language forms that would be appropriate for the child at that point of development, but that had not yet been acquired.

INTERVENTION APPROACHES

The basic goals under discussion in this chapter traditionally have not been targeted by language clinicians except as attempts to help language impaired children to generalize the use of newly trained content-form interactions. As pointed out in Chapter 8, even in these cases, primary emphasis has been on the child's use of the language form, not on the use of that form to enhance communicative effectiveness or efficiency. Therefore, the number of approaches that address these goals specifically are fewer in number, and they have been the subject of experimental investigation only in recent years. In the remaining sections of this chapter, I will present the procedures that have been used and examine the available evidence of their effectiveness. Where the procedures differ significantly from those presented in Chapters 8, 9, and 10, they will be discussed in sufficient detail so that clinicians who are unfamiliar with the procedures conceivably could put them to use.

Trainer-Oriented Approaches

When a clinician selects any of the basic goals that are the subject of this chapter, a very difficult problem arises. From a traditional trainer-oriented perspective, the following question will probably be asked: "What can I do to *make* the child talk more *spontaneously?*" It can be noted that the two italicized words in this question are contradictory. How can a behavior be viewed as truly spontaneous when another person has done something intentionally to *make* that behavior occur (e.g., presenting an imitative model, asking a question, requesting that the child guess about a picture)? This problem is what Hubbell (1981) has called the *"be spontaneous" paradox*. As soon as the clinician demands or requests a verbal production from the child, that production can no longer be judged an initiation, and the basic and specific goals of this chapter would not necessarily have been addressed. Trainer-oriented approaches to the problem of getting children to use language more frequently and spontaneously are attempts at *first-order change* (Hubbell, 1977, 1981), and they seem to run headlong into the "be spontaneous" paradox. Lovaas (1977), who developed an operant program for nonverbal autistic children, indicated his awareness of this problem when he stated, "Strange as this may seem to some, we actually built a program to help the child become more spontaneous" (p. 87).

Operant Approaches

Table 11-1 contains several of the procedures designed by Lovaas (1977) to facilitate the use of spontaneous verbalizations by the autistic children enrolled in his intervention program. It is important to note that these procedures are begun as early as possible in the child's course of language training, and they are carried out simultaneously with procedures developed to enrich the child's vocabulary and repertoire of grammatical skills. Thus, they may function as attempts to help generalize newly acquired behaviors as well as to facilitate the child's spontaneous use of behaviors already present in her repertoire. This is especially true of "spontaneity training" and "expressing desires," both of which become a part of the general program at the very outset of intervention.

A close examination of the activities in Table 11-1 makes it clear that, even though these exercises might have a positive influence on the child's language use, they are all dependent on some initiation and instruction on the part of the clinician. The child is not really taking the initiative to speak; she is being required to talk under conditions that are in some cases only remotely related to naturally occurring conversational contexts. With the exception of "expressing desires," those factors that typically motivate language normal children to share information through language are conspicuous in their absence from these tasks. As was the case for the use of operant trainer-oriented procedures to teach new content-form interactions, then, the clinician must be concerned about getting these behaviors generalized to extraclinic contexts.

To this end, it is important that in this and most trainer-oriented operant programs, *any* spontaneous communicative bids be reinforced throughout the program. That is, the clinician should be prepared to provide verbal praise, attention, time, and willingness to engage in activities that the child enjoys, and, possibly, tangible reinforcers such as food and hugs when the child initiates communicative acts at any time during the program—not just during planned activities. The home-based operant programs reported by Hemsley and co-workers (1978), and Howlin (1981a,b) have emphasized parents' use of questions and prompts to evoke appropriate speech, reinforcement of correct productions, and corrections of the child's errors during activities that the child enjoys.

Evaluation of the Procedures. In those few cases in which children's use of spontaneous, socially directed verbalizations have been isolated as dependent variables, highly structured operant programs have been reasonably successful in increasing children's rates of linguistic and nonlinguistic communicative bids (Hemsley et al., 1978; Howlin, 1981a,b; Lovaas, 1977; Lovaas, Koegel, Simmons, and Long, 1973). Howlin (1981a,b) presents a compelling case for the view that operant procedures are more effective in facilitating autistic children's *use* of *existing* language behaviors than in training *new* language forms. She observed only small gains in the length and complexity of utterances produced by her subjects that could be interpreted as the direct result of the operant intervention programs. Marked gains in the frequency of comprehensible utterances and communicative speech as well as significant reductions in nonverbal utterances were noted after six months of training, however. The rates of language use remained fairly stable over the next 12 months, a time period during which procedures were implemented almost exclusively by parents in the home. Importantly, of the communicative acts that improved, the greatest gains were in spontaneous information-giving utterances and questions (both assertive acts) and in answers. The report of Hemsley and co-workers (1978) on these same subjects showed that the parents who were involved in the home-based treatment spent no more time with their children during the intervention period than they had prior to treatment. This finding suggests that the children's increases in initiatory conversational acts were due to the nature of the treatment rather than to the effects of more frequent contacts with adults.

Although Lovaas and colleagues (1973; Lovaas, 1977) claim that their subjects made significant gains in "spontaneous" language, their measures do not make clear exactly what types of verbal and nonverbal stimuli typically preceded those acts viewed as "spontaneous" and "appropriate." Furthermore, Lovaas (1977) notes that "Even though some of our data support the notion of increase in spontaneous language, we do not have the data we needed to show that our spontaneity training program produced an overall, generalized use of everyday spontaneous behavior" (p. 170). Thus, although increases in children's use of assertive conversational acts occurred after several months of training (around 8 months in the investigation by Lovaas et al. [1973]), it is not clear which aspects of the training program were responsible for these changes.

As might be expected, operant approaches have not been limited to attempts to increase children's spontaneous and functional use of existing behaviors. The same procedures that were discussed in Chapter 8 and are given in Table 11-1 have been used to train children to produce assertive conversational acts not currently part of the child's communicative repertoire. For example, Lovaas (1977) reports having spent a great deal of time in teaching children to initiate conversations. For example, questions about the immediate environment such as "Is this a table?" and "Is this a chair?" were trained early in the

Table 11–1. Four Programs Designed to Facilitate Spontaneous Verbalizations Among Autistic Children*

Social Questions

Goal: To facilitate the child's answering of simple social questions and to encourage the child to follow them up with similar questions designed to evoke a social response from the partner.

1. The clinician asks the child a question (e.g., "How are you?" "What is your name?" "What did you do this morning?").

2. If the child does not answer correctly, an imitative prompt is used (e.g., Clinician: "How are you? Say, 'fine.' " Child: "Fine").

3. If the child responds correctly, reinforcement is provided and a prompt is given for the child to pose the same question of the adult (e.g., Child: "Fine." Clinician: "Say, How are you?" Child: "How are you?" Clinician: "Fine").

4. The same question is repeated and the prompts are gradually faded. Eventually, reinforcement should be provided only following the child's answer *and* subsequent question.

5. New questions are added in the same manner until reinforcement is contingent on complete chains of questions and answers (e.g., Adult: "How are you?" Child: "Fine. How are you?" Clinician: "Fine. What is your name?" Child: Larry. What is your name?").

Giving and Seeking Information

Goal: To help the child discriminate between those questions for which she has answers and those for which she does not. To encourage the child to seek needed information from a third party and then relay it to the original party.

1. The clinician asks one of many possible questions, some of which the child can answer and some of which she cannot (e.g., "How old are you?" or "Who will pick you up after speech?").

2. If the child answers correctly, reinforcement is provided (e.g., "Good!" "Good boy!") and another question is asked.

3. If the child cannot answer, the clinician prompts, "Say, 'I don't know.' "

4. The child is then prompted to ask the same question to a third person present in the room (e.g., "Ask Richie, 'Who will pick me up after school?' ").

5. The third party answers the child's question and prompts the child to tell the clinician (e.g., "Your brother. Tell Don, 'My brother' ").

6. The child is reinforced and the clinician asks another question.

7. Gradually, prompts are faded and the reinforcement schedule is reduced so that the child is reinforced only after the entire sequence is produced correctly.

Spontaneity Training

Goal: To increase the amount of information supplied spontaneously in responses to questions (i.e., to facilitate the child's use of topic extensions with multiple topic-relevant utterances).

1. The child is shown a set of posters, each containing a single object, and the clinician asks "What is this?" or "What do you see?"

2. The child is reinforced for each label until criterion is met.

3. Posters with *two* pictures are shown and similar questions are asked. After the child labels one picture, prompts are provided to see that the second picture is also labeled.

4. Gradually, the number of pictures per poster is increased and the number of prompts is reduced, thus requiring more labels per each poster in response to only a single initial question.

Table 11-1   (continued)

5. Eventually, the stimuli presented are shifted to real stimulus arrays from the immediate environment and the child is manded to "Tell me what you see on the table/in the room/on the shelf," "What are you playing?" "Tell me about your toys," "Tell me about yourself," and so forth.
6. If the child produces minimal responses, prompts such as pointing to unnamed pictures, toys, or body parts as well as open-ended questions like "What else?" are used.
7. Gradually, prompts are faded and reinforcement is contingent on the child's production of a lengthy and complete response.

Expressing Desires

Goal: To increase the child's use of spontaneous requests for action.

1. In the beginning, the clinician asks the child "What do you want?" and the child responds by pointing. Food items are recommended as stimuli.
2. The same verbal and non-verbal stimuli are used and the child is prompted to label the food item desired. This food is then provided to the child.
3. Once responding is reliable, the clinician fades out all prompts and *waits* patiently for the child to produce a spontaneous request.

*Based on Lovaas (1977).

Lovaas (1977) program. Although teaching questions as a form of obtaining unavailable information has considerable merit, it is difficult to imagine the types of circumstances in which questions such as these could be viewed as truly socially appropriate. Operant techniques are certainly not limited to teaching this type of question, however. For example, at a very early point of their program, Guess and colleagues (1976) trained the question, "What's that?" in response to new objects not previously labeled. Twardosz and Baer (1973) demonstrated very clearly that operant techniques can be used to train severely retarded children to ask questions to obtain unknown information. They trained their two adolescent subjects, who produced only a few short phrases prior to training, to ask the question "What letter?" in response to cards containing letters of the alphabet that they did not know by name. The subjects never asked this question when a stimulus card contained a letter that they could already label.

Still, there is very little evidence that training these sorts of behaviors using operant procedures in a formal context will be generalized to typical settings in which the need to obtain information arises naturally. Once the child learns a new assertive conversational behavior in a formal clinic setting, the clinician is still faced with the classic problem of getting the child to use the new behavior in more typical everyday contexts. For children who are nonassertive in communicative situations (passive conversationalists and inactive communicators), this problem is of special significance.

There is some evidence that when the stimulus conditions in a trainer-oriented teaching context are made more natural, the clinician can expect better stimulus generalization. For example, Simic and Bucher (1980) attempted to train the production of the form "I want a [point to food item desired]" to six mentally retarded children, aged 7 to 11. These children acquired and generalized the use of this form to a new context more completely and efficiently when, in training, the food items to be requested were actually placed out of reach of the child than when they were placed directly in front of the child. In other words, the operant procedures were more effective when the stimulus situation actually involved a need to communicate using the target conversational act. This suggests that efforts to enhance the naturalness of trainer-oriented procedures may prove to be more effective in facilitating the acquisition of new conversational acts than more formal tasks that are frequently used.

Obviously, much more research is needed in this area. At this time, we can conclude that for severely impaired autistic children, significant gains in spontaneous language use occur following the use of operant-based intervention programs that address themselves, at least to some extent, to the spontaneous use of initiatory communicative acts. When training is restricted to responsive contexts, however, increases in the child's use of assertive behaviors cannot be assumed (Blank and Milewski, 1981). It appears that in order for increases in the use of available verbal behaviors to remain stable over time, it is important that training procedures be continued by parents in the home (Howlin, 1981a,b; Lovaas et al., 1973).

The autistic children described by Lovaas (1977) and Howlin (1981a,b) are probably more severely involved (i.e., more passive or inactive, with more pathological behaviors in areas other than language) than many language impaired children. The procedures discussed in this section may have some degree of effectiveness for less severely impaired children as well. When these procedures are used to facilitate language use, however, the "be spontaneous" paradox should always be of concern to the clinician. For many children who do not require the tight control over the situation offered by these techniques, other procedures may be more appropriate.

Modeling Approaches

I am unaware of any experimental efforts to use modeling procedures to teach new conversational acts to young language impaired children or to increase their rate of use of existing acts in meaningful conversational contexts. As with operant procedures, the emphasis has been on training new content-form relationships. This is unfortunate because modeling procedures, as described in Chapter 8, would appear to have a great deal of potential for increasing children's use of already existing verbal behaviors. Models can be provided to demonstrate not only the types of utterances to be produced but also the verbal and nonverbal conditions in which specific conversational acts are appropriate. In fact, in observational learning experiments with language normal children, that is how the procedure has most often been used (Bandura and Harris, 1966; Carroll, Rosenthal, and Brysh, 1972; Odom, Liebert, and Hill, 1968; Rosenthal and Carroll, 1972; Zimmerman and Pike, 1972). In these experiments, children from the second to the seventh grades were required to produce sentences following a series of modeled sentences. The procedures were highly successful in getting children to use the same types of sentences as those of the model. Importantly, the *forms* these children used were not *acquired* through these procedures. Rather, the children learned the types of sentences that were valuable in the experimental context and made more frequent use of them.

Whether the gains in experiments of observational learning have any long-term influence on children's *use* of specific conversational acts in naturalistic social contexts is not known. For this type of approach to be successful, it would seem to be very important to give children models not just of the sentences to be used, but also of the conditions in which target conversational acts can be of significant social benefit to the user. This has not been done routinely in experiments of observational learning of language. For example, Zimmerman and Pike (1972) modeled questions for children and reinforced their use. But in their training procedure, they did not answer the children's questions! There is no question that children can learn what to say using this type of a procedure. It is highly unlikely that they will gain any insight as to *when* to make use of the target conversational act, however. The clinician must modify the modeling procedures that have been used experimentally with language normal children to enhance the naturalness of the activity.

Enhancing the Naturalness of Trainer-Oriented Procedures

In Chapter 8, several principles were discussed for enhancing the naturalness of trainer-oriented approaches. My intent in that chapter was to illustrate ways in which the clinician can maintain a high degree of control over the clinical situation and still offer to the child models of target behaviors and requests for their use under conditions that have parallels with less structured conversational settings. These same principles are of special relevance in the present context. By implementing these principles, the clinician can demonstrate to the child that language use has important positive social consequences. The discussions in Chapter 8 of "informativeness" and "creating conditions in which there is a real need to communicate" are especially significant in the present context. Three additional examples of ways in which the principles for enhancing naturalness can be employed to reach the basic goals of this chapter are discussed in the following paragraphs.

Facilitating the Use of Requests for Clarification. In Table 11-2, an example is provided of an activitiy designed either to teach or to increase the frequency of use of "What?" or "Huh?" as simple requests for clarification. In this activity, the model and child must listen to a story and use available props to "act the story out." At first, every request that the clinician produces contains one or more words that are pronounced incorrectly or one or more references that are incomplete or otherwise ambiguous. In these cases, the clinician knows that the child cannot possibly interpret these requests accurately. Thus, a communication breakdown has been established, and the model (and, eventually, the child) must produce a request for clarification. No external reinforcement should be necessary under such circumstances. Assuming that the child is willing to play the game, there is a real need to obtain the clarified information—without it, the story cannot proceed. Under these conditions, the natural consequences to the request for clarification should be reinforcing.

After the child begins to recognize the need to produce clarification requests to repair such breakdowns, the proportion of ambiguous and unclear messages in the clinician's story is gradually reduced. In the final stages of this type of approach, the child will be listening to and processing discourse not unlike that characteristic of a common learning situation in the preschool or grade school classroom. Importantly, the child will have a strategy for behaving appropriately when her understanding is not complete.

In the example in Table 11-2, a story was told. It is not difficult to see how this procedure could be used in tasks in which the child draws pictures, folds paper, constructs models, bakes cookies, and so forth, following the instructions of the teacher or clinician. When the child has finished such an activity, the completed product serves as tangible evidence to the child that language is a powerful tool that serves important and useful functions. By listening carefully, trying to understand, and repairing faulty communication attempts, the child can accomplish goals that may be otherwise unattainable (drawing, paper folding, baking, etc.).

Table 11–2.   A Sample Activity Designed to Encourage a Child to Use Simple Requests for Clarification More Consistently*

Clinician	Model
I'm going to tell a story about this boy and this dog. You listen carefully. Then you act out all the things that happen in the story. Are you ready?	
One day, a boy walked up to his dog. The boy said, [habo].	
	What?
The boy said, "hello."	
	(Moves boy to dog) Hello.
Then, he [pIpt] the dog.	
	Huh?
The boy petted the dog.	
	(Makes boy pet dog)
Next, he gave the dog a [badnit].	
	What?
The boy gave the dog a bone to eat.	
	(Pretends to give dog a bone)
Then, it was time for tricks. The boy said, [dop] dog	
	What did you say?
The boy told the dog to jump.	
	"Jump." (Makes dog jump)
The boy said, [pedat].	
	Huh?
The boy said, "Play dead."	
	(Makes dog play dead)
Then, the boy [lupt] at the dog.	
	What?
He laughed at the dog.	
	(Pretends to laugh)
The dog didn't like that. He [grupt] at the boy.	
	Huh?
The dog growled.	
	(Makes a growling sound)
Then he [bot] the boy on the [nad].	
	What?
The dog bit the boy on the nose.	
	(Laughs and makes dog bite the boy)

*The child is told to listen to the model to see how she gets the clincian to say things more clearly. A similar type of story would then be told with the child acting it out.

It should also be pointed out that even though the activity in Table 11–2 involves modeling, operant procedures could have been used just as easily. Instead of providing many models before requesting that the child take a turn, the child would listen to each unintelligible or ambiguous sentence. Then, the child would be required to imitate a command such as, "Say 'what?' " or "Say 'huh?' " Which of these procedures will work best is not known. A clinician's decisions on which procedures to use will depend on her past experiences with various procedures as well as her theoretical assumptions on language and language learning. The key to the activity in the table, though, is that a situation is created in which the child has a real need to communicate and that the target conversational act can immediately satisfy that need.

Facilitation of the Use of Requests for Information. Table 11–3 contains an illustration of an activity that can be used to increase the frequency of requests for information. To create a need for a request for information, the clinician performs several complex actions very quickly so that the child cannot possibly observe them all. As in the activity presented in Table 11–2, if the child is interested in the activity, language must be used. In this case, the language required is some form of a request—probably a question. The model gives the child a demonstration of many types of questions that can be used to obtain the required information. Then, the child is asked to watch the clinician and perform a similar type of activity. Since the basic goal is to increase the frequency of assertive conversational acts, the clinician would probably respond to any request for information or action. Only requests for information would be modeled, however. The activity illustrated in Table 8–10 in Chapter 8 could also be used to reach this basic goal. To reach the present goals, however, stimuli presented by the clinician on one side of an opaque barrier could be varied in many ways to evoke questions of all types, not just those of a particular form.

Facilitating the Use of Statements. Table 11–4 provides an example of a task that may have merit in teaching young language impaired children to make more frequent use of *rules*, a particular type of statement. In this example, models of many different types of rules (and protests) are provided. It is assumed that many or most of these forms are in the child's repertoire, but they are used infrequently. If the child had never made use of rules in her spontaneous speech, the model might present examples of only one or two forms so that the child would have a basis for learning what to say as well as when to say it.

For a goal such as the use of rules or requests for action, the social context is very important. In this particular example, the model (and then the child) gives instructions to a baby puppet. The use of a baby puppet or doll may be important, because the opportunity to state rules and to give multiple requests and instructions is much greater with a young child who does not have the knowledge of how to perform a particular task. Again, the emphasis is placed on showing the

Table 11–3.   A Sample Activity Designed to Increase a Child's Frequency of Use of Requests for Information*

Clinician	Model
Today we're going to make a paper airplane. Watch me so that you can make one just like it.	
(The airplane is then folded so quickly that the child cannot follow all of the steps)	
Now you make one.	
	How did you do that?
Fold it like I did.	
	I didn't see.
	Where do you fold first?
Right here.	
	Like this?
Yeah.	
	Now what?
Fold the corner to the middle like this.	
	Do the other side too?
Yep.	
	Is yours a point like mine?
Uh huh.	
	Can I see yours?
No, you're doing fine.	
	What do I do now?
Put the sides together. Then pull one side down like this.	
	Is this right?
You've got it!	
	Is the other side the same?
Yep.	
	Is it ready to fly?
It sure is.	
	Can I try it?
Go ahead!	

*The child is told to listen to the model and see how she learns by asking questions. Following a series like this, the child gets a try at folding the paper and must ask questions (or make other requests) to get the details.

child the types of situations in which the target conversational act is socially appropriate. It may be useful to assist the child in seeing how rules can be used in this type of structured context and then observe the child in less constraining activities with a younger child. Specific behaviors with which the child has difficulty in the interactions with the younger child could then be targeted in a more structured context. In this way, child-oriented or hybrid procedures (see later discussion) can be combined profitably with modified trainer-oriented approaches to attain specific and basic goals.

Table 11–4.   A Sample Activity Designed to Facilitate a Child's Use of Rules and Other Directives*

Clinician	Model
	The big one goes on first.
(Reaches to pick up small ring)	
	No, you need the big one. You hafta put the big one on.
(Puts on the big ring)	
	That's right. Now, you gotta do the orange one.
(Picks up yellow ring)	
	No, you hafta do orange. It goes like this.
(Puts on the yellow ring) (Reaches for blue ring)	
	No, you can't put on the little one. It's not time yet. You hafta listen to me. Put the green one on.
(Puts green ring on)	
	Now, the little one goes on. You can try the little one now. It's okay.
(Puts the little ring on)	

*The clinician tells the child to listen to see how the model helps the baby (a puppet) learn how to place colored rings on a spindle. The recalcitrant baby is operated by the clinician. After a series such as this, the child might be required to teach the baby another task, such as stacking blocks to make a house.

In sum, although a clinician might appear to be caught in the "be spontaneous" paradox when using trainer-oriented procedures, there is some evidence that operant procedures can be useful in achieving general increases in autistic children's use of language forms that are currently within their repertoires. Both operant and modeling procedures appear to have potential in helping children to acquire new assertive behaviors. It is likely, though, that significant modifications in the activities in which the procedures are typically employed will be needed to reach the basic goal of increased frequency of usage of assertive behaviors. In this section, a few suggestions were provided as to how traditional procedures can be modified to this end. By illustrating for the child circumstances in which assertive acts can have sizable payoffs, and by the showing the child the types of benefits that can be obtained through the use of these acts, it is not unreasonable to expect that the child will begin to use these acts spontaneously in extra-clinic environments.

Child-Oriented Approaches

Hubbell (1977, 1981) argued convincingly that child-oriented procedures are likely to be maximally useful when the clinician's goals are to induce talking in nonverbal children or to increase the rate with which the child makes use of assertive conversational behaviors. The rationale for the use of these techniques is presented in detail in Chapter 9. Basically, the clinician's intent with this type of approach is not to *make* the child do anything. Rather, the clinician adopts a role in which she is maximally responsive to the child. The child is allowed the freedom to select her own toys, activities, and conversational topics. In this way, the clinician can avoid the "be spontaneous" paradox. The stage is set for a *second-order change* that will occur under the child's own terms rather than those of the clinician.

Evaluation of the Procedures

Seitz and Hoekenga (1974) found that their program was successful in getting parents of 2 to 4 year old language impaired children to reduce their total number of utterances, to increase their positive responsiveness to their children (e.g., interactions and praise), and to reduce their negative responsiveness (e.g., criticism, physical punishment). These modifications resulted in significant increases in the compliance and interaction of the children at the posttest, which was held after completion of an 8 week parent-training program. For three of the four children, marked increases in the frequency of utterances were noted. The other subject produced only about half as many utterances in the posttest session as in the pretest, however.

Seitz and Marcus (1976) trained a mother of a 20 month old multiply handicapped child to use facilitative play techniques. Following training, which resulted in reductions in the mother's amount of talking and an increase in her responsiveness to the behaviors of her child, the child vocalized more, began producing different sounds, and was more responsive to the parent. Similar results were observed by Seitz and Riedell (1974) following their training of child-oriented procedures to the mother and father of a severely retarded child in the early stages of language learning. In general, the parents decreased their use of questions, their attempts to interrupt the child's play by shifting her focus of attention, and their use of physical contact to move the child. As a result, the child spent more time in independent play and was more responsive to the parents. Hetenyi (1974, cited in Hubbell, 1977) trained a mother of a language impaired child to increase her use of comments and statements that did not require a response and to decrease her use of questions and commands. These changes were related to very large increases in the child's rate of verbal productions.

The results of these investigations suggest that, when the clinician's basic goal is a general increase in the child's frequency of use of conversational behaviors already represented in her repertoire, a child-oriented approach is a valuable alternative to more common trainer-oriented approaches. We too have observed that when the pressure to talk is removed, many children increase their use of non-solicited conversational bids. Positive responses by the clinician to the child's initiatives typically lead not only to more verbal interaction but also to longer verbal exchanges between child and adult that are focused on the same topic.

I should hasten to add that for some children, these positive changes in language use do not occur in the first session or even the first several sessions. Children who are used to playing a passive and subordinate role with adults do not and should not be expected to make sudden changes in their willingness to communicate. The relationships in facilitative play between the child and the adult are different than relationships that the child has had with most adults in the past. Often, it takes time before the child learns to feel comfortable with these new conditions. In my view, this time is not wasted. Much can be learned about a child by observing her behavior in play, and this information is virtually always of some use in developing the child's intervention program. Furthermore, the clinician can make frequent use of simple utterances that are closely fitted to the child's focus of attention. These utterances may have a significant influence on the child's comprehension and, perhaps, even on the child's expressive skills.

As stated in the section on trainer-oriented approaches, child-oriented procedures need not be used exclusively of trainer-oriented or hybrid procedures. In the ecologically valid environment created through the use of child-oriented procedures, the child is free to initiate as little or as much as she likes. Such contexts should be ideal for monitoring the child's use of target conversational acts that have focused on more structured contexts. Weaknesses that become apparent in the child's interactions with others in the facilitative play context could conceivably become the focus of attention in more structured intervention sessions.

Hubbell (1977) points out that this type of approach may not be effective with some types of children. As an example, he cites autistic children. For autistic children who are not verbal, I would have to agree that facilitative play procedures probably do not hold much promise. Especially beyond the age of 5 or 6, however, it is not clear that any intervention approach that focuses on spoken language has been particularly successful with autistic children (Fay and Shuler, 1980; Howlin, 1981a,b; Lovaas et al., 1973).

Nevertheless, for at least some verbal autistic children who are passive conversationalists or inactive communicators, child-oriented procedures probably have a role to play in facilitating spontaneous talking, at least as part of a more comprehensive program that also includes trainer-oriented or hybrid procedures, or both. Prizant (1983) noted that "modeling language in a context of active involvement and in synchrony with relevant action patterns is a powerful teaching strategy for autistic children" (p. 75). If this is so, child-oriented procedures would seem to be well suited to the task. The techniques of following the child's lead, using parallel talk, build-ups, and breakdowns, and limiting the complexity of utterances used to address the child should maximize the child's comprehension potential. If the child can understand comments that are related to the immediate context, she may be more willing and able to interact verbally.

One of the basic principles of child-oriented procedures involving adults is that the child's behaviors should be interpreted as having communicative significance. The clinician then responds in a contingent fashion. These procedures would seem to fit in well with recent proposals that many overtly abnormal responses of autistic children (e.g., immediate echoing of questions) appear to be serving some personal or social function (Prizant and Duchan, 1981; Hurtig, Ensrud, and Tomblin, 1982). Duchan (1983) noted that to help some autistic children to interact in conversations, it may be important, at least occasionally, to adopt a "nurturing mode" of interaction.

> Unstructured activities or interactions that would elicit interactive initiative and cognitive interest from Robbie [an autistic child] would provide the adults with opportunities to use language that is semantically contingent, as well as offer Robbie more opportunity to make a connection between his meanings and ours. (p. 60)

The population of autistic children is extremely heterogeneous. For those autistic children who have a verbal repertoire but who rarely initiate verbal interactions, a child-oriented approach represents a theoretically reasonable but, as yet, largely untested clinical alternative to the use of more formal procedures and activities.

Interactions with Younger Children. At least by age 4, many language normal children increase their proportional use of questions and commands when they interact with younger children (Sachs and Devin, 1976; Shatz and Gelman, 1973). Fey and Leonard (1984) presented evidence indicating that some specifically language impaired children with primary impairments of expressive syntax and morphology can also make these adjustments when addressing younger children. It is possible that part of the problem with some passive conversationalists and inactive communicators is that they do not have much experience in certain social contexts, such as playing with younger children, in which their adoption of an assertive, superordinate role is both necessary and appropriate.

On the basis of this possibility and some limited empirical evidence presented later, I believe that another type of child-oriented approach warrants careful consideration and study when the basic goal is to increase the child's use of assertive conversational behaviors. In this approach, the child would take part in dyadic interactions with a younger child instead of an adult. Interactions with younger children who may lack the social skills needed to initiate and sustain social interactions may provide these children with just the type of social experience they lack.

Furman, Rahe, and Hartup (1979) used this type of approach to increase levels of social interaction of preschool children described as being socially withdrawn. Prior to treatment, the withdrawn, or isolate, children engaged in social interactions with peers in the classroom in an average of 26 per cent of all observation periods. This was only approximately half of the average rate for these children's classroom peers.

The treatment consisted of 10 dyadic interactions between the isolates and children who were 12 to 20 months their juniors. During the 20 minute sessions, the two children were free to play with toys that were selected for their potential to maximize social interaction. No adult intervention was used at any time. Another group of isolates received identical treatment, except that their partners were same-age peers.

The results of this 4 to 6 week treatment were that children in both treatment groups increased their overall rates of social interaction with peers in the classroom to levels that did not differ significantly from those of their normal classroom peers. A group of control isolates who received no treatment exhibited no changes over the treatment period. The gains were greatest for the children who interacted with a younger partner. At posttest, these children differed significantly in their interaction rates from the control children, whereas the isolates who interacted with same-age peers did not. In fact, seven of the eight children who interacted with younger children increased their interaction rates by 50 per cent or more.

Most of the gains made by the children who received treatment were in behaviors categorized as "reinforcement." This involved giving help, guidance, praise, cooperative play, and so forth. On the basis of the dependent measures used, it is impossible to tell whether there were increases in the assertive *conversational* behaviors of these children, although the authors' descriptions and interpretations suggest that this was the case.

The play sessions must have provided the isolates with experiences that occurred infrequently in the classroom. We believe these experiences included the opportunity to be socially assertive (i.e., to direct social activity). . . . The play sessions may have fostered increased peer interaction because they provided situations in which assertive behaviors met with a higher probability of success than in the classroom. Experiences with younger children, as contrasted with experiences with age mates, would provide the isolate with the most opportunities to initiate and direct social activity. (p. 921)

At present, there is no evidence to indicate that this type of treatment would be equally effective in increasing the *verbal* assertiveness of passive conversationalists or inactive communicators. When a child's nonassertive conversational style presents a significant barrier to the development of language and social skills, however, clinicians may be forced to attempt models of intervention that differ significantly from those with which they are most familiar. The theoretical rationale behind the use of planned interactions with younger children appears to me to be rather strong. What little experimental evidence is available is supportive. In my view, the approach deserves the attention of the clinician-experimenter working with nonassertive language impaired children.

By arranging for interactions between language impaired and younger language normal children in which little or no assistance is provided by an adult, the clinician might accomplish one or more of three possible objectives. First, such contexts would give the language impaired child many opportunities to use available assertive conversational acts. Spontaneous increases in the child's use of requests for action, information, clarification, attention, and so forth, might occur as a result of her attempts to engage the younger child in some activity and maintain her attention to the task. Second, regular dyadic contacts with a younger child would provide the language impaired child with an ecologically valid environment in which to practice the use of new conversational acts and forms that have been trained in more structured contexts. For example, if the transposing of the subject and auxiliary in yes-no questions has been selected as a target goal, interactions with younger children would provide numerous naturally occurring contexts in which the child could practice this new form (e.g., "Do you like this?" "Is that hard?" "Are you okay?" "Can you do this?"). Third, as mentioned earlier in this chapter, careful observation of the language impaired child in this type of context may reveal specific deficits in the child's production of particular conversational acts or with language forms that are frequently needed in addressing the younger child. These behaviors might then be the focus of intervention using a trainer-oriented or hybrid approach.

Hybrid Approaches

One element common to most hybrid approaches is the clinician's attempt to create contexts in which the child is motivated to communicate. At the very least, the clinician tries to set up situations in which it might reasonably be expected that a language normal child would produce the target behavior. The most general principle for accomplishing these goals is for the clinician to cease playing the role of provider to the child and to begin to think of herself as a creator of obstacles or, in Lucas' (1980) term, as a "saboteur." When hybrid approaches are chosen to facilitate the child's use of assertive behaviors, this new role is especially important. In this section the effectiveness of several hybrid approaches will be discussed. These approaches have been designed with the express intent of facilitating the use of spontaneous communication among language impaired children.

Incidental Teaching. Hart and Rogers-Warren (1978) noted that one of the goals of incidental teaching was to increase the child's use of initiatory verbal behaviors. The experiments that have been performed to date all support the efficacy of this approach in achieving this goal (see Chapter 10 for details on the procedures used). Hart and Risley (1968, 1974, 1975) observed increases in the use of targeted language forms in assertive conversational acts following the use of incidental teaching procedures. It should be recalled, however, that the subjects in these studies were relatively high functioning children from low income family backgrounds.

In the Hart and Risley investigation (1975), once the children were producing high levels of compound sentences directed to the teachers, a new twist was added. Following a child request to the teacher, the desired materials were given to one of the child's peers, and the child was told to "Ask Bill for it" or was given some similar cue. The same incidental procedures were then used to help the child use compound sentences in their requests to other children. The results of this new dimension were that the number of compound sentences directed to teachers dropped to levels that were still well above baseline, and the numbers addressed to other children increased to the same level as for teachers. This high level of requesting using the target structure was maintained during a follow-up baseline period during which access to the materials was contingent only on using a noun label for the desired object. Prompts for the target sentences were used very infrequently, especially after the first few treatment sessions.

Hart and Risley (1980) reexamined the transcripts of the children they had studied earlier and observed that the incidental teaching used in the earlier investigation had some positive general effects that had not been anticipated. First, the children used more than twice as many words during free play at the end of the 9 month preschool program than at the beginning. These were not simple repetitions of the same words because the rate of use of *different* words nearly doubled on the average as well. Second, there were increases in the use of simple, compound, and complex sentences such that, by the end of the study, the children who received treatment produced levels of sentences that were comparable with those sampled from a group of upper middle-class children in another nursery. These middle-class children began the year with much higher rates of verbalizations than the children who received the intervention. The finding of increased usage of a variety of different types of sentences is especially compelling because the sentence types that were trained by Hart and Risley (1975) were excluded from the analysis. Thus, these increases in sentence usage were not simply a function of increasing the children's use of target utterances.

That these unplanned improvements in language usage occurred as a direct result of incidental teaching can be inferred on the basis of a comparison with the performance of a control group of children in a Head Start classroom. These children were comparable to the treatment group in all respects at the beginning of the investigation. They did not receive incidental teaching through their preschool program. Their performance on all of the dependent variables remained constant across the year and, therefore, they were well below the children who received incidental teaching in language use and elaboration at the end of the year.

The value of incidental teaching for facilitating the use of assertive acts among more severely language impaired children has also been demonstrated. Olswang, Kriegsmann, and Mastergeorge (1982) developed an extremely comprehensive plan for encouraging the use of requests in an "autistic-type" child 4 years 10 months of age. This child had an MLU of 2.6, but rarely used language for social purposes. His spontaneous utterances typically were related neither to his own nor to his partner's prior utterances. On the basis of the description provided, this child would seem to fit the pattern for inactive communicators presented in Chapter 5.

The basic goal selected for this child was to increase his use of requests. Specific goals included requests for action, requests for objects, and requests for information. A subgoal, the elicitation of at least five requests of each type per session, was also established. A horizontal goal attack strategy was employed; that is, all three specific goals were addressed as opportunities arose throughout each session.

Thirty minute sessions were held three times weekly. After the child met a criterion of 10 requests for action and 10 requests for objects in each of three sessions, individual treatment continued for requests for information, and the child's teacher was given instructions regarding ways to elicit requestive behaviors in the classroom.

The individual treatment sessions involved reasonably natural activities (e.g., painting). The clinician manipulated the environment in ways that made the child's use of verbal requests necessary. The five specific forms of elicitation used are illustrated in Table 11–5. When the child produced a request, the clinician avoided praise for talking (e.g., "Good talking!"), but responded quickly and appropriately to the child's request. The clinician also modeled appropriate lexical items throughout the sessions in an effort to get the child to increase the lexical diversity of his requests.

These procedures were highly successful in getting the child to increase his use of all three types of requests in the classroom in response to the eliciting stimuli presented in Table 11–5. Spontaneous requesting (i.e., requests produced in response to stimuli other than those designed to evoke a request) also showed marked gains for requests for objects and actions, but not for requests for information. Furthermore, the child exhibited use of requests in all six classroom activities monitored, instead of only the two activities in which requests were observed before treatment. Careful analysis indicated that the child used a diverse vocabulary in producing requests—the requests were not stereotyped. These gains were still in evidence two months following the termination of intervention, although rates of request productions had decreased somewhat.

Owings, Workman, Price, Dayhuff, and Taylor (1983) used a similar procedure to facilitate the use of protests and requests for objects. Their subject was a nonverbal child, aged 3 years 6 months, who was functioning at Piaget's sensorimotor substage VI. At pretest, this child used no vocal or verbal communicative acts, although some gestural acts were produced. Intervention was provided daily for at least 10 minutes over a 3 week period. The clinician gave the child a desirable object and let him play with it. Then the object was taken from the child and placed where it was visible but out of reach. As another alternative, an object that the child did not want was substituted for an object with which the child was playing. In either case, if the child requested the object gesturally, vocally, verbally, or in any combination, it was provided immediately. If the child protested or if, after a 10 second pause, the child did not respond, the clinician asked, "What do you want?" and responded appropriately to the child's answer, if one was offered. This sequence was repeated with new objects if the child

Table 11–5. Adult Elicitation Behaviors to Facilitate the Use of Requestives by an Inactive Communicator*

1. *Direct Model:* Adult provides direct verbal model of request for an object, action, or information; the content word(s) referring to the requested object, action, or information must be linguistically coded by the adult. The adult also must directly elicit the imitation from the child.
    "M, tell me 'zip jacket please.' "
    "Ask me 'where's my coat.' "
    "M, you say 'need another brush.' "

2. *Direct Question:* Adult asks question which elicits a request for an object, action, or information.
    "What do you want?"
    "What do you need?"
    "Do you need me to help you with something?"

3. *Indirect Model:* Adult provides a verbal model of a request for an object, action, or information. The child is not asked to imitate. Thus, the adult may provide a model, followed by an elicitation statement, or give the child a choice of requests.
    "If you want more colors, let me know."
    "I'll get the scissors if you want them."
    "Would you like to color or paint?"

4. *Obstacle Presentation:* A direct verbal instruction (command) is given to a specific child, but some type of obstacle is provided. The obstacle may be in the form of a barrier to an object or action or an absent object.
    "Get the clay." (clay missing)
    "Can you push the truck?" (truck broken)
    "Do you want to paint?" (no paint)
    "Finish the puzzle." (piece missing)
    "Get the car." (car in sealed or closed container)
    "Please pour the juice." (cannot open juice container)

5. *General Statement:* This is a verbal comment directed to either a specific child or group of children which refers in a general way to an object or ongoing activity that the children or the child might want to request. It is designed to give the children a general option to/for request—which they may or may not pursue—*not* to model a specific request.
    "This book looks like it might be fun to read."
    "We could make a snowman."
    "I have some cutters for cookies."
    "I have a snack if anyone is hungry."

*Adapted from Olswang, L., Kriegsmann, E., and Mastergeorge, A. (1982). Facilitating functional requesting in pragmatically impaired children. *Language, Speech, and Hearing Services in Schools, 13,* 219. Reprinted with permission.

failed to respond after three attempts to elicit a request or protest. As a result of this brief program, the child made significant gains in his overall use of requests for objects. Interestingly, of the 20 requests produced in the posttest free play session, 16 were verbal. That is, even though verbal requests were not stressed in intervention, the child began spontaneously to make his requests more explicit by using words.

Waiting. Assuming that the clinician has designed an activity in which the need to communicate arises frequently and naturally, and that the child has some available linguistic forms to use, only one other condition must obtain in order to expect that the child will talk: The child must be given enough time to generate a response. This simple fact is so fundamental it seems trite. Still, it is surprising how frequently adults, including clinicians, anticipate the language impaired child's needs and provide the necessary assistance or information before the child indicates her needs verbally. MacDonald (1985) reported that

> Our almost ubiquitous finding is that parents, and often teachers, of a severely language-delayed child regularly communicate rhetorically and short circuit the child's communicative turn. That is, they expect the child not to communicate in a certain way; then, when the child fulfills their prophecy, they dominate the interaction and provide inadequately matched signals and insufficient time for the turn-taking exchanges for language to emerge. (p. 117)

There is evidence that systematic waiting when the child is in need of assistance or information is, in itself, an effective procedure in increasing rates of spontaneous talking among language impaired children.

Halle, Marshall, and Spradlin (1979) used the simple technique of "waiting" to get six severely and profoundly mentally retarded children to make requests (e.g., "want apple," "tray, please") to obtain their trays on which their meals were placed. In this study, the children were called to the counter, where they typically received their trays. In these cases, however, the trays were withheld for 15 seconds until some verbal request was performed by the child. Four of the six children exhibited substantial increases in their use of appropriate requests at mealtimes using only the waiting technique. Two of these children required additional incidental teaching (e.g., imitative prompts) to stabilize their increased response rates. The two remaining children also required incidental teaching to achieve significant increases in the use of spontaneous requests.

Halle, Baer, and Spradlin (1981) followed up this original study with two investigations that were more extensive in their scope. In the first study, the subjects were six 3 and 4 year old children with Down's syndrome. All six children were producing at least single-word responses. Intervention took place daily for 20 minutes in each of three different activities: free play, snack, and lunch. All intervention took place in the classroom and was conducted by the two classroom teachers.

During the baseline period, the children made limited use of requests. It was also noted, however, that the teachers typically anticipated the children's needs and then either supplied the needed service (e.g., by helping the child with her coat) or asked questions (e.g.,

"What do you need?"). Both of these behaviors preempted the children's opportunities to use assertive conversational acts. The teachers were then instructed to approach the children when they were aware of their needs, but to delay for 5 seconds if the child did not initiate a verbal request. An imitative stimulus was to be provided if no response was forthcoming. After this instruction, the teachers markedly increased the number of opportunities for child requests by waiting for a request at opportune times. All six children's rates of initiations increased dramatically as a result of this simple intervention.

These results were then replicated in a second experiment with six 5 to 9 year old mentally retarded children. It was also shown that teachers spontaneously used the delay procedure in contexts not specifically targeted for intervention. After the completion of the experiment, however, teacher rates of use of the waiting procedure declined substantially. This finding was observed in the first experiment as well.

It is clear from these studies of hybrid approaches that the nonassertive profiles of at least some language impaired children are maintained by their environments. That is, their environments are sufficiently benevolent to make regular use of assertive language behaviors unnecessary. The subjects in these investigations did not learn new responses. Instead, they learned the types of appropriate contexts in which their existing behaviors were necessary and functional. As a means of assisting children in their spontaneous use of available conversational acts, incidental teaching in its myriad forms provides a powerful procedural framework.

The Mand-Model Procedure

Rogers-Warren and Warren (1980) observed that, following the use of the mand-model procedure (see details in Chapter 10) in the classroom, their three subjects increased their rates of appropriate verbalizations. This finding led these investigators to believe that the procedure might have considerable potential for facilitating spontaneous language use among language impaired children who were passive or inactive in conversations. To test this hypothesis, Warren, Mcquarter, and Rogers-Warren (1984) used the mand-model procedures with three children (aged 2 years 11 months to 3 years 7 months) who were social isolates in free play. Their exemplary descriptions of the social-conversational characteristics of their subjects suggest that one child was a passive conversationalist, and the other two had traits more characteristic of children I have described as inactive communicators.

The results of this experimental intervention paralleled those of the original study (Rogers-Warren and Warren, 1980). Child verbalizations during free play increased dramatically for all three children. For the passive conversationalist, a significant increase was noted for utterances that were not responses. The other two subjects also showed increases in initiations. These were marginal for one subject and appear not to have been significant for the other, however—at least during the phase of the study in which mands and models were no longer presented by the teachers. The only measure of utterance form in this study was MLU. All three children showed some gains, and for the passive conversationalist and one of the other children, these gains were maintained even after mands and models were discontinued.

Rogers-Warren and Warren (1980) suggested that this procedure may be more effective than incidental teaching for passive conversationalists and inactive communicators because the clinician has greater control over the number of teaching opportunities that will occur. If the child does not initiate a communicative attempt, the clinician requires one. Ideally, these mands should be used only when the expected target response is appropriate and meaningful in the present situation. Apparently, these methods do make it possible for children to produce longer, more complex sentences, and they do not necessarily foster the continuation of the passive or inactive styles of isolate children. To the contrary, they may lead to higher rates of initiations, at least in children who are responsive at the outset of intervention.

Still, Hart (1985) claims that if clinicians expect the child's new language acquisitions to come to truly functional use, the child must learn to use them at appropriate times in response to nonlinguistic as well as linguistic stimuli. Therefore, an important aspect of the clinician's responsibility must be to ensure that the child's target forms can be produced in self-initiated conversational acts as well as responses. As noted throughout this book, this is a position with which I am especially sympathetic. If the mand-model procedure is to be used to the benefit of passive conversationalists and inactive communicators, the clinician must be careful to ensure that the child is making appropriate use of new language forms in the production of assertive as well as responsive conversational acts. At some point, after the child is initiating utterances more regularly, adoption of some other, less constraining hybrid approach seems advisable (Warren et al., 1984).

CONCLUSION

For some language impaired children, the basic goal of training new content-form interactions may have to take a back seat to goals that deal with the children's inability or unwillingness to use available linguistic forms to fulfill a wide variety of functional, conversational acts. The question is not really whether these children need to and can learn more complex language forms. Most of them will have deficits in language form and will need to have intervention directed toward these problems at some point in the intervention program. The most basic question, however, is whether these children will make use of new forms even if they can be acquired. In my experience, the answer to this question has been a resounding "no." Again, I am not suggesting that work on language form should be neglected (e.g., see basic goal No. 3 for passive conversationalists). I am merely claiming that with some children, we may be more successful in reaching our most basic goal, improving the child's ability to communicate, if we address their basic deficits in the spontaneous use of the language that they already have available.

The approaches presented in this chapter make it clear that a clinician can emphasize the child's use of assertive conversational acts in an intervention setting that is also appropriate for facilitating the acquisition of new language forms. For example, in the incidental teaching paradigm, even though the primary basic goal may be to increase the child's use of socially directed, spontaneous verbalizations, the nature of the activities makes it highly likely that other aspects of the child's language system will be influenced as well. In their intervention program, Olswang and colleagues (1982) made it a point to use new vocabulary in a fashion not unlike that characteristic of a focused stimulation approach (see Chapter 10). The result was not only increased use of requests but also increases in the diversity of vocabulary used to form those requests. Hart and Risley (1980) presented compelling evidence that increased language use to teachers and to peers in the classroom can lead to general increases in the complexity and novelty of the children's spontaneous utterances. In other words, as passive and inactive children begin to talk more, the need for more specific vocabulary and for more efficient means of encoding complex semantic notions may also increase. For at least some children, then, initiating more frequent communicative attempts may force them to stretch the limits of their existing knowledge of language. It may also motivate their search for new forms that can more effectively and efficiently meet their needs.

Much more research is needed into ways in which clinicians can be more effective and efficient in their attempts to facilitate children's use of assertive conversational behaviors. Judging by the success reported thus far for the procedures presented in this chapter, it appears that a firm foundation for this future work has already been laid.

Chapter 12

Facilitating Positive Social Interactions with Peers

Fostering language development with inactive communicators as well as with many passive conversationalists may depend heavily on getting these children more into the social mainstream. When they begin to participate more actively in social contexts with adults and peers, the need to interpret and generate functional linguistic responses should increase. In turn, these needs should foster an intensification of the child's motivation to discover more effective and efficient means of communicating.

The potential gains arising from more appropriate interactions with the social environment extend well beyond the realm of language structure, however. For example, there is evidence of both a correlational and an experimental nature that children who use a "positive interactional style" (Putallaz and Gottman, 1981) in peer interactions become the recipients of more positive behaviors from their peers than do children who use a less positive style (Charlesworth and Hartup, 1967; Keller and Carlson, 1974; Strain, Shores, and Kerr, 1976). A positive interactional style involves frequent use of the following types of behaviors: (1) giving attention and approval in a positive manner; (2) giving affection and personal acceptance; (3) offering things to other children; and (4) complying with the desires of other children. Preschool children who use such a style are rated higher by peers on sociometric scales than are children who use positive behaviors infrequently (Hartup, Glazer, and Charlesworth, 1967). These findings suggest that language impaired children who do not develop and use a broad repertoire of appropriate social behaviors may be at risk not only for continued lags in their language development but also for significant problems of social adaptation.

Therefore, I am in agreement with the following claims of Alpert and Rogers-Warren (1985) regarding autistic children; however, I would extend these claims to include all language impaired children who exhibit deficits in social-interactional skills.

> Ultimately, communication is a social behavior and without an established repertoire of interactive behaviors the development of communication and remediation of communicative deficits will be much more difficult. Since the autistic child's deficits in language are closely linked to his social behavior, attention to *developing appropriate social interactions should not be considered to be outside the realm of language intervention.* (p. 143, emphasis added)

The primary basic goal that I suggested for inactive communicators in Chapter 5 was

1. Increase the child's frequency of positive social bids (verbal and nonverbal) in a variety of social contexts.

This goal reflects the general sociocommunicative deficit of these children, including their failure to respond appropriately to their social partners with the expected frequency. As noted in Chapter 5, it can be viewed as an extension of the first basic goal recommended for passive conversationalists: Increase the frequency of use of assertive conversational acts in a variety of social contexts. It is important that both of these goals state explicitly the intention to improve the child's communicative performance *across social contexts.*

With few exceptions (e.g., Hart and Risley, 1975, 1980), however, clinical experiments that have dealt successfully with language impaired children's conversational assertiveness and responsiveness have not determined the extent to which these children's improved performance has generalized to different social contexts, such as with peers (see Chapter 11). Paul (1985) noted that "The child who is not interacting with peers sufficiently may not generalize behavior from adult-child to child-child interaction" (p. 305). To reach the basic goals stated earlier, then, it may be necessary with some passive conversationalists—and perhaps with all inactive communicators—to institute procedures designed specifically to get the children to increase the rate, duration, and overall quality of interactions with peers. The focus of this type of intervention would be on verbal and nonverbal social acts that lead to the development of more positive peer interactions and greater peer acceptance. Goals of language content-form interactions would be deemphasized in such an approach. Once the child begins interacting more frequently and positively, specific deficits in conversational skills will likely become evident and can be treated in ways that were discussed in Chapters 8 through 11. In this chapter, some of the procedures that have been used to increase children's production of positive social behaviors will be presented and discussed.

DIRECT INSTRUCTION—COACHING

Several investigators have suggested that a very direct approach in which children are "coached" to use positive social behaviors with peers may be effective in training social skills (Asher and Renfrew, 1981; Gottman, Gonso, and Schuler, 1976; Ladd, 1981; Oden and Asher, 1977). The basic components of this type of intervention are (1) verbal instruction of the social skill concepts that are to be trained (e.g., asking questions, giving suggestions and directions, giving support, participating, sharing, cooperating); (2) providing opportunities to practice these skills with a peer (e.g., in simple table games) or with an adult who is playing the role of a peer; and (3) a verbal review of what happened in the practice sessions and how the new behaviors worked.

The use of procedures such as these have consistently been successful in increasing ratings of peer acceptance among isolated preschool- and school-aged children who are not language impaired (Gottman et al., 1976; Ladd, 1981; Oden and Asher, 1977). Of these studies, however, only Ladd (1981) has shown that these increases were the result of the children's acquisition and use of the new social skills that were trained. Specifically, Ladd's program was successful in increasing children's use of positive questions and leading behaviors (e.g., suggestions and directions) toward peers and decreasing their use of nonsocial behaviors that did not involve their peers. These behavioral improvements and gains in sociometric status were maintained at a 4 week follow-up. Increases in sociometric status that have been observed following coaching have been shown to be stable for as long as 1 year (Oden and Asher, 1977).

Craig (1983) suggested that coaching may be an appropriate method for training important social-conversational behaviors to specifically language impaired children. This approach has not been tested in any systematic fashion. Because of the highly verbal nature of the instruction, these methods would probably be of greatest use with children who were functioning linguistically at a fairly high level, at least in comprehension. The children would also have to attend closely to and cooperate with the coach. However, with some language impaired children, failure to attend to and comply with adults and peers constitutes the main factor that makes intervention on social skills necessary. These children would not be likely candidates for this form of intervention.

Gottlieb and Leyser (1981) noted that these procedures might be adaptable for use with mildly mentally retarded children, but significant changes would be required. A great deal of demonstration and practice would probably be needed to replace the abstract, verbal descriptions and reviews that typify the coaching procedures used to date. This is likely to be the case for most language impaired children as well.

MODELING

Modeling would appear to have significant advantages over coaching, at least for lower-functioning children. Social behaviors such as approaching other children and offering to share play materials, playing cooperatively, asking simple questions, providing suggestions and directions, and so forth, could be modeled. It might even be possible to arrange such demonstrations by socially adept children with poor formal language skills. In this way, children could observe how positive social advances and responses can be made without using complex language. Very little language would be required to follow and understand such a presentation. The child would be required only to attend to the actions and verbalizations of the models.

Modeling has been used successfully in a number of experiments to enhance the social interactive skills of isolated children. O'Connor (1969) developed a 23 minute film with 11 scenes involving the social interactions of nursery school children. The basic principle underlying each scene was one child observing two or more children who were engaged in some social activity. The child then approaches the group in some appropriate manner and is rewarded by the responses of the group members. For example, group members smile at the child, talk to her, and indicate their approval by having her join the group, share play materials, and so forth. To make the modeling cues more salient, a narrator

> called attention to the child's intentions to interact (eight utterances), described how to interact for positive consequences (twenty-seven utterances), gave descriptions of ongoing behavior (twenty-four utterances), and described the positive consequences of interactions (twenty-eight utterances). (Asher and Renshaw, 1981, p. 282)

This film was shown to a group of preschool children who were described by their teachers as socially withdrawn and who were observed by the experimenters to spend less than 15 per cent of their time throughout the school day in social interactions with other children. Following observation of the modeling film, these children produced rates of social interaction in the classroom that were over five times greater than their pretreatment rates. In fact, their posttreatment rates did not differ from those of a group of randomly selected children who were not regarded by their teachers as socially isolated.

These findings have been replicated by Evers and Schwarz (1973), Keller and Carlson (1974), and O'Connor (1972). The results of each of these investigations also indicated that the effects of modeling were maintained at follow-up observations roughly 3 to 6 weeks after the children had observed the film. Evers and Schwarz (1973) and O'Connor (1972) both included conditions in which praise and attention from adults was made contingent on the child's social bids toward others. In both cases, contingent praise and attention failed to enhance the positive effects of modeling.

To the best of my knowledge, Gottman (1977) has carried out the only experiment in which attempts to increase children's positive social behaviors using the type of modeling film just described were not successful. In general, then, it seems that the rate of preschool children's positive interactions can be increased through modeling procedures. Of course, the really important question is "How do language impaired children respond to this type of modeling treatment?" Unfortunately, the answer to this question is not known at present.

The modeling procedures discussed in this section differ in an important way from the modeling paradigm often used to facilitate the acquisition of new language forms, as discussed in Chapter 8. In all of the studies described in the foregoing paragraphs, a narrator used a number of verbal cues to help the children focus on the nature of the social problem, on behaviors that might be useful in overcoming the problem, and on the positive consequences of using these types of prosocial behaviors. To follow and profit from these cues, the child must possess considerable language skills—and these may not be available for many language impaired children who have low social-interactional abilities.

The extent to which verbal cues are necessary to teach new social skills using modeling is not known. I am aware of only one study that can provide some insight into this issue. Guralnick (1976) used a modeling approach to enhance the social play of two preschool children who had IQs of 58 and 78. The language abilities of these children were not described, although some delays in development were probably present. Prior to intervention, both of these children spent most of their time in solitary play. Intervention consisted of five sessions in which the subjects observed two nonhandicapped children as they played with toys primarily in a cooperative fashion. No cues, verbal or otherwise, were used to draw the children's attention toward the other children's positive social bids. This form of treatment had no observable influence on either child's play behavior. Guralnick suggested that this approach may not have been systematic enough in its demonstration of the necessary social behaviors to teach their acquisition or use to the two children in his study. Like coaching, then, the potential of modeling to train the use of peer-directed positive social behaviors to language impaired children remains untapped.

COACHING AND MODELING: A COMBINED APPROACH

Actually, most descriptions of coaching have included some elements of symbolic modeling, and the narratives that have accompanied modeling films could be viewed as a form of coaching as well. It may be that conscious efforts to combine the two approaches could be highly effective for some language impaired children who have limited formal linguistic abilities.

Cole (1982) has suggested such a method to teach social approach and response behaviors to language impaired children, although she offers no support of its effectiveness. In her discussion of helping children respond to the ouvertures of other children, she states

> For a while, the adult may need to participate as a partner with the language-disordered child, at first assuming the child's role, then giving the child direct suggestions about how to respond, and finally withdrawing as the child learns to act appropriately in his or her own behalf. (p. 123)

The intervention would take place during free play with several other children present. The clinician could sit down and play with the child and then wait for other children to approach them. As other children came along, the clinician would respond appropriately (e.g., "There's Sue. She likes our blocks. Sue, wanna play?") After this type of play invitation has been modeled for the child several times, the clinician can encourage the child to make the offer (e.g., "Hi, Billy. Jenny, Billy sees our big house. Ask him if he wants to build a house"). Eventually, the clinician withholds her directions and waits for the child to respond spontaneously.

Table 12–1 contains a set of procedures designed to train peer confederates to initiate play with inactive communicators (see description later in this chapter). These procedures and modifications of them might also be applicable in training social skills directly to language impaired children. Direct teaching and modeling are combined in a highly systematic fashion that is much more formal than that suggested by Cole (1982). Some language impaired children may be able to extract social principles from this type of demonstration, instruction, and practice in much the same way that they have been shown to extract rules of language form by observing numerous consecutive models of that form. At present, however, this is only speculation.

Table 12–1. A Procedure for Training Peer Confederates to Serve as Agents in Interventions that are Designed to Increase the Use of Positive Social Behaviors by Socially Isolated Children*

1. A mature, socially adept child who can participate regularly in intervention sessions is selected as a confederate.

2. The child is instructed to try her best to get the target child to play with her.

3. The clinician role-plays the part of the isolate child in four 20-minute practice sessions.

    A. The clinician models some possible ways of asking the child to play, (e.g., "Come play," "Let's play this," "Wanna stack blocks?")

    B. The child is instructed to try asking the clinician to play. This continues until the confederate has made 10 attempts.

        1. On every other attempt of the confederate, the clinician provides social praise (e.g., "That was a good one," "Yeah, that might get them to play") and responds in an appropriate fashion to the child's request.

        2. The clinician ignores the remaining bids of the confederate for 10 seconds and then says "The children often won't want to play. But don't worry. You need to keep on trying to get them to play with you."

    C. The confederate is told that it often helps to offer toys to the children to play with. The clinician then models appropriate behaviors and asks the confederate to try to give her something when she asks the clinician to play (e.g., the clinician gives the child a ball and says "Wanna play ball?" "Come play with me," "Let's roll it"). Twenty practice opportunities are provided.

        1. As above, the clinician responds to and praises every other confederate attempt and ignores the remaining bids.

*Based on Strain, Shores, and Timm (1977).

CONTINGENT ADULT PRAISE AND ATTENTION

Whether they are language impaired or not, many children who are socially isolated have at least some contacts with their peers. Furthermore, these contacts may not always be negative. For example, the child might occasionally play in parallel fashion near her social partners and might even share play materials under certain circumstances. In less severe cases, cooperative play between children may even be observed. The *frequency* with which these positive interactions occur is dramatically less than that observed for other children, however.

According to operant theory, it should be possible to increase the rate of these positive social episodes by associating them with very pleasant contingencies. If social interactions are extremely infrequent, a teacher or clinician may resort to some active means of manipulating the social environment so that positive social episodes will occur.

Then the child could be reinforced for participation in these teacher-contrived activities. This general approach to increase the overall rate of positive social interactions among isolate children has been used in numerous investigations with considerable success (Allen, Hart, Buell, Harris, and Wolf, 1964; Buell, Stoddard, Harris, and Baer, 1968; Hart, Reynolds, Baer, Brawley, and Harris, 1968; Kirby and Toler, 1970). It would appear to be highly applicable to many language impaired children, because it places relatively small demands on the children's memories or on their attentional, perceptual, or linguistic resources.

Strain and co-workers (1976) used prompts to encourage social interaction and social praise to reinforce the appropriate social initiations and responses of three children with delayed speech and language. These 4 year old children exhibited extreme "opposition to and withdrawal from parents and peers" (p. 32). All intervention took place during free play in a language classroom with seven other children whose language delays ranged from mild to severe. Some of the children with mild delays had no behavioral disturbances, but others displayed social profiles that were as negative as those of the target children.

A description and some examples of the teacher prompts and social reinforcement used by Strain and co-workers are given in Table 12-2. This table also contains a description of the system used by Strain and colleagues in a number of investigations to code the social behaviors of the children. Each child behavior was coded as (1) an initiation or a response; (2) motor-gestural or vocal-verbal; and (3) positive or negative. Use of a system such as this results in the loss of a great deal of important qualitative information that is included in analysis systems such as that described in Chapter 5. However, this type of system has the distinct clinical advantages of efficiency and practicality. When the goal is a general increase in positive social initiations and responses, such a coding system has great potential for clinical application.

The use of the prompting and reinforcement approach of Strain and co-workers (1976) led to dramatic increases in the target children's use of positive social behaviors during free play. The effects were most clearly marked for those children who produced higher rates of social behaviors at the outset of the experiment, however. For the two children who used negative behaviors during the baseline period, substantial reductions in negative behaviors also occurred during intervention. In addition, it was noted that when the target children increased their use of positive behaviors, social acts by peers that were

Table 12–2. A System for Coding Teacher and Child Behaviors for an Intervention Program Designed to Enhance the Child's Social-Interactional Skills*

Teacher Behaviors

1. *Prompting:* All physical and verbal acts designed to foster interactions between the target child and peers.

   A. Physical prompts include moving a child into closer proximity to other children, manipulating the child's body in some way to contact other children or to assist the child in offering toys and other materials to peers, and so forth.

   B. Verbal prompts include suggestions, directives, and explanations of rules with the intent of encouraging some positive social contact between children. For example, "Let's work together," "It's more fun to build with Ada," "We have to play in the sand with Linda," and so forth.

2. *Reinforcement:* All praise and comments of approval as well as positive physical behaviors (e.g., hugging) that are contingent on the child's *positive* social behavior. For example, "That's nice how you can play together," "Tom, you're really helping Cindy," "It's great the way you share your toys, Liz," and so forth.

Child Behaviors

1. *Decision One: Initiation or Response*

   A. Initiations include all behaviors that are emitted 3 seconds or more after a social behavior by a partner.

   B. Responses include all behaviors that are emitted within 3 seconds of a social behavior by a partner.

2. *Decision Two: Motor-Gestural or Vocal-Verbal*

   A. Motor-gestural includes all behaviors that move the child into some form of contact with another child, either directly or indirectly through touching another child's toy, offering toys, gaining attention by waving, and so forth.

   B. Vocal-verbal includes all vocalizations produced while the child is facing another child and is within 3 feet of that child. All vocalizations that can be viewed as being socially directed by virtue of their accompanying gestures or their semantic content are also included.

3. *Decision Three: Positive or Negative*

   A. Motor-gestural

      1. Positive behaviors include touching gently, hugging, holding hands, waving, playing cooperatively, offering toys, and so forth.

      2. Negative behaviors include hitting, pinching, grabbing others' toys, opposing positive social advances of others, and so forth.

   B. Vocal-verbal

      1. Positive behaviors include all social vocalizations excluding screaming, shouting, crying, and so forth and other utterances that can be viewed as rejecting, oppositional behavior.

      2. Negative behaviors include all of the behaviors that are excluded from the "positive" category.

---

*Based on Strain, Shores, and Kerr (1976).

directed toward the target children increased. Thus, there appeared to be an increase in the reciprocal social involvement of treated and untreated peers as a result of intervention. Unfortunately, when the teacher discontinued her use of the intervention procedures, the children's rates of positive social acts dropped significantly, and negative behaviors increased to approximately baseline levels.

The report of Strain and colleagues (1976) contains no information on whether (and to what extent) these general increases resulted from more frequent child initiations or on whether they were simply responses to the teacher and peers. If no increases in initiations were observed, it is not too surprising that when the teacher discontinued her use of prompts, the child's rate of interaction dropped to near baseline levels. It is also unclear whether the results involved greater increases in motor-gestural or vocal-verbal social acts. Since at least one child who made significant gains was apparently functioning primarily with single-word utterances, much of his improvement may have been due to increases in nonverbal social responding. It may be that these procedures are effective in increasing the positive nonverbal behaviors of children with extremely limited verbal repertoires.

In sum, contingent praise and attention from adults has been shown to be effective with children who interact with peers at a lower than normal rate. However, it seems that gains that occur as a result of this type of treatment disappear when the procedures are discontinued (Hart et al., 1968; O'Connor, 1972; Strain et al., 1976). A gradual "thinning" of reinforcement across a period of days or weeks may help to ensure the stability of gains made in positive social behaviors as a result of this type of treatment (Hart et al., 1968; Timm, Strain, and Eller, 1979).

USING PEERS AS CONFEDERATES

The use of teacher prompting and contingent social reinforcement places extreme demands on the teacher's time and other resources. A more efficient and perhaps more effective method might be to make use of peers to assist in the intervention process. (Although the term "peer" is typically used in the literature and will be used here as well, it should be clear that what is meant by the term in this context is a child who is similar in age, but who is much more socially adept than the child to whom intervention is directed.) In a number of experiments, peers have been trained to prompt and, in some cases, to reinforce the positive social behaviors of isolate children (Guralnick, 1976; Ragland, Kerr, and Strain, 1978; Strain, 1977; Strain, Kerr, and

Ragland, 1979; Strain and Shores, 1977a,b; Strain, Shores, and Timm, 1977).

Perhaps the most important aspect of this type of intervention is the training of the peer confederate. Table 12-1 contains an outline of the steps used by Strain and colleagues to teach confederates to initiate social interactions with the isolated children. Similar steps can be used to train confederates to provide contingent social reinforcement (Strain et al., 1979). This training format has been uniformly successful in modifying the confederates' behavior toward even extremely socially isolated children. The procedures contain elements of both modeling and coaching as discussed previously in this chapter.

With some qualifications, peer confederates have been very effective as agents of social change in programs involving socially isolated children. Strain (1977) trained a 4 year old confederate with a Stanford-Binet IQ of 130 to make use of the initiatory behaviors described in Table 12-1. The subjects were three behaviorally disturbed children between the ages of 43 and 51 months described as displaying "delayed language patterns and extreme opposition to adults' requests" (p. 447). The Stanford-Binet IQs of these children were 47, 50, and 55. Intervention sessions took place for 15 minutes each day in an experimental room. Observations were also made during free play in the classroom as a check on carry-over to nonintervention contexts. The confederate was not involved in these sessions.

During the intervention sessions, two of the children made impressive increases in their use of positive social behaviors. Approximately 20 per cent of this increase was composed of initiations, and the rest were responses. The percentage of increases in initiations and responses that were vocal-verbal is not reported. The subject who showed the lowest rate of positive behaviors during the first baseline made only minimal changes in social responding. As has been the case with other procedures, once the confederate stopped initiating interactions, the rates of positive social responding decreased to approximately baseline levels.

This same pattern of results was observed in the generalization sessions in the classroom. During the periods of intervention, social interactions involving these children in the classroom increased for two boys, but not for the one who showed only small gains in the intervention sessions. Approximately 50 per cent of the increase in positive social bids involved initiations. Unfortunately, when intervention was terminated, performance in the classroom also decreased for the two boys who had exhibited progress.

Very similar findings have been observed in the use of these procedures with other moderately to severely retarded children with language delays (Strain et al., 1977) and with extremely isolated and oppositional autistic children (Ragland et al., 1978; Strain et al., 1979). As a result of peer confederate intervention, most of these children have increased their use of positive social behaviors and reduced their use of negative behaviors. The retarded children have shown marked increases in their use of initiatory as well as responsive behaviors following this treatment (Strain, 1977; Strain et al., 1977). In contrast, the gains made by autistic children have been primarily in responses to the confederate (Ragland et al., 1978). Only the children who began with almost no positive behaviors in their social repertoires have failed to show some improvement. Even the children who have made progress, however, have returned to baseline levels of performance following discontinuation of treatment. It appears that, if these procedures are to be used, some modifications may be required to ensure carry-over to extraclinic environments and to ensure maintenance of the new pattern of social performance.

CONCLUSION

It is clear from the discussion above that very little information is available about the effectiveness of interventions that are designed to foster positive social interactions between children and their peers. The few studies that apparently have involved language impaired children have provided very limited descriptions of their language skills at the outset of the investigation. Therefore, they are difficult to evaluate. Any conclusions that are drawn must be viewed with caution.

On the basis of what little information we have, it appears that several procedures can be used to enhance the social responsiveness of language impaired children toward their peers. Coaching, modeling, and combinations of these approaches have been successful with socially isolated children who, presumably, were not language impaired. They may also be effective with language impaired children who are reasonably cooperative with adults. Although these procedures have led to lasting changes among social isolates with normal language, experience in other areas of language intervention suggests that we must be skeptical of the stability and generalizability of any intervention outcomes with language impaired children.

For children who are extremely withdrawn or who reject the social advances of adults and peers, other procedures will probably be necessary. Teacher- or peer-initiated prompts for interaction have been reasonably successful in getting these children to interact more positively, but the short-lived nature of these gains has been well documented. With severely disturbed autistic children, the social initiations of a peer confederate have led only to increases in the children's frequency of responding to the confederate, not to generalized social responding or initiating.

There are several possible ways in which the gains made during intervention might be enhanced. These include lengthening the period of intervention, changing adult and peer agents on a regular basis to give the child more positive experience with different individuals or combining several or even all of the procedures discussed earlier. There is some evidence that gradually reducing the rate of adult or peer prompts and rates of reinforcement enhances the durability of intervention gains (Timm et al., 1979). Finally, procedures such as those discussed in this chapter could be combined with procedures presented and evaluated in Chapter 11 that were designed to increase spontaneous talking.

I have argued throughout this book that much of what language interventionists do is experimental. There is probably no other aspect of intervention that is more experimental than attempting to facilitate positive social relationships between young language impaired children and their peers. Given the critical nature of positive interactions with others for social, emotional, cognitive, and linguistic development, it may be that there is no other aspect of intervention on which research is so desperately needed.

Chapter 13

Facilitating Responsiveness to the Conversational Partner

Until the last chapter, the emphasis in this book has been on facilitating children's use of assertive language behaviors. There is good reason for this—if language impaired children are not shown how new language behaviors can be used spontaneously to influence others in a social context, they often will use them only when obligated by their partner to do so. Under these circumstances, the basic intervention goal of improved communicative performance may not have been attained.

But successful communication depends on more than the willingness to verbalize and the ability to produce grammatically well formed sentences. When two (or more) individuals enter into a conversation, they accept a number of responsibilities. The following list is not exhaustive by any means. First, the verbal and nonverbal behaviors of the other partner must be attended to carefully. Second, when one person speaks, the listener must assume that a communicative attempt is being made and make some effort to interpret and respond appropriately to the speaker's semantic and pragmatic intent. By the same token, the speaker must carefully assess the linguistic and nonlinguistic context and, on the basis of this assessment, adjust the general topic of conversation and select a form of expression to meet the needs of the listener and the situation. Third, the speaker and the listener must monitor each other's behaviors to ensure that the speaker's intentions have been accurately expressed and comprehended. Fourth, both participants must cooperate in efforts designed to repair communication breakdowns when they occur. Fifth, each participant must play a role in extending the topic of conversation by adding new, but semantically related information, when appropriate.

At least some language impaired children either are not aware of some or all of these responsibilities or they choose not to accept them. Trying to communicate with these children can be an exercise in frustration for all concerned. The basic goals that were recommended in Chapter 5 for these children, to whom I refer as verbal noncommunicators, are repeated here.

1. Increase the relatedness of the child's responses to the assertive acts of the partner.
2. Facilitate the child's production of sequences of utterances that are topically related to one another.
3. Encourage the child to establish referents in a clear and unambiguous fashion.

Despite the recognized need for intervention with children who exhibit this type of conversational problem (Cole, 1982; Longhurst and Reichle, 1975; Lucas, 1980; Muma, 1978b; Shewan, 1975; Warr-Leeper, 1982), there has been very little clinical research in the area. In this chapter, I will provide a brief overview of some of the procedures that may be useful for attaining goals such as these.

A WORD ON COMPREHENSION

When a child fails to respond appropriately to the questions, comments, statements, and so forth, of adults and peers, the clinician must be concerned with the child's comprehension skills. If the child cannot comprehend particular words or sentence types, appropriate responses to these types of conversational acts cannot be expected. For example, a child might answer a question such as "Where are you going over Christmas?" with a related, but semantically inappropriate response (e.g., "a new bike"). A more tangential response to the same question that conceivably could result from poor comprehension skills might be "Santa Claus is coming." Children who respond in this manner appear to be willing to take part in the conversation, and they understand their obligation to respond; however, they often do not have the necessary knowledge of language content-form interactions to process this type of utterance and respond in an appropriate manner.

It may be that at least part of this type of child's general difficulty in responding appropriately is a result of the language that is addressed to the child by her parents and teachers. These individuals may be using language that is too complex and that is produced in such a way that the child cannot make use of nonlinguistic contextual cues to aid her language comprehension processes. This possibility should be investigated carefully. If the hypothesis is borne out, an appropriate intervention would involve helping significant members of the child's social environment to reduce the complexity of their speech to the child. This is a basic component of child-oriented approaches (see Chapters 9 and 14). Alternatively, or in addition, the clinician may opt to select as goals the particular content-form interactions that pose the greatest obstacles to successful communication for the child. Chapter 8 contains relevant information regarding how these specific goals could be selected. Chapters 8 through 10 provide detailed information on facilitating the child's understanding and use of these forms.

OPERANT APPROACHES: QUESTION-ANSWER PAIRS

Because contingent responses to questions typically precede contingent responses to comments, statements, and other assertive acts in development (Bloom et al., 1976), and because question-answer pairs are relatively easily controlled by the clinician, questions are often selected as the focus of attention in dealing with nonresponsive children. Many of the operant procedures discussed in Chapter 8 that have been used to train new content-form interactions use a format whereby the clinician asks the child a question about some nonlinguistic stimulus and then provides the answer for the child to imitate (Gray and Ryan, 1973; Hester and Hendrickson, 1977; MacDonald et al., 1974). Gradually the imitative prompt is faded, so that the child must answer the question on her own.

Table 13–1 contains several examples of each step of the approach taken by Blank and Milewski (1981). This approach is unique in that it reduces the redundancy of many question-response formats. In phases 1 to 3, the emphasis is on teaching the child to respond appropriately to basic types of questions and simple permutations of these questions (e.g., "Who is that?" "What is this?"). Once a new basic form and its permutations are acquired (following phase 3), it is mixed with other forms already acquired to form sequences of questions. As can be seen from the examples in the table, this forces the child to listen closely and make careful discriminations of the semantic and grammatical details of the questions. At each step along the way, the child is reinforced for all efforts to attempt the task.

Blank and Milewski (1981), Hemsley and co-workers (1978), Howlin (1981a,b), and Lovaas and co-workers (1973) have all observed increases in autistic children's verbal responsiveness to the questions of clinicians or parents following similar types of question-response activities using operant procedures. For very severely impaired children such as the autistic children in these studies, the tight control of-

Table 13–1. Examples of the Question-Answer Paradigm to Facilitate Appropriate Responding by a 4½ Year Old Autistic Child*

Clinician	Child
Phase 1: Imitation	
That is a boy.	
	That is a boy.
This is a dog.	
	This is a dog.
Phase 2: Answering Questions (Imitation)	
Who is that? That is a boy.	
Who is that?	
	That is a boy.
What is this? This is a dog.	
What is this?	
	This is a dog.
Phase 3: Answering Questions (Nonimitation)	
Who is that?	
	That is a boy.
What is this?	
	This is a dog.
Phase 4: Answering "Mixed" Forms of Questions	
Who is this?	
	This is a boy.
What is he doing?	
	He is playing ball.
What is that?	
	That is a dog.
What can he do?	
	He can jump.
What are they doing now?	
	They are running.

*Based on Blank and Milewski (1981).

fered by the operant paradigm helps to ensure the child's attention and maximizes success. For many emotionally disturbed children, intrusions into their own rigid means of responding to the world can bring about very dramatic, negative reactions (Blank and Milewski, 1981; Yudkovitz, Lewiston, and Rottersman, 1975). The high rate of success that can be achieved with operant procedures may help to minimize the possibility of such responses.

Interactive Language Development Teaching (ILDT) (Lee et al., 1975) involves basically operant procedures in a question-answer framework, but it has some other desirable features that may be useful in reaching the basic goal of improved responsiveness to partner conversational acts (see procedural details in Chapter 8). It will be recalled that in this procedure, the clinician asks questions about an ongoing story. Therefore, the child must listen to more than just sequences of questions in order to respond correctly. The fact that this is a group procedure is also an advantage. Not only does the child have opportunities for responding to questions related to the story, but in addition she has many opportunities for observing the question-answering acts of other children. The child receives vicarious reinforcement by observing the clinician's favorable reaction to and praise of other children who respond appropriately. Ratusnik and Ratusnik (1976) used ILDT with four psychotic children and observed improvements in the ability to engage in discourse as a result. This was only one part of the program for these children, though, so it is difficult to determine the extent to which gains in conversational skills resulted from the use of this intervention paradigm or from other aspects of the children's program.

MODELING AND COACHING

Modeling could be used to increase the relatedness of the child's response to prior discourse, although I am aware of no studies that have used modeling for this purpose. As an example of how this could be done, let's take a case of a child who frequently produces sequences of rambling sentences that appear incoherent and meaningless. The child would observe a model whose task might be to describe a picture or to tell a simple story such as "The Three Bears." After each sentence or two, the clinician could "reinforce" the model with feedback (e.g., "Oh, I see," "Yeah, you're telling a great story," "Let's see. Goldilocks tried the Papa Bear's porridge? Okay, I've got it. Go ahead"). The target child's attention could be drawn to off-target responding by having the model produce one tangential or unrelated sentence in every four or five total sentences. These utterances would be responded to negatively (e.g., "Wait a minute. That doesn't make sense!").

It is easy to see how coaching could be worked into such a procedure. For example, before presenting the models, the clinician could instruct the model to be very careful and "stay on the topic." Each time the model produced an inappropriate response, the clinician could reinstruct, (e.g., "I caught you. You went off the topic, didn't you? You said 'The baby's bottom was bare,' but that's not part of this story. Finish the story and stay on the topic"). After modeling the story, the child would get a turn.

AUDITORY SELF-MONITORING

Yudkovitz and Rottersman (1973) and Yudkovitz and co-workers (1975) suggested a procedure that contains many of the same principles found in modeling and coaching. This approach is purportedly based on the theoretical notion that many of the language-related symptoms of childhood schizophrenia are due to impaired auditory monitoring skills. Table 13–2 illustrates three of the basic steps found in this general approach with examples relevant to the specific goal of increasing appropriate responses to requests for information. In this approach, the child is sensitized to the particular types of errors that she makes. Once aware of her inappropriate responding, the child may be able to monitor conversations more adequately and generate more appropriate topic maintaining and extending acts. Yudkovitz and co-workers have had reasonable success using this strategy with four psychotic adolescents who were high-functioning cognitively and verbally. It is not clear how well preschool- and early school–aged children who are not adequately responsive, but who are not psychotic, might respond to this form of treatment.

THE BARRIER GAME

Several authors have recommended the use of a referential communication task such as that used by Glucksberg and Krauss (1967) to improve the communication skills of language impaired children (Longhurst and Riechle, 1975; Muma, 1978b; Yudkovitz et al., 1975). To the best of my knowledge, there have been no clinical experiments designed to test the effectiveness of this type of game in facilitating the extraclinic communicative skills of language impaired children.

The game should be especially useful for the specific goals of getting the child to respond to partner comments and requests for action. It should also help to facilitate children's production of and responses to requests for clarification. Finally, it requires children to produce often very lengthy sequences of utterances related to a particular topic. The child will fail in this task unless the perspective of the listener is carefully considered in all the child's descriptions.

In the original scheme of Glucksberg and Krauss (1967), a child on one side of an opaque screen were required to describe a set of abstract geometric figures to a child on the other side of the screen. This child was to stack the figures in the same order as they were described by the speaker. Because abstract stimuli that were similar in many aspects were used, the task required children to think of novel ways to

Table 13–2.   Illustration of Three of the Six Steps in a Communication Therapy Program Designed For Use with Schizophrenic Children*

I. *General Error Sensitivity:* The errors that the child must detect are unrelated to her own errors.

    A. The clinician reads a story, a paragraph or so in length, in its correct form. The story is then repeated and the child must listen for errors. These might consist of associating the wrong sound with animals (e.g., the cow said "bow-wow"), describing pictures in the story incorrectly (e.g., "Then the cow came in," while showing a picture of a cat), or making comments about pictured events out of sequence.

    B. The child must indicate to the clinician when an error has been made.

II. *Interpersonal Scanning for Error*

    A. The clinician selects a target error found in the child's conversational behavior (e.g., responding inappropriately to questions).

    B. The clinician reads or talks to the child, occasionally making this error. For example, the clinician could tape a set of questions about a picture book. The clinician would answer some of these questions appropriately. On many occasions, however, the clinician would make the same types of off-topic or tangential errors frequently made by the child. The child must indicate when an error occurs.

        1. At first, the clinician may have to give the child extra cues. For example, each question could be answered correctly one time. Immediately after this, the same question might be repeated with a highly inappropriate response.

III. *Intrapersonal Scanning for Error*

    A. Tapes of conversations with the child are edited to produce a master tape consisting of samples of the child's own speech. Some of these examples will be correct and others will contain the child's target error. The child must scan these stimuli and point out her own errors. For example, questions by the child's co-conversationalists followed sometimes by appropriate responses and other times by off-target responses could be included.

    B. Alternatively, the clinician can record verbal interactions with the child. Immediately after each relevant production by the child, the taped sample would be reviewed for instances of the target error.

    C. When the child becomes capable of finding almost all errors on tape playback, she is required to monitor her on-line conversational acts for instances of the target error.

        1. These interactions should be taped so that review and validation of the child's errors are possible. This also makes it possible to show the child that she can converse in an appropriate manner when she carefully monitors the partner's and her own verbal and nonverbal behavior.

*Based on Yudkovitz, Lewiston, and Rottersman (1975).

describe the figures. The potential for miscommunication was very high. Once the speaker was satisfied with the descriptions and the listener had manipulated all of the figures as instructed by the speaker, the barrier was removed and the children checked their stacks of figures to determine the adequacy of the speaker's descriptions.

The task must be modified for most language impaired children. For example, for most of these children, describing abstract figures is too complex and does not foster the use of long sequences of semantically related utterances. Situations or scenes involving dolls and other props that are created by the clinician are usually more effective. These can be described by one child and recreated using identical materials by the other. Furthermore, because these children are likely to have difficulties both in sending the messages and in receiving them, the clinician will need to help the children throughout the task by providing feedback on the accuracy of messages. The clinician can also assist the listener by providing cues as to when requests for clarification may be useful.

Table 13-3 provides an illustration of a barrier task in which the subgoal for the speaker is to produce a sequence of ten or more utterances related to the topic with no off-topic responses. The specific goal for the listener is to follow the instructions of the speaker, producing requests for clarification where they are required. As the table indicates, this activity creates a fairly naturalistic type of communication activity that demands careful description, consideration of the listener's perspective, highly discriminating listening skills, and the use of and response to frequent requests for clarification.

A very interesting and useful variation on the barrier game is called the "over-the-shoulder" game (Muma, 1978b). In this variation, the speaker sits behind the listener and watches the listener respond to his verbal descriptions and instructions. This is a major advantage over the barrier game. If the listener follows an instruction incorrectly, the speaker becomes aware of this immediately and can begin an appropriate repair sequence rather than having to wait until all of the necessary actions have been described. Thus, the task places fewer demands on the children's memory for what was actually said in the instructions. Arguments about who was right and who was wrong can be avoided for the most part in this approach.

CHILD-ORIENTED APPROACHES

With only slight modifications, the child-oriented procedures discussed in Chapter 9 may be highly effective in attacking all of the error behaviors outlined in the basic goals for verbal noncommunicators, at least for some children. First, using this approach, the clinician observes the child closely and follows her lead. The clinician uses language that is well within the child's ability to comprehend. This, in itself, may reduce the amount of inappropriate speech produced by some children. Furthermore, because the clinician is so closely attuned to the child's focus of attention, the child's meaningful verbal efforts are more likely to be consequated in the fashion desired by the child. The message sent to the child is, "Make sense, and you will get what you want from others."

Second, using these procedures, the clinician must make an earnest effort to interpret everything that the child says. In effect, the clinician views the child as a co-conversationalist and places on her the responsibility of communicating meaning. When the child produces an utterance that is not appropriate within the present speaking context or that contains pronouns or nonspecific nouns and verbs whose referents cannot be determined, the clinician initiates procedures to determine the source of the communication breakdown. The following example illustrates this basic idea.

Child:	I like to play ball. That's not too funny.
Clinician:	*What's* not too funny?
Child:	I threw a ball once.
Clinician:	And what happened?
Child:	It broke a window.
Clinician:	Well, that wasn't funny at all, was it?
Child:	No.

Of course, not all children who are verbal noncommunicators will respond to the clinician's attempts to get them back on track, and not all attempts by the clinician to derive meaning from the child will be as successful as the one in the foregoing example. Even when they are not immediately effective, however, the clinician, family members, teachers, and other individuals who continually query the child's off-target or nonspecific productions may be telling the child that what she says is going to be interpreted by the conversational partners. Therefore, more planning of utterance form and content may be required. In a slightly more direct approach, the basic conversational rule can actually be provided for the child (e.g., "I don't know what you mean. You have to tell me what you mean!").

The following example involves a modification of the basic child-oriented procedures in which questions that are contingent on the child's utterances are frequently asked.

Child:	I want blue clay.
Clinician:	What are you going to make?
Child:	A robin have a red breast.
Clinician:	No, I *asked* you! *What are you going to make?*
Child:	A bird.
Clinician:	Oh, great! I'll make a birdhouse.

Here, the child's response to the clinician's first question did not fulfill her social obligation to provide the information that was queried

Table 13–3. A Sample Barrier Activity Involving Two Language Impaired Children and a Clinician*

Emily	Terri
(The clinician proceeds to make a cat using different colors of Play-Doh)	
You get some Play-Doh. Then you roll it.	
	(Looks confused)
Clinician: Terri, do you know what color you need?	
	No.
Clinician: You'd better ask.	
	What color?
Uh, red. I saw a firetruck.	
Clinician: Are we talking about firetrucks?	
No.	
Clinician: Then, tell Terri what to do next.	
You make a red ball. Then get some blue and make another ball. Then, put it on.	
	Huh?
This is fun.	
Clinician: Terri asked you something.	
What?	
	What ball goes on?
Put the blue one on the red one.	
Now make a yellow ball. It's very small. Put it on top.	
	It's a snowman.
Wait! Take some yellow and roll a big, long wormy-wormy.	
Now put it on the blue ball.	
	I can't!
It's a tail!	
Clinician: Terri, do you get it?	
	Yeah.
Clinician: Well, tell Emily then.	
	I get it now.
Now you pinch the ball.	
	Where?
On the top, you silly.	
Clinician: Maybe Terri doesn't know which ball to pinch.	
Oh. Pinch the top one. It's like a ears.	
	Oh.

Table 13–3 (continued)

Now make a nose and a eyes.

    Clinician: Okay. Now let's look and see.
                Did Emily tell you all of the in-
                structions, Terri?

(The two cats are compared and the appropriateness of the instructions from Emily and the feedback from Terri are discussed)

---

*The activity involves making an animal out of Play-Doh. The clinician is on the side of the speaker (Emily), and the listener (Terri) is on the other side of the barrier. Emily is required to describe the clinician's actions to Terri. Three cans of Play-Doh (one blue, one red, and one yellow) are on each side of the barrier. The barrier precludes visual inspection of the Play-Doh activities by the individuals on the opposite sides, but the speaker and the listener can see each other's faces.

by the question. The clinician then pointed out in no uncertain terms that the child was under obligation to provide a relevant response. Yudkovitz and co-workers (1975) caution that this type of intrusion by adults may result in highly negative reactions from some psychotic children. As noted above, more structured procedures that carefully program frequent success may be more appropriate for these individuals at first. Once they become capable of monitoring their errors in trainer-oriented procedures such as those of Yudkovitz and co-workers, however, it would seem highly appropriate to remind them continually that what they say must have some logical and easily identifiable association with the present speaking context to be regarded as acceptable.

We have found this type of query into children's stereotypical utterances to be quite effective in extinguishing them. For example, we worked with an adolescent girl who was moderately mentally retarded. She frequently used the phrase "It's getting crazy" or "It's gonna get crazy, now" or some other variant of this expression when she became excited about new activities or experiences. Our approach is exemplified in the following example.

    Clinician: Now, we're going to play a new game.
    Child: (laughing) It's getting real crazy now.
    Clinician: *What's* getting crazy?
                (Child looks at the clinician and laughs)
    Clinician: I think this game will be fun.
    Child: Yeah, it will be fun.

My interpretation of this example and many others like it is that the child was surprised by the fact that she had been held accountable for an utterance that had been used so habitually and thoughtlessly in the past. Since she did not really know what the utterance meant, she had no way of responding to our persistent queries. Of course, if the utterance had really been meaningful to the child, our approach gave her the opportunity to replace her unacceptable utterance with something more appropriate. For example, she might have said, "That means I'm happy" to which we might have responded, "Oh, I'm happy too. This game will be fun." As a result of our use of this procedure over a period of a few weeks, the child stopped using this stereotypical utterance at home and, as far as we could tell, at school as well. During clinic activities, she began to substitute more appropriate utterances in these contexts (e.g., "This will be fun," or "I'm ready now").

CONCLUSION

At present, we have only scattered anecdotal reports and case study information to demonstrate the effectiveness of most of the procedures that have been described in this chapter. Which procedures are selected for any particular child most likely will be based more on the clinician's theoretical perspectives on these children's problems and on past successes with children exhibiting similar symptoms than on any available experimental literature. Because of this, it is especially important to implement procedures such as those discussed in Chapter 7 for evaluating the success of treatment with verbal noncommunicators.

The conversational analyses proposed in Chapter 5 yield quantitative measures that can be used as dependent variables in these clinical experiments. For example, the clinician may want to determine the average proportions of requests for action, information, clarification, and so forth, that the child follows up with a responsive. It should also be worthwhile to determine the average proportion of nonrequestives that are followed by maintaining and extending acts as opposed to initiating and tangential acts. These variables could then be used as a metric for judging the child's response to treatment. Whatever specific goals are selected for a particular child, improved communicative performance *in actual conversational contexts* is the desired outcome of intervention with verbal noncommunicators as with all other language impaired children. I do not believe that we can be satisfied with anything less.

Chapter 14

Involving the Family in the Intervention Process

Regardless of the theoretical orientation adopted, it is a simple fact that the language impaired child spends much more time at home with family members and friends than she could ever spend at the clinic. Therefore, the child's needs to use language arise much more frequently at home and at school than in any clinical setting. Furthermore, these needs arise under conditions that are often difficult to simulate in the clinic. As has been discussed in the last several chapters, the most productive loci of learning may be those times when the child is highly motivated to communicate. It follows, then, that intervention that takes place in the home and involves the child's parents and family members may be beneficial, if not crucial, in reaching the child's basic and specific goals. If language skills are facilitated in the child's home by the child's family members, problems of extra-clinic generalization that have been the nemesis of language interventionists possibly could be circumvented.

There are several other potential advantages to incorporating parents into the child's intervention program. Because language intervention is so frequently a long-term process, and because so many children are in need of services, it makes sense to search for intervention approaches that can make the most effective use of the clinician's valuable time. Training parents to become intervention agents may be a viable time-saving alternative to clinic-centered services in which the clinician has direct contact with the child. This would allow the clinician to treat more children at a significantly lower cost per child (Baker, 1976; Cooper, Moodley, and Reynell, 1974, 1978, 1979; Manolson, 1979; McConkey, Jeffree, and Hewson, 1979; Reisinger, Ora, and Frangia, 1976).

If parent training procedures are truly cost-efficient and if they are effective, they may be ideally suited for use in cases of language impairment that are relatively low caseload priorities and otherwise might not be eligible for services. Similarly, they may make it possible for children who live long distances from the nearest speech, language, and hearing clinic to receive appropriate intervention. Parents could receive consultative assistance from the clinician and then report back for reevaluation at some later point in time. An appropriately designed home program may not only facilitate the child's development but also serve to inform the parents about their child's capabilities, normalize their expectations of the child's abilities and prognosis, and, generally, reduce their anxieties and frustrations. Such programs may make parents feel that something *can* be done to help their child and that they themselves are a positive factor in the helping process.

Finally, enlisting the assistance of parents in the intervention process may be an effective way of extending services to a child when formal intervention in the clinic must be terminated. For a variety of reasons, it is often necessary to stop clinic-centered intervention. The family may move, the child may have met all established goals, the child's progress may have plateaued, and so forth. In many such instances, a home intervention program may ensure that the child continues to develop with the greatest speed possible under any of these circumstances.

There is little disagreement among clinicians that, at some point, soliciting the help of family members in intervention is desirable, if not necessary. As we will see, disagreements arise concerning the optimal point in the child's program at which the parents should become involved and exactly what their role should be.

PARENTS AS CAUSAL AGENTS OF LANGUAGE IMPAIRMENT

Parents of language impaired children often wonder about the extent to which their own child-rearing practices have *caused* their children's difficulties in language learning. When a clinician suggests that she would like the parents to come in for some training and practice in intervention techniques that are designed to facilitate the child's language development, some parents are relieved. They are happy finally to receive professional guidance in helping their children. Other parents take such suggestions as confirmation of their own suspicions that they have been responsible in some way for their child's language learning difficulties. Clinicians must be aware of parents' sensitivities and take steps to ensure that their well-intentioned efforts to integrate parents into the intervention process reduce rather than exacerbate the parents' feelings of guilt, anxiety, and frustration.

One important step in avoiding such problems is to provide the parents with as much information as possible about the role of parents as factors in their children's language impairments. Unfortunately, we do not have a great deal to go on. The results of several investigations indicate that parents typically interact with their language impaired children in ways that are quite similar to the interaction patterns displayed by parents of younger, normally developing children with similar language skills (Conti-Ramsden and Friel-Patti, 1983; Cramblit and Siegel, 1977; Lasky and Klopp, 1982; MacPherson and Weber-Olsen, 1980; Rondal, 1978). However, in several studies, investigators have noted what appear to be problematic styles of interaction between mothers and their developmentally delayed (Cunningham et al., 1981; Marshall et al., 1973; Peterson and Sherrod, 1982) and specifically language impaired children (Lasky and Klopp, 1982; Newhoff, Silverman, and Millet, 1980; Peterson and Sherrod, 1982; Siegel et al., 1979; Wulbert et al., 1975). The most consistent observations in these studies have been that the parents of language impaired children tend to use more directive speech acts (e.g., questions and commands) and produce significantly fewer utterances that are semantically related to the child's utterances than do parents of language normal children. There is widespread agreement that these features have a negative impact on language development and that this style of interaction should be modified, whenever possible.

We must be cautious in our interpretation of these findings, however. Because of the reciprocal nature of social-communicative interaction, the direction of the influence is difficult to ascertain. In other words, it can be argued that the child's behavior has caused some extraordinary parental reaction just as easily as it can be claimed that the child's difficulties have arisen because of the inadequate performance of the parent (Cunningham et al., 1981; Peterson and Sherrod, 1982; Siegel et al., 1979; Wulbert et al., 1975).

In most cases that we have observed, there has been no evidence to suggest that the parents' behavior caused the child's language learning problems. This has been true even when the parents were highly unresponsive to the child's initiatives and rigidly constrained her behavior. Laying blame on the parents in these cases is counterproductive and contraindicated. Thus, I believe that clinicians should be very discreet in their use of highly judgmental terms like "clinical mothers" (Clezy, 1979) to describe parents who exhibit what might be viewed as maladaptive patterns of interaction with their children. Furthermore, I do not believe that parent participation in the child's intervention program should depend on the clinician's judgment of parental inadequacy in social interactions with their child. In her review of the literature on parent training research, Howlin (1984) concluded that

> although parents cannot be held responsible in any way for the delayed development of their children it is possible that modifying their interactions with their children might help to create a more beneficial language environment. Hence, their direct involvement in language intervention programmes would seem to be important for success. (p. 200)

This is exactly the message that we attempt to convey to the parents of the language impaired children with whom we have the good fortune of working.

THE PARENTS' ROLE IN INTERVENTION

Just as there is no one intervention procedure that is right for every child at all times, there is no parent intervention program that is right for every parent. Fortunately, there are several options available to the clinician for including parents in the child's intervention program. The roles that parents are asked to play differ significantly in the amount of time and mental and emotional energy that they require from the parents as well as the clinician.

Parents as Aides

The basic rationale for using parents as aides in the intervention program is to provide the child with more of the same type of treatment that is offered in the clinic. If within-clinic intervention is helping the child, a larger dose of the same procedures should result in greater effectiveness. Furthermore, this procedure should effect greater extraclinic generalization because the child develops and practices new behaviors in at least two different locations with at least two different interventionists.

There are three traditional ways of employing parents as aides. First, the parents may be involved from the outset of training. In this case, their efforts in the home serve to supplement the clinician's efforts in the establishment and automatization of a new behavior. For example, Zwitman and Sonderman (1979) instructed the parents of their language impaired clients in the use of their training procedure and recommended that they use it 10 to 15 minutes daily to supplement once weekly sessions held in the clinic (see Chapter 8 for details on this operant program). Sandler and co-workers (1983) trained a group of mothers to work on the goals of their children's Individual Education Plans in language as well as in four other areas. The training tasks were essentially the same as those used by the teachers in the children's school.

A second method of involving parents as training aides is through sequential modification (see Chapter 8). In this approach, the parent is trained to carry out activities designed to elicit target structures only after the child has reached a high level of performance in the clinic. The parent extends an established training program while the clinician initiates a new program in the clinic. The emphasis in this case is on the generalization of a trained behavior to more naturalistic contexts. Gray and Ryan (1973) made use of this procedure in a home carry-over program in which the parents conducted eight 5 to 10 minute formal sessions in the home over a 2 week period. Parents were trained to evoke target responses from their children as they casually looked through books and magazines. They scored the child's responses using standard recording sheets and then reported back to the clinician. Mulac and Tomlinson (1977) used Gray and Ryan's procedures to teach "is" questions and found that this type of home program was insufficient. In a more extensive sequential modification program developed by these investigators, parents observed the clinician's attempts to evoke the target structure in activities outside the training context and practiced these procedures immediately after the clinician's efforts. They were then assigned to use the procedures in the home (see Chapter 8 for a more detailed description of procedural aspects of this study).

As a third model of parents as aides, parents and family members often can assist the clinician within clinic sessions even when no attempt is made to train them to administer formal procedures on their own. We often bring family members into the clinic sessions to serve as models, to heighten the child's attention, to help the clinician to motivate and reinforce the child, to help create more naturalistic intervention contexts, and, generally, to assist the clinician in any way possible. Very little training is required in these cases because the clinician is always present to provide feedback and the parent is not required to administer training in formal contexts at home.

Effectiveness of the Procedures

Because the clinician still has the major responsibility for intervention, using parents as aides does not always represent major time savings to the clinician. Furthermore, because no effort is made to train the parents to make use of general teaching principles or incidental teaching techniques, it is unlikely that they will develop the ability to design and implement intervention goals and activities on their own. The parents are completely dependent on the clinician and, therefore, the clinician accepts a relatively long-term commitment to direct service delivery in this type of intervention. It is true, however, that if parents are trained to supplement in-clinic intervention with a home program, it may be possible to reduce the number of sessions required in the clinic.

The effectiveness of instructing parents to carry out formal procedures to meet objectives identical to those being trained in the clinic has not yet been tested adequately. Zwitman and Sonderman (1979) noted some positive results from their intervention program, but it is impossible to determine the extent to which the parent program was a factor. The children in the experiment by Sandler and colleagues (1983) demonstrated no improvements in their language behavior with respect to a control group who received only in-school treatment.

In our own experience, we have found that cursory attempts to involve the parents with supplemental "homework" for the child often result in parental confusion and frustration. More frequently, the procedures either are used incorrectly by the parents, or they are not implemented at all. As discussed in detail throughout the rest of this chapter, if any parent intervention is to succeed, the clinician must be willing to invest a good deal of time and energy in parent training and program evaluation.

In some cases, however, generalization of behaviors trained in the clinic to extraclinic environments may depend on some form of sequential modification. One advantage of the sequential modification approach is that the amount of time the parents have to commit to intervention is limited; for some families, greater involvement in formal teaching is not realistic because of the time and energy commitments involved. A second advantage is that the target linguistic behavior has already been established by the child by the time parent intervention begins. Therefore, some correct responding on the child's part is likely from the outset. Because of this, the parent's job is made much easier, as is the clinician's job of training the parent.

The simplest form of parental participation as intervention aides consists of having the parents take part in the clinic sessions. In many cases, this form of intervention will be prohibitive because it requires that the parent attend the clinic sessions regularly. Nevertheless, it is useful because it makes it easier for the clinician to design more natural activities. Furthermore, it allows parents to feel more a part of their child's program while actually requiring very little other than their presence.

No quantitative evidence for the utility of this type of parental participation exists; however, we have found that, when they are available and willing, and the children do not resist, parents often can be strong motivators of their children and reinforcers of their success. Since children typically identify closely with their parents and siblings, alternating these individuals as models may enhance observational learning through modeling procedures.

Of course, there are times when having the parent in the therapy room is disruptive. For example, the child may cling to the mother and refuse to perform when she is present. This type of parental involvement is contraindicated in such cases.

Parents as Primary Intervention Agents

There have been numerous attempts to train parents to take on major intervention responsibilities. They have been trained to use trainer-oriented techniques to manage their children's behavior problems and to facilitate acquisition and development of self-help, preacademic, and speech and language skills in the home (Arnold, Sturgis, and Forehand, 1977; Baker, 1976; Baker, Heifetz, and Murphy, 1980; Bidder, Bryant, and Gray; 1975; Forehand and Atkeson, 1977; Harris, Wolchik, and Weitz, 1981; Hemsley et al., 1978; Howlin, 1981a,b; Kemper, 1980; Kysela, Hillyard, McDonald, and Ahlston-Taylor, 1981; MacDonald et al., 1974; Reisinger, Ora, and Frangia, 1976; Salzberg and Villani, 1983). There also have been many reports of programs involving parent administration of child-oriented language intervention procedures (Fey et al., 1978; Hubbell, 1981; Mash and Terdal, 1973; Seitz and Hoekenga, 1974; Seitz and Marcus, 1976; Seitz and Riedell, 1974) and hybrid procedures (Cheseldine and McConkey, 1979; Clezy, 1979; Cooper et al., 1974, 1978, 1979; Culatta and Horn, 1981; Lombardino and Mangan, 1983; Manolson, 1979; McConkey et al., 1979; McDade, 1981; Wulz, Hall, and Klein, 1983). For each of these approaches, the parents become the sole providers of direct intervention following a period of training. This is in sharp contrast with the more subordinate roles that parents play as intervention aides. The role that the parent fills is markedly different in each intervention approach.

In trainer-oriented approaches, the parents are trained to take on the role of the child's teacher. Although attempts are often made to teach the parents how to make use of behavior modification principles in naturalistic contexts, some formal training of the target behaviors to the child is required several times per week. Parents are given training in the administration of specific procedures (e.g., modeling, prompting, reinforcing, fading) and activities designed by the clinician to facilitate the development of specific linguistic behaviors. The parents typically are trained to record the child's responses. They then report back regularly to the clinician so that progress can be evaluated and new activities can be developed.

In child-oriented interventions, no direct teaching of any specific language behavior is attempted, and no specific language structures are selected as goals. Hubbell (1981) states that

> Our goal in working with parents, then, is not to teach the parent to teach the child. Rather, it is to establish transactional patterns between child and parents that maximize the opportunities for language growth in the child. (p. 275)

Through modifications in the characteristic patterns of interaction between the child and family members, the child is expected to increase her rate of spontaneous talking and use of initiatory behaviors such as questions and commands. Gains in formal linguistic abilities as measured globally by MLU or, perhaps, Developmental Sentence Scores (Lee, 1974) are also anticipated as a result of improved social relationships and more frequent, less highly constrained opportunities to communicate.

Parents are trained to make use of child-oriented procedures as they interact with their children at all times during the day, in the home, and elsewhere. These procedures include parallel talk, self-talk, expansions, and expatiations, as well as reducing the use of highly constraining behaviors such as commands and questions that are not contingent on the child's own utterances. In general, the parent is trained to be more patient, to wait for the child to initiate some behavior, whether communicative or not, and to operate on those child-selected behaviors, using simple, but complete utterances. The successful implementation of this type of home intervention program represents a dramatic change of role for the clinician, the parent, and the child.

In hybrid approaches to parent intervention, specific goals are selected by the clinician, often in collaboration with the parents. In this regard, they are similar to trainer-oriented procedures. They are much more like child-oriented approaches, however, in that parents are shown how to reach the selected specific goals by using nondirective forms of interaction and highly responsive patterns of verbalization. Prompts and attempts to evoke target structures from children are generally limited to contexts in which the child has initiated some act that renders use of the target structure appropriate. Teaching contexts are never highly programmed as in trainer-oriented approaches.

Effectiveness of the Procedures

Trainer-Oriented Approaches. Programs designed to enlist parents as language teachers, using trainer-oriented procedures, generally have been successful in accomplishing the specific goals of the training programs (Arnold et al., 1977; Bidder et al., 1975; Forehand and Atkeson, 1977; Harris et al., 1981; Hemsley et al., 1978; Howlin, 1981a,b; Kemper, 1980; Kysela et al., 1981; MacDonald et al., 1974), although the gains have often been modest. Many of these programs have not only succeeded in reaching goals designed by the clinician for the child, they have also resulted in the same general improvements in the parents' adjustment toward their children and in their own abilities to deal with their children's special problems (Arnold et al., 1977; Baker, 1976; Baker et al., 1980; Bidder et al., 1975; Holmes, Hemsley, Rickett, and Likierman, 1982; MacDonald et al., 1974).

Despite the encouraging results obtained thus far, there is still a great deal that we do not know about parents as primary language trainers, and some caution is advised. First, with few exceptions (e.g., Arnold et al., 1977), the children trained have been severely language impaired, and the language behaviors trained by parents have been words or simple language structures. Efforts to train more complex morphological and syntactic structures have not always been successful. For example, Howlin (1981a,b; see also Hemsley et al., 1978) taught parents to use operant techniques to train a variety of linguistic forms to their autistic clients, aged 3 to 11 years. Over an 18 month period, most significant gains were observed in the spontaneous use of socially directed utterances. Few gains were observed in the acquisition of new linguistic forms. Clements, Evans, Jones, Osborne, and Upton (1982) reported that their preschool-aged and early school-aged developmentally delayed children showed only minimal gains following 16 to 18 months of home intervention administered by the parents, and these gains were no greater than those of a control group. These investigators noted that the improvements that were observed tended to be within a developmental level (i.e., single words, two words) rather than across developmental levels. At present, we know very little about the effectiveness of parents in the training of more complex language forms to children who have only mild or moderate delays in their development.

Second, although it is reasonable to assume that behaviors that are acquired through parent training in the home setting are likely to generalize to other contexts, there is very little evidence to support this assumption. This may be due to the fact that so few studies have been concerned about setting generalization. Yet, of those few studies that have examined generalization effects of behaviors trained by parents using trainer-oriented procedures, the results have not been encouraging. For example, Kysela and associates (1981) reported that the positive results of their parent-centered direct teaching program did not generalize to other persons and settings. Therefore, they taught parents to use the incidental teaching procedures of Hart and Risley (1968, 1974, 1975) as a complement to direct teaching. In their analysis of the generalization effects of 45 parent training studies, Forehand and Atkeson (1977) observed that many studies had reported positive results, but that procedures used to evaluate generalization had not always been adequate. Among those studies using more controlled evaluation measures, generalization was shown not to be as extensive as had been hoped.

It seems that as long as highly formal, nonnaturalistic behavioral teaching techniques are being used, generalization should be expected to be a problem, regardless of who administers the programs or where the training takes place. Siegel and Spradlin (1978) noted that "Parents as teachers in the home environment help make the clinic more similar to the home and increase the chance that similar reinforcement contingencies will be applied in both settings" (pp. 392–393). Based on the findings of the behavior management projects reviewed by Forehand and Atkeson (1977), however, it might be asked whether using parents as trainers helps make the clinic more like the home or whether it helps make the home more like the clinic! Steps must be taken to ensure that parent training results in more than the creation of stimulus conditions and contingencies in the home that are every bit as artificial as those often created in the clinic.

A third area of concern with trainer-oriented approaches is that there are very few studies that have sampled children's behaviors over extended periods of time following training. Of those that have, the results have not always been reassuring. In their studies with autistic children, Harris and co-workers (1981), Hemsley and colleagues (1978), Holmes and co-workers (1982), and Howlin (1981a,b) observed rapid gains followed by a relative plateau in learning. This pattern could have resulted from two factors. First, it may be a function of the children who received training. In general, although some provocative results have been reported, the use of operant techniques has resulted in only limited success in training oral language behaviors to autistic children except when the children possessed some functional language at the outset of training (Howlin, 1981a,b).

The early plateaus reported in studies with autistic children have not been observed by MacDonald and colleagues in their use of the

ELIS procedures primarily with nonautistic retarded children (Mac-Donald, 1978; MacDonald et al., 1974). As we shall see, ELIS training typically focuses a great deal of attention on application of the procedures in naturalistic contexts throughout the day. Still, the gains recorded by MacDonald and his associates have not been followed up over extended periods as long as a year, to the best of my knowledge. It is not clear whether the early improvements observed are maintained and continued over such long periods of time.

Second, failures to observe continued progress with some children in parent intervention programs may be due to the parents' failure to continue to use the procedures. I will have more to say about this problem in the next section on parent training methods.

Child-Oriented Approaches. To date, most attempts to train parents to make use of child-oriented procedures have been successful in at least some important respect. Following training, children have been shown to interact more and, in Seitz and Hoekenga's investigation (1974), to use higher MLUs than they did prior to training. Parents have consistently reported that, following intervention, they viewed their children as more competent; therefore, they were more comfortable in letting their children explore their environments without parental interference. When they became confident that their children could respond, they became more comfortable with waiting and following the child's lead with contingent behavior. Therefore, these procedures would seem to be especially applicable to parents of children who produce low rates of initiatory communicative acts (e.g., passive conversationalists and inactive communicators).

Perhaps the greatest advantage of training parents to use child-oriented techniques is that their use in the home requires no extra time on the parents' part. They can and should be used as the child is getting dressed, eating, boarding the bus for school, and riding in the car. The real challenge, then, is to help parents realize that what they learn in the clinic can be adapted to almost any situation. This is not as easy as it may sound because regular, opportunistic usage of these procedures requires considerable mental energy—something that is often hard for tired, busy parents to muster as they carry out their daily activities. Nevertheless, the use of these procedures has demonstrated that parents can be trained to become the major factor in their child's language intervention program without forcing them into the traditional role of teacher, a role in which many parents do not feel comfortable (MacDonald et al., 1974).

Despite the positive outcome of the parent intervention studies reviewed earlier, there is room for caution in relying solely on a child-oriented parental involvement approach to intervention. First, investigations of the effectiveness of child-oriented procedures have involved very small numbers of children and have been weak methodologically (see Chapter 8 for more detailed criticisms of experimental procedures). Second, as with trainer-oriented approaches, most examples of child-oriented interventions have involved young or severely language impaired children at very early levels of language learning. The effectiveness of these procedures with older, more linguistically advanced children is not known.

Third, although it is logical on theoretical grounds to assume that the positive results of child-oriented programs will generalize to all relevant speaking contexts, there is no empirical support for this assumption. As noted in Chapter 8, it is possible that the child's gains in communicative ability will be restricted to those contexts in which the child's social partners play a nonconstraining role in the interaction.

One final problem that we have encountered with training child-oriented procedures to parents is that clinicians who use the facilitative play procedures appropriately often get rapid positive results. During the observation phase of training, parents are often very impressed with what they see from their children. When the parents begin to take a turn, however, the child often reverts to her more typical passive style of interaction. We have seen this occur even when the parents are administering the procedures with admirable proficiency. It is understandable that they find this very disturbing and frustrating. In these cases, we explain to the parents that they are using a style of interacting with their child that is markedly different from that which the child expects. It often takes a period of a few weeks before the child can accept the parent in their new role and begin to adapt to it. Once this happens, though, highly favorable changes on the child's part usually ensue.

Hybrid Approaches. Reports of the outcomes of parent intervention using hybrid procedures have been consistently positive (Cheseldine and McConkey, 1979; Cooper et al., 1974, 1978, 1979; Culatta and Horn, 1981; McConkey et al., 1979). Like child-oriented procedures, most hybrid procedures offer the significant advantage of practicality in naturalistic contexts. Although clinician-designed activities are typically assigned several times weekly, the activities are play-oriented and often do not differ significantly from activities commonly performed by parents with their children throughout the day.

Because specific goals are selected prior to intervention, it is relatively easy to demonstrate through the use of multiple baseline treatment designs that the child's progress following treatment was the effect of the intervention and not some other, uncontrolled variables.

Two studies have taken advantage of this feature (Cheseldine and Mc-Conkey, 1979; McConkey et al., 1979). Although the use of a multiple baseline design involved only a combined total of three children in these studies, the outcomes of these experiments indicate that parent administration of hybrid procedures does lead to significant gains on the children's specific goals. Furthermore, these studies provide some of the only convincing evidence that the promising results of facilitative play techniques actually stem from parental adoption of a less constraining, more responsive style of interaction.

The descriptive analysis of Cooper and associates (1979) is based on a larger number of subjects, many of whom were specifically language impaired. The data presented indicate that hybrid procedures administered in the home can result in gains in language skills commensurate with the child's gains in chronological age. However, some children who received no professional intervention at all made similar gains. The nature of the statistics used to analyze the data makes it impossible to conclude with confidence that the gains of the children receiving intervention actually exceeded those who received no intervention or those who received more "traditional" treatment in the language clinic. Furthermore, because of the design of the study, it is impossible to determine which aspects of the intervention procedure were responsible for the children's improvements.

The problems associated with training parents to use hybrid procedures are similar to those of the other approaches discussed. With the exception of the program of Cooper and associates (1979), most of the available reports deal with developmentally delayed or deaf children at very early stages of language development. Claims for the effectiveness with older, more linguistically advanced children or with children with basic goals other than the facilitation of content-form interactions are largely speculative. Another highly significant problem involves generalization of gains observed in the child's linguistic behavior. Even the reasonably well controlled study of McConkey and co-workers (1979) suffers from the fact that measures were always collected from parent-child interactions in the game settings within which intervention took place. Whether the chilren's new verbal skills were used in other social and physical contexts is not known.

METHODS OF TRAINING PARENTS AS THE PRIMARY AGENTS OF INTERVENTION

The need for more carefully controlled research on the effectiveness of parent interventionists is great. Nevertheless, the results of many studies, taken together, indicate that all three intervention approaches involving parents have promise. In this section, the methods that have been used to train parents as interventionists will be presented and evaluated.

Trainer-Oriented Approaches

The trainer-oriented methods that have been used to date have been behaviorally oriented and, in most cases, very highly structured. For example, Kysela and associates (1981) successfully trained parents to use an operant conditioning program with their developmentally delayed infants and toddlers. The program involved tightly programmed steps for evoking gross and fine motor imitations and sound and word imitations as entry skills for the operant language program of Guess and co-workers (1976). Rather extensive training schemes typically are required to get parents to implement these procedures adequately. The length of training varies, but most programs are spread over a period of several weeks or months.

An outline of a clearly described and reasonably well documented parent training paradigm, that associated with the Environmental Language Intervention Strategy (ELIS) (MacDonald et al., 1974), is provided in Table 14-1 (see Chapter 8 for discussion of intervention goals and procedures). The ELIS procedures have also been taught successfully to parents of developmentally delayed children using slight modifications of the procedures shown in the table. MacDonald (1978) cites several methodological adaptations conducted by his students and colleagues. For example, a 7 week parent training program used by Manolson (1976) included one session in which general principles of behavior management were discussed, two sessions in which video-recorded training sessions involving the mother and her child were viewed and assessed, and two evening sessions in which the fathers were instructed in the use of the procedures. Nickols (1976) demonstrated that ELIS procedures could be trained effectively even when the child was not involved in the parent training sessions. Children of mothers trained with clinician-mother role play made gains that were equivalent to those made by children of mothers who received practice with their own children.

There is evidence that more time-efficient group training procedures are also highly effective in training ELIS procedures and in inducing marked gains in children's MLU and use of targeted semantic relations. Kemper (1980) reported a successful implementation of ELIS procedures in a 12 week parent training program involving the parents of five language impaired children. In this program, an orientation meeting was held in which the general purposes of the pro-

Table 14–1. The Parent Training Phase of the Environmental Language Intervention Strategy*

1. Session 1: Imitation training
    a. Clinician role-plays imitation training with mother and demonstrates recording of responses.
    b. Parent takes role as teacher with clinician playing child's role.
    c. Clinician models the procedure with the child, and mother records responses.
    d. Mother performs the procedure with child and records responses.
2. Parent is instructed to carry out the procedure at home with the child daily.
3. Session 2: Conversation training
    a. Procedures are identical to those of session 1, except that principles of the conversation phase of training are taught.
4. Parent is instructed to carry out conversation training daily at home.
5. Session 3: Play training
    a. Procedures are identical to those of sessions 1 and 2 except that principles of the play phase of training are taught.
6. Sessions 4 through 10
    a. Practice combining all three phases, imitation, conversation, and play within the same session.
    b. Discuss with the parent any difficulties they are experiencing, program adjustments required, need to modify recording, and so forth, as well as evaluation of the child's progress.
    c. Through modeling, role-playing, and feedback to the parent, stress development of new ways to create nonlinguistic stimuli that require the child's target structures.
    d. Stress the use of appropriate reinforcement of correct responses and punishment of incorrect responses.
7. Sessions 11 through 14
    a. Use modeling and reinforcement to help parents learn to develop nonlinguistic and linguistic contexts that are more typical of everyday needs and interests of the child and to expand training to new semantic relations.

*Sessions between clinician and parents are held twice weekly. Based on Mac-Donald, Blott, Gordon, Spiegel, and Hartmann (1974).

gram and the extent of parent involvement were discussed. Parents signed a contract stating that they agreed to attend 12 weekly meetings and that they would administer two 15 minute sessions at least 3 days a week. Videotapes of each parent using the procedures with their own child were made periodically in the clinic. The parent wore a miniature FM receiver during the session, and the clinician provided on-line encouragement and feedback as he watched through a one-way mirror. At each meeting, the videotape of one parent was presented and discussed.

MacDonald (1978) noted briefly that positive results had been obtained in each of five independent projects with parent groups. He suggested that group training paradigms appear to be equally effective and more time-efficient than individual training programs.

Child-Oriented Approaches

The parent training programs for child-oriented interventions have tended to be nondirective. An outline of procedures adapted from Seitz and Hoekenga (1974) and Fey and co-workers (1978) is presented in Table 14–2. In this paradigm, the parents are not told explicitly what to do to facilitate their child's language. Rather, they are led to discover those intervention techniques that result in greater responsivity and longer, more complex utterances in the child's behavior through observation of the clinician. The clinician points out positive exchanges between the child and clinician, and the parents are asked to describe and analyze these events.

Seitz and Hoekenga (1974) and Seitz and Riedell (1974) made use of the parents' own children in their training sessions. Fey and co-workers (1978) obtained positive results when parents observed and practiced their new interactional patterns with language impaired children other than their own. This finding suggests that interventions involving role play between the clinician and parents or even observation of prepared films of other parents with other children may also be effective.

Although much of their general program was trainer-oriented, Mash and Terdal (1973) demonstrated the effectiveness of videotapes in training facilitative, nondirective forms of play to five groups of mothers. Eight to 10 mothers participated in each group, and all groups met for ten 1 hour sessions. Facilitative play techniques were the topic of two of these sessions. Videotaped examples of *other* parents interacting with *other* children, 10 to 60 seconds in length, were shown to illustrate ways of increasing the number of mother-child interactions during play. Examples of the effects of frequent questioning and commanding were also shown. Parents then discussed these illustrative examples and uncovered the principles of interaction underlying them.

Hybrid Approaches

The hybrid parent intervention approaches to be discussed here are of two slightly different varieties. In one form, specific goals are selected at the outset of intervention. The parent is instructed in the use of facilitative forms of verbal interaction within specially designed activities as a means of reaching these objectives. In the alternative approach, the program begins by training child-oriented procedures as discussed in the last section. Then, specific goal-directed activities that are often initiated by the adult are introduced. The application of child-oriented methods within the specific adult-selected activities is then stressed. The training option, then, is really one of starting out specific and becoming more broad through the introduction of more and more activities and goals (Cheseldine and McConkey, 1979; Clezy, 1979; Culatta and Horn, 1981; Lombardino and Mangan, 1983; McConkey et al., 1979) or of starting very generally in child-selected activities and activities of daily living and progressing to increasingly more specific goal-directed activities (Cooper et al., 1974, 1978, 1979; Manolson, 1979; McDade, 1981).

McConkey and associates (1979) selected goals, including vocabulary items and early semantic relations, for 10 developmentally delayed children. In one parent training session, 1 to 1¼ hours in length, parents were acquainted with a simple game and instructed in how to stimulate their child by producing high rates of comments about the child and her actions. Their task was to follow the child's lead rather than to use questions and commands to direct the child's attention and actions. Training procedures involved the now familiar sequence of explanation, modeling the procedures with the parent's child, and parental practice with feedback from the clinician. A written outline of the goals and procedures was given to the parents, and they were instructed to play the games for 10 minutes or so each day. Parents were encouraged to audiotape these sessions whenever possible. Follow-up contacts were arranged in the clinic every 2 weeks. At these meetings, feedback on the parents' use of procedures was provided, and new activities were described and demonstrated. Over the 5 month intervention period, seven of the 10 parents whose language was analyzed exhibited significant increases in the use of nonconstraining statements over the course of treatment. Two of the three parents who showed no positive change took part in one session in which the clinician pointed out "good" and "less helpful" behaviors of the parent in a videotaped interaction with their child. This single session resulted in large increases in the use of comments that were maintained over 10 sessions. The parents of one child did not use the procedures and eventually dropped out of the program.

Cheseldine and McConkey (1979) demonstrated that lengthy, parent-training programs are not always necessary. They provided parents of seven preschoolers with Down's syndrome with toys and other play materials and with a set of specific goals, such as a small set of verbs and simple word combinations involving these verbs. No formal instructions or demonstrations were given. Mothers and fathers were each asked to carry out and tape record at least four play sessions in the home over a period of 1 to 2 weeks. Two parents who were unsuccessful in facilitating their child's use of target structures on

Table 14–2. An Outline of the Nondirective Parent Training Procedures Used to Train Nonconstraining, Language-Facilitating Forms of Parent-Child Interaction*

1. Tell the parents that you would like to observe the child with them to see how the child uses language when she is with a familiar adult. This interaction should last approximately 15 minutes and should be videotaped, if possible. Several observations of this type of interaction should be made.

2. Transcribe the taped session including the utterances of both the parent and child and analyze the interaction using categories of behavior such as those given below.

   a. Questions: Any form of question, regardless of intent.

      † (1) Contingent on the child's speech or vocalizations.

      (2) Noncontingent on the child's speech or vocalizations.

   b. Commands: Any imperative forms, including attempts to redirect the child's attention (e.g., "Look at this!").

   c. Comments: Descriptions, identifications, statements, and so forth, that are typically delcarative in intent.

      † (1) Contingent on the child's speech or vocalizations—expansions, expatiations, and imitations.

      (2) Noncontingent on the child's speech or vocalizations.

         † (a) Focused on the child's behavior.

         † (b) Focused on the parent's behavior.

         (c) Focused on some object or event external to the interaction context.

   † d. Responses to the child's requests.

   e. Other verbal behaviors.

3. Explain to the parents that the program is designed to increase their use of ways of interacting with their children that are believed to be most effective in getting language impaired children to talk more and to use longer, more complex sentences.

4. Demonstrate the use of the behaviors marked with a dagger in No. 2 above. Emphasis is on verbal responsiveness to the child's behaviors.

   a. Throughout the demonstration, call the parent's attention to specific interchanges that are positive (i.e., those in which a facilitative behavior of the clinician is used). Focus on those episodes that result in some positive response by the child. Have the parents write these exchanges down for use in later discussions. Aim for 10 to 15 examples per session (Fey et al., 1978).

5. At regular conferences, discuss the positive behaviors and have the parents verbalize their understanding of what the clinician is doing. Emphasize how the child is responding to these behaviors. Written or videotaped records should facilitate these discussions.

6. After approximately six sessions, allow the parents to interact with the child. Videotape, when possible.

   a. Record some positive and negative episodes for later analysis and discussion. Negative episodes are those in which a constraining behavior is used, and the child either does not respond or responds in a simple, short utterance.

   b. Provide positive feedback throughout the interaction following episodes in which the child has responded favorably to positive parent behaviors.

   c. Discuss the parent-child interaction using the specific examples recorded as topics. Focus on instances in which the child responds positively to the parent's positive behaviors.

Table 14–2 (continued)

7. Videotape several parent-child interactions again at the completion of the 5 to 8 week program.

*Sessions are held 3 times weekly.

†Dagger (†) indicates nonconstraining, facilitative behaviors.

Based on Seitz and Hoekenga (1974) and Fey, Newhoff, and Cole (1978).

their own became successful facilitators after only a 30 minute discussion with the clinician. During this session, the clinician provided written and oral instructions to use the target forms in a stimulating but nondemanding manner.

Culatta and Horn (1981) trained four mothers to use focused stimulation to teach new words to their hearing impaired toddlers. Each mother observed at least eight sessions in which the clinician used the exposure procedures. This was followed by three sessions designed to teach the word "open." In the first two sessions, mothers observed the clinician and acted as aides and models. In the third session, the mother practiced the procedure by opening a variety of containers and modeling the word for the child. No efforts were made to get the child to respond. Following training, the mothers were asked to think of examples of activities in which the word "open" could be used repeatedly. The mother and clinician also discussed the child's performance and ways to increase the frequency of presenting models of the target word. Formal training ended by instructing the mothers to use these procedures for a new verb during six 5 minute periods per day for a week and to make use of this word wherever appropriate in naturalistic contexts. At the end of this week another word was assigned.

The Hanen Early Language Program (Manolson, 1979; 1983) is a prototype hybrid procedure that begins with training on general facilitative play and incidental teaching techniques and proceeds to more specific goal-related activities. The program, spread over a 12 week period, involves ten 3 hour group meetings, two individual videotaped consultations, and two follow-up consultations. In the first two sessions, nonconstraining, facilitative procedures are discussed. Assignments are given to use the procedures three times daily and to note changes in the child's responses. Incidental teaching techniques in response to child requests are role-played in the third session. Session 4 is a videotaped home visit used for assessment of parent and child progress. Recommendations for parent modifications are made. These tapes are shared and critically assessed by the group in the fifth session. In sessions 6 to 8 parents are instructed in the development of specific goals and in the use of procedures such as instructing, prompting, shaping, and reinforcing their children. They role play activities and learn to score their children's responses. Session 9 is another home videotaping session designed to assist in evaluation of the parents' use of the structured teaching procedures. These tapes are shared with the group in session 10. Sessions 11 and 12 involve extension of the child's skills into new activities, such as play and music, and into more diverse everyday activities. Finally, a review of program goals and an evaluation conclude the treatment.

The Efficiency of the Procedures

A brief overview of the procedures used to train parents reveals that the similarities both across and within the three intervention approaches are far more striking than the differences. Modification of parental behavior has been successful using some version of the following sequence of procedures: (1) explanation of the program and its rationale; (2) modeling of the procedures by the clinician with the child or in role play with the parents themselves; (3) parental practice of the procedures with the child or in role play with the clinician; (4) feedback from the clinician to the parent concerning the adequacy of administration of the training procedures; (5) discussions with the parents concerning any difficulties they may be having; (6) the parents' administration of the program in the home; and (7) follow-up on a regular basis to answer any further questions, to discuss the child's progress, and to plan and practice new procedures. Cheseldine and McConkey (1979) demonstrated that not all of these steps are necessary with all parents. At present, however, we have no way of knowing for certain which parents will respond to less rigorous treatments. The prudent approach would appear to be the inclusion of at least some form of all seven steps. This type of training takes a good deal of time and effort, but given the general effectiveness of the procedures, it still represents a highly efficient use of the clinician's time.

Although the nondirective discovery methods of Seitz and Hoekenga (1974) and of Fey and colleagues (1978) appear to have been effective, there is no evidence to show that they are more beneficial than more direct methods of training child-oriented procedures to parents (cf. Mash and Terdal, 1973). In addition, more direct methods may result in more rapid changes in parental behaviors. The studies of McConkey and co-workers (1979) and Cheseldine and McConkey (1979) indicate quite convincingly that, when activities are simple, goals are clearly identified, and parents are willing to participate in home intervention, facilitative play techniques can be taught in one session that may involve nothing more than the introduction of appropriate toys and a description of specific goals.

One way of increasing the efficiency of all types of parent training is to work with parents in groups. Group procedures appear to be at least as effective as individual parent training programs and may offer significant advantages. Baker (1976) sums up these advantages succinctly:

> Parents can derive peer support and encouragement for their own teaching efforts as well as information from others in the group about their child-rearing practices and about available services. A group format also makes more feasible a structured curriculum utilizing films, tapes, modeling, role playing, group problem solving, and mini-lectures; some of these would be impossible in one-to-one training, others possible but cumbersome. (p. 707)

Do Parents Implement the Procedures in the Home?

Although the reported changes in parental behavior following training are impressive, many studies reported have not carefully monitored how well the parents actually implemented the procedures in the home. When such monitoring has been done, the results sometimes indicate that parents do not administer highly programmed steps as planned or as trained. For example, Kysela and associates (1981) made videotape records of parents' teaching sessions. Their report of the results is sketchy, but at least one parent required a good deal of assistance throughout the training period to perform the procedures accurately.

In their follow-up of 14 parents of autistic children who had participated in a trainer-oriented parent-intervention program, Holmes and co-workers (1982) reported that four parents had not wholeheartedly believed in the behavioral principles used, two had thought that their own methods were better, one was extremely upset with the use of time-out procedures used to punish the child, and one found that the use of external reinforcers such as candy was meaningless to her child. Hubbell (1981) also reported a case in which a family rejected the clinician's efforts to get them to use operant procedures. Holmes and co-workers conclude "it could be that for some parents, the use of behavioral principles requires just too much of a shift from their own views about child care, and so may never be successful" (p. 340).

It is not likely that child-oriented or hybrid procedures would be perceived by parents as being as objectionable as the tightly programmed and highly constraining methods of operant conditioning. Still, parental attitudes can pose problems in the use of even these procedures. For example, McConkey and associates (1979) had to use special procedures to modify the highly constraining behaviors of one pair of parents who admitted that they did not believe that the suggestions of the clinicians would work!

It is likely that contacts with the parents will have to be frequent and regular during the parent training period, and following that time, to ensure that the teaching strategies are being carried out appropriately. McConkey and associates (1979) and Cheseldine and McConkey (1979) have shown that audiotaping of home sessions can be helpful in this regard. This procedure has several major assets; it makes it possible to obtain many baseline samples collected in the home, it provides for a careful check on the parents' use of the procedures, and it offers the clinician a simple and efficient means of monitoring the child's progress over multiple sessions. Salzberg and Villani (1983) used audiotaping of home intervention as a helpful component of a program designed to assist in the transfer of parents' use of operant procedures from the clinic to play contexts.

Are Changes in Parental Behavior Maintained Over Time?

If parent training programs are to reach their potential as time-saving alternatives to direct clinician-child contacts, it is necessary to show that parents can and will continue their use of the teaching strategies well beyond the point at which the formal parent-training program has been completed. The implementation of formal trainer-oriented procedures and, to some extent, hybrid procedures, takes time. Even parents involved in highly successful interventions have reported that these sessions are difficult to carry out (Baker et al., 1980; Holmes et al., 1982; MacDonald et al., 1974). In their follow-up study 14 months after the completion of a large scale parent intervention project, Baker and co-workers found that most of the parents had retained the information trained on behavioral principles and teaching strategies. However, only 44 per cent of the families were still using the trained procedures in any useful way. The parents reported that the time involved in formal sessions was the major obstacle to home intervention. Harris and associates (1981) and Holmes and co-workers (1982) report highly similar findings.

Failure to continue use of trained procedures is not limited to highly structured approaches, however. There is virtually no evidence that parents continue their use of child-oriented or hybrid procedures at home in naturalistic contexts following the termination of clinician-parent contacts. Hubbell (1981) cited two examples in which highly successful interventions had been conducted with two families in their own homes. In both cases, the children had made notable progress, and the parents had indicated their pleasure. Yet two months after treatment was concluded, neither parent was still using the procedures. The mother who was trained by Seitz and Riedell (1974) to make significant reductions in her controlling behaviors "had returned to many of her old ways of interacting with the child" (p. 302) at a 3 month follow-up session.

Therefore, clinicians cannot assume that parents will carry out appropriate intervention procedures on a regular basis just because they have attained a high level of proficiency in the use of the clinical procedures. It appears that they are far more likely not to do so. If this is true for some parents who are highly motivated to become involved in the intervention process, it has major implications for programs involving parents who do not have a high level of interest. Indeed, it suggests that such programs are not likely to be successful.

Holmes and co-workers (1982) recommend follow-up visits at least one time every 6 months or regular meetings between groups of parents. This type of follow-up would provide parents with the opportunity to ask questions and to receive assistance in handling new problems. Hubbell (1981) points out the absolute necessity of regular follow-up sessions, even when the procedures trained to parents can be used incidentally in naturally occurring contexts. Furthermore, he recommends that a contract outlining the parents' and clinician's responsibilities and specifying the period during which the contract is in effect be established at the outset of training. Such a contract commits the participants to cooperate in the program for the specified period and, according to Hubbell, minimizes the parents' fear of the unknown. Contracts may also be useful following termination of parent training to increase the likelihood that the behaviors learned by the parents are actually practiced in the home.

In their follow-up investigation, Baker and associates (1980) observed that, of the families that were still doing some teaching 14 months after program completion, most teaching was done incidentally, not formally. They suggested that it may be important to emphasize incidental teaching if clinicians are to have any realistic expectation of long-term use of procedures in the home by the parents and family. One exemplary aspect of the program of MacDonald and co-workers (1974) and other ELIS-based training regimens is the emphasis on extending instruction to help parents take advantage of naturally occurring opportunities for using the ELIS teaching procedures. This is also an important feature of the Culatta and Horn (1981) procedure. Following these programs, parents have demonstrated the ability to create new contexts for training and to initiate training on new language structures in naturalistic environments. This fact may be responsible in part for the uniformly positive results arising from the use of this procedure. Still, whether this level of parental involvement is maintained over any significant period of time following training is not known.

SUMMARY AND CONCLUSION

The findings of most studies reviewed in this chapter suggest that, if they are properly trained and appropriate precautions are taken, parents can serve as powerful and effective agents of intervention. The benefits of parent participation often are not restricted only to the child but extend to the parents as well. Anecdotal reports are scattered throughout the literature of parents developing more positive attitudes toward their children and themselves following their participation in an intervention program. Furthermore, even though successful parent training programs often involve a large investment of the clinician's time, there is little question that such programs can increase the clinician's overall efficiency. The time saved through approaches involving less direct contact with children makes it possible for the clinician to treat more children. In most cases, then, the inclusion of parents in some capacity is highly recommended.

Unfortunately, the picture is not quite as simple as this optimistic evaluation might suggest. For example, not all parents are alike. They differ dramatically in the levels of guilt that they bear and anxiety that they exhibit, in their willingness and ability to learn to administer clinical procedures, in the time and energy they have to devote to the implementation of these procedures in the home on a regular basis, in their existing methods of child care and views of development, in their relationships with their children and their understanding of their children's problems, and in a number of other ways. We do not know precisely how these differences influence the likelihood of success of various types of parent intervention. Because of these differences among parents, however, it is clear that clinicians should not expect any single parent intervention approach to be successful for all parents.

I believe that clinicians must be very tolerant and accepting of these differences among parents. This acceptance can be reflected by discussing with parents from the outset the benefits that can accrue from their participation and the various ways in which they may help. These discussions should include a careful delineation of the responsibilities associated with various parent intervention options and the time and energy commitments associated with each. If parents are aware of all of the options and are allowed to be a part of the selection process, it may be much easier to count on their enthusiastic participation in whatever role they choose. There is no time savings for the clinician, and there is no benefit for the child, if attempts are made to train parents to use procedures that are beyond their degree of willingness or capability to administer.

Some parents initially agree to participate only in a limited fashion, such as working with the child at home in a sequential modification program on targets already reached in the clinic. Giving these parents a small and manageable role in the initial stages of intervention may encourage them to take on even more substantial responsibilities at some later time. Their roles as interventionists can be modified gradually in a manner that is compatible with their self-selected lifestyle.

In some cases, the options that are available for parent involvement may be severely limited owing to caseload restrictions or logistical problems. For example, children who are mildly impaired or those who are functioning at a linguistic level roughly commensurate with their level of cognitive abilities may be considered to be low priorities for direct services provided on a regular basis by the clinician. Similarly, it is unlikely that children who live great distances from the nearest clinic can participate regularly in a traditional in-clinic program. Direct, ongoing clinician-child contact may not be a viable option in such cases. Often, the only way to reach these children may be to train the parents as the primary intervention agents.

It is also possible that characteristics of the child will limit the range of options available for parent participation. For example, with a preschool child who has a severe language impairment and a large gap between cognitive and linguistic abilities, I am reluctant to hand over complete responsibilities for the child's intervention to the parents at the outset of intervention. I prefer to see children with this type of problem regularly and to work with them directly for a period of several weeks or months. This provides me with the opportunity to examine in great detail their strengths and weaknesses and to determine the procedures to which they respond most readily. In this type of case, I simply do not provide parents with the option of taking complete control of the child's program in the early stages of treatment. This does not mean that the parents cannot be involved. It just means that, initially, their role is likely to be one of some type of aide to the clinician. Alternatively, the parents could be trained to use child-oriented procedures at home while the clinician is using more specific trainer-oriented or hybrid procedures in the clinic. As the clinician becomes more comfortable with the intervention plan, it may be possible gradually to shift the major responsibilities from the clinician to the parent.

Regardless of the option selected by the clinician and the parents to make the parents a part of the child's intervention program, there are several steps that can be taken to enhance the likelihood that trained intervention procedures will be applied correctly and routinely in the home over an extended period of time.

1. Outline basic and specific goals and discuss them with the parents before beginning treatment.
2. Involve both parents, if possible, as well as any other caretakers or siblings, when they are able and willing to participate.
3. Draw up contracts that delineate the parents' and clinician's responsibilities and the length of time over which the contract is in effect.
4. Train the parents thoroughly using each of the following steps: (a) explanation of the purposes of the procedures; (b) collection of baseline data on the child *and* the parent; (c) demonstration of the procedures for the parents; (d) observation of the parents' use of the procedures; (e) feedback concerning the parents' performance. The use of filmed presentations and group training sessions can greatly increase efficiency without significantly reducing program effectiveness when parents are being trained to accept the role of primary intervention agent.
5. Monitor the parents' use of the procedures and the child's use of targeted behaviors in the home. Audiotaping in the home may be very useful in this regard when home visits are not possible.
6. Train parents to make incidental use of the training procedures in situations that occur naturally during the routine daily activities of the family.
7. Maintain regular, periodic contacts with the parents concerning their use of the intervention procedures after intensive parent-clinician sessions have been discontinued. Parents can be assigned to call the clinician by phone on a regular basis, say once every 3 months, if face-to-face meetings are not possible. Do not assume that the parents will continue their use of the procedures even when the parent training program has been highly successful.
8. Take whatever steps are necessary (see Chapter 7) to demonstrate that procedures used by parents are having the desired effects on the child. There is no justification for the continued use, without modification, of procedures that do not have the desired effect on the child's communicative potential.

In closing, this last point deserves some emphasis. Taken at face value, the research literature paints a very positive picture of parent language intervention programs. As was pointed out in preceding sections, however, many of the available studies have serious methodological weaknesses. By and large, experimenters have overlooked some very critical variables such as the generalization of parent and child behaviors to nontraining contexts and the extent to which parents continue to use the procedures after training sessions have concluded. The *promise* of greater effectiveness at lower cost with parent intervention programs should never be taken as *proof* of that effectiveness. Clinicians should approach parent programs with the healthy skepticism of a highly objective and careful clinical researcher. I am in complete agreement with Baker (1976) in his statement that "Any parent training program should make a methodologically sound effort to assess its effects. To do so is not a luxury but a basic component of service if that service is to be responsible and ethical" (p. 716). In this respect, parent intervention programs are no different from any other form of service delivery.

References

Akmajian, A., and Heny, F. (1975). *An introduction to the principles of transformational syntax.* Cambridge, MA: MIT Press.

Allen, K. E., Hart, B., Buell, J., Harris, F., and Wolf, M. (1964). Effects of social reinforcement on isolate behavior of a nursery school child. *Child Development, 35,* 511–518.

Alpert, C., and Rogers-Warren, A. (1985). Communication in autistic persons: Characteristics and intervention. In S. Warren and A. Rogers-Warren (Eds.), *Teaching functional language: Generalization and maintenance of language skills.* Baltimore: University Park Press.

Aram, D., Ekelman, B., and Nation, J. (1984). Preschoolers with language disorders: 10 years later. *Journal of Speech and Hearing Research, 27,* 232–244.

Aram, D., and Kamhi, A. (1982). Perspectives on the relationship between phonological and language disorders. *Seminars in Speech, Language, and Hearing, 3,* 101–114.

Aram, D., and Nation, J. (1980). Preschool language disorders and subsequent language and academic difficulties. *Journal of Communication Disorders, 13,* 159–170.

Arnold, S., Sturgis, E., and Forehand, R. (1977). Training a parent to teach communication skills. *Behaviour Modification, 1,* 259–276.

Asher, S., and Renshaw, P. (1981). Children without friends: Social knowledge and social skill training. In S. Asher and J. Gottman (Eds.), *The development of children's friendships.* Cambridge: Cambridge University Press.

Baer, D., and Guess, D. (1973). Teaching productive noun suffixes to severely retarded children. *American Journal of Mental Deficiency, 77,* 498–505.

Baker, B. (1976). Parent involvement in programming for developmentally disabled children. In L. Lloyd (Ed.), *Communication assessment and intervention strategies.* Baltimore: University Park Press.

Baker, B., Heifetz, L., and Murphy, D. (1980). Behavioral training for parents of mentally retarded children: One-year follow-up. *American Journal of Mental Deficiency, 85,* 31–38.

Bandura, A. (1977). *Social learning theory.* Englewood Cliffs, NJ: Prentice-Hall.

Bandura, A., and Harris, M. (1966). Modification of syntactic style. *Journal of Experimental Child Psychology, 4,* 341–352.

Bangs, T. (1982). *Language and learning disorders of the preacademic child.* Englewood Cliffs, NJ: Prentice-Hall.

Barnes, S., Gutfreund, M., Satterly, D., and Wells, G. (1983). Characteristics of adult speech which predict children's language development. *Journal of Child Language, 10,* 57–65.

Bates, E. (1976). *Language and context: Studies in the acquisition of pragmatics.* New York: Academic Press.

Bates, E., Benigni, L., Bretherton, I., Camaioni, L., and Volterra, V. (1977). From gesture to first word: On cognitive and social prerequisites. In M. Lewis and L. Rosenblum (Eds.), *Interaction, conversation, and the development of language.* New York: John Wiley and Sons.

Bates, E., and MacWhinney, B. (1979). A functionalist approach to the acquisition of grammar. In E. Ochs and B. Schieffelin (Eds.), *Developmental pragmatics.* New York: Academic Press.

Bates, E., and MacWhinney, B. (1982). Functionalist approaches to grammar. In E. Wanner and L. Gleitman (Eds.), *Language acquisition: The state of the art.* Cambridge: Cambridge University Press.

Beisler, J., and Tsai, L. (1983). A pragmatic approach to increase expressive language skills in young autistic children. *Journal of Autism and Developmental Disorders, 13,* 287–303.

Belkin, A. (1983). Facilitating language in emotionally handicapped children. In H. Winitz (Ed.), *Treating language disorders: For clinicians by clinicians.* Baltimore: University Park Press.

Bellugi, U. (1967). The acquisition of negation. Unpublished doctoral dissertation. Cambridge, MA: Harvard University.

Bidder, R., Bryant, G., and Gray, O. (1975). Benefits to Down's syndrome children through training their mothers. *Archives of Disease in Childhood, 50,* 383–386.

Blank, M., Gessner, M., and Esposito, A. (1979). Language without communication: A case study. *Journal of Child Language, 6,* 329–352.

Blank, M., and Milewski, J. (1981). Applying psycholinguistic concepts to the treatment of an autistic child. *Applied Psycholinguistics, 2,* 65–84.

Blasdell, R., and Jensen, P. (1970). Stress and word position as determinants of imitation in first language learners. *Journal of Speech and Hearing Research, 13,* 193–202.

Bloom, L. (1970). *Language development: Form and function in emerging grammars.* Cambridge, MA: MIT Press.

Bloom, L. (1973). *One word at a time.* The Hague, Netherlands: Mouton.

Bloom, L., Hood, L., and Lightbown, P. (1974). Imitation in language development: If, when and why. *Cognitive Psychology, 6,* 380–420.

Bloom, L., and Lahey, M. (1978). *Language development and language disorders.* New York: John Wiley and Sons.

Bloom, L., Lightbown, P., and Hood, L. (1975). Structure and variation in child language. *Monographs of the Society for Research in Child Development, 40* (Serial No. 160).

Bloom, L., Rocissano, L., and Hood, L. (1976). Adult-child discourse: Developmental interaction between information processing and linguistic knowledge. *Cognitive Psychology, 8,* 521–552.

Braine, M. (1976). Children's first word combinations. *Monographs of the Society for Research in Child Development, 41* (Serial No. 164).

Branston, M. (1979). The effect of increased expansions on the acquisition of semantic structures in young developmentally delayed children: A training study. Unpublished doctoral dissertation. University of Wisconsin-Madison.

Bricker, W., and Bricker, D. (1974). An early language training strategy. In R. Schiefelbusch and L. Lloyd. *Language perspectives: Acquisition, retardation, and intervention.* Baltimore: University Park Press.

Brown, L., Sherbenou, R., and Dollar, S. (1983). *Test of nonverbal intelligence.* Austin, TX: Pro-Ed.

Brown, R. (1973). *A first language: The early stages.* Cambridge, MA: Harvard University Press.

Buell, J., Stoddard, P., Harris, F., and Baer, D. (1968). Collateral social development accompanying reinforcement of outdoor play in a preschool child. *Journal of Applied Behavior Analysis, 1,* 167–173.

Camarata, S., Newhoff, M., and Rugg, B. (1981). Perspective taking in normal and language disordered children. Paper presented at University of Wisconsin symposium on research in child language disorders, Madison, WI.

Campbell, C. R., and Stremel-Campbell, K. (1982). Programming "loose training" as a strategy to facilitate language generalization. *Journal of Applied Behavior Analysis, 15,* 295–301.

Carroll, W., Rosenthal, T., and Brysh, C. (1972). Social transmission of grammatical parameters. *Journal of Educational Psychology, 63,* 589–596.

Carrow, E. (1973). *Test for auditory comprehension of language.* Austin, TX: Learning Concepts.

Carrow-Woolfolk, E., and Lynch, J. (1982). *An integrative approach to language disorders in children.* New York: Grune and Stratton.

Chapman, R. (1978). Comprehension strategies in children. In J. Kavanagh and P. Strange (Eds.), *Language and speech in the laboratory, school and clinic.* Cambridge, MA: MIT Press.

Chapman, R. (1981a). Exploring children's communicative intents. In J. Miller, *Assessing language production in children: Experimental procedures.* Baltimore: University Park Press.

Chapman, R. (1981b). Mother-child interaction in the second year of life: Its role in language development. In R. Schiefelbusch and D. Bricker (Eds.), *Early language: Acquisition and intervention.* Baltimore: University Park Press.

Chapman, R. (1983). Deciding when to intervene. In J. Miller, D. Yoder, and R. Schiefelbusch (Eds.), *Contemporary issues in language intervention.* Rockville, MD: American Speech-Language-Hearing Association.

Charlesworth, R., and Hartup, W. (1967). Positive social reinforcement in the nursery school peer group. *Child Development, 38,* 993–1002.

Cheseldine, S., and McConkey, R. (1979). Parental speech to young Down's syndrome children: An intervention study. *American Journal of Mental Deficiency, 83,* 612–620.

Chomsky, N. (1957). *Syntactic structures.* The Hague, Netherlands: Mouton.

Chomsky, N. (1965). *Aspects of a theory of syntax.* Cambridge, MA: MIT Press.

Chomsky, N. (1975). *Reflections on language.* New York: Pantheon.

Clements, J., Evans, C., Jones, C., Osborne, K., and Upton, G. (1982). Evaluation of a home-based language training program with severely mentally handicapped children. *Behaviour Research and Therapy, 20,* 243–249.

Clezy, G. (1979). *Modification of the mother-child interchange in language, speech, and hearing.* Baltimore: University Park Press.

Cole, P. (1982). *Language disorders in preschool children.* Englewood Cliffs, NJ: Prentice-Hall.

Connell, P. (1982). On training language rules. *Language, Speech, and Hearing Services in the Schools, 13,* 231–248.

Connell, P., Gardner-Gletty, D., Dejewski, J., and Parks-Reinick, L. (1981) Response to Courtright and Courtright. *Journal of Speech and Hearing Research, 24,* 146–148.

Connell, P., Spradlin, J., and McReynolds, L. (1977). Some suggested criteria for evaluation of language programs. *Journal of Speech and Hearing Disorders, 42,* 563–567.

Constable, C. M. (1983). Creating communicative context. In H. Winitz (Ed.),

Treating language disorders: For clinicians by clinicians. Baltimore: University Park Press.

Conti-Ramsden, G., and Friel-Patti, S. (1983). Mothers' discourse adjustments to language-impaired and non-language-impaired children. *Journal of Speech and Hearing Disorders, 48,* 360–368.

Cooper, J., Moodley, M., and Reynell, J. (1974). Intervention programmes for preschool children with delayed language development: A preliminary report. *British Journal of Disorders of Communication, 9,* 81–91.

Cooper, J., Moodley, M., and Reynell, J. (1978). *Helping language development: A developmental programme for children with early language handicaps.* London: Edward Arnold Publishing.

Cooper, J., Moodley, M., and Reynell, J. (1979). The developmental language programme: Results from a five year study. *British Journal of Disorders of Communication, 14,* 57–69.

Costello, J. (1983). Generalization across settings: Language intervention with children. In J. Miller, D. Yoder, and R. Schiefelbusch (Eds.), *Contemporary issues in language intervention.* Rockville, MD: American Speech-Language-Hearing Association.

Courtright, J., and Courtright, I. (1976). Imitative modeling as a theoretical base for instructing language-disordered children. *Journal of Speech and Hearing Research, 19,* 655–663.

Courtright, J., and Courtright, I. (1979). Imitative modeling as a language intervention strategy: The effects of two mediating variables. *Journal of Speech and Hearing Research, 22,* 389–402.

Courtright, J., and Courtright, I. (1981). Some comments on validity, tautology and methodology: A reply to Connell et al. *Journal of Speech and Hearing Research, 24,* 148–150.

Craig, H. (1983). Applications of pragmatic language models for intervention. In T. Gallagher and C. Prutting (Eds.), *Pragmatic assessment and intervention issues in language.* San Diego: College Hill Press.

Cramblit, N., and Siegel, G. (1977). The verbal environment of a language-impaired child. *Journal of Speech and Hearing Disorders, 42,* 474–482.

Cromer, R. (1981). Reconceptualizing language acquisiton and cognitive development. In R. Schiefelbusch and D. Bricker (Eds.), *Early language: Acquisition and intervention.* Baltimore: University Park Press.

Cross, T. (1978). Mothers' speech and its association with rate of syntactic acquisition in young children. In N. Waterson and C. Snow (Eds.), *The development of communication.* New York: John Wiley and Sons.

Crystal, D., Fletcher, P., and Garman, M. (1976). *The grammatical analysis of language disability: A procedure for assessment and remediation.* London: Edward Arnold.

Culatta, B., and Horn, D. (1981). Systematic modification of parental input to train language symbols. *Language, Speech, and Hearing Services in the Schools, 12,* 4–13.

Culatta, B., and Horn, D. (1982). A program for achieving generalization of grammatical rules to spontaneous discourse. *Journal of Speech and Hearing Disorders, 2,* 174–181.

Cunningham, C., Reuler, E., Blackwell, J., and Deck, J. (1981). Behavioral and linguistic developments in the interactions of normal and retarded children with their mothers. *Child Development, 53,* 62–70.

DeAjuriaguerra, J., Jaeggi, A., Guignard, F., Kocher, F., Maquard, M., Roth,

S., and Schmid, E. (1976). The development and prognosis of dysphasia in children. In D. Morehead and A. Morehead (Eds.), *Normal and deficient child language*. Baltimore: University Park Press.

DeMaio, L. (1984). Establishing communication networks through interactive play: A method for language programming in the clinic setting. *Seminars in Speech and Language, 5*, 199–211.

Dore, J. (1974). A pragmatic description of early language development. *Journal of Psycholinguistic Research, 3*, 343–350.

Dore, J. (1979). Conversational acts and the acquisition of language. In E. Ochs and B. Schieffelin (Eds.), *Developmental pragmatics*. New York: Academic Press.

Duchan, J. (1983). Autistic children are noninteractive: Or so we say. *Seminars in Speech and Language, 4*, 53–63.

Duchan, J., and Erickson, J. (1976). Normal and retarded children's understanding of semantic relations in different verbal contexts. *Journal of Speech and Hearing Research, 19*, 767–776.

Dunlap, G., and Koegel, R. (1980). Motivating autistic children through stimulus variation. *Journal of Applied Behavior Analysis, 13*, 619–627.

Dunn, L. (1965). *Peabody picture vocabulary test*. Circle Pines, MN: American Guidance Service.

Dunn, L., and Smith, J. (1965). *Peabody language development kits*. Circle Pines, MN: American Guidance Service.

Du Preez, P. (1974). Units of information in the acquisition of language. *Language and Speech, 17*, 369–376.

Erreich, A., Valian, V., and Winzemer, J. (1980). Aspects of a theory of language acquisition. *Journal of Child Language, 7*, 157–179.

Evers, W. L., and Schwarz, J. C. (1973). Modifying social withdrawal in preschoolers: The effects of filmed modeling and teacher praise. *Journal of Abnormal Child Psychology, 1*, 248–256.

Fay, W., and Schuler, A. (1980). *Emerging language in autistic children*. Baltimore: University Park Press.

Fey, M., and Leonard, L. (1983). Pragmatic skills of children with specific language impairment. In T. Gallagher and C. Prutting (Eds.), *Pragmatic assessment and intervention issues in language*. San Diego: College-Hill Press.

Fey, M., and Leonard, L. (1984). Partner age as a variable in the conversational performance of specifically language-impaired and normal-language children. *Journal of Speech and Hearing Research, 27*, 413–423.

Fey, M., Leonard, L., and Wilcox, K. (1981). Speech style modifications of language-impaired children. *Journal of Speech and Hearing Disorders, 46*, 91–96.

Fey, M., Newhoff, M., and Cole, B. (1978). Language intervention: Effecting changes in mother-child interactions. Paper presented at the American Speech and Hearing Association Annual Convention, San Francisco.

Fluharty, N. (1974). Fluharty screening test for preschool children. *Journal of Speech and Hearing Disorders, 1*, 75–88.

Folger, J., and Chapman, R. (1978). A pragmatic analysis of spontaneous imitations. *Journal of Child Language, 5*, 25–39.

Folger, M., and Leonard, L. (1978). Language and sensorimotor development during the early period of referential speech. *Journal of Speech and Hearing Research, 21*, 519–527.

Forehand, R., and Atkeson, B. (1977). Generality of treatment effects with parents as therapists: A review of assessment and implementation procedures. *Behavior Therapy, 8,* 575–593.

Friedman, P., and Friedman, K. (1980). Accounting for individual differences when comparing the effectiveness of remedial language teaching methods. *Applied Psycholinguistics, 1,* 151–171.

Fristoe, M. (Ed.) (1975). *Language intervention systems for the retarded: A catalogue of original structured language programs in use in the U.S.* Montgomery: State of Alabama Department of Education.

Furman, W., Rahe, D., and Hartup, W. (1979). Rehabilitation of socially withdrawn preschool children through mixed-age and same-age socialization. *Child Development, 50,* 915–922.

Gallagher, T., and Prutting, C. (Eds.) (1983). *Pragmatic assessment and intervention issues in language.* San Diego: College-Hill Press.

Garcia, E. (1974). The training and generalization of a conversational speech form in non-verbal retardates. *Journal of Applied Behavior Analysis, 7,* 137–149.

Garcia, E., Guess, D., and Byrnes, J. (1973). Development of syntax in a retarded girl using procedures of imitation, reinforcement, and modelling. *Journal of Applied Behavior Analysis, 6,* 299–318.

Glucksberg, S., and Krauss, R. (1967). What do people say after they have learned how to talk? Studies of the development of referential communication. *Merrill-Palmer Quarterly, 13,* 309–216.

Gottlieb, J., and Leyser, Y. (1981). Friendship between mentally retarded and nonretarded children. In S. Asher and J. Gottman (Eds.), *The development of children's friendships.* Cambridge: Cambridge University Press.

Gottman, J. (1977). The effects of a modeling film on social isolation in preschool children: A methodological investigation. *Journal of Abnormal Psychology, 5,* 69–78.

Gottman, J., Gonso, J., and Schuler, P. (1976). Teaching social skills to isolated children. *Journal of Abnormal Child Psychology, 4,* 179–197.

Gottsleben, R., Tyack, D., and Buschini, G. (1974). Three case studies in language training: Applied linguistics. *Journal of Speech and Hearing Disorders, 39,* 213–224.

Gray, B., and Fygetakis, L. (1968a). Mediated language acquisition for dysphasic children. *Behaviour Research and Therapy, 6,* 263–280.

Gray, B., and Fygetakis, L. (1968b). The development of language as a function of programmed conditioning. *Behaviour Research and Therapy, 6,* 455–460.

Gray, B., and Ryan, B. (1973). *A language program for the nonlanguage child.* Champaign, IL: Research Press.

Greenfield, P., and Smith, J. (1976). *The structure of communication in early language development.* New York: Academic Press.

Greenfield, P., and Zukow, P. (1978). Why do children say what they say when they say it? An experimental approach to the psychogenesis of presupposition. In K. E. Nelson (Ed.), *Children's language,* Vol. I. New York: Gardner Press.

Greenwald, C., and Leonard, L. (1979). Communicative and sensorimotor development of Down's syndrome children. *American Journal of Mental Deficiency, 84,* 296–303.

Groht, M. (1958). *Natural language for deaf children.* Washington, DC.: Alexander Graham Bell Association for the Deaf.

Guess, D. (1969). A functional analysis of receptive language and productive speech: Acquisition of the plural morpheme. *Journal of Applied Behavior Analysis, 2,* 55–64.

Guess, D., and Baer, D. (1973). An analysis of individual differences in generalization between receptive and productive language in retarded children. *Journal of Applied Behavior Analysis, 6,* 311–329.

Guess, D., Keogh, W., and Sailor, W. (1978). Generalization of speech and language behavior. In R. Schiefelbusch (Ed.), *Bases of language intervention.* Baltimore: University Park Press.

Guess, D., Sailor, W., and Baer, D. (1974). To teach language to retarded children. In R. Schiefelbusch and L. Lloyd (Eds.), *Language perspectives: Acquisition, retardation, and intervention.* Baltimore: University Park Press.

Guess, D., Sailor, W., and Baer, D. (1978). Children with limited languages. In R. Schiefelbusch (Ed.), *Language intervention strategies.* Baltimore: University Park Press.

Guess, D., Sailor, W., and Baer, D. (1976). *Functional speech and language training for the severely handicapped.* Part I. Lawrence, KS: H & H Enterprises.

Guralnick, M. (1976). The value of integrating handicapped and nonhandicapped preschool children. *American Journal of Orthopsychiatry, 46,* 236–245.

Hall, P. K., and Tomblin, J. B. (1978). A follow-up study of children with articulation and language disorders. *Journal of Speech and Hearing Research, 43,* 227–241.

Halle, J., Baer, D., and Spradlin, J. (1981). Teachers' generalized use of delay as a stimulus control procedure to increase language use in handicapped children. *Journal of Applied Behavior Analysis, 14,* 389–409.

Halle, J., Marshall, A., and Spradlin, J. (1979). Time delay: A technique to increase language use and facilitate generalization in retarded children. *Journal of Applied Behavior Analysis, 12,* 431–439.

Halliday, M. A. (1975). *Learning how to mean: Explorations in the development of language.* New York: Elsevier North-Holland.

Halliday, M., and Hasan, R. (1976). *Cohesion in English.* London: Longman.

Handleman, J. (1979). Generalization by autistic-type children of verbal responses across settings. *Journal of Applied Behavior Analysis, 12,* 273–282.

Harris, S. (1975). Teaching language to nonverbal children with emphasis on problems of generalization. *Psychological Bulletin, 82,* 565–580.

Harris, S., Wolchik, S., and Weitz, S. (1981). The acquisition of language skills by autistic children: Can parents do the job? *Journal of Autism and Developmental Disorders, 11,* 373–384.

Hart, B. (1985). Naturalistic language training techniques. In S. Warren and A. Rogers-Warren (Eds.), *Teaching functional language: Generalization and maintenance of language skills.* Baltimore: University Park Press.

Hart, B., Reynolds, N., Baer, D., Brawley, E., and Harris, F. (1968). Effect of contingent and non-contingent social reinforcement on the cooperative play of a preschool child. *Journal of Applied Behavior Analysis, 1,* 73–76.

Hart, B., and Risley, T. (1968). Establishing use of descriptive adjectives in the spontaneous speech of disadvantaged preschool children. *Journal of Applied Behavior Analysis, 1,* 109–120.

Hart, B., and Risley, T. (1974). Using preschool materials to modify the language of disadvantaged children. *Journal of Applied Behavior Analysis, 7,* 243–256.

Hart, B., and Risley, T. (1975). Incidental teaching of language in the preschool. *Journal of Applied Behavior Analysis, 8,* 411–420.

Hart, B., and Risley, T. (1980). In vivo language intervention: Unanticipated general effects. *Journal of Applied Behavior Analysis, 13,* 407–432.

Hart, B., and Rogers-Warren, A. (1978). A milieu approach to teaching language. In R. Schiefelbusch (Ed.), *Language intervention strategies.* Baltimore: University Park Press.

Hartup, W., Glazer, J., and Charlesworth, R. (1967). Peer reinforcement and sociometric status. *Child Development, 38,* 1017–1024.

Hegde, M. (1980). An experimental-clinical analysis of grammatical and behavioral distinctions between verbal auxiliary and copula. *Journal of Speech and Hearing Research, 23,* 864–877.

Hegde, M., and Geirut, J. (1979). The operant training and generalization of pronouns and a verb form in a language delayed child. *Journal of Communication Disorders, 12,* 23–34.

Hegde, M., and McConn, J. (1981). Language training: Some data on response classes and generalization to an occupational setting. *Journal of Speech and Hearing Disorders, 46,* 353–358.

Hegde, M., Noll, M., and Pecora, R. (1979). A study of some factors affecting generalization of language training. *Journal of Speech and Hearing Disorders, 44,* 301-320.

Hemsley, R., Howlin, P., Berger, M., Hersov, L., Holbrook, D., Rutter, M., and Yule, W. (1978). Treating autistic children in a family context. In M. Rutter and E. Schopler (Eds.), *Autism.* New York: Plenum Press.

Hester, P., and Hendrickson, J. (1977). Training functional expressive language: The acquisition and generalization of five-element syntactic responses. *Journal of Applied Behavior Analysis, 10,* 316.

Hetenyi, K. B. (1974). Interactions between language-delayed children and their parents—a case study. Paper presented at the annual convention of the American Speech and Hearing Association, Las Vegas.

Hodson, B., and Paden, E. (1983). *Targeting intelligible speech: A phonological approach to remediation.* San Diego: College-Hill Press.

Holland, A. (1975). Language therapy for children: Some thoughts on context and content. *Journal of Speech and Hearing Disorders, 40,* 514–523.

Holmes, N., Hemsley, R., Rickett, J., and Likierman, H. (1982). Parents as cotherapists: Their perceptions of a home-based behavioral treatment for autistic children. *Journal of Autism and Developmental Disorders, 12,* 331–343.

Hood, L., McDermott, R., and Cole, M. (1980). "Let's try to make it a good day"—some not so simple ways. *Discourse Processes, 3,* 155–168.

Horgan, D. (1977). *Individual differences in rate of language acquisition.* Paper presented at the second annual Boston University conference on language development, Boston.

Hovell, M. F., Schumaker, J. B., and Sherman, J. A. (1978). A comparison of parents' models and expansions in promoting children's acquisition of adjectives. *Journal of Experimental Psychology, 25,* 41–57.

Howe, C. (1976). The meanings of two-word utterances in the speech of young children. *Journal of Child Language, 3,* 29–49.

Howlin, P. (1981a). The effectiveness of operant language training with autistic children. *Journal of Autism and Developmental Disorders, 11,* 89–105.

Howlin, P. (1981b). The results of a home-based language training programme with autistic children. *British Journal of Disorders of Communication, 16,* 73–87.

Howlin, P. (1984). Parents as therapists: A critical review. In D. Muller (Ed.),

Remediating children's language. San Diego: College-Hill Press.

Hubbell, R. (1977). On facilitating spontaneous talking in young children. *Journal of Speech and Hearing Disorders, 42,* 216–232.

Hubbell, R. (1981). *Children's language disorders: An integrated approach.* Englewood Cliffs, NJ: Prentice-Hall.

Hughes, D., and Carpenter, R. (1983). *Effects of two grammar treatment programs on target generalization to spontaneous language.* Paper presented to the American Speech-Language-Hearing Association annual convention, Cincinnati.

Hurtig, R., Ensrud, S., and Tomblin, J. B. (1982). The communicative function of question production in autistic children. *Journal of Autism and Developmental Disorders, 12,* 57–69.

Ingram, D. (1981). The transition from early symbols to syntax. In R. Schiefelbusch and D. Bricker (Eds.), *Early language: Acquisition and intervention.* Baltimore: University Park Press.

Jeffree, D., Wheldall, K., and Mittler, P. (1973). Facilitating two-word utterances in two Down's syndrome boys. *American Journal of Mental Deficiency, 78,* 117–122.

Johnston, J. (1982a). The language disordered child. In N. Lass, L. McReynolds, J. Northern, and D. Yoder (Eds.), *Speech, language, and hearing.* Philadelphia: W. B. Saunders.

Johnston, J. (1982b). Generalization: The nature of change. *Proceedings from the third Wisconsin symposium on research in child language disorders* (pp. 45–61), Madison.

Johnston, J. (1983). What is language intervention? The role of theory. In J. Miller, D. Yoder, and R. Schiefelbusch (Eds.), *Contemporary issues in language intervention.* Rockville, MD: American Speech-Language-Hearing Association.

Johnston, J., and Schery, T. (1976). The use of grammatical morphemes by children with communication disorders. In D. Morehead and A. Morehead (Eds.), *Normal and deficient child language.* Baltimore: University Park Press.

Karmiloff-Smith, A. (1979). *A functional approach to child language: A study of determiners and reference.* Cambridge: Cambridge Univerity Press.

Keller, M., and Carlson, P. (1974). The use of symbolic modeling to promote social skills in preschool children with low levels of social responsiveness. *Child Development, 45,* 912–919.

Kemp, J. (1983). The timing of language intervention for the pediatric population. In J. Miller, D. Yoder, and R. Schiefelbusch (Eds.), *Contemporary issues in language intervention.* Rockville, MD: American Speech-Language-Hearing Association.

Kemper, R. (1980). A parent-assisted early childhood environmental language intervention program. *Language, Speech, and Hearing Services in Schools, 11,* 229–235.

King, R., Jones, C., and Lasky, E. (1982). In retrospect: A fifteen-year follow-up report of speech-language-disordered children. *Language, Speech, and Hearing Services in Schools, 13,* 24–33.

Kirby, F., and Toler, H. (1970). Modification of preschool isolate behavior: A case study. *Journal of Applied Behavior Analysis, 3,* 309–314.

Kirk, S., McCarthy, J., and Kirk, W. (1968). *Illinois test of psycholinguistic abilities* (rev. ed.). Urbana, IL: University of Illinois Press.

Kolvin, I., and Fundudis, T. (1981). Elective mute children: Psychological development and background factors. *Journal of Child Psychology and Psychiatry, 22,* 219–232.

Kysela, G., Hillyard, A., McDonald, L., and Ahlsten-Taylor, J. (1981). Early intervention: Design and evaluation. In R. Schiefelbusch and D. Bricker, *Early language: Acquisition and intervention.* Baltimore: University Park Press.

Ladd, G. (1981). Effectiveness of a social learning method for enhancing children's social interaction and peer acceptance. *Child Development, 52,* 171–178.

Lahey, M., and Bloom, L. (1977). Planning a first lexicon: Which words to teach first. *Journal of Speech and Hearing Disorders, 42,* 340–350.

Lasky, E., and Klopp, K. (1982). Parent-child interactions in normal and language-disordered children. *Journal of Speech and Hearing Disorders, 47,* 7–19.

Lee, L. (1969). *Northwestern syntax screening test (NSST).* Evanston, IL: Northwestern University Press.

Lee, L. (1974). *Developmental sentence analysis.* Evanston, IL: Northwestern University Press.

Lee, L., Koenigsknecht, R., and Mulhern, S. (1975). *Interactive language development teaching.* Evanston, IL: Northwestern University Press.

Leiter, R. (1979). *Leiter international performance scale.* Chicago: Stoelting.

Leonard, L. (1972). What is deviant language. *Journal of Speech and Hearing Disorders, 37,* 427–446.

Leonard, L. (1973). Teaching by the rules. *Journal of Speech and Hearing Disorders, 38,* 174–183.

Leonard, L. (1974). A preliminary view of generalization in language training. *Journal of Speech and Hearing Disorders, 39,* 429–436.

Leonard, L. (1975a). The role of nonlinguistic stimuli and semantic relations in children's acquisition of grammatical utterances. *Journal of Experimental Child Psychology, 19,* 346–357.

Leonard, L. (1975b). Developmental considerations in the management of language disabled children. *Journal of Learning Disabilities, 8,* 232–237.

Leonard, L. (1975c). Relational meaning and the facilitation of slow-learning children's language. *American Journal of Mental Deficiency, 80,* 180–185.

Leonard, L. (1975d). Modeling as a clinical procedure in language training. *Language, Speech, and Hearing Services in the Schools, 6,* 72–85.

Leonard, L. (1976). *Meaning in child language.* New York: Grune and Stratton.

Leonard, L. (1979). Language impairment in children. *Merrill-Palmer Quarterly, 25,* 205–231.

Leonard, L. (1981). Facilitating linguistic skills in children with specific language impairment. *Applied Psycholinguistics, 2,* 89–118.

Leonard, L. (1983). Defining the boundaries of language disorders in children. In J. Miller, D. Yoder, and R. Schiefelbusch (Eds.), *Contemporary issues in language intervention.* Rockville, MD: American Speech-Language-Hearing Association.

Leonard, L., Cole, B., and Steckol, K. (1979). Lexical usage of retarded children: An examination of informativeness. *American Journal of Mental Deficiency, 84,* 49–54.

Leonard, L., and Fey, M. (1979). The early lexicons of normal and language-disordered children: Developmental and training considerations. In N.

Lass (Ed.), *Speech and language advances in basic research and practice*. New York: Academic Press.

Leonard, L., Schwartz, R., Chapman, K., Rowan, L., Prelock, P., Terrell, B., Weiss, A., and Messick, C. (1982). Early lexical acquisition in children with specific language impairment. *Journal of Speech and Hearing Research, 25,* 554–559.

Leonard, L., Schwartz, R., Folger, M., Newhoff, M., and Wilcox, M. (1979). Children's imitations of lexical items. *Child Development, 50,* 19–27.

Leonard, L. B., Steckol, K. F., and Panther, K. M. (1983). Returning meaning to semantic relations: Some clinical applications. *Journal of Speech and Hearing Disorders, 48,* 25–36.

Liebergott, J., Bashir, A., and Schultz, M. (1983). Dancing around and making strange noises: Children at risk. In A. Holland (Ed.), *Language disorders in children* (pp. 37–56). San Diego: College-Hill Press.

Lombardino, L., and Mangan, N. (1983). Parents as language trainers: Language programming with developmentally delayed children. *Exceptional Children, 49,* 358–361.

Longhurst, T., and Reichle, J. (1975). The applied communication game: A comment on Muma's "Communication Game: Dump and Play." *Journal of Speech and Hearing Disorders, 40,* 315–319.

Lovaas, O. (1977). *The autistic child: Language development through behavior modification.* New York: Irvington Publishers.

Lovaas, O., Koegel, R., Simmons, J., and Stevens-Long, J. (1973). Some generalization and follow-up measures on autistic children in behavior therapy. *Journal of Applied Behavior Analysis, 6,* 131–166.

Lucas, E. (1980). *Semantic and pragmatic language disorders: Assessment and remediation.* Rockville, MD: Aspen Systems Corporation.

Lund, N., and Duchan, J. F. (1983). *Assessing children's language in naturalistic contexts.* Englewood Cliffs, NJ: Prentice-Hall.

Lutzker, J., and Sherman, J. (1974). Producing generative sentence usage by imitation and reinforcement procedures. *Journal of Applied Behavior Analysis, 7,* 447–460.

MacDonald, J. (1978). *Environmental language inventory.* Columbus, OH: Charles E. Merrill.

MacDonald, J. (1985). Language through conversation: A model for intervention with language-delayed persons. In S. Warren and A. Rogers-Warren (Eds.), *Teaching functional language: Generalization and maintenance of language skills.* Baltimore: University Park Press.

MacDonald, J., and Blott, J. (1974). Environmental language intervention: The rationale for a diagnostic and training strategy through rules, context and generalization. *Journal of Speech and Hearing Disorders, 39,* 244–256.

MacDonald, J., Blott, J., Gordon, K., Spiegel, B., and Hartmann, M. (1974). An experimental parent-assisted treatment program for preschool language-delayed children. *Journal of Speech and Hearing Disorders, 39,* 395–415.

MacPherson, C., and Weber-Olsen, M. (1980). Mother speech input to deficient and language normal children. *Proceedings from the First Wisconsin Symposium on Research in Child Language Disorders,* (pp. 59–81), Madison.

Mahoney, G. (1975). Ethological approach to delayed language acquisition. *Exceptional Children, 80,* 139–148.

Manolson, A. (1979). Parent training: A means of implementing pragmatics in early language remediation. *Human Communication, 4,* 275–281.

Manolson, A. (1983). *It takes two to talk—A Hanen early language parent guide book.* Toronto: Hanen Early Language Resource Centre.

Maratsos, M. P., and Chalkley, M. A. (1980). The internal language of children's syntax: The ontogenesis and representation of syntactic categories. In K. E. Nelson (Ed.), *Children's language.* New York: Gardner Press.

Marshall, N., Hegrenes, J., and Goldstein, S. (1973). Verbal interactions: Mothers and their retarded children vs. mothers and their nonretarded children. *American Journal of Mental Deficiency, 77,* 415–419.

Mash, E., and Terdal, L. (1973). Modification of mother-child interactions. *Mental Retardation, 11,* 44–49.

Matheny, N., and Panagos, J. (1978). Comparing the effects of articulation and syntax programs on syntax and articulation improvement. *Language, Speech, and Hearing Services in Schools, 9,* 57–61.

McCauley, R., and Swisher, L. (1984). Psychometric review of language and articulation tests for preschool children. *Journal of Speech and Hearing Disorders, 49,* 34–42.

McConkey, R., Jeffree, D., and Hewson, S. (1979). Involving parents in extending the language development of their young mentally handicapped children. *British Journal of Disorders of Communication, 14,* 203–218.

McCormick, L., and Schiefelbusch, R. (Eds.) (1984). *Early language intervention.* Columbus, OH: Charles E. Merrill.

McDade, H. (1981). A parent-child interactional model for assessing and remediating language disabilities. *British Journal of Disorders of Communication, 16,* 175–183.

McGee, G., Krantz, P., Mason, D., and McClannahan, L. (1983). A modified incidental teaching procedure for autistic youth: Acquisition and generalization of receptive object labels. *Journal of Applied Behavior Analysis, 16,* 329–338.

McGivern, A., Rieff, M., and Vender, B. (1978). *Language stories: Teaching language to developmentally disabled children.* New York: John Day Company.

McLean, J. (1983). Historical perspectives on the content of child language programs. In J. Miller, D. Yoder, and R. Schiefelbusch (Eds.), *Contemporary issues in language intervention.* Rockville, MD: American Speech-Language-Hearing Association.

McLean, J., and Snyder-McLean, L. (1978). *A transactional approach to early language training.* Columbus, OH: Charles E. Merrill.

McReynolds, L. (1983). Evaluating program effectiveness. In J. Miller, D. Yoder, and R. Schiefelbusch (Eds.), *Contemporary issues in language intervention.* Rockville, MD: American Speech-Language-Hearing Association.

McReynolds, L., and Engmann, D. (1974). An experimental analysis of the relationship of subject and object noun phrases. *ASHA Monographs, 18,* 30–47.

McReynolds, L., and Kearns, K. (1982). *Single subject experimental designs in communication disorders.* Baltimore: University Park Press.

Meline, T. (1980). The application of reinforcement in language intervention. *Language, Speech, and Hearing Services in Schools, 11,* 95–102.

Miller, J. (1978). Assessing children's language behavior: A developmental process approach. In R. Schiefelbusch (Ed.), *Bases of language intervention.* Baltimore: University Park Press.

Miller, J. (1981a). *Assessing language production in children: Experimental procedures.* Baltimore: University Park Press.

Miller, J. (1981b). Early psycholinguistic acquisition. In R. Schiefelbusch and D. Bricker (Eds.), *Early language: Acquisition and intervention.* Baltimore: University Park Press.

Miller, J., Chapman, R., Branston, M., and Reichle, J. (1980). Language comprehension in sensorimotor stages V and VI. *Journal of Speech and Hearing Research, 23,* 284–311.

Miller, J., and Yoder, D. (1974). An ontogenetic language teaching strategy for retarded children. In R. Schiefelbusch and L. Lloyd (Eds.), *Language perspectives: Acquisition, retardation and intervention.* Baltimore: University Park Press.

Morehead, D., and Ingram, D. (1976). The development of base syntax in normal and linguistically deviant children. In D. Morehead and A. Morehead (Eds.), *Normal and deficient child language.* Baltimore: University Park Press.

Moulton, J., and Robinson, G. (1981). *The organization of language.* Cambridge: Cambridge University Press.

Mulac, A., and Tomlinson, C. (1977). Generalization of an operant remediation program for syntax with language delayed children. *Journal of Communication Disorders, 10,* 231–243.

Mulligan, M., and Guess, D. (1984). Using an individualized curriculum sequencing model. In L. McCormick and R. Schiefelbusch (Eds.), *Early language intervention.* Columbus, OH: Charles E. Merrill.

Muma, J. (1971). Language intervention: Ten techniques. *Language, Speech, and Hearing Services in Schools, 5,* 7–17.

Muma, J. (1973). Language assessment: The co-occurring and restricted structure procedure. *Acta Symbolica, 4,* 12–29.

Muma, J. (1978a). Letter: Connell, Spradlin, and McReynolds: Right, but wrong! *Journal of Speech and Hearing Disorders, 43,* 549–552.

Muma, J. (1978b). *Language handbook: Concepts, assessment, intervention.* Englewood Cliffs, NJ: Prentice-Hall.

Nelson, K. (1973). Structure and strategy in learning to talk. *Monographs of the Society for Research in Child Development, 38* (Series No. 141).

Nelson, K. (1982). Social cognition in a script framework. In J. Flavell and L. Ross (Eds.), *Social cognitive development: Frontiers and possible futures.* Cambridge: Cambridge University Press.

Nelson, K., and Gruendel, J. (1979). At morning it's lunchtime: A scriptal view of children's dialogues. *Discourse Processes, 2,* 73-94.

Nelson, K. E. (1977). Facilitating children's syntax acquisition. *Developmental Psychology, 13,* 101–107.

Nelson, K. E., Carskadden, G., and Bonvillian, J. (1973). Syntax acquisition: Impact of experimental variation in adult verbal interaction with the child. *Child Development, 44,* 497–504.

Newhoff, M., Silverman, L., and Millet, A. (1980). Linguistic differences in parents: Speech to normal and language disordered children. *Proceedings of the First Wisconsin Symposium on Research in Child Language Disorders,* (pp. 44–59), Madison.

Nickols, M. (1976). Two models for parent language training of retarded children. Unpublished master's thesis. Columbus, Ohio State University.

Nippold, M., and Fey, S. (1983). Metaphoric understanding in preadolescents having a history of language acquisition difficulties. *Language, Speech, and*

Hearing Services in Schools, 14, 171–180.

O'Connor, R. (1969). Modification of social withdrawal through symbolic modelling. *Journal of Applied Behavior Analysis, 2,* 15–22.

O'Connor, R. (1972). Relative efficacy of modeling, shaping, and the combined procedures for modification of social withdrawal. *Journal of Abnormal Psychology, 79,* 327–334.

Oden, S., and Asher, S. (1977). Coaching children in social skills for friendship making. *Child Development, 48,* 495–506.

Odom, R., Liebert, R., and Hill, J. (1968). The effects of modeling cues, reward, and attentional set on the production of grammatical and ungrammatical syntactic constructions. *Journal of Experimental Child Psychology, 6,* 131–140.

Olswang, L., Bain, B., Dunn, C., and Cooper, J. (1983). The effects of stimulus variation on lexical learning. *Journal of Speech and Hearing Disorders, 48,* 192–201.

Olswang, L., Kriegsmann, E., and Mastergeorge, A. (1982). Facilitating functional requesting in pragmatically impaired children. *Language, Speech, and Hearing Services in Schools, 13,* 202–223.

Orazi, D., and Wilcox, M. (1982). *The modification of spontaneous communicative behaviour in language-disordered children.* Paper presented at the American Speech and Hearing Association Convention, Toronto.

Owings, N., Workman, S., Price, M., Dayhuff, S., and Taylor, S. (1983). *Developing communicative intentions in a language delayed preverbal child.* Paper presented at the American Speech and Hearing Association Convention, Cincinnati.

Panagos, J. (1982). The case against the autonomy of phonological disorders in children. *Seminars in Speech, Language, and Hearing, 3,* 172–182.

Panagos, J., and Prelock, P. (1982). Phonological constraints on the sentence productions of language-disordered children. *Journal of Speech and Hearing Research, 25,* 171–177.

Panagos, J., Quine, M., and Klich, R. (1979). Syntactic and phonological influences on children's articulation. *Journal of Speech and Hearing Research, 22,* 841–848.

Paul, L. (1985). Programming peer support for functional language. In S. Warren and A. Rogers-Warren (Eds.), *Teaching functional language: Generalization and maintenance of language skills.* Baltimore: University Park Press.

Paul, R., and Shriberg, L. (1982). Associations between phonology and syntax in speech-delayed children. *Journal of Speech and Hearing Research, 25,* 536–547.

Peterson, G., and Sherrod, K. (1982). Relationship of maternal language to development and language delay of children. *American Journal of Mental Deficiency, 86,* 391–398.

Philips, G., and Dyer, C. (1977). Late onset echolalia in autism and allied disorders. *British Journal of Disorders of Communication, 12,* 46–58.

Prelock, P., and Panagos, J. (1980). Mimicry versus imitative modeling: Facilitating sentence production in the speech of the retarded. *Journal of Psycholinguistic Research, 9,* 565–578.

Prelock, P., and Panagos, J. (1981). The middle ground in evaluating language programs. *Journal of Speech and Hearing Disorders, 46,* 436–437.

Prinz, P., and Ferrier, L. (1983). "Can you give me that one?" The comprehension, production, and judgement of directives in language-impaired children. *Journal of Speech and Hearing Disorders, 48,* 44–54.

Prizant, B. (1983). Echolalia in autism: Assessment and intervention. *Seminars in Speech and Language, 4,* 63–79.

Prizant, B., and Duchan, J. (1981). The function of immediate echolalia in autistic children. *Journal of Speech and Hearing Disorders, 46,* 241–249.

Putallaz, M., and Gottman, J. (1981). Social skills and group acceptance. In S. Asher and J. Gottman (Eds.), *The development of children's friendships.* Cambridge: Cambridge University Press.

Ragland, E., Kerr, M., and Strain, P. (1978). Effects of peer social initiations on the behavior of withdrawn autistic children. *Behaviour Modification, 2,* 565–578.

Ratusnik, C., and Ratusnik, D. (1976). A therapeutic milieu for establishing and expanding communicative behaviors in psychotic children. *Journal of Speech and Hearing Disorders, 41,* 70–92.

Rees, N. (1972). Bases of decisions in language training. *Journal of Speech and Hearing Disorders, 31,* 283–304.

Rees, N. (1978). Pragmatics of language: Applications to normal and disordered language development. In R. Schiefelbusch (Ed.), *Bases of language intervention.* Baltimore: University Park Press.

Reisinger, J., Ora, J., and Frangia, G. (1976). Parents as change agents for their children: A review. *Journal of Community Psychology, 4,* 103–123.

Rice, M., and Kemper, S. (1985). *Child language and cognition.* Baltimore: University Park Press.

Rizzo, J., and Stephens, M. (1981). Performance of children with normal and impaired oral language production on a set of auditory comprehension tests. *Journal of Speech and Hearing Disorders, 46,* 150–159.

Rogers-Warren, A., and Warren, S. (1980). Mands for verbalization: Facilitating the generalization of newly trained language in children. *Behavior Modification, 4,* 230–245.

Rondal, J. (1978). Maternal speech to normal and Down's syndrome children matched for mean utterance length. In C. Meyers (Ed.), *Quality of life in severely and profoundly mentally retarded people: Research foundations for improvement.* Washington, DC: American Association on Mental Deficiency.

Rosenthal, T., and Carroll, W. (1972). Factors in vicarious modification of complex grammatical parameters. *Journal of Educational Psychology, 63,* 174–178.

Rowan, L., Leonard, L., Chapman, K., and Weiss, A. (1983). Performative and presuppositional skills in language-disordered and normal children. *Journal of Speech and Hearing Research, 26,* 97–105.

Rubin, B., and Stolz, S. (1974). Generalization of self-referent speech established in a retarded adolescent by operant procedures. *Behavior Therapy, 5,* 93–106.

Ruder, K. (1978). Planning and programming for language intervention. In R. Schiefelbusch (Ed.), *Bases of language intervention.* Baltimore: University Park Press.

Sachs, J., and Devin, J. (1976). Young children's use of age-appropriate speech styles. *Journal of Child Language, 3,* 81–98.

Salvia, J., and Ysseldyke, J. (1978). *Assessment in special and remedial education.* Boston: Houghton Mifflin.

Salzberg, C., and Villani, F. (1983). Speech training for parents of Down's syndrome toddlers: Generalization across settings and instructional contexts. *American Journal of Mental Deficiency, 87,* 403–413.

Sandler, A., Coren, A., and Thurman, S. (1983). A training program for parents of handicapped preschool children: Effects upon mother, father and child. *Exceptional Children, 49,* 355–357.

Scherer, N., and Olswang, L. (1984). Role of mothers' expansions in stimulating children's language production. *Journal of Speech and Hearing Research, 27,* 387–396.

Schery, T., and Lipsey, M. (1983). Program evaluation for speech and hearing services. In J. Miller, D. Yoder, and R. Schiefelbusch (Eds.), *Contemporary issues in language intervention.* Rockville, MD: American Speech-Language-Hearing Association.

Schumaker, J., and Sherman, J. A. (1970). Training generative verb usage by imitation and reinforcement procedures. *Journal of Applied Behavior Analysis, 3,* 273–287.

Schwartz, E. (1974). Characteristics of speech and language development in the child with myelomeningocele and hydrocephalus. *Journal of Speech and Hearing Disorders, 39,* 465–468.

Schwartz, R., Chapman, K., Prelock, P., Terrell, B., and Rowan, L. (1985). Facilitation of early syntax through discourse structure. *Journal of Child Language, 12,* 13–25.

Schwartz, R., Chapman, K., Terrell, B., Prelock, P., and Rowan, L. (1985). Facilitating word combination in language-impaired children through discourse structure. *Journal of Speech and Hearing Disorders, 50,* 31–39.

Schwartz, R., and Leonard, L. (1982). Do children pick and choose? Phonological selection and avoidance in early lexical acquisition. *Journal of Child Language, 9,* 319–336.

Schwartz, R., Leonard, L., Folger, M., and Wilcox, M. (1980). Evidence for a synergistic view of linguistic disorders: Early phonological behaviour in normal and language disordered children. *Journal of Speech and Hearing Disorders, 45,* 357–377.

Scollon, R. (1976). *Conversations with a one year old.* Honolulu: University Press of Hawaii.

Seitz, S., and Hoekenga, R. (1974). Modelling as a training tool for retarded children and their parents. *Mental Retardation, 12,* 28–31.

Seitz, S., and Marcus, S. (1976). Mother-child interactions: A foundation for language development. *Exceptional Children, 42,* 445–449.

Seitz, S., and Riedell, G. (1974). Parent-child interactions as the therapy target. *Journal of Communication Disorders, 7,* 295–304.

Shatz, M., and Gelman, R. (1973). The development of communication skills: Modifications in the speech of young children as a function of the listener. *Monographs of the Society for Research in Child Development, 38* (Serial No. 152).

Shewan, C. (1975). The language-disordered child in relation to Muma's "Communication game: Dump and play." *Journal of Speech and Hearing Disorders, 40,* 310–314.

Siegel, G., and Spradlin, J. (1978). Programming for language and communication therapy. In R. Schiefelbusch (Ed.), *Language intervention strategies.* Baltimore: University Park Press.

Siegel, L., Cunningham, C., and van der Spuy, H. (1979). *Interaction of language delayed and normal preschool children and their mothers.* Paper presented to Society for Research in Child Development, San Francisco.

Simic, J., and Bucher, B. (1980). Development of spontaneous manding in language deficient children. *Journal of Applied Behavior Analysis, 13,* 523–528.

Simon, C. (1976). The environmental language intervention strategy: A laudatory comment regarding the versatility of its clinical applications. *Journal of Speech and Hearing Disorders, 41,* 557–558.

Simon, C. (1980). Communicative competence: Photo diagrams. In C. Simon,

Communicative competence: A functional-pragmatic language program. Tucson: Communication Skill Builders.

Skarakis, E., and Greenfield, P. (1982). The role of new and old information in the verbal expression of language disordered children. *Journal of Speech and Hearing Research, 25,* 462–467.

Smeets, P., and Streifel, S. (1976). Training the generative usage of article-noun responses in severely retarded males. *Journal of Mental Deficiency Research, 20,* 121–127.

Snow, C. (1979). Conversations with children. In P. Fletcher and M. Garman (Eds.), *Language acquisition.* Cambridge: Cambridge University Press.

Snyder, L. (1978). Communicative and cognitive abilities and disabilities in the sensori-motor period. *Merrill-Palmer Quarterly, 24,* 161–180.

Snyder, L. (1982). Defining language disordered children: Disordered or just "low verbal" normal? *Proceedings of the Third Wisconsin Symposium on Research in Child Language Disorders* (pp. 197–209), Madison.

Snyder, L. (1984). Communicative competence in children with delayed language development. In R. Schiefelbusch and C. Pickar (Eds.), *Communicative competence: Acquisition and intervention.* Baltimore: Univerity Park Press.

Spradlin, J., and Siegel, G. (1982). Language training in natural and clinical environments. *Journal of Speech and Hearing Disorders, 47,* 2–6.

Stark, R., and Tallal, P. (1981). Selection of children with specific language deficits. *Journal of Speech and Hearing Disorders, 46,* 114–123.

Steckol, K. F. (1983). Are we training young language delayed children for future academic failure? In H. Winitz (Ed.), *Treating language disorders: For clinicians by clinicians.* Baltimore: University Park Press.

Stein, A. (1976). A comparison of mothers' and fathers' language to normal and language deficient children. Unpublished doctoral dissertation, Boston University.

Stevens-Long, J., and Rasmussen, M. (1974). The acquisition of simple and compound sentence structure in an autistic child. *Journal of Applied Behavior Analysis, 7,* 473–479.

Stokes, T., and Baer, D. (1977). An implicit technology of generalization. *Journal of Applied Behavior Analysis, 10,* 349–367.

Strain, P. (1977). An experimental analysis of peer social initiations on the behavior of withdrawn preschool children: Some training and generalization effects. *Journal of Abnormal Child Psychology, 5,* 445–455.

Strain, P., Kerr, K., and Ragland, E. (1979). Effects of peer-mediated social initiations and prompting/reinforcement procedures on the social behavior of autistic children. *Journal of Autism and Developmental Disorders, 9,* 41–54.

Strain, P., and Shores, R. (1977a). Social interaction development among behaviorally handicapped preschool children: Research and educational implications. *Psychology in the Schools, 14,* 493–502.

Strain, P., and Shores, R. (1977b, May). Social reciprocity: A review of research and educational implications. *Exceptional Children,* 526–530.

Strain, P., Shores, R., and Kerr, M. (1976). An experimental analysis of "spillover" effects on social interaction among behaviorally handicapped preschool children. *Journal of Applied Behavior Analysis, 9,* 31–40.

Strain, P., Shores, R., and Timm, M. (1977). Effects of peer social initiations on the behavior of withdrawn preschool children. *Journal of Applied Behavior Analysis, 10,* 289–298.

Stremel, K., and Waryas, C. (1974). A behavioral-psycholinguistic approach to language training. In L. McReynolds (Ed.), *Developing systematic procedures for training children's language.* ASHA Monographs, No. 18.

Terrell, B., Schwartz, R., Prelock, P., and Messick, C. (1984). Symbolic play in normal and language-impaired children. *Journal of Speech and Hearing Research, 27,* 424–430.

Timm, M., Strain, P., and Eller, P. (1979). Effects of systematic, response-dependent fading and thinning procedures on the maintenance of child-child interaction. *Journal of Applied Behavior Analysis, 12,* 308.

Tomblin, J. B. (1983). An examination of the concept of disorder in the study of language variation. *Proceedings from the Fourth Wisconsin Symposium on Research in Child Language Disorders* (pp. 81–109), Madison.

Twardosz, S., and Baer, D. (1973). Training two severely retarded adolescents to ask questions. *Journal of Applied Behavior Analysis, 6,* 655–661.

Tyack, D. (1981). Teaching complex sentences. *Language, Speech, and Hearing Services in Schools, 12,* 49–56.

Tyack, D., and Gottsleben, R. (1974). *Language sampling, analysis, and training: A handbook for teachers and clinicians.* San Francisco: Consulting Psychologists Press.

Van Riper, C. (1963). *Speech correction: Principles and methods,* (4th ed.) Englewood Cliffs, NJ: Prentice-Hall.

Warren, S., McQuarter, R., and Rogers-Warren, A. (1984). The effects of mands and models on the speech of unresponsive language-delayed preschool children. *Journal of Speech and Hearing Disorders, 49,* 43–52.

Warr-Leeper, G. (1982). *The language management library: Therapy procedures for the treatment of pragmatic disorders.* London, Ontario: Mariner Graphics and Communications.

Watson, L. (1977). *Conversational participation by language deficient and normal children.* Paper presented to American Speech and Hearing Association, Chicago.

Watzlawick, P., Weakland, J., and Fisch, R. (1974). *Change: Principles of problem formation and problem resolution.* New York: W. W. Norton.

Weiner, P. (1974). A language delayed child at adolescence. *Journal of Speech and Hearing Disorders, 39,* 202–212.

Weir, R. (1962). *Language in the crib.* The Hague, Netherlands: Mouton.

Weiss, A., Leonard, L., Rowan, L., and Chapman, K. (1983). Linguistic and nonlinguistic features of style in normal and language-impaired children. *Journal of Speech and Hearing Disorders, 48,* 154–163.

Weiss, R. (1981). INREAL intervention for language handicapped and bilingual children. *Journal of the Division of Early Childhood, 4,* 40–51.

Welch, S., and Pear, J. (1980). Generalization of naming responses to objects in the natural environment as a function of training stimulus modality with retarded children. *Journal of Applied Behavior Analysis, 13,* 629–643.

Wellen, C., and Broen, P. (1982). The interruption of young children's responses by older siblings. *Journal of Speech and Hearing Disorders, 2,* 204–209.

Wells, G. (1974). Learning to code experience through language. *Journal of Child Language, 1,* 243–269.

Westby, C. (1980). Assessment of cognitive and language abilities through play. *Language, Speech, and Hearing Services in Schools, 11,* 154–169.

Wheeler, A., and Sulzer, B. (1970). Operant training and generalization of a verbal response form in a speech-deficient child. *Journal of Applied Behavior Analysis, 3,* 139–147.

Wilcox, M. (1984). Developmental language disorders: Preschoolers. In A. Holland (Ed.), *Language disorders in children*. San Diego: College-Hill Press.

Wilcox, M., and Leonard, L. (1978). Experimental acquisition of Wh-questions in language disordered children. *Journal of Speech and Hearing Research, 21,* 220–239.

Willbrand, M. (1977). Psycholinguistic theory and therapy for initiating two word utterances. *British Journal of Disorders of Communication, 12,* 37–46.

Winitz, H. (1973). Problem solving and the delaying of speech as strategies in the teaching of language. *ASHA, 15,* 583–586.

Winitz, H. (1976). Full time experience. *ASHA, 18,* 404.

Winitz, H. (1983). Use and abuse of the developmental approach. In H. Winitz (Ed.), *Treating language disorders: For clinicians by clinicians*. Baltimore: University Park Press.

Winokur, S. (1976). *A primer of verbal behavior: An operant view*. Englewood Cliffs, NJ: Prentice-Hall.

Wollner, S. G. (1983). Communicating intentions: How well do language-impaired children do? *Topics in Language Disorders, 3,* 1–14.

Wulbert, M., Inglis, S., Kriegsman, E., and Mills, B. (1975). Language delay and associated mother-child interactions. *Developmental Psychology, 11,* 61–70.

Wulz, S., Hall, M., and Klein, M. (1983). A home-centered instructional communication strategy for severely handicapped children. *Journal of Speech and Hearing Disorders, 48,* 2–11.

Yudkovitz, E., Lewiston, N., and Rottersman, J. (1975). Communication therapy in childhood schizophrenia: An auditory monitoring approach. *Psychosocial Process: Issues in Child Mental Health, 4.*

Yudkovitz, E., and Rottersman, J. (1973). Language therapy in childhood schizophrenia: A case study of a monitoring and feedback approach. *Journal of Speech and Hearing Disorders, 38,* 520–532.

Zimmerman, B., and Pike, E. (1972). Effects of modeling and reinforcement on the acquisition and generalization of question-asking behavior. *Child Development, 43,* 892–907.

Zwitman, D., and Sonderman, J. (1979). A syntax program designed to present base linguistic structures to language-disordered children. *Journal of Communication Disorders, 2,* 323–335.

Author Index

Subject Index